MOVIE-MADE AMERICA

A CULTURAL HISTORY OF AMERICAN MOVIES

ROBERT SKLAR

VINTAGE BOOKS/A DIVISION OF RANDOM HOUSE/NEW YORK

FOR LEONARD AND SUSAN

Published in the United States by Random House, Inc., New York, and simultaneously in Canada by Random House of Canada Limited, Toronto.
Originally published by Random House, Inc., in 1975.

Library of Congress Cataloging in Publication Data
Sklar, Robert.
Movie-Made America.
Bibliography: p.

Includes index.
1. Moving-pictures—United States—History. I. Title.
[PN1993.5.U6S53 1976] 791.43'0973 76-8945
ISBN 0-394-72120-9

Manufactured in the United States of America

PREFACE

This book, as is often the case, is not the book I intended to write when I began it. In the late 1960s I had reached a point in my work as a historian and critic of twentieth-century American culture when I felt the need to explore the role of movies as an art form, and as an influence on other arts. As I immersed myself in the subject, however, I soon began to see that the approach I was taking would not lead me to the heart of the matter. Its conception of both movies and culture was too narrow. One had to go beyond the handful of major directors and the few dozen classic films, and even beyond the great inchoate mass of movies as a whole, to try to understand motion pictures in their largest sense, as a mass medium of cultural communication.

In the process of expanding my approach to movies I also began to redefine my ideas of culture, shifting my focus from artists and their creations to people and their lives. From this perspective, the advent of movies on the American cultural scene at the beginning of the twentieth century clearly posed a challenge to existing cultural policies and institutions, and to elucidate the story of that challenge and the responses to it became a primary purpose of this book.

That task has led me to examine, among other topics, the invention of motion-picture technology; the nature and evolution of the motion-picture audience; the organization and business tactics of the movie trade; the design and economics of theaters; the social and professional lives of movie workers; government policies toward movies, and the attitudes and strategies of censorship groups; and the cultural influence of movies at home and overseas.

In my research I sought to explore the cultural aspects of American movies as broadly as possible through published and unpublished materials (these sources are detailed in the Notes on Sources; only direct quotations are cited in the text). I have also screened hundreds of films from all periods and have tried—with only a few exceptions—to refer in the book solely to movies I have seen or re-seen since I began this work half a dozen years ago.

I am acutely aware that subjects to which I devote a paragraph or a page could with justice receive far more extensive treatment; and other topics of considerable interest (for example, the influence of movie set and clothing designers on consumer tastes) I was unable to find room for at all. There are a number of important directors whom I greatly admire, in particular John Ford, Josef von Sternberg and Orson Welles, to whom I should have liked to give far more attention.

The lack of cultural studies, however, persuaded me of the value of writing a single volume covering the cultural history of American movies from the 1890s to the present, to provide a broad framework for understanding their significance. It is important to begin with a recognition that movies have historically been and still remain vital components in the network of cultural communication, and the nature of their content and control helps to shape the character and direction of American culture as a whole.

My understanding of the structure and transformations of American culture in the twentieth century is still far from complete. At various times I have found myself obliged to use such terms as "dominant order" or "dominant ideology" without fully explaining what groups and concepts in the culture these phrases represent. One of the tasks of cultural historians is to elucidate the nature of cultural power in the modern United States, and more important, its connections with economic, social and political power. I hope this book makes a contribution to that subject, at least to illuminate its complexity, its imperviousness to simple answers.

In the case of movies, the ability to exercise cultural power was shaped not only by the possession of economic, social or political power but also by such factors as national origin or religious affiliation, not to speak of far more elusive elements, such as celebrity or personal magnetism. The movies were the first medium of entertainment and cultural information to be controlled by men who did not share the ethnic or religious backgrounds of the traditional cultural elites: that fact has dominated their entire history, engaging them in struggles on many fronts, and sometimes negating the apparent advantage enjoyed by men who otherwise adhered faithfully to the proper capitalist values and conservative political beliefs.

They say movies are a collaborative art and writing is solitary, but this book could not have been written without the assistance of so many people they amount almost to a cast and crew.

I have first of all to thank those who enabled me to screen the many films I studied in the course of preparing this work. Gary Carey instructed and encouraged me in my first extended use of the Museum of Modern Art Film Study Department in 1968, and Charles Silver did the same five years later. John Kuiper and his staff at the Library of Congress Motion Picture Division helped me to study films from their Paper Print Collection, and Dan Ross set up facilities for me to screen the Academy of Motion Picture Arts and Sciences' collection of early American movies. I am grateful to David R. Smith of the Walt Disney Archives for his assistance in screening Disney's 1930s short cartoons, and to James L. Limbacher of the Henry Ford Centennial Library, Dearborn, Michigan, for providing me access to his library's collection. In addition, Newman Film Library,

Detroit; Columbia Cinemateque, New York; Twyman Films, Dayton, Ohio; Universal 16, Chicago; and Audio Film Center-Brandon Films, LaGrange, Illinois, also generously screened or made available films for me.

The Horace H. Rackham School of Graduate Studies, University of Michigan, provided crucial support and encouragement in the form of research grants at both the beginning and end of the project. I was also significantly aided by a fellowship from the John Simon Guggenheim Memorial Foundation in 1970–1971; I am grateful to the foundation and its president, Gordon N. Ray, for their support.

Among the many librarians who assisted me I have especially to thank Mildred Simpson and her staff at the library of the Academy of Motion Picture Arts and Sciences; Mary Rollman, Mary George and many others in the interlibrary loan service of the University of Michigan Library; and David L. Kapp of Baker Library, Graduate School of Business Administration, Harvard University. Eileen Bowser introduced me to the D. W. Griffith materials in the Museum of Modern Art Film Department's collection. Mary Yushak Corliss of the Film Stills Archive, Museum of Modern Art; Charlotte LaRue of the Museum of the City of New York; Victor R. Plukas, historian of the Security Pacific National Bank, Los Angeles; George M. Barringer of the Georgetown University Library; and Cinemabilia helped me gather the illustrations.

Charles Eastman, James Frawley, Monte Hellman, Peter Bogdanovich, Jack Nicholson and others gave me the benefit of their knowledge and experience of contemporary Hollywood in talks during the summer of 1971; the editors of *Ramparts* encouraged the investigations that led to my article, "Hollywood's New Wave," in their November 1971 issue. The Yale University American Studies Program and its graduate students provided the occasion for my first efforts to explore the social myths in Frank Capra's films; I thank especially Alan Trachtenberg and Neil Shister.

I am indebted to John Higham, Sidney Fine, Frank B. Freidel, Kenneth S. Lynn and Russell Gregory for their support of this project. Sylvia Jenkins Cook, Patricia Finch, Daniel Sell and Gary Rothberger ably assisted me in gathering research materials. Anne Freedgood of Random House was a patient and supportive editor and considerably improved the manuscript with her exceptional editorial skills. Sam Bass Warner, Jr., instructed me on the transformations of American urban life and criticized an early version of the manuscript. Marilyn Blatt Young gave both early and late versions the benefit of her sense of style and human experience. Kathryn Kish Sklar encouraged the project over many years and helped at many points to clarify its language and conceptions. Alice Kessler-Harris gave the project her support and the benefit of her fine grasp of social theory and American social life. Leonard Sklar and Susan Sklar saw more movies than they wanted to and helped me to remember that there are more important things in life than bright screens in darkened rooms. These and many other persons have helped to remove many shortcomings from the work; those that remain are the author's sole responsibility.

March 1975 R. S.

CONTENTS

THE RISE OF MOVIE CULTURE

1

THE BIRTH OF A MASS MEDIUM

For the first half of the twentieth century—from 1896 to 1946, to be exact—movies were the most popular and influential medium of culture in the United States. They were the first of the modern mass media, and they rose to the surface of cultural consciousness from the bottom up, receiving their principal support from the lowest and most invisible classes in American society.

They were not foreordained to flourish in this way. Under slightly different circumstances the motion-picture camera and projector might as easily have become primarily instruments of science, like the microscope, or of education and family entertainment, like the lantern slide, or of amateur photography, or of amusement-park diversion. In 1890, before his laboratory had perfected any motion-picture apparatus, Thomas A. Edison predicted that moving pictures and his phonograph would provide home entertainment for families of wealth. It turned out differently for one fundamental reason: movies developed during critical years of change in the social structure of American life when a new social order was emerging in the modern industrial city.

The two decades from 1890 to 1910 span the gap from the beginning of motion pictures to their firm establishment as mass entertainment; they are also the years when the United States transformed itself into a predominantly urban industrial society. Many American cities doubled their populations; millions of South and East European immigrants brought their unfamiliar languages, religious institutions and cultural customs to create diversity such as the nation had never before seen; long parallel lines of horsecar and streetcar tracks pushed out from the city centers to the open land where residential suburbs began to grow. Industry moved in downtown, and the middle classes moved out, leaving their old houses or properties to be occupied by foreigners and migrants from the countryside.

The change was not simply a matter of growth. There were basic alterations in the character of cities. The older American city, for all its gradations of caste and class, had been a place where people of all income levels and occupations lived close to each other and intermingled. The emerging social structure of twentieth-century cities did away with such proximity and encounter. Increasingly, areas of cities were segregated by social class; how much money you made, the clothes you wore at work, the kind of job you did, the country of your origin, set the boundaries of where you lived. The old American city, which had been a single community, became the new American city of many communities, separated from each other by social barriers.

We have abundant information on the amusements and pastimes of the cultivated classes in the new social order. The books and magazines of the time are filled with reports on their fears and aspirations, and comments on the state of their theaters, the pleasures of their country clubs, their athletic games and sports. Of working-class life we know much less. In the early-twentieth-century city, the respectable classes managed to get around without entering the immigrant ghettos and workers' neighborhoods, and sometimes—as was the case with the nickelodeon movie theaters—several years went by before the general public acquired knowledge of new social or cultural phenomena among the lower orders. Here and there the invisible wall around the working-class districts was breached by settlement-house projects like Jane Addams' Hull House in Chicago, and sociological investigations by scholars like W. E. B. Du Bois in Philadelphia's black ghetto. Their reports told us much of what we know about working-class life at the turn of the century.

Obviously the overwhelming fact of life for these men and women was work itself—half of every twenty-four hours was spent on the job, eleven hours in the best of circumstances, punching in at six or sometimes seven, checking out again at six, in winter never seeing sunlight off the job. The settlement-house workers wrote glowingly of clubs and lodges in the workers' neighborhoods, of church and fraternal organizations to provide wholesome recreation and camaraderie, but few working people had the energy or time to organize activities. They preferred ready-made, prepackaged recreation that provided instant gratification for every nickel and dime.

The place to go for pleasure in a working-class district was first and foremost the neighborhood saloon. For young people there were dance halls and roller-skating rinks, and club rooms where young men could play pool; police and reformers sometimes clamped down on these as centers of vice, and when times were hard they closed. There were also bowling alleys and shooting galleries, and that pretty well exhausted the neighborhood's diversions. Around 1890 new forms of entertainment began to appear in and around the growing cities—amusement parks like Coney Island, major-league baseball, dime museums, continuous vaudeville, but these were rare treats for workers and their families.

Then, in 1893, came Edison's kinetoscope peep show, and in 1896, large-screen motion-picture projection. The movies moved into vaudeville houses and penny arcades, and within a decade had found a secure and profitable home in working-class neighborhood storefront theaters. The urban workers, the immigrants and the poor had discovered a new medium of entertainment without the aid, and indeed beneath the notice, of the custodians and arbiters of middle-class culture. The struggle for control of the movies was to begin soon thereafter, and it continues to the present day. But movies have never lost their original character as a medium of mass popular culture.

To please the people was the last thing in the minds of the men who invented motion pictures. They were nineteenth-century men of science, and they became interested in the principles of photography and motion toys because they were seeking a way to make visible what was not apparent to the human eye. They needed to find or build a research tool that could master movement and control time. When they had perfected the techniques they needed, they lost interest in the further development of motion pictures. Neither of the two men who conceived the idea and performed the significant work that made motion pictures possible—the French scientist Étienne Jules Marey and the British-born American photographer Eadweard Muybridge—lived long enough to realize that the general public was drawn to movies for the same reasons as they: because movies subjected time and motion to the human will.

The history of motion pictures has been traced back two thousand years and includes in modern times the scores of nineteenth-century toys and devices that created the visual illusion of motion; but the story of the photographic motion picture begins with Marey and Muybridge. Unknown to each other, one in Paris and the other in Palo Alto, California, each provided the other with the solution to the problem he could not solve.

Marey's problem was set by his vast and honorable ambition: he wanted to perfect a scientific method to prove Charles Darwin's theory of evolution by natural selection. Having begun his career as a physician, he made a name for himself by inventing a graphic instrument to record pulse and blood pressure, and by writing a treatise on the circulation of the blood. This earned him his appointment in 1867 as professor of natural science at the Collège de France, where he began to apply the graphic method to the study of animal and human locomotion. Once the proper techniques had been worked out, Marey believed, the graphic recording of organic functions such as movement could show over time how alterations in function brought about organic change—in other words, evolution. Furthermore, Marey contended, if the scientist could learn to understand nature's methods, he could reproduce them. By learning precisely how birds fly, one could build a flying machine on the same principles.

Marey's studies swiftly moved beyond the making of graphic records to the visual reproduction of human and animal movements. In the laboratory, Marey and his co-workers set a man to walking while he wore an apparatus that recorded his movements on a graph. Then physiologists and anatomists made drawings representing sixteen progressive stages in his movements. These drawings were placed around the circumference of a wheel on Plateau's phenakistoscope, a motion device; when the wheel was rotated, it produced the illusion of the man walking. The illusion itself was no feat; motion toys had been doing that for years. What was important for Marey was to slow down the wheel so that he could observe and analyze the succession of movements.

The method worked for the relatively simple motions of a cooperative subject like a man. Animals were another story. Even so essential and commonly observed a movement as a horse's gait was difficult to reproduce, let alone the precise movements of a bird on the wing. Scientists filled their journals with arguments about the pace of the horse; it was as if today no one could agree on how an internal-combustion engine works. Despairing of seeing a horse's legs in motion, they tried to describe the rhythm of its movements by attaching differently pitched bells to each leg and recording the succession of strides from the sound of the bells. Marey went them one better and successfully produced graphs of a horse's movements by placing rubber bulbs in specially constructed shoes and recording when each hoof touched the ground. But none of that helped an artist who was trying to draw a horse in motion; the legs still moved too fast to see.

In the fall of 1878 Marey talked about his unsolved problem at a French scientific meeting. Before the end of the year he had his solution. In its December issue the French scientific journal *La Nature*, with unconcealed excitement, printed for the first time anywhere Eadweard Muybridge's instantaneous photographs of horses in motion, taken earlier that year at Palo Alto. Marey acknowledged at once that the accuracy of Muybridge's photographs far superseded his own graphic method. He wrote an admiring letter about the pictures to *La Nature*, and Muybridge graciously replied in a letter to the journal, intimating that Marey's book *Animal Mechanism* had inspired the horse breeder, railroad tycoon and former governor of California, Leland Stanford, to finance his costly experiments in photographing horses in motion.

If only history supported such just symmetries. Unfortunately, it doesn't. Stanford had hired Muybridge in 1872, a year before Marey's book was published and two years before it was translated into English. What Stanford wanted to find out was whether a horse lifted all four legs off the ground while trotting, a subject Marey never mentioned, and he turned to Muybridge because of his notable landscape photographs taken in California for the U.S. Coast and Geodetic Survey. But Muybridge's 1872 photographs of horses did not settle the point, and he and Stanford parted ways. Two or three years later, in all likelihood, Stanford read Marey's book and decided that a more scientific approach could give him comprehensive knowledge of his trotters' gaits.

In 1877 he re-engaged Muybridge and built a special track, a camera house for a battery of twelve electrically operated cameras, and a specially marked fence along the track to give precise measurements of a horse's position in each shot. Each camera was fitted with an electromagnetic shutter, and various devices were used so that sulkies or horses tripped a series of wires, causing photographs to be taken in succession. The results this time were spectacular. Not only did Stanford get his proof that horses simultaneously lifted all four legs off the ground; he and Muybridge had made a critical breakthrough in the visual study of motion, which the French leaders in the field were the first to acclaim.

For a time, curiously, they were almost the only acclaimers. Muybridge's work was more often ridiculed than praised. Artists had vested interests to protect in their "hobby-horse" illustrations of horses galloping with legs extended front and back. But the photographs were also rejected because they demanded a radical reordering of visual expectations and experience. The histories of the arts are filled with such efforts to nullify the new by derisive laughter: disdain as self-defense. "Some of these positions seem grotesque," J. D. B. Stillman argued in his book about Muybridge's photographs sponsored by Stanford, "but for no other reason than because their action is not understood."[1] About criticism of his own photographs Marey later wrote: "Is it not that the ugly is only the unknown, and that truth seen for the first time offends the eye?"[2]

Important as Muybridge's still photographs of objects in motion were, Marey never forgot that they were only a means to an as yet unattained goal—to produce an illusion of motion. In his first response to the Palo Alto photographs he said that beautiful zoetropes (the name of a common motion device) could be made from them. Muybridge quickly followed up on this suggestion. In 1879 he doubled the number of cameras he used, from twelve to twenty-four, and developed a machine, the zoopraxiscope, which could project the images large-size on a screen from a motion wheel. He toured England and the Continent in 1881–1882, projecting his twenty-four photographs of horses and other animals in motion, and everywhere stimulating inventors and technicians to work on similar projects. In Paris the photographer Muybridge met the scientist Marey, though their paths were already beginning to diverge.

Marey wanted not merely illusions of motion, but illusions that could meet his rigorous standards of scientific accuracy, and he had become convinced that the photographer's work failed that critical test. In 1878 Muybridge's achievement had overshadowed the fact that his photographs had never been taken at exact intervals of time. But subsequent photographs of birds in flight, taken by Muybridge's battery of cameras at Marey's urging, revealed the imprecision in Muybridge's method, and Marey found them unusable for scientific analysis. He needed a camera that could take rapid photographs through a single lens at precise intervals.

The idea of such a camera had first been suggested to him by the French astronomer Pierre Janssen's invention in 1873 of a revolver camera to record the transit of Venus across the sun. Marey set out to construct "a kind of photographic gun" with which to photograph birds

---

[1] *The Horse in Motion* (1882), p. 102.

[2] *Movement* (1895), p. 183.

ACADEMY OF MOTION PICTURE ARTS AND SCIENCES

Thomas L. Tally, pioneer Los Angeles motion-picture exhibitor, stands at the left in the city's first movie "parlor" (top), which opened at 311 S. Spring Street in 1896. A decade later (the photo dates from 1909 or 1910) he was operating at Sixth and Broadway (bottom) in a theater that gained a kind of immortality when it appeared in Harold Lloyd's 1923 comedy, *Safety Last* (see the still on p. 118).

ACADEMY OF MOTION PICTURE ARTS AND SCIENCES

in flight.[3] In 1882 he perfected a camera the size and shape of a rifle, capable of taking twelve photographs on one plate in one second's time, with each exposure 1/720 of a second. It was small, light and mobile enough to photograph birds in their natural surroundings, following their flight as they moved. Thus Marey's photographic gun may be called the first camera to take motion pictures.

Over the next decade Marey continued to make improved motion-picture cameras, increasing the number of exposures, the mobility of large-size cameras, and with the introduction of transparent film, using long strips of film to increase the length of time a movement could be photographed. In 1892 he developed the first projector to use celluloid film on an endless belt, an important step beyond the zoetrope projection devices, which were limited to the number of pictures that could be placed around a wheel. Marey's projector lacked a reliable mechanism, however, to make the film move steadily past the lens. The first satisfactory large-screen projector was completed by the Lumière brothers in France in 1895.

To the end of his career Marey remained a scientist first and an inventor second. His goal was to study movements the eye could not see, and reproductions of motion interested him only as a means to that end. When he had attained high-speed multiple photographs of movement on the same plate, he found the movements appeared too close together to be distinguished one from another. To overcome the problem he dressed a man in black, with strips of silver lace attached to his clothes at his head and along an arm, leg and foot, and photographed the man running against a dead black background. The resulting photograph shows only white lines of movement, compressed closely together but with each separate line distinct.

Before his death in 1904, Marey was working through motion photography to obtain geometrical drawings of motion. "Animated projections," he wrote, referring to the commercial motion pictures which had become popular in the major cities of Europe and America, "interesting as they are, are of little advantage to science, for they only show what we see better with our own eyes."[4]

Thomas Alva Edison, like Marey, was an inventor, but he was also an entertainer and entrepreneur, and none of his biographers has yet made clear which of these roles he pursued most vigorously. What distinguished Edison from the dozens of other successful inventors of late-nineteenth-century America and Europe was his imperial cast of mind. Like Columbus, he planted his flag and laid claim to everything he could imagine. And most of the territory he dreamed about, he also conquered.

---

[3] "Une sorte de *fusil photographique*": Marey, letter to *La Nature* (December 28, 1878), p. 54.

[4] Marey, "The History of Chronophotography," Smithsonian Institution, *Annual Report for 1901* (1902), p. 329.

By 1890 Edison's wizardry had given the American people and the world the telephone transmitter, the phonograph and the electric light: only his rival inventors knew enough to doubt his magic touch. What if he altered dates and facts to make it appear that he had invented the movies? What if he told the press in 1891 that he was near to perfecting a television-like apparatus, when in fact he hadn't done any work on the idea? The thought, after all, was what mattered. It wasn't his fault that this particular dream was a generation or two too soon.

Edison maintained his remarkable half-century reign as an American hero by a judicious combination of real accomplishment and the tantalizing promise of even more amazing inventions just around the corner. A credulous press and public came to believe that Edison's fantasies were more real than any other man's working invention; the inventor of a motion-picture projector agreed to market his machine under Edison's name when he was persuaded that no one would want his product because buyers were waiting for Edison to come out with his own. No wonder Edison was sometimes tempted to abuse this public trust by giving false information to reporters, in private letters, and even in caveats and patent applications filed with the government Patent Office. If the myth still persists that Edison was the principal instigator of the idea and the practical mechanisms of motion pictures, it is because his associates, his admirers and Edison himself worked diligently to create and perpetuate it, even against the weight of facts and adverse court decisions.

From the moment of his invention of the phonograph in 1877 Edison probably had in mind some link between his talking machine and projected photographs. But it was not until a decade later, when Edison's laboratories moved from Menlo Park to West Orange, New Jersey, that they actually began motion-picture work. Significantly, Edison turned first to Eadweard Muybridge. The photographer and the inventor met in West Orange early in 1888 and discussed uniting the zoopraxiscope with the phonograph. Neither machine, however, was capable of accomplishing their goal, "to combine, and reproduce simultaneously, in the presence of an audience, visible actions and audible words," as Muybridge later described it.[5] The phonograph could not yet project to an audience, and Muybridge's projector was limited to a few dozen still photographs.

As a result of their meeting Edison purchased a set of photographs of humans and animals in motion that Muybridge had taken between 1884 and 1887 at the University of Pennsylvania. These Edison assigned to an assistant, William K. L. Dickson, with instructions to devise a machine capable of projecting them. Dickson worked with celluloid reprints of Muybridge's photographs on a cylindrical device resembling the early phonograph, to no avail. On a trip abroad, meanwhile, in 1889, the "Wizard of Menlo Park" met Marey and was shown the French scien-

---

[5] *Animals in Motion* (1899), pp. 4–5.

tist's work with transparent film strips. Thereupon Edison instructed Dickson to abandon the unsuccessful cylinder and use strip film. Eventually the Edison laboratories produced their one major contribution to motion-picture technology, the perforation of the film strip at equidistant intervals so that the film would run smoothly past the lens. This improvement was incorporated into the kinetoscope, Edison's "peep show" viewing machine, which showed actual short motion pictures of up to a minute's duration and was widely used between 1893 and 1896, until large-scale projectors superseded it.

The range of Edison's imagination was never limited by the technical difficulties of invention. At various times in the early 1890s Edison told the press or inquirers that he was producing or experimenting with synchronized sound, exact colors and stereoscopic (three-dimensional) effects for his motion pictures. With the exception of synchronized sound, which had interested him from the beginning, these claims were all contrary to fact, and the sound experiments had not been successful. Other inventors had been working on such projects, however, and the principles of both color photography and stereoscopy were widely known. It seems clear that Edison made his claims principally to discourage his competitors.

The mark of a wizard, however, may be his ability to see the future more clearly than the present. In 1890 Nathaniel Hawthorne's son-in-law, George Parsons Lathrop, proposed to Edison that they collaborate on a science-fiction book. Edison made some notes for the project. Naturally thinking to promote his principal commercial product, he envisioned a day when well-to-do owners of phonographs would also have visual reproductions of operas and stage productions to accompany their recordings. The phonograph publishing houses would employ their own companies of stars to make "kinetographic phonograms" for family use.[6] Live drama or opera before theatrical audiences would be a thing of the past. It was these notes, rather than any research or experimentation, that formed the basis for Edison's claim the following year that he was within a few months of achieving direct transmission of live events into the home.

Edison's ideas, widely reported in the newspapers, were probably already familiar to their readers from a different source. Edward Bellamy's famous utopian novel, *Looking Backward: 2000–1887*, was just at that moment at the peak of its popularity, selling at the rate of half a million copies a year. Bellamy describes his Bostonians of the year 2000 listening to a radio-like device that carried live music into the home over telephone wires; on Sundays, of course, it featured sermons. Another Bellamy vision, also published in a popular national monthly just before Edison made his notes for Lathrop, pictured a future society where the phonograph record (sometimes accompanied by a viewer showing a

---

[6] Edison's notes quoted in Gordon Hendricks, *The Edison Motion Picture Myth* (1961), p. 99.

series of still photographs) had completely replaced the book as the principal medium of communications.

Three quarters of a century later, people throughout the world were using media much like those Edison and Bellamy had forecast. Television, radio, phonographs and tape recorders all possessed, to a greater or lesser degree, the qualities the inventor and the reformer had stressed in their future media: private and individual use, personal comfort, variety of choice. What had not come completely true was the opposite pole of their predictions: the obsolescence of public gatherings, the demise of theatrical performances before an audience—even, in Bellamy's case, the end of churchgoing. One can easily understand the appeal of personal and private forms of entertainment, information and culture; in later years Edison talked less about the wealthy and emphasized instead the opportunities for working people to experience the theretofore exclusive higher arts. But what we can only guess is how much the visions of home-entertainment media were impelled by fear or antipathy toward the downtown theater districts, crowded suddenly by strangers from another continent.

Edison was not the only man in the late nineteenth century who thought that the illusion of motion ought to be as lifelike as possible, with a human-size picture, synchronized sound, color and three-dimensionality. The French movie critic André Bazin has called this desire "the myth of total cinema"—the quest for a medium that could re-create the world in its own image, record and preserve human lives and events in as realistic a manner as possible.[7] For Bazin the goal of every mechanical reproduction device was ultimately, in a psychoanalytic sense, to overcome the fact of death, in the same way that the Egyptians embalmed their dead.

But technical difficulties and commercial imperatives made the myth of total cinema impractical. After 1890, inventors in at least four countries—the United States, Great Britain, France and Germany—were racing toward the achievement of working motion-picture cameras and projectors. There was no time to perfect everything when your competitors might beat you to the market with something adequate but less complete. A medium thus began to emerge that was only a pale shadow of the inventors' dreams. It was a two-dimensional, black-and-white (with occasional prints color-tinted by hand) silent medium, first projected no more than an inch square in viewing machines, later on large screens in theaters and improvised halls. Inventors never ceased their efforts to attain full color, synchronized sound and three-dimensionality, and eventually they perfected each of these. But meanwhile the paying audiences reacted of necessity to what appeared before their eyes, and a different set of psychic responses and possibilities took precedence over what might have been had the movies been more successfully "real."

---

[7] *What Is Cinema?* (1967), pp. 17 ff.

Though the actual work in his laboratory fell far short of his widely publicized advance promises, Edison did manage to meet his commitments to the Chicago World's Columbian Exposition in 1893, and thus was first in the market with a commercial motion-picture machine. The Edison machine exhibited at the Chicago fair was his kinetoscope, a peep-show viewer capable of showing unenlarged 35-mm. black-and-white pictures with a maximum running time of about ninety seconds. At the same time Edison was arranging for production and an extensive distribution network for his machines, and many were sold and set up in storefront locations throughout the country in 1894 and 1895. Most of the kinetoscope parlors, as they were called, had from five to ten viewers, perhaps including several "kinetophones," machines that played a recording of nonsynchronized accompaniment music while the picture was shown.

Edison made his profit through sale of the machines, and it was a case of buyer beware. The Wizard seemed to know they would be a nine days' wonder when he overruled his attorneys and didn't bother to secure patent protection for the viewers in Great Britain, where the machine fell into the public domain. Customers indeed quickly lost interest in them. Though Edison for a time managed to drum up admiring notices from the press extolling the lifelike realism of the motion pictures, the novelty of the kinetoscope films that people remarked about was their unreality, the curious illusion of life in tiny human beings. Since the film subjects were largely vaudeville performers, customers could see the real thing if they preferred.

As the kinetoscope business began to wane, a second American motion-picture producer came on the market with a competing machine. This was the American Mutoscope and Biograph Company with its mutoscope viewing machine, which contained postcard-size flip cards rather than strip film; mutoscopes can occasionally be found in amusement parks to this day. The technical expert behind the new company was none other than W. K. L. Dickson, the man who had done the actual motion-picture work at West Orange, and who left Edison's employ in 1895.

Dickson and Edison, competitors now, were among several inventors in Europe and America working to achieve large-scale motion-picture projections. In the winter of 1895–1896 at least two such efforts came to fruition, the Lumière brothers' projector in France and a device developed by Thomas Armat and C. Francis Jenkins in the United States, which Edison contracted to market under his own name as the Vitascope; Dickson's Biograph projector followed in the fall of 1896.

The natural places to find large and willing audiences for large-screen motion pictures were the vaudeville theaters. Edison premiered the Vitascope at Koster and Bial's house in New York, and the other machines followed in rival houses. Vaudeville managers noted not only a doubling of weekly receipts but also a more "select" class of patrons coming, at least temporarily, to see the novelty. Motion pictures became a fixture on vaudeville programs, usually the concluding number. When the seats were filled and patrons were lined up outside waiting to get in, managers sometimes threw movies on the screen before their regular place on the bill, falsely signaling that the program was over. Thus movies earned a reputation as vaudeville "chasers," though in later years this has sometimes been erroneously understood to mean that movies were unpopular. The opposite was, in fact, true. In 1900, vaudeville performers went on strike to protest the managers' new practice of taking out 5 to 10 percent of their salaries as agents' fees. The managers filled their programs entirely with motion pictures and kept audiences coming in; the strike was broken.

Vaudeville patrons, however, comprised only a small proportion of the potential audience for movies. They were mainly middle-class Americans in the larger cities, housewives on a shopping trip downtown, office workers during their lunch break or out for an evening, people who could afford a quarter or more for their entertainment. Such people existed, too, in the small towns and countryside of America, and enterprising motion-picture companies sent projectionists out in touring road shows, which often set up out of doors on pleasant evenings. Around 1900 one promoter began offering small-town theater managers an evening of motion pictures to book into their houses, as an alternative to touring vaudeville or stock-company melodrama.

For how many people in the United States, at the dawn of the twentieth century, was a quarter an impossible extravagance? When you add to that the cost of streetcar fare, of paying for a friend or a family, and perhaps above all the cost in time—in getting there and back, in the length of the program, in sleep lost—it includes nearly all the men and women who worked long hours for low pay in the factories and shops. If their craving for diversion in their few free hours could be successfully tapped, there was money to be made; but their entertainment had to be inexpensive, brief and, especially, accessible. One had to bring it to them where they lived. Here and there, immigrant entrepreneurs hit upon the idea of penny arcades, with slot machines and other games, mutoscope flip-card viewers and perhaps a movie for a nickel in a curtained-off corner of the store in back. The movies proved popular. Nickels made more profits than pennies. So the same enterprising businessmen made over empty stores into movie theaters. Nicolets they were called in one city, nickeldromes in another, nickelodeons more frequently elsewhere. And a vast new audience for movies was born.

Credit has generally been given to two Pittsburgh men for opening the first neighborhood storefront theater in McKeesport, Pennsylvania, sometime in the summer or fall of 1905. But provenance does not matter. There were storefront movie theaters as early as 1896 in New Orleans and New York, and all-movie "electric" theaters had opened in downtown Los Angeles and Chicago in 1902. What was important was the new audience and the way it responded. Within a year there were dozens of working-class neighborhood theaters, and then hundreds. The

THE BYRON COLLECTION, MUSEUM OF THE CITY OF NEW YORK

New York's early movie district clustered around Union Square. The Automatic One-Cent Vaudeville (top, photographed around 1904) was at 48 E. Fourteenth Street, the Comet Theatre (bottom, around 1910) at 100 Third Avenue, between Twelfth and Thirteenth. By the 1930s the Comet had become the Lyric (see photo, p. 163), and in 1974 it was still operating—as the Jewel, showing male homosexual films.

QUIGLEY PHOTOGRAPHIC ARCHIVE, GEORGETOWN UNIVERSITY LIBRARY

growth was nothing short of phenomenal. Statistics are few, however, and not necessarily reliable. One pioneer filmmaker reported in his memoirs that net profits in 1906 were three times what they had been in 1905, and doubled again the following year—a more than 600 percent increase in the space of two years. In 1908, investigators for civic groups found more than six hundred nickel theaters in greater New York, with a daily attendance roughly estimated at between three and four hundred thousand admissions, and gross annual receipts running over $6 million for New York City alone.

As a business, and as a social phenomenon, the motion pictures came to life in the United States when they made contact with working-class needs and desires. "The ideal location" for a nickel theater, wrote the author of a handbook for managers and operators in 1910, "is a densely populated workingmen's residence section, with a frontage on a much-traveled business street."[8] He specifically warned that locating in a wealthy neighborhood or in a section where churchgoers lived would give scant patronage; and in small towns one would likely encounter public indifference or constant interference from the pulpit and the weekly press. Contrast this to Great Britain, where a similar handbook advised prospective managers that "the comfortably-positioned artizan or middle classes . . . are the greatest supporters of the picture theater," and the "great unwashed" present the exhibitor nothing but problems.[9]

In America the problems posed by the "great unwashed" who paid their nickels so freely were generally those of ethnic and racial antagonism. Theaters in "mixed" neighborhoods, according to the American handbook, sometimes experienced friction between groups, and patronage from lower-class Italians or Negroes would drive away other customers. There was no sign, however, that proprietors of the early nickel theaters ever suffered from a lack of audience. It was found that business was best where four or five storefront theaters crowded together on the principal shopping block or main thoroughfare of a working-class district. Some of the theaters opened early in the morning, but most ran their programs from noon until late in the evening. They had garish lights and posters, perhaps a barker with a megaphone, or a phonograph blaring music from the entrance.

The programs lasted no more than fifteen or twenty minutes, short enough for a housewife to leave a carriage in the vestibule and carry her baby inside, for children to drop in after school, for factory workers to stop and see a show on the way home from work. In the evening and on Saturday afternoon whole families went together, sometimes taking in all the neighborhood programs in a single outing. The middle-class investigators for the famous Pittsburgh Survey were appalled in 1908 to find patient lines of working-class men and women waiting to get into the nickel theaters on Saturday afternoon. The researchers wanted to see

[8] F. H. Richardson, *Motion Picture Handbook* (1910), p. 160.

[9] *How to Run a Picture Theatre* (1914), pp. 9, 20.

what the show was like, but they were not willing to stand so long in line.

Inside, they might have been just as disconcerted by what was on the screen—not, for the moment, by the movies' contents, to which we will return, but rather by the quality of projection. Even a dozen years after the first large-screen projections, the intermittent feed mechanism on the early projectors made the screen image pulse or flash with an eye-straining flicker effect. Also, the film itself deteriorated rapidly from use. And the rate of movement on the screen changed constantly because the cameras were operated by hand, so from reel to reel there were wide variations in the rate of frames per second. Projectionists could compensate by adjusting the projection speed, but this often only exacerbated the problem of screen images moving faster or slower than their real-life counterparts.

Although they could do little about the flicker problem and were sometimes indifferent to the deterioration of the film, exhibitors learned to capitalize on audience enthusiasm for tampering with reality. One could project a film of a train at twice the normal speed, and no one would know a slow train had been made to appear fast. But how much better to earn laughter and applause for a trick the audience could appreciate. Films run deliberately in slow or fast motion produced a grotesque comic effect—for example, a person washing dishes at breakneck speed, or a prize fighter taking a knockout punch and falling to the canvas with leisurely deliberation. It was even funnier to run films backward, to watch swimmers leap feet-first out of a pool and end up on the diving board, or see cars racing in reverse up city streets.

The flickering black-and-white images that appeared on theater screens in the first years of the twentieth century were a far cry from the "myth of total cinema" that Edison and others had foreseen—even from the heightened pictorial realism that theatrical producers and critics, caught up in the late-nineteenth-century aesthetic of realism, hoped to gain from motion pictures. They were instead, as one or two of the early writers on motion pictures began to explain, merely a series of two-dimensional still photographs, to which the viewer through his or her own senses and imagination gave depth, motion and continuity.

But the need for active participation by the spectator did not deter the working-class men and women in the early motion-picture audience. As much as scientists like Marey, they demonstrated an appetite for mastery over time and motion. Though their taste had to be satisfied in crowded, dark and smelly rooms, few would forgo such opportunities for pleasure and vicarious power. They took hungrily to the movies and turned, by their nickels, an instrument of science and amusement into the first mass entertainment medium.

2

NICKEL MADNESS

The sudden appearance of storefront movie theaters, by the scores and even by the hundreds, in the working-class districts of American cities went unnoticed by the chroniclers of business enterprise, social life and culture. Newspapers and magazines had expended all too much credulence on the new medium back in the 1890s. As the claims and predictions of inventors and showmen came nowhere near fulfillment, they appeared in retrospect no more than wishful thinking or simple self-promotion. References to movies disappeared from print, except for occasional notices in scientific journals about mechanical improvements. When working-class men and women discovered the wonders of the motion-picture machine, no one was there to record their feelings—no one but a few exhibitors who realized they had struck a gold mine and were telling only their friends. Like many of the critical encounters in twentieth-century society where technology and culture have come together and produced new modes of behavior, leisure, desire and consciousness, the significance of the moment was recognized belatedly, long after the changes had become accomplished facts.

In the case of storefront movie theaters, nearly two years passed, from 1905 to 1907, before the news seeped up to the middle class. Usually the information was relayed by a reformer or policeman with cries of astonishment, indignation and alarm. To these guardians of public morality the movie theaters were one more example of corrupt institutions and practices that had grown up in the poor and immigrant districts of the new industrial city; they belonged in the same class as brothels, gambling dens and the hangouts of criminal gangs. In a way they were worse, for the movies appeared to some merely as harmless amusements and thus were an even more insidious trap for the unwary. As the Progressive movement began to take form early in the century, it drew much of its energy from the middle classes' discovery that they had lost control over—and even knowledge of—the behavior and values of the lower orders; and the movies became prime targets of their efforts to reformulate and reassert their power.

The storefront movie theaters were a shocking revelation to the middle classes in another way as well. The movies were not simply gathering places where, according to some reformers, sins were committed; they were centers of communication and cultural diffusion. What was most galling to many in well-to-do city districts, suburbs and small towns was the idea that workingmen and immigrants had found their own source of entertainment and information—a source unsupervised and unapproved by the churches and schools, the critics and professors who served as caretakers and disseminators of the official American culture. In that atmosphere of middle-class hostility it was difficult to suggest that working-class people had been fortunate to find some entertainment, impossible to say that they had chosen their entertainment well. Even one who wished to defend movies as innocent amusement found it necessary to describe them as a form of mass delirium called "nickel madness."[1]

It would have taken an outsider with extraordinary empathy for the needs and desires of common people to come to a different conclusion. The educator, clergyman or charity worker who went exploring among the storefront theaters was likely to have his or her worst suspicions confirmed. Amid the din on a busy street in a working-class district, one found crowds of men and women, unescorted girls and unsupervised young children studying lurid posters, streaming into one theater and out of another. Inside a theater one's first impression was of stale, still air and the smell of sweat and unwashed bodies. It was totally dark, save for the screen and the shaft of projector light below the ceiling. Perhaps someone stood in front and narrated the story in English or a foreign language; perhaps the only sound came from a phonograph in the lobby. The observer might notice, or might simply imagine, some couples paying more attention to each other than to the movie, and in the most indecorous way.

Clearly, there was a fallow field here for reform. One could propose laws requiring more lighting and ventilation. One could prohibit unescorted children from attending in the evening. One could demand more stringent supervision of theaters by police, fire officials and license bureaus. But there were those who quickly saw that regulation and improvement of theaters dealt only with symptoms, not with the disease. The root of the problem lay in the movies themselves, and the road to control over motion pictures went beyond exhibitors to the producers who financed and made them.

In the earliest days of motion pictures the terms "producer" and "filmmaker" could almost have been synonymous. Only the Edison and Biograph companies were large enough for a division of labor, and that was because they had begun as manufacturers of equipment, expanding into production in order to supply purchasers of their projectors. Otherwise the filmmakers were free-lance cameramen who sold their films to the manufacturing companies, or if they were more ambitious, set up producing companies on their own. Almost to a man they came to movie work, both in the United States and Great Britain, from a background in technical trades, with experience in electrical work or photography and

---

[1] Barton W. Currie, "The Nickel Madness," *Harper's Weekly*, Vol. 51 (August 24, 1907), p. 1246.

an aptitude for mechanical innovation. Free-lance or employed by a manufacturer, they performed the same tasks, writing, casting, directing, photographing, editing, and perhaps even developing and printing their own movies.

It would be interesting to know how these men responded to the rapid proliferation of storefront theaters after 1905 and the dramatic change in both the size and the social character of their audience. Unfortunately, there is no evidence that they noticed any difference at all. Business assuredly got better. But they were busy men, preoccupied with the complex task of making movies. They did not have time to stand on the bridge and survey the social and cultural scene. They worked far below deck in the boiler room of culture, and they experienced the sudden expansion of the working-class audience chiefly as a demand for more steam.

This is not to say that filmmakers were not aware of the desires of the audience or interested in improving the quality of their product. They were technicians first, but they were also showmen, and many of them, like Edwin S. Porter, who made *The Great Train Robbery*, got their start as vaudeville or touring projectionists who had watched and listened to the reactions of urban and small-town audiences.

In the beginning the limits of motion-picture technology forced them to make movies little more than a minute in length. At the Edison laboratories in West Orange, where the first extensive motion-picture production was begun in 1894 inside the "Black Maria," a black tar-papered studio on a circular track, the cameraman W. K. L. Dickson knew that his films would appear no more than an inch square within the peep-show viewer.

He turned naturally to familiar amusement subjects: vaudeville acts, sporting contests, curiosities and grotesques. Performers were persuaded to ferry over from Manhattan to appear before Edison's camera, often for no more than a promise of celluloid immortality. The first films displayed in peep-show viewers in New York included as subjects Eugene Sandow, the Austrian strong man; a wrestling match; a Highland dance; a trapeze act; a cock fight; and two films of Bertholdi, the vaudeville contortionist. Within the first year of production Dickson photographed Buffalo Bill; boxing cats; Mexican, Indian, Arab, Oriental and black vaudeville performers; performing dogs; a trained-bear act; a gun spinner; dancers, acrobats, tumblers, prize fighters.

When large-screen projection began in 1896, vaudeville managers put about a dozen of these one-minute films together to make up a motion-picture vaudeville turn. But what value was it for audiences to watch a sixty-second black-and-white silent movie of a performer they might very well have seen live, vocal and in color on the same bill? What excited audiences of the earliest large-screen projections was not films of vaudeville acts but scenes never before seen inside a theater—crashing sea waves, onrushing locomotives, the wonders of nature and machines, far-off places, rare and unusual sights.

Dickson had already begun to vary his subjects at the Edison studio when he found that comic scenes of everyday life were popular with peep-show customers—fun in a blacksmith shop, a dentist's office, a barroom, a barbershop, a Chinese laundry. These, of course, were not so different from vaudeville or variety-show skits. Later, when he joined Biograph, Dickson made for its October 1896 debut films of Niagara Falls, the Empire State Express, and two showing Republican presidential candidate William McKinley at his home in Canton, Ohio.

But it remained for Dickson's successor at West Orange, Alfred Clark, to make the first discovery of what film could do that no other medium could match. In the fall of 1895 Clark took his camera out of doors and made several costume films, including one about Joan of Arc, one featuring a duel, and three on American Indian and frontier themes. The most significant, however, was *The Execution of Mary, Queen of Scots.* Mary (played by a man) rests her head on the block, and the executioner raises his ax to strike. At this point Clark stopped the camera, put a dummy in place of the actor and resumed cranking. The ax came down and lopped off Mary's head.

Clark had hit upon perhaps the most profound and complex resource of the cinema—its ability to give viewers access to events that happened when they were not there, to the dangerous, the fantastic, the grotesque, the impossible, at a close but safe remove. The repetition of this scene in the BBC television production *Elizabeth R* in the early 1970s indicates how strong a hold this elemental function of movies still has for us, fulfilling the wish, as Stanley Cavell has written, "for the magical reproduction of the world by enabling us to view it unseen."[2]

Mary's severed head started no trends. How widely it was seen, in a season of declining kinetoscope peep-show business, is open to question. Other filmmakers later had to repeat Clark's discovery for themselves. For the moment, the needs of their customers were pulling them in other directions. In the spring of 1896, movies began their vaudeville career, and scenes of life in the world were in demand. The men with the movie cameras set up their tripods at the beach, on the dock, along the road, in the city street, and cranked out a minute's worth of the scene before them. One film out of twenty might by skill or chance rise above an ordinary view and present an effective pictorial composition of everyday life in motion. But retrospective aesthetic judgments are beside the point. In the first year or two of motion pictures, movies of horse-drawn ambulances, or bathers splashing in a pool, or a hundred other sights of daily industry and amusement, fully satisfied the vaudeville audiences' appetite for wonder.

The filmmakers could not afford to repeat themselves for too long, however. The search for novelty began as early as 1897 when an enterprising company staged a religious drama, *The Passion Play*, before a camera on a New York rooftop. Their fifty-five-minute film ran for six

---

[2] *The World Viewed* (1971), p. 101.

months at the Eden Musée in New York and was shown throughout the country by traveling projectionists. Except for a championship prize fight filmed in its entirety in 1899, no other motion picture of such length was attempted for nearly fifteen years.

The war with Spain in 1898 gave regular film producers their first prime opportunity for spectacle. Patriotic fervor ran so high that it was easy to sense audience receptivity to films about the war, even if some were as obviously fabricated as a flag-raising before a painted backdrop, called by Edison *Raising Old Glory Over Moro Castle* (1899). Fabrication was, of course, the point: no motion-picture films were made of the fighting in Cuba. What was important was how filmmakers responded to the challenge of reproducing the war for the benefit of vaudeville audiences. An unknown cameraman for the Edison company recapitulated Alfred Clark's discovery when he simulated an execution by firing squad in *Shooting Captured Insurgents, Spanish-American War* (1898). Again the film medium showed itself capable of re-creating extreme moments of life and death for an audience safe in auditorium seats.

Every image on the screen possessed this element of magic; why then shouldn't the movies become explicitly a medium for magical entertainment? The first person to take this logical step was the French conjurer and illusionist Georges Méliès, for whom magical motion pictures were a natural extension of his theatrical work. It is perhaps more significant that Méliès, a caricaturist and magician by trade, should have begun his filmmaking career by taking scores of outdoor shots of urban scenes and landscapes, just as his American counterparts were doing. But when Méliès began to explore the capacity of motion pictures for a magical form of spectacle, he turned not to history or current events but to his own specialty, one of the few ways, before movies, to produce the appearance of effects beyond the bounds of human power.

The mechanical properties of the motion-picture camera gave Méliès the chance vastly to expand his repertoire. By stopping the camera and altering the scene before resuming (as Clark had done with *Mary*), or by splicing separate films together, he created illusions of magical transformation, appearance and disappearance. Characters shrank or grew or turned into animals. Anything at all could happen in a Méliès film, but he never permanently violated the moral or physical order of everyday life. A man might lose his head, and unlike Mary, Queen of Scots, get along very nicely without it; the head and body might go their separate ways and survive many comic misadventures, yet in the end they were safely reunited and all was as before. From his long experience as a performer, Méliès sensed or knew that fantasy and magic, like dreams and nonsense language, have a structure and logic of their own, and to deviate from their forms is a sure way to lose an audience.

American filmmakers paid Méliès a high but dubious compliment: when his films appeared in the United States they immediately copied them. Since a motion-picture copyright law was not passed until 1912, there was no prohibition against stealing another person's idea—or simply buying a print of his film and putting your name on it, as was sometimes done. (Filmmakers did submit more than three thousand prints on paper rolls to the Library of Congress, on the possibility that they could gain protection as still photographs; and the restoration of those prints in the 1950s, after their negatives had long since crumbled to dust, brought back a fair proportion of early American movies from the lost past.)

The Edison company began making direct or very close copies of Méliès films with *Vanishing Lady* in 1898, *Strange Adventure of a New York Drummer* in 1899 and *Uncle Josh's Nightmare* in 1900. Trick films, as they were called, became the latest novelty and continued their popularity for nearly a decade. When middle-class magazines began to write about movies after 1907, they gave considerable space to revealing how the trick effects were attained.

Around 1900, American producers began to make risqué, bawdy, low-life films. Although there is no precise evidence about the changing standards of popular entertainment at that time, the beginning of sexual themes in the movies coincides with a rapid expansion of urban amusements, the proliferation of vaudeville into smaller cities and the advent of the golden age of burlesque theater. The major vaudeville theaters and the circuits they controlled were reputed to maintain "polite" standards at all times, but the smaller independent theaters and the new penny arcades may have been looking for broader fare. And the morality tale of urban dangers, designed to shock and forewarn as well as to titillate, might have found favor anywhere. Edison made *Tenderloin at Night* in 1899 and then retold the same story in 1902 as *How They Do Things on the Bowery*: loose women lure country rubes into saloons, drug their drinks and steal their money.

More often, movies with sexual innuendo were comic or had come-on titles to lure customers but ultimately to trick them. *What Happened on 23rd St., NYC* (1901) was a strong wind that blew up skirts, and *What Demoralized the Barbershop* (1901) was a raised skirt. *The Pouting Model* and *Water Nymphs* (both 1902) offered, respectively, a nude little girl with her back to the camera and infants in a fountain.

But some films delivered more or less what they promised, particularly to an urban audience composed in the early twentieth century of a large number of bachelors. In *Trapeze Disrobing Act* (1901) a woman strips to a leotard; in *Birth of a Pearl* (1903) a woman also appears in a leotard; and a series of 1903 movies—*The Corset Model, The Pajama Girl, The Physical Culture Girl, At the Dressmaker's, From Showgirl to Burlesque Queen* are a few among many—show women in various stages of undress. More overt sexual activity came in with *The Typewriter* (1902), a film that repeated the often exploited comic possibilities in the double meaning of the word that referred at that time to both the machine and the person who used it. *The Typewriter* shows an employer kissing his secretary and being discovered by his wife. *Be Good* and *The Girl at the Window* (both 1903) show kisses and caresses without benefit of plot.

The opening in 1902 of a storefront "electric" theater in Los Angeles may have been a reaction against the showing of salacious films as standard motion-picture vaudeville turns. Thomas Tally, the owner, pointedly advertised programs especially for ladies and children, and with a downtown location and a ten-cent admission he was, unlike the later nickelodeons, in direct competition for vaudeville's middle-class audience. One may wonder where Tally found the wholesome films to fill up the hour of entertainment he promised. The only movies mentioned by name in his inaugural advertisement were *Capture of the Biddle Brothers* and *New York City in a Blizzard.*

Both films had been produced early that same year by the Edison company and photographed by the filmmaker most recently employed by Edison, Edwin S. Porter. *Capture of the Biddle Brothers* is no more than a two-minute-long shot of a gun battle and capture, a primitive Western. *New York City in a Blizzard* marks its maker as someone special. Composed of four separate shots (a shot is the basic unit of filmmaking, the single image that is made from the time the camera begins running to the time it stops running), the film combines effective camera movement with interesting movement in the scene. Tally had prophetically recognized in Porter a filmmaker who could provide the "up-to-date, high class moving picture entertainment" he advertised.[3] A year later Porter was to create the first classic American work of the new medium, *The Great Train Robbery.*

Despite the homage and attention given to his most famous film, Edwin S. Porter remains an enigmatic figure in the early history of American movies. In a business where ballyhoo was from the beginning as essential a raw material as celluloid film, Porter was simply too quiet, modest and unambitious a man. Or perhaps he knew his limitations better than anyone else. After a ten-year period, from 1899 to 1909, when he was the most important filmmaker in the United States, Porter could not, or would not, adapt himself to the more exalted but more limited role of director in a rapidly changing motion-picture industry. Perhaps the producer Adolph Zukor was right when he described Porter as an artistic mechanic rather than a dramatic artist, a man who liked to work with machines better than people. Porter began his motion-picture career as an electrician and projectionist and ended it as an inventor and designer of cameras and projectors, and president of a projector manufacturing firm. In the years between as a filmmaker, he successfully demonstrated most of the techniques that were to become the basic modes of visual communication through film.

Porter was nearly thirty when he joined the Edison company in 1899, following several years as a touring projectionist in the West Indies and South America, Canada and the United States. Besides his skills in elec-

---

[3] Tally's advertisement is reproduced in Kenneth Macgowan, *Behind the Screen* (1965), p. 128.

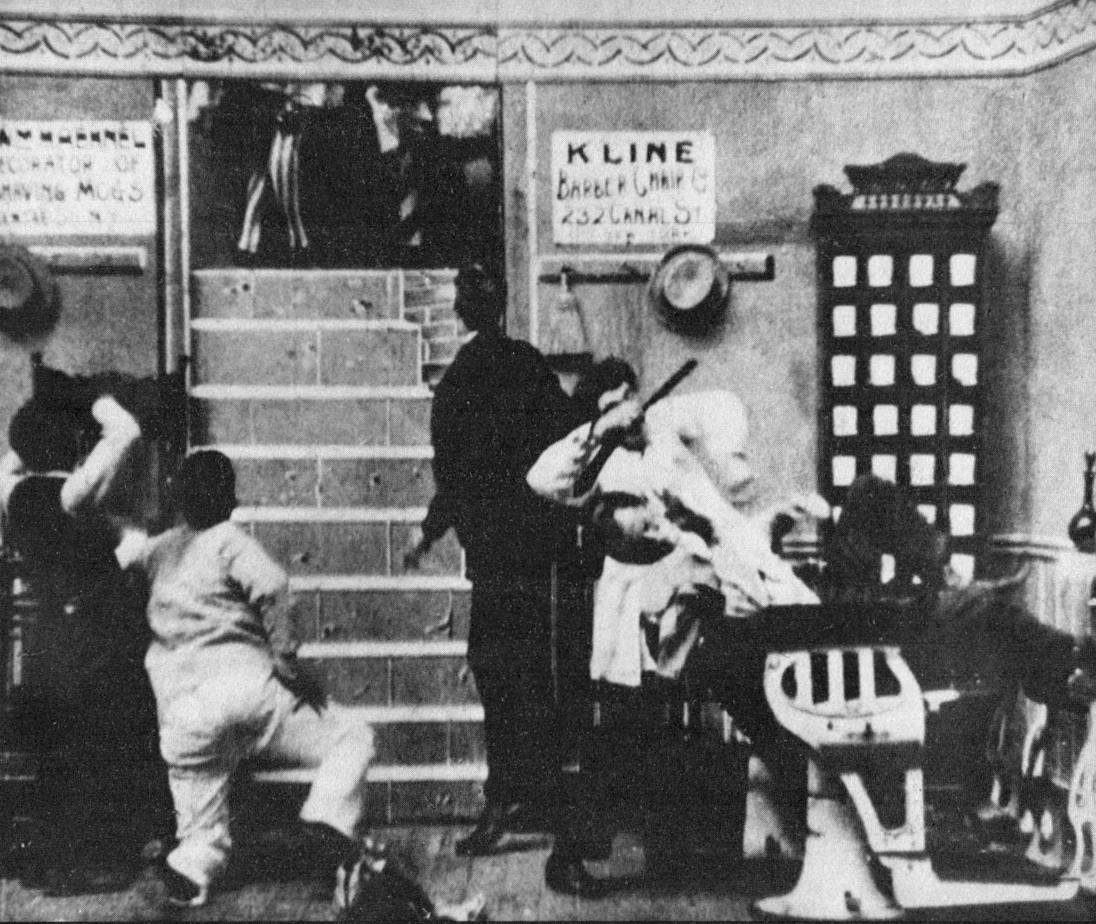

ACADEMY OF MOTION PICTURE ARTS AND SCIENCES

What Demoralized the Barbershop, an Edison film of 1901, was one of scores of risqué and titillating movies made in the early days for peep-show viewers and vaudeville patrons. The demoralizing sight was a woman adjusting her stockings and showing off her calves.

tronics and projection he brought to Edison an extensive knowledge of the tastes of motion-picture audiences, gained behind the projector at fair grounds and in open fields. Edison soon put him in complete charge of production at his New York studios, which meant that Porter was responsible for the entire filmmaking operation—selecting the subjects, operating the camera, directing the actors and assembling the final print.

He began by making trick films and comedies, and though much of his work was inspired by other people's movies, he quickly showed an original imagination of his own. He proved himself particularly adept at light satire. His *Terrible Teddy, the Grizzly King*, of February 1901, poked fun at the then Vice-President-elect Theodore Roosevelt. In *Uncle Josh at the Moving Picture Show* (1902), a country bumpkin gets so excited over a kissing scene that he tears down the screen. (Jean-Luc Godard used this same idea for a scene in *Les Carabiniers* in 1963.)

Porter's *Jack and the Beanstalk* (1902) borrowed from Méliès' films of popular fairy tales, and *Life of an American Fireman* (1903) was probably patterned after an effective British film by James Williamson, *Fire* (early 1902). Once again, however, he did not simply copy others' work, he improved on what he used. In these two films Porter's chief contribution was a technical innovation: instead of using abrupt splices or cuts between shots, he created dissolves, gradual transitions from one image to another. This slowed succession of images worked particularly well in *Life of an American Fireman.* Its nine separate shots depicting the rescue of a mother and child from a burning house made it the most complex outdoor-location movie yet assembled.

Then came *The Great Train Robbery*. Nothing Porter had done before, no movie by British or continental filmmakers, prepared audiences for its astonishing impact. The capacity of the medium for spectacle had first been expended on scenes from everyday life, then on magic and trick effects, then on urban sex play and titillating glimpses of women. Porter was the first to unite motion-picture spectacle with myths and stories about America that were shared by people throughout the world.

He had begun in a tentative way with the brief *Capture of the Biddle Brothers*, and had also made a film, just before *The Great Train Robbery*, of *Uncle Tom's Cabin.* He was reaching beyond the vaudeville turn, the burlesque skit and the magic act into the realm of the dime novel and the stage melodrama, the picture book and ballad, the uncharted ground of American popular culture where folklore and commercial entertainment met and mingled. Everyone knew the story of Little Eva and Uncle Tom, and Porter made it an impressive motion-picture spectacle, though his movie essentially took the form of a filmed stage production. The Western story of banditry and retribution was also familiar to all, and in Porter's hands it became something to marvel at: who had ever before witnessed a fight between bandit and trainman from a close vantage point on a swiftly moving train; who had watched while an innocent passenger made a false move and was coolly shot to death? In *The Great Train Robbery*, Porter gave life to legend, and to audiences of 1903 it was an astounding new way to encounter the world.

From the little evidence we have, *The Great Train Robbery* was not nearly so important to Porter as it was to its audience. Always the technician, he seemed to regard *Life of an American Fireman* as his major breakthrough and later films simply as elaborations on the principles he had worked out there. In a way he was right: from a technical standpoint the earlier movie was the greater triumph and even the more interesting film. But to an audience the merely quantitative developments of more shots and more locations, combined with the powerful appeal of a story, could produce a totally different viewing experience.

The Great Train Robbery used twenty separate shots, not counting the close-up of a bandit firing at the camera (sometimes used at the beginning, sometimes at the end, and often at both). The story unfolded over nearly a dozen different locations, indoors, in or on the train, beside the train and in hilly, wooded terrain. No movie before it contained such a variety of scene or such swift movement from place to place. For the first time, a motion picture demonstrated the speed and spaciousness required of a storytelling medium.

While *The Great Train Robbery* was touring the country with spectacular success, Porter continued to try new themes and techniques. But his innovations never led him anywhere; for all the methods he mastered, he remained essentially where he had begun. His first effort at social commentary, *The Ex-Convict* (1904), was made up of eight separate single-shot episodes, each with its own title, and there was no cutting or editing at all. *The Kleptomaniac* (1905) told two parallel stories to illustrate how the legal system favors wealthy people over poor. In *The Seven Ages* (1907) he illuminated a scene with side lighting from a fireplace, used close-ups and created more than one shot for a scene, one of the earliest examples of a filmmaker breaking away from the theatrical analogy of one shot for each scene.

Yet, having effectively demonstrated an extraordinary range of what were to become basic film techniques, Porter rarely used any more than once and never put them all together as a style. In the following decade other filmmakers borrowed or rediscovered the same techniques and claimed them as their own. Porter did not dispute them. He was finding himself more and more out of his depth. Hired by Adolph Zukor in 1913 to direct the first American five-reel feature films, Porter insisted on turning the camera crank himself, as if he were still back making one-minute Uncle Josh comedies. *The Prisoner of Zenda,* the first of his features to be released, though acclaimed in its time, is no more than a conventional photographed stage play, containing none of the techniques Porter had pioneered.

In the years of his greatest success, 1903 to 1905, Porter's principal legacy to his fellow filmmakers came from the combination of suspense and movement. Will firemen get to the burning building in time to save mother and child? Will the posse capture the bandits before they get

THE MUSEUM OF MODERN ART/FILM STILLS ARCHIVE

THE MUSEUM OF MODERN ART/FILM STILLS ARCHIVE

Audiences marveled when Edwin S. Porter's *The Great Train Robbery* (1903) depicted sights they had never witnessed before, like the sudden violent death of a man. In these frame enlargements, a passenger breaks from the crowd (top) and a robber wheels and shoots him in the back; he slowly succumbs (bottom) as the robber already has the crowd covered again.

away? Rescue movies like *Life of an American Fireman* and Cecil Hepworth's British film *Rescued by Rover* (1905)—the latter second in popularity only to *The Great Train Robbery* in both Britain and the United States—were races against time. But in Porter's Western film there were two groups racing, one against the other—or more precisely, one with a head start and the other trying to catch up, a chase. Chases provided at least twice as much opportunity for more shots, locations and movement, and after 1904 they became the new fad in motion-picture spectacle.

Chases worked especially well in comedies, and by 1904, comedies had become the staple of motion-picture production. With comedy the film-maker was held back only by the limits of his inventiveness, and he could add as many pratfalls, accidents and comic near-disasters as time and film allowed. Even lack of imagination was no insurmountable hardship. When Biograph made a funny film, *Personal* (1904), about a Frenchman who advertised in the paper for a wife and then was chased around Grant's Tomb and through Riverside Park by more than a dozen husband-seeking women, the Edison company made its own version, same story, same location, and called it *How a French Nobleman Got a Wife Through the New York Herald Personal Column.* Another manufacturer simply copied the Biograph print and sold it as its own.

But no one in this period made comedies better than the French company Pathé Frères, until World War I the world's largest motion-picture producer. Like Méliès, the Pathé firm excelled at fairy tales and fantasies, but it surpassed Méliès by taking its stories into the open air and giving them sweep and movement. When the first all-movie theater opened in London in 1907—two years after the proliferation of nickelodeons in the United States—its programs consisted exclusively of two hours of Pathé films. In 1909, according to figures drawn from a British motion-picture trade paper, French producers supplied 40 percent of the new films released in Great Britain, and American producers came next with 30 percent. There are no comparable figures for the United States, but it is likely that Pathé Frères also became the single largest producer of films shown in nickelodeons. Pathé profits jumped dramatically from 1905 to 1907 (though no more, on a percentage basis, than the profits of Vitagraph, the largest American producer). In his book of reminiscence, *The Movies in the Age of Innocence*, Edward Wagenknecht recalls that his neighborhood nickelodeon in Chicago showed only Pathé films.

Pathé's success in the American market did not notably affect either the content of American films or opportunities for American producers. Comedy chases, trick and fantasy films, and risqué movies of women dressing and undressing (which Biograph in particular continued to produce in number) made up the bulk of the programs. One action or melodramatic film was usually part of every show. Producers began to make Western, crime and romance films in increasing number. In this they were emulating not only the popularity of *The Great Train Rob-*

bery and its imitators, but also the American culture of which the major producers were undeniably a part.

From 1905 to 1907—the years of nickelodeon expansion free from middle-class observation—the book-buying public was making best sellers of Western novels by Rex Beach and Zane Grey; realistic works on contemporary American urban life like O. Henry's *The Four Million*, Upton Sinclair's *The Jungle* and Edith Wharton's *The House of Mirth*; and Elinor Glyn's controversial novel of adultery, *Three Weeks*. Motion-picture content rarely differed much from the accepted subjects of other popular forms of entertainment—vaudeville, stage melodrama, burlesque, dime novels—and was much closer to the average novel or legitimate stage play than middle-class opponents of the movies ever admitted. What was distinctive about the movies as they entered their second decade, over and above their actual or potential capacity for creating new forms of visual experience, was their success in providing entertainment and information to an audience that did not need English or even literacy to gain access to urban popular culture for the first time.

The growing notoriety of nickelodeons brought movies to the attention of the middle-class men and women who served the institutions of social control—the churches, reform groups, some segments of the press, and ultimately the police. When they investigated they found that the producers of the new entertainment were people with backgrounds and tastes similar to their own, as opposed to theater managers, who, like their customers, were often recently arrived immigrants. Although they wanted to exert their authority over the producers, it was clear that the exhibitors were both a more vulnerable and a more acceptable target for attack.

Police raids, padlocks and confiscated property were vital signs of moral endeavor to those who were outraged by the immoral potentialities of motion pictures, far more satisfying than quiet efforts to influence producers in private. Moreover, to close a theater or seize a film cut off revenue for all segments of the movie trade, from theater owners to producers. A campaign against theaters for showing movies considered disreputable would get the message to producers without the difficulty of confronting them directly.

Suppression began erratically with seizures in some cities and police censorship in others. It reached an early culmination in New York City, the center of motion-picture production and the largest market, when every movie theater in the city was suddenly ordered closed during Christmas week 1908.

The background of this confrontation was a city ordinance which, along with high population density in the tenement districts, had stimulated the rapid spread of nickelodeons by allowing them to be licensed as common shows for $25 instead of the $500 required for vaudeville and stage theaters. Moreover, the ordinance had placed movies under the licensing bureau's jurisdiction rather than the police's. These arrangements were open to criticism because they provided no means of enforcing health and safety standards in the nickelodeons. It was also clear that the demand for movie licenses afforded considerable opportunity for graft in the licensing bureau, where employees were alleged to be demanding cash payments from applicants.

At the police department's request, Mayor George B. McClellan called a hearing, and on the basis of testimony he heard, he immediately revoked every nickelodeon license, more than six hundred in all. The exhibitors quickly fought back. Led by William Fox, they successfully petitioned the courts for injunctions allowing their theaters to reopen. As a result of the controversy, however, new laws were passed raising the license fee, placing nickelodeons under police jurisdiction and controlling children's attendance.

McClellan had set an example which, if repeated in cities where exhibitors were weaker and courts less forthcoming, could create chaos for the young motion-picture business. The producers got the message. The nine principal producing companies had just organized a Motion Picture Patents Company with the intention of creating a complete monopoly over all phases of motion-picture production, distribution and exhibition; now, assessing both their new strength and their demonstrated vulnerability, they decided, like many other industries faced with public criticism during the Progressive era, to try to prevent outside interference by joining in the creation of a regulatory body of their own choice. This tactic also set a pattern for the movie industry's behavior on later occasions.

The critical role in setting up a regulating agency that might satisfy both sides was played by The People's Institute, a New York reform organization which had gone against the grain of its kind by recognizing the value of movies as popular recreation. It brought ten New York civic organizations together to sponsor a motion-picture censorship board, and early in 1909 the producers gave it their approval. They agreed to submit all films to the board prior to making final release prints, and to excise any footage the board wanted cut, even to junking a film entirely.

The New York Board of Motion Picture Censorship soon changed its name to the National Board of Review of Motion Pictures, to indicate that it did not approve of censorship—undoubtedly a concession to the producers, who feared they might be establishing a precedent for other, less cooperative censorship bodies. They hoped the board's seal of approval—originally an open pair of scissors superimposed on a four-pointed star—would put a stop to local censorship when it appeared on motion pictures.

The censors worked in the screening room of the Motion Picture Patents Company. Every morning half a dozen or more volunteers, dignified women in broad-brimmed flowered hats and dour-faced men, sat down to watch seven or eight of the producers' latest offerings. Some 20 percent of the films they saw they refused to approve. Often they required cuts in the films they passed. Obscenity was their prime target, but they never defined the word, assuming that a respectable person knew obscenity when he or she saw it. Films of women in corsets and leotards, kidnapping, gruesome crimes, and films that might give instructions on how to commit a crime, were taboo. A theatrical suicide, with beating of breast and rolling of eyes, could pass; a leap from the Brooklyn Bridge could not.

The sign of the open scissors did not achieve its primary end. Agitation for local censorship boards continued, and in Chicago, where police censorship had been set up before the New York board was established, police frequently cut scenes or even prohibited whole films that carried the national board's endorsement.

But the board's operations unexpectedly won for the producers more important friends than the Chicago police. In New York the cultural establishment was impressed by the producers' willingness to abide by the wisdom of the charitable, educational and religious leaders who made up the board, even when it meant additional expense or lost revenue. Such cooperation seemed unmistakably to indicate a disposition to be guided by respectable opinion. National magazines published in New York began to give movies more attentive and usually more favorable notice.

It was not what movies were but what they might become that attracted the spokesmen for middle-class culture. They were fascinated by the audience the movies had won over and could command. Initially they had been disturbed by the discovery of working-class people taking part in a culture of which they had no knowledge and over which they exercised too little authority. Now the possibility of gaining control over movies suddenly opened vast new horizons, kindled impossible cultural dreams. The industrial revolution had erected barriers of experience, environment and culture between the middle and the working classes. Not since the Elizabethan Age in England had the high culture of the middle and upper classes been a truly popular culture, accessible to all social groups. But the nickelodeons could restore the past: movies would bring high culture back to the people. No longer was there need for persons of culture to fear or despise the movies: the medium lay close to their grasp, to reshape and uplift.

There was one basic flaw in this middle-class dream: it rested on the continued dominance of the medium by the Patents Company producers who, despite their apparent monopolistic power, proved unable over the succeeding decade even to survive. And as power changed hands in the motion-picture industry it passed not to middle-class reformers and cultural custodians, but to members of the very immigrant ethnic groups they sought to influence and control.

3

EDISON'S TRUST AND HOW IT GOT BUSTED

"Now it cannot be denied," the first motion-picture yearbook admitted candidly in 1912, "that in the beginning many inferior elements crowded into this business; that the appeal was often to the morbid and the vulgar and that some men made, and others exhibited, pictures which catered to the lowest instincts of humanity."[1] This may be the earliest recorded confession of sins by anyone connected with the movie trade; it was to be followed regularly over a span of several decades by similar, almost ritual repudiations of the past.

Every charge made by reformers, the clergy, politicians or the press against the moviemakers was admitted to be accurate—in the past. "The rolling stones, the lovers of pure adventure, the gamblers, the fellows with the grub-stake and a thirst for sudden wealth" had indeed been the disgraceful movie pioneers, acknowledged a writer in 1923; but long ago they had been forced out by a better sort.[2]

The movie leaders and their publicity men may have believed this version of their industrial development, or may simply have adopted it for tactical purposes. In either case, they did not do justice to the actual history of the motion-picture enterprise. To put forward the idea that the men who founded the movie trade were lawless buccaneers and unscrupulous fortune hunters obscures the essential fact that before 1910 the movies were as completely in the hands of respectable, established Anglo-Saxon Protestant Americans as they were ever to be.

The men who ran the motion-picture industry in its first decade closely resembled the average American businessman at the beginning of the twentieth century. The largest American company, Vitagraph, was headed by two men who had been born in England and raised in the United States, Albert E. Smith and J. Stewart Blackton. Biograph (officially the American Mutoscope and Biograph Company, which had been founded in the 1890s by Henry Marvin, an upstate New York manufacturer, and W. K. L. Dickson, the Englishman who had done the motion-picture work at Edison's laboratory) was taken over in 1908 by a New York banker; D. W. Griffith, son of a distinguished ante-bellum Kentucky family, began his career as a director there. Edwin S. Porter,

[1] *Moving Picture Annual and Yearbook for 1912* (1913), p. 7.

[2] John Amid, *With the Movie Makers* (1923), pp. 110–11.

the son of a small-town Pennsylvania merchant, directed production at Edison's new studios in Manhattan and the Bronx until 1909. These three New York companies were the most important in the trade. But there were also three in Chicago, one in Philadelphia, and a handful of small producers scattered around the country.

The most famous name in the industry was, of course, Thomas Alva Edison. After the turn of the century, Edison inexorably consolidated his control over the products and personnel in the field. If middle-class reformers had realized how great an influence Edison wielded, they might have moderated their criticisms, for where could they have found an American industry run by a leader more admired, trusted and indeed revered than Edison? But for his own good reasons Edison let it be known that he took no interest in day-to-day filmmaking activities. At the same time that he was moving behind the scenes to subordinate his competitors, he carefully managed his public image so that he would appear to the public as a solitary, unworldly inventor, interested only in his continuing quest to link phonograph and camera and attain sound motion pictures.

Edison's entrepreneurial efforts came to fruition in December 1908, with the creation of the Motion Picture Patents Company. His behavior on the occasion of his triumph, as related by his latest biographer, was a study in unbusinesslike indifference. Representatives of the companies involved in forming the patents agreement gathered in the library of Edison's West Orange laboratory for dinner and a formal signing, which would be recorded for posterity by their own motion-picture cameramen. The inventor is said to have eaten rapidly, excused himself and rested on a cot in a corner of the room while the last details were hammered out. When the moment was at hand he rose, signed, shook hands all around and then returned to his experiments, saying, "Good-by boys. I have to get back to work," thereby tacitly denying his arduous endeavors in achieving the patents agreement.[3]

The rise and fall of the Motion Picture Patents Company is a fascinating episode in the history of American business enterprise, but the full story has never been told. The most complete accounts in motion-picture literature—in Terry Ramsaye's *A Million and One Nights* (1926) and Benjamin B. Hampton's *A History of the Movies* (1931)—were both written during Edison's lifetime, when it would have been impolitic to challenge the motives or tactics of a man considered by many the greatest living American. Ramsaye, in fact, took the opposite tack and exalted Edison. One is always a little shocked to learn that a hero has feet of clay. Yet the evidence is overwhelmingly clear: the roots of the motion-picture monopoly lay in Thomas A. Edison's greed and dissimulation; and the results of it were a complete debacle for the Wizard, his leadership and his social class.

Edison wanted complete domination of the motion-picture field. But

---

[3] Quoted in Matthew Josephson, *Edison* (1959), p. 402.

instead of driving his competitors out of business, he tried to force them to use only his cameras under license, and to sell or rent films only to the exchanges and exhibitors who agreed to use licensed products exclusively. The advantages he could not get through the U.S. Patent Office he pursued through the federal courts. It was his practice, as Gordon Hendricks has extensively demonstrated in *The Edison Motion Picture Myth* (1961), to claim as much as he could in his patent applications. If the patent examiners rejected his applications, he would revise them until they were approved. Thereafter he began to harass his competitors with lawsuits. None of them had a fraction of the financial resources or legal talent that Edison could bring to bear from his widespread business ventures, and gradually most of them capitulated. By 1907 all the American producers, Méliès and Pathé Frères were under license to Edison, with one exception—Biograph.

Biograph could stay out because it had a patent for a camera of its own. In 1901 Edison had sued Biograph for patent infringement and won his case in federal circuit court. It was appealed, and in 1902 the lower court was dramatically overruled. "It is obvious," declared Judge William J. Wallace, "that Mr. Edison was not a pioneer. . . ."[4] He had not invented the film, he had not invented a camera capable of taking a successive series of pictures, nor a camera that could take motion pictures at high speeds and precise intervals. (The judge gave credit for the latter where it belonged, to Marey.) Edison had been first in the field commercially and had probably invented a successful way to make other people's inventions work rapidly and properly; this the judge would grant him, and nothing more.

Undaunted, Edison reapplied for a new patent, claiming only what the judge allowed—the sprocket mechanism for moving the film intermittently and steadily past the lens. When the revised patent was issued, he took Biograph to court again. In 1906 he lost again, and on appeal in 1907 he lost yet another time, although the appeals court gave him a minor victory when it held that the Warwick camera, used by some of Biograph's overseas associates, did infringe on Edison's reissued patent. Biograph's successful defenses against Edison, however, threatened to be ruinous. The company was not in a financial position to survive if Edison took his case to the Supreme Court. Even when he was in the wrong, Edison was too powerful to lose. In 1908 Biograph agreed to negotiate a truce. The Motion Picture Patents Company was the result.

The Patents combine consisted of nine producing companies—Edison, Biograph, Vitagraph, Essanay, Kalem, Selig, Lubin, Pathé Frères and Méliès—and one importer of films, George Kleine. They pooled some sixteen patents: one for film, two for cameras, and thirteen for projectors. The company was designed to fulfill the goal Edison had been working toward, a complete monopoly of motion-picture activity in the United States. It entered into an agreement with Eastman Kodak, the

---

[4] *Edison v. American Mutoscope Company*, 114 Fed. Rep. 926 (1902), at 934-35.

sole American manufacturer of raw film stock, limiting sales to licensed producers. These producers could rent their films only to exchanges (the distributing firms) that handled licensed films exclusively, and exchanges could make films available only to theater exhibitors who showed nothing but licensed films. Any distributor or exhibitor who broke these rules was blackballed. Exhibitors were also required to pay $2 a week to the Patents Company for the privilege of renting licensed films. Edison got the major portion of these royalties, and his net profits from motion-picture operations soared to over $1 million a year, which may have been the aim of his struggle to control the movies in the first place.

In the Progressive era, business combinations like the Patents Company, which monopolized an industry, were called trusts, and they were deplored at least rhetorically by a great majority of the American people. But the Patents Company appears to have accepted the name of "trust" (The Trust, in the motion-picture trade papers) with equanimity and even with pride. In 1910 it made itself a more perfect trust by establishing its own rental exchange, the General Film Company, which by 1912 had taken over nearly sixty licensed distributors and virtually cornered the market in the rental of licensed films. The Trust's self-confidence did not, however, take into account the vagaries of a presidential election year.

In July 1912 the Democratic party picked as its candidate Woodrow Wilson, who accused the incumbent Republicans of favoring big business and promised a return to competition and opportunities for the little man. Six weeks later, almost as if in response to Wilson's nomination, the Republican Administration filed suit against the Motion Picture Patents Company, charging it with restraint of trade in violation of the 1890 Sherman Antitrust Act. No other industry, after all, was as vulnerable, or regarded with as great suspicion by the middle-class public, for whose votes the parties were competing.

In its defense the Patents Company argued that the controls it imposed were necessary to establish order and higher standards for the motion-picture trade. The members had wanted to relieve each other of the odium of patent infringement, they said, to end the legal conflicts that were diverting their energies from making better pictures, and to protect the morals of the public, as evidenced by their cooperation with the National Board of Review. Nevertheless, in 1915 the federal court declared the Motion Picture Patents Company an illegal conspiracy in restraint of trade.

The irony of it was that the Trust did not end competition, it fostered it. It gave regulation and direction to a continually shrinking segment of the motion-picture industry, while outside its narrowing circle others were developing entirely different methods of filmmaking, promotion and exhibition. It did not notably improve the quality or morality of motion pictures, but it inspired others to do so. The Patents Company's most significant contribution was one it chose not to invoke in its defense: by its tactics of exclusion and harassment it brought into being a growing opposition, composed principally of former nickelodeon managers from the urban ghettos of New York and Chicago. Since it believed it could easily monopolize the industry, the Trust was surprised to find itself in a struggle against energetic and innovative foes. The federal court ruling of 1915 was almost irrelevant. By then the Patents Company had already lost the battle. Control of the industry had passed into the hands of the immigrant groups that had provided the first big audience for movies.

By 1912, the fourth year of the Patents Company, its share of total film production and importation had fallen from virtually 100 percent at the end of 1908 to slightly more than half. The so-called independent firms, outside the orbit of the Trust, accounted for the remainder. Significantly, the independents were responsible for all the feature films of three reels or more.

This unusual accomplishment by newcomers was even more remarkable in light of the obstacles put in their way. The independents were denied access to American-made raw film stock. If they could obtain it elsewhere, they still faced the problem of finding a workable camera not covered by the Trust's patents; if they went ahead and used an infringing camera, they were vulnerable to the Trust's ubiquitous investigators and lawsuits. And any film they managed to complete was barred from the screens of all the theaters licensed to show the Trust's films. Nevertheless, the independents defeated the Trust and brought about a revolution in motion-picture leadership.

The struggle of the independents, indeed their very existence, had its roots in the strategy chosen by the Trust. For a variety of reasons, the Trust decided not to swallow the industry whole but to control only selected parts, expecting the remainder to collapse from lack of market or supply. Four or five American producers were left out chiefly because they were too small to bother about. By the terms of the Trust agreement, several of the leading British and Italian producers were to be kept out of the American market, apparently because they had angered Edison by siding with Biograph in the earlier patents dispute. Only two European companies (except for the two French producers who were members of the Trust), one British and one French, were allowed entry, and at the greatly reduced rate of three reels per week for both. As far as distribution went, the Trust seems at first to have offered licenses to all the existing exchanges, but later organized its own exchange and bought or drove out all but one of its licensees. Most important, the Trust licensed only a half to two thirds of the six thousand movie theaters in the United States.

On the filmmaking side of its operations the Trust planned to stand pat; it continued to produce inexpensive one-reel films, moving to two reels only after great hesitation. On the marketing end, however, it saw opportunities for profitable improvement. Motion-picture distribution and exhibition could hardly have been more chaotic than they were in 1909. Nickelodeons, bunched together, showed a half-hour program of three one-reel films and changed their program every day. Each of the six thousand theaters required twenty-one films a week, and the exchanges did not always give satisfactory service; often they sent broken, scratched or deteriorated films, made late deliveries or none at all, or provided theaters next door to each other with the same program. In its efforts to improve distribution service, the Trust sensed an opportunity to transform the motion-picture audience.

Why cater to the poorest sectors of American society when a more well-to-do audience offered lucrative possibilities for greater profits? The Trust gave special consideration to exhibitors moving into better neighborhoods or downtown locations, promising preferential bookings to theaters that would hold films for longer runs and charge a dime. Through local newspaper advertising and reviews and by building up a reputation for quality prints of pre-censored films, the Patents Company hoped gradually to shift the social foundations of movie patronage. Anywhere from two to three thousand storefront nickelodeons were therefore left unserviced by the Trust. Their need provided a clear opportunity for anyone capable of breaking the Trust's blockade.

Probably only one man in the industry had the resources—Carl Laemmle, a Chicago-based distributor. Laemmle owned six exchanges in major Midwestern, Rocky Mountain and West Coast cities, including Chicago, Minneapolis, Omaha, Salt Lake City, and Portland, Oregon. He had close contacts with exhibitors in all those cities and their hinterlands, and a supply of films he had purchased when producers operated on a direct-sale as well as rental basis. He was a German-born Jew in his early forties who had had a nondescript career as a clothing-store manager until, like scores of other immigrant businessmen, he opened a storefront nickelodeon. More skillful and ambitious than most, he built the largest distributing concern in the United States within three years. He was licensed by the Trust, but it refused him any voice in industry decisions. For three months his resentment grew and then, in April 1909, he declared his independence.

Laemmle's first problem was to secure a regular source of new films. He found it in the International Projecting and Producing Company, formed in the aftermath of the Trust agreement to import the films of excluded European producers to the few American exchanges that remained outside the Trust. But Laemmle needed new American films as well, and the small group of independent producers could come up with hardly more than a film a week. A new opportunity presented itself when Lumière began to make its raw film stock available in the United States. Laemmle immediately launched a production company, the Independent Moving Picture Company, known as Imp.

The Patents Company's indifference to the storefront nickelodeons stirred the hopes of other motion-picture men as well. Where the major producers had not had significant competition before they organized the

Trust, within a year perhaps a dozen new producing companies entered the field, knowing they had an open market in independent exchanges and nonlicensed theaters. The New York Motion Picture Company was the first new firm, founded early in 1909 by the independent distributors Adam Kessel and Charles O. Baumann and the producer-director Fred Balshofer. They made Western films under the Bison trademark. Then Edwin S. Porter left Edison and joined a new company, Defender; later he established the Rex Film Company with the same partners. David Horsley, a pre-Trust independent producer, reorganized as the Nestor Company. Patrick Powers, a former distributor, began a production company bearing his own name. Kessel and Baumann's New York Company, Laemmle's Imp, and Powers became the big three of the independents.

Using Lumière film stock, the independent producers tried to work with noninfringing European cameras, but since the results were unsatisfactory, they began using Edison machines surreptitiously. The Trust retaliated by hiring spies to gather evidence of patent infringement and even tried forcibly to disrupt independent production activities. The independents camouflaged their cameras, engaged bodyguards to protect their cameramen and eventually scattered to locations in Cuba, Florida, Arizona and California, where they had the advantages of year-round sunshine and distance from the Trust.

The Trust, well versed in Edison's tactics, harried the independents into court. Laemmle himself, according to his biographer, was the target of 289 separate legal actions, which cost him more than $300,000 in defense expenses. The Trust, like Edison before it, had more losses than victories in the courts, and this time the defendants had the resources and stamina to hold out; unlike Edison's earlier opponents, they had no alternative except to go out of business. In 1910 the Trust lobbied in Congress to have duties raised on imported film stock. It lost. J. J. Murdock, president of the International Projecting and Producing Company, persuaded the legislators to lower duties on both raw and manufactured film in the otherwise infamous Payne-Aldrich tariff bill.

Year by year the independents grew stronger. In 1910, with Laemmle and Kessel and Baumann taking the lead, they organized the Motion Picture Distributing and Sales Company, designed to consolidate the movement of films from producers to exchanges. At first a number of the small companies refused to join, but a compromise was arranged, and the Sales Company became the sole outlet for independent films. By mid-1910 the Sales Company and its affiliated exchanges could offer theaters a choice of twenty-seven films a week. Building on their solid base of storefront nickelodeon customers, the independents began to lure licensed exhibitors away from the Trust. Laemmle's associate, Robert C. Cochrane, waged a devastating campaign of ridicule against the Trust in trade-paper ads, attacking its strong-arm tactics and especially the $2 weekly royalty.

In 1912, the year the independents nearly equaled the Trust in total film production, they split into two rival camps. Harry E. Aitken, a Wisconsin distributor, organized the Mutual Film Corporation, with the intention of buying exchanges and becoming sole national distributor of several production companies. Ten independent producers went with Aitken, and seven others formed their own corporation, the Universal Film Manufacturing Company, to succeed the Sales Company and continue supplying films to independent exchanges.

Laemmle, Kessel and Baumann, and Powers were again the central figures in Universal, but they soon quarreled over who was first among equals, and Kessel and Baumann quit. Laemmle and Powers then demonstrated what they had learned in their struggle with the Trust: they claimed that the assets of the New York Motion Picture Company had been signed over to Universal in exchange for stock, and tried to seize its property in New York and Los Angeles by force. Eventually Universal lost the battle in court, gaining only the Bison trademark. By the time the Justice Department filed suit against the Trust in 1912, the independents may have deserved scrutiny just as much.

But the independents were on the ascendancy. They consistently demonstrated the initiative and innovative energy that the Trust producers lacked, most particularly in their swift adoption of a "star" system, similar to the traditional billing in the theater and vaudeville. The Trust producers had not identified their players; and many actors and actresses, hoping some day to achieve "legitimate" success in the theater, were glad of the anonymity. But the growing movie public picked their favorites anyway and wrote fan letters to "The Biograph Girl" or "The Lone Indian" of the Bison company. Laemmle decided to capitalize on this audience desire for stars.

In 1909 he hired "The Biograph Girl," Florence Lawrence, away from Biograph and gave her star billing by name in Imp films. The next year he lured Mary Pickford from the same company by nearly doubling her salary. And he discovered that stars sold pictures as nothing else could. So long as theaters changed their programs daily—and the practice persisted in neighborhood theaters and small towns until the early 1920s—building up audience recognition of star names was almost the only effective form of advance publicity.

When word got out that the independents offered opportunities to build a career, talent came to them from the Trust producers, from vaudeville and from other trades, and by the mid-1910s they had the three leading filmmakers. Thomas H. Ince left vaudeville in 1910 to join Imp and was hired away by Kessel and Baumann's company, where he became one of the first important producer-directors. Kessel and Baumann also lured Mack Sennett from Biograph to Keystone. When Biograph refused to let D. W. Griffith make films longer than two reels, he resigned to work for Harry E. Aitken's Mutual company.

The defeat of the Trust was, however, above all a victory for the men who ran and supplied the storefront nickel theaters. Among them were a considerable number of East European Jews who had come to the

United States as youths and struggled up the economic ladder, specializing in businesses like clothing and expensive accessories such as furs and jewelry, where skill in meeting and pleasing the public and a flair for fashion were essential to success. Some entered the amusement business as a sideline, others in escape from a dead end, but both groups quickly learned that providing inexpensive commercial entertainment was a necessary service, and far more profitable than selling apparel. The Trust threat led the most ambitious and talented among them to seek power over their own destiny. Laemmle was their pathfinder and prototype. More than any other man he had established the independents and kept alive the neighborhood theaters in the ghettos. But Laemmle's triumph, important as it was, was only a stepping stone. Waiting in the wings were others who had stood aloof from the independents' struggle, for their ambitions ranged far beyond the needs of nickelodeons.

The first titans to emerge were two New York showmen, William Fox and Adolph Zukor, both Hungarian Jews. Even before the Trust was formed they had raised a question of untold portent: if businessmen could make tens of thousands of dollars, even hundreds of thousands, showing movies for a nickel to the lowest classes in American society, what could they make if everyone went to the movies? The Trust took up their ideas, at least partially, and both men were content to cooperate with it until it became, in Fox's case, hostile, and in Zukor's, ineffectual. They were younger than Laemmle—Zukor by six years, Fox by twelve—and closer to other sectors of the amusement world that catered to the middle and even to the leisure class.

Fox made the first breakthrough into middle-class audiences. He had not yet turned thirty when he led New York exhibitors in opposing Mayor McClellan's 1908 order closing the nickelodeons, by which time he owned more than a dozen neighborhood theaters and had startled the New York amusement world by taking over established vaudeville houses and successfully showing movies as half the program. His nickel and dime admissions filled large houses that had been playing to small audiences and brought him greater profits despite the lower price. He not only made vaudeville accessible to the working classes, his use of larger and more comfortable theaters attracted the vaudeville-going middle classes to movies.

When Fox expanded his operations into motion-picture distribution, he came into conflict with the Trust. At first his was a licensed exchange; but as it began its efforts to take over all licensed distributors, the General Film Company tried to buy him out. He refused to sell, and his license was canceled. He took the Trust to court—a switch on the usual procedure—and won the right to keep his license, becoming the only distributor to resist takeover successfully. This experience convinced Fox that a distributor should have his own source of film supply, and he went into production. Thus he pioneered in the vertical integration of the movie industry, combining production, distribution and exhibition under single or affiliated ownership—a development that soon became standard in the industry, until the Justice Department won another antitrust suit thirty-three years after the Patents Company decision.

While Fox was preoccupied with his battle against the Trust, Zukor observed his success in combining inexpensive movies and vaudeville. In 1908 Zukor was operating on a smaller but nevertheless comfortable level with a string of nickel theaters. Having attained wealth as a furrier, he had gone into amusements as a penny-arcade operator, then failed disastrously as an exhibitor of Hale's Tours—a short-lived idea before the advent of nickelodeons, with a theater built like a railroad car and scenic views projected as if one were traveling on a track.

That failure probably held back his progress while Fox advanced and Zukor's friend Marcus Loew became a dominant figure in the low-priced vaudeville field. In 1910 Zukor merged part of his holdings into Loew's Consolidated Enterprises and became treasurer of Loew's growing theatrical empire, meanwhile keeping separate several theaters he owned with the theatrical manager William A. Brady. More than any other exhibitor of his time, Zukor had contact with the entire range of popular entertainment, its audience, finances, problems and opportunities. He began to set his sights on an audience still outside the reach of either Fox or Loew.

European producers, catering from the beginning to a class rather than a mass audience, started around 1911 to make films of up to five reels—more than an hour in length. Zukor was among the first to believe the European features could draw the same class of patrons in the United States. Until then he had worked in harmony with the Trust, but as soon as he raised the issue of European features he realized that its conservatism about production costs and film lengths contradicted its desire to attract middle-class audiences.

Zukor believed that the best way to make movies appealing to the middle classes would be to produce longer and more expensive films modeled after familiar middle-class forms of entertainment. Even better than spectacle films, which the Italians in particular were exporting to the United States, would be films of plays, starring well-known stage actors and actresses. The crucial element of voice would be missing, but that would not matter if Zukor could make movies that fulfilled his slogan: "Famous Players in Famous Plays."

He started at the top by purchasing the American rights to a four-reel French film, *Queen Elizabeth*, the only motion-picture appearance of the era's most famous actress, Sarah Bernhardt. In aesthetic terms it was nearly as primitive as any movie made before *The Great Train Robbery*, with the camera so far from the action that the players' features were hardly discernible, and with individual shots of interminable length. But that was precisely what Zukor wanted, a film that looked as if one were watching a play from the twenty-fifth row.

Queen Elizabeth was no nickel-and-dime proposition. Zukor's first in-

THE MUSEUM OF MODERN ART/FILM STILLS ARCHIVE

The man who forged the first motion-picture trust and two ambitious immigrant entrepreneurs who broke with him and later tried some trust-building of their own: Thomas A. Edison with Adolph Zukor (bottom), and William Fox (top) in the garden of his Long Island estate. In a caption supplied with Fox's picture, his publicity department described him as "The Man Who Forgets to Sleep."

THE MUSEUM OF MODERN ART/FILM STILLS ARCHIVE

stinct was to make it available, following the theatrical pattern, on a road-show basis, booking the film into legitimate theaters and furnishing projection equipment and publicity in return for a percentage of the gross. This did not work: hardly anyone believed you could sell reserved seats for a feature motion picture at prices comparable to live drama. An aspiring salesman, Al Lichtman, convinced Zukor that a "states' rights" system of distribution would be better. This involved selling or leasing the film to an exchange with the exclusive right to market it in a specified state or territory, thus putting the burden of convincing theater managers on the distributor. This system had worked for several Italian spectaculars, beginning in 1911, and with Lichtman handling *Queen Elizabeth*, it worked for Zukor as well.

By the time *Queen Elizabeth* opened in New York in July 1912, Zukor had launched the Famous Players Film Company. He made Daniel Frohman, a well-known theatrical producer, his partner, to ensure his lines of contact to the stage world, and brought in Edwin S. Porter as head of production after D. W. Griffith turned him down; having made so many advances in motion-picture technique, Griffith did not want the strait jacket of Zukor's stage formula. Porter was acquiescent and began making films of famous plays with famous players—*The Count of Monte Cristo* with James O'Neill, father of Eugene, and *The Prisoner of Zenda* with James K. Hackett, produced second but released first, in 1913.

Others quickly followed Zukor's lead. Griffith made a four-reel feature for Biograph, *Judith of Bethulia*, based on a famous play, though unlike Porter he completely discarded stage conventions in the filming. Biograph did not release it until 1914, after Griffith had resigned to direct and supervise features for the Reliance and Majestic companies, subsidiaries of Harry Aitken's Mutual distributors.

Jesse L. Lasky, a vaudeville manager, joined with his brother-in-law, Samuel Goldfish (later Goldwyn), a Polish-born glove salesman, to found the Jesse L. Lasky Feature Play Company. They added as director Cecil B. DeMille, an actor from a theatrical family, and went to California to make a film of a long-time stage favorite, *The Squaw Man*. Totally inexperienced, they punched the sprocket holes on their negative film incorrectly, so when the positives were printed and projected, each frame was slightly off, causing feet to appear above heads. They took their problem to Siegmund "Pop" Lubin, a pioneer from the 1890s and one of the Trust producers, who immediately recognized the cause and told them how to solve it. It is a famous story in film history: Father Time assisting at the birth of the new era.

Zukor proved to be right: features began to attract the middle class to movies. Even people who rarely went to the legitimate theater made the excursion downtown to see an Italian epic or an American film of a popular play or novel. By and large they liked what they saw and came back. But at least one or two motion-picture exhibitors suspected that movies needed a new environment before they could win over the steady patronage of a new class: the tastes and expectations of a cultivated audience required an atmosphere of elegance that only newly conceived and constructed movie theaters could provide.

Such theaters, planned as important works of architecture in their own right, had been going up in Berlin, Germany, since 1911. There the middle and leisure classes had made up the bulk of the movie audience from the start. Berlin had only 168 movie theaters in 1913, compared to Chicago, a city of similar population, with over 400 theaters in 1909 and many more by 1913—most of them, of course, storefronts. In Berlin even the neighborhood theaters were specially constructed, some as small, intimate theaters in hotels or office buildings, others ornate museumlike edifices seating more than a thousand, with individual cushioned armchairs for seats, and with elaborately designed and decorated foyers, stairways, ceilings and walls.

The first American theater built especially for motion pictures, the Regent, at 116th Street and Seventh Avenue in New York, opened in February 1913. Compared to even the average Berlin movie theater, it was neither architecturally distinguished nor sumptuous. Built like a vaudeville theater, and in competition with the vaudeville houses in its neighborhood, it almost failed because it showed only Trust-produced short films. This frightened the owners of another new theater under construction, the Strand, at Forty-seventh Street and Broadway. Before it opened, in April 1914, they considered booking vaudeville, variety, and even grand opera before deciding at the last minute on movies.

What convinced them to commit their house to movies—or rather, who convinced them—was S. L. "Roxy" Rothapfel (later Rothafel), the first great showman of motion-picture exhibition. He had taken over the Regent and made it successful showing features, and he was immediately hired to work his magic on the Strand. Rothapfel's credo was "Don't 'give the people what they want'—give 'em something better," and he did it with spectacular flair: special lighting, orchestral music, uniformed ushers, rest rooms fitted and furnished with royal splendor.[5] Theaters run by "Roxy" were more memorable for their service than for their design.

This difference between German and American movie theaters was in keeping with the difference between their audiences. Although American movies won new patronage from the middle classes, their prosperity continued to rest on a foundation of working-class support. Exhibitors quickly discovered that working-class people appreciated amenities as much as anyone else: the larger and more pretentious the theaters, the greater numbers they drew. "Although the motion-picture theater is a democratic institution," one observer commented, "the well-to-do working classes prefer to patronize the classy building which has been exclusively erected for motion-picture entertainments. It is not because they refuse to associate with their poor brothers and sisters; quality is the

---

[5] Quoted in Ben M. Hall, *The Best Remaining Seats* (1961), p. 37.

deciding factor. For five or ten cents more they see a longer and better program, amid more comfortable surroundings."[6]

By 1917 it was assumed that new movie houses would be popular-priced theaters for the masses, and as a manual on theater construction that year recommended, "palatial in design, of colossal dimensions."[7] Richly appointed, imaginative, even bizarre lobbies and interiors, it was thought, would help remove patrons from the workaday world and put them in a suitable frame of mind for the fantasies on the screen. All classes and castes might come together in the American picture palace to dream as equals in the dark.

Adolph Zukor's aim, according to a biographer in the 1920s, had been to "kill the slum tradition" in the movies.[8] In this he succeeded, but not quite in the way he had expected or the middle-class cultural spokesmen before him had hoped. The movies expanded into the middle classes without leaving their storefront audiences behind. In the realm of motion-picture attendance, the class distinctions of American society began slowly to fade. The earlier hopes of the cultivated classes were at least partially attained when feature pictures conveyed their values to the lower orders. But the possibility of restoring cultural unity to American society through movies had slipped beyond the reach of the middle class. If anyone had the power to forge such a unity, it was the producers, many of them foreign-born Jewish immigrants, and their efforts would be not in the name of high culture but rather of mass entertainment.

This was a galling fact to many middle-class Americans, and they continued for decades their struggle to gain control if not of the industry, then over the content of its final products, the movies themselves. Others regarded the rise of the storefront-theater managers to fabulous wealth and power with a mixture of awe and amusement. The term "movie mogul" came into use around 1915, nicely describing the immigrant producers in the eyes of the public—part splendid emperors, part barbarian invaders. Their foreignness, their language, their alleged ignorance, were the subjects of a thousand jokes. "I've got something big," says a scenario writer. "I've got the film rights to *Pudd'nhead Wilson.*" No good, replies the mogul. "Ve don't want to knock the President."[9]

World War I completed the process of making American motion pictures a giant business. In the prewar years, French and Italian film-makers had been acknowledged as the best in the world. The war cut their production, as well as that of England and Germany. American companies took over the Japanese market from the Italians and the Latin American from the French, not to speak of doing better in their own

---

[6] Ernest A. Dench, *Advertising by Motion Pictures* (1916), p. 200.

[7] Edward Bernard Kinsila, *Modern Theatre Construction* (1917), p. 98.

[8] Will Irwin, *The House That Shadows Built* (1928), p. 151.

[9] Homer Croy, *How Motion Pictures Are Made* (1918), p. 104.

theaters, where Pathé Frères had been the most popular producer, and Italian spectaculars, important drawing cards for the middle class. American motion-picture exports rose from 36 million feet in 1915 to nearly 159 million in 1916, an almost fivefold increase. By the end of the war, the United States was said to produce some 85 percent of the films shown throughout the world and 98 percent of those shown in America; motion pictures were variously called (though with considerable exaggeration) the fourth, fifth or sixth largest American industry. The leaders of the field had succeeded as businessmen, entrepreneurs and showmen, beyond their wildest dreams. What could be said, however, of their primary product, the image on the screen, the movies with their much debated potential as a new form of art?

4

D. W. GRIFFITH AND THE FORGING OF MOTION-PICTURE ART

Long before anyone thought movies could be art, a new generation of thinkers and artists had begun to explore the principles of motion pictures for analogies to their own innovations in philosophy, science, painting and literature. What interested these early-twentieth-century modernists was movement, and the relativity and multidimensionality of space and time. The invention of cameras and projectors to record and reproduce images of motion coincided with the development of modernism, and in some cases may have fostered it.

The French philosopher Henri Bergson was most explicit in using a cinematic analogy. As early as 1902–1903, in a series of lectures in Paris, he compared what he called "the mechanism of conceptual thought" to the way motion pictures work. We perceive the entire world, he said, as if taking a rapid series of shots like the separate still frames of motion-picture film. These remain still until we give them motion by our process of thought, setting them moving as a projector does and creating an imitation of living reality in our minds. "We hardly do anything else," said Bergson, "than set going a kind of cinematograph inside us."[1]

One did not even need to be conscious of motion pictures to apply their principles. Describing her early writing in a retrospective lecture, Gertrude Stein explained that she was doing what the cinema was doing, "making a continuous succession of the statement of what that person was." The result was not separate things but one thing, just as individual frames become one moving image. It did not matter that she was not thinking about movies when she wrote this way, and had probably never seen one. "This our period was undoubtedly the period of the cinema and series production," she said. "And each of us in our own way are bound to express what the world in which we are living is doing."[2]

In the years after 1900, what the world was doing—at least the world of modernist art and literature—was what motion pictures were doing. Not only did an observer at the 1913 New York Armory Show compare Marcel Duchamp's *Nude Descending a Staircase* to E. J. Marey's studies of men in motion; more hostile critics at the same show attributed the flat perspectives and multiple images in cubist works by Picasso, Braque,

[1] *Creative Evolution* (1911), p. 306.

[2] *Lectures in America* (1935; Vintage ed. 1975), pp. 176–77.

Léger and others to a "distorted Bergsonian philosophy."[3] Wylie Sypher, studying the development of twentieth-century arts, has concluded: "It may well be that according to the law of technical primacy —the theory that in each era all the arts fall under the influence of one of the arts—the cinema has technical primacy during the years between the rise of cubism and the present."[4]

What these important acknowledgments leave unclear is whether they grant that movies themselves—as opposed to the principle, techniques or forms of cinematic reproduction—can be art. By the cinema, Sypher made clear, he did not mean commercial motion pictures, where the camera is used "merely to record a nineteenth-century plot," but rather "an artistic technique of presenting things as they exist in time by means of a composite perspective."[5] Presumably this technique is available to filmmakers as well as to visual artists and prose writers, but not if they work in the motion-picture industry.

Perhaps the most succinct statement of this view was made by Bernard Shaw in 1924. "All industries," Shaw said, "are brought under the control of [businessmen] by Capitalism. If the capitalists let themselves be seduced from their pursuit of profits to the enchantments of art, they would be bankrupt before they knew where they were. You cannot combine the pursuit of money with the pursuit of art."[6] (A Hollywood publicist brilliantly reversed this condemnation and reworked it into a famous *bon mot* attributed to Shaw when he refused a contract offer from Samuel Goldwyn: "The trouble, Mr. Goldwyn, is that you are only interested in art, and I am only interested in money.")[7]

The question is still not settled. Whether art can be created in a setting where maximum profit is the primary goal remains an issue throughout the mass-entertainment industries. What credence can be given, therefore, to the claims of a man who asserted as early as 1913 that he had founded the modern techniques of motion-picture art? He was an overworked employee of a company engaged in illegal restraint of trade, for whom he produced an average of nearly two films a week over a five-year period. His principal aesthetic allegiance was to the nineteenth-century plot. Was David Wark Griffith nevertheless an artist and modernist, comparable in some measure to Gertrude Stein and Pablo Picasso?

* * *

---

[3] Frank Jewett Mather, Jr., quoted in Milton W. Brown, *American Painting from the Armory Show to the Depression* (1955), p. 55.

[4] *Rococo to Cubism in Art and Literature* (1960), p. 266.

[5] *Ibid.*

[6] Bernard Shaw and Archibald Henderson, "The Drama, The Theater, and the Films," *Harper's*, Vol. 149 (September 1924), p. 426.

[7] Quoted in Norman Zierold, *The Moguls* (1969), p. 128.

The story of Griffith's pilgrimage along the path of movie progress, his early triumphs and late disasters, has in recent years become familiar to everyone interested in the medium: the pioneer days of growth and innovation at Biograph, the controversial epic of white supremacy, *The Birth of a Nation*; the second epic, *Intolerance*, still acclaimed by many as the greatest movie ever made; years of fame, leadership and productivity, his own studio, more classics like *Broken Blossoms* and *Way Down East*; then financial setbacks, loss of independence, humiliation and failure, drink, lonely years in Kentucky and the pastel stucco houses of Southern California, and finally death in the Hollywood Knickerbocker Hotel.

It is one of many Hollywood morality tales, perhaps the most significant. But what is important is how Griffith's life and work appear from the vantage point not of Hollywood, but of society, history, culture, the arts. The moguls, after all, were businessmen as well as motion-picture men and have their counterparts in bankers, brokers, automobile manufacturers. Where, outside the hermetic world of Hollywood, are there comparisons to fit the first and greatest of American directors?

It has often been said that young people or newcomers to a field, with little commitment to its traditions and rules of procedure, achieve the leaps of discovery and creation that change its fundamental method and direction. Often they bring with them or find elsewhere the ideas or perceptive modes that can revolutionize a field from within. Thus Picasso and Stein and other early twentieth-century modernists used principles derived from technology and psychology to reshape the styles and visions of painting and prose.

Everyone working in movies was, of course, more or less a newcomer. And as the years went by, many were willing to claim that they had been the innovators and forged the movies as an art by advancing beyond trick films and chases into the realm of drama. Indeed, the drive to attain status for the movies by imitating the drama grew so powerful that as more and more people entered the movies from theatrical backgrounds, knowledge of cinematic principles grew steadily weaker, and the movies were in danger of becoming mere records of stage performances.

One might have expected nothing more from Griffith, for he came to movies as another failed playwright and actor, looking for a job. But few people have brought more to the films than he.

There is a story, which may or may not be true, told by Linda Arvidson, the first Mrs. Griffith, in her memoir, *When the Movies Were Young*. In October 1908, five months and twenty-nine films after his start as a director at Biograph, Griffith made a film, *After Many Years*, that left his co-workers astonished and uneasy. The plot was taken from Tennyson's *Enoch Arden*, a story of a shipwrecked man who returns many years later to find his wife remarried and his children grown.

Watching it in the screening room, the Biograph staff was aware that it was a movie unlike any made before. The camera had been moved so close to the actors that human figures filled the frame. In some shots they were actually larger than the frame and were shown only from the knees up. For the first time viewers could see facial expressions throughout the film. At one point there were three separate shots of the same scene to keep the actor close to the camera as he moved in open space. And the most startling novelty was that the movie, like Tennyson's original, told two parallel stories, switching from the wife to the marooned husband.

"How can you tell a story jumping about like that?" Griffith's employers asked him, according to Arvidson. "The people won't know what it's about." And Griffith answered, "Well, doesn't Dickens write that way?"[8] Griffith had found his inspiration for moving freely through space and time not from *Mary, Queen of Scots* and *The Great Train Robbery*, but in the traditional novel and epic poem. The nineteenth-century plot, at one central moment, served as the vehicle for the rediscovery of cinema's fundamental resources. This time, through the growth and development of D. W. Griffith's cinematic style, they would not be lost again.

Griffith turned naturally to Dickens and Tennyson because his principal ambition had been, and probably in October 1908 still was, to be a writer. Acting was something he had done to make a living. He was lean and austerely handsome, with a deep voice and a flamboyant style. Because he looked and sounded like an actor he became one, though never a good one. On stage—and also at Biograph—he called himself Lawrence Griffith, using his real name, David, and his family name, Wark, for his writing.

He came out of the defeated South, born in Kentucky in 1875 to genteel poverty and a sense of better times gone by. His early years were spent in the presence of an aging, wounded and impoverished father, who had been a power in ante-bellum Kentucky and a heroic Confederate officer in the Civil War, and who retained until his death in 1885 his stentorian manner and aura of a lost past. Griffith was a far cry from the men of science and technology who were the first to make a mark on the movies. He was a whole-souled American romantic. Like a character in Theodore Dreiser's novels of the period he yearned for success, but also for an indefinable something more, some form of contentment, fulfillment, security.

He had been an actor for twelve years with little to show for it when he entered movies. His career as David Wark Griffith had perhaps gone a little better than his work as Lawrence Griffith. In 1906, age thirty-one, newly married to an actress and settled in New York, he suddenly began to succeed: he sold a play for $1,000, had a poem published in *Leslie's Weekly* and a short story accepted by *Cosmopolitan*. But the play, *A Fool and a Girl*, set in the California hop fields where Griffith had once worked between acting assignments, closed after a week's run

---

[8] Mrs. D. W. Griffith (Linda Arvidson), *When the Movies Were Young* (1925; Dover ed., 1969), p. 66.

in Washington and another week in Baltimore. Griffith went back to his desk to begin a historical drama on the American Revolution and back to the pavements to find an actor's job.

The movie studios were looking for actors and stories. At Edison in the Bronx, Edwin S. Porter used him once, in *Rescued from an Eagle's Nest.* At Biograph on East Fourteenth Street both Griffiths found work, and in addition to acting, he sold several synopses—short summaries of stories that could be made into one-reel films. He became known as an actor with ideas, and when Biograph's regular director became ill and his replacement proved unsatisfactory, the company managers accepted an employee's suggestion to try Griffith. Griffith agreed, provided he could return to acting should he fail.

He knew very little about movies. He had not even been a particularly satisfactory film actor, for he sometimes moved with such speed and exaggerated gestures that he appeared blurred on the screen. But at Biograph he would not be required to do the complete filmmaking job that men like Porter did. Biograph had pioneered in the separation and specialization of filmmaking tasks, largely because it employed a skillful cameraman, G. W. "Billy" Bitzer, who preferred to run his camera and let someone else take care of the actors.

Bitzer took charge of placing the camera, establishing the field of vision, and telling the director where to place the chalk marks that indicated the area within which action could be filmed in focus. Other employees were being increasingly used to supply story ideas or synopses and to assemble the completed film following the director's notes. The director at Biograph was left with casting, rehearsing if there was time, and coaching and cajoling the actors from the sidelines while the camera ran.

A film director had one more task, however, which had no precise counterpart in literature or drama: he had to provide the film with continuity. At the basic level, continuity meant telling a story without confusing the audience. In the early years of motion pictures there was persistent concern about how much audiences could understand and how much they had to be shown or told about changes in time or location or the mere movement of characters from room to room. Theatergoers could find this information in the program, in the division of a play into acts and scenes. Readers of novels had chapter breaks. Directors of the early silents came more and more to use printed titles for such stage directions—"They Return Home" or "Five Years Later."

But continuity also had a deeper meaning: it signified the form of motion-picture narrative, the complex of stylistic devices used in telling a screen story. Continuity encompassed the entire craft of filmmaking—the choice of setting and lighting, the placement of camera and actors, the intercutting of shots and the timing of scenes, the pace and interest of the plot. Continuity was not merely keeping audiences clear about what was happening, it was holding their attention, perhaps making them excited, captivated, enthralled. Griffith's unsuccessful predecessor at Biograph was a synopsis writer who could tell a story in words but not in pictures: his separate scenes did not connect well enough, did not move the action forward. Griffith's literary background might have prepared him with ideas, but he would have to show that he had visual skills as well.

His first film, a gypsy melodrama called *The Adventures of Dolly*, satisfied his employers. Within a fortnight he was assigned to direct the entire Biograph output, which meant two one-reel films a week and an additional half-reel comedy or short melodrama. He maintained this schedule for more than a year and a half, after which he gave up the shorter films and some of the one-reelers to new directors he had trained.

At first his films followed the conventions of moviemaking in 1908. They were composed of a dozen or fewer separate shots of consecutive action. Even in outdoor scenes their sense of space was limited, as if bordered by the invisible walls of the proscenium stage, and much of interest to the story seemed to be taking place elsewhere, out of camera range. Yet there was something about the films he directed that immediately marked them as out of the ordinary. They moved swiftly, they had an aura of intensified emotion and heightened energy. Griffith's imagination was as florid and extravagant as his personal and acting style, and it seemed to work with visual images even better than with words.

His taste in stories ran to the exotic. He made films about American Indians, Mexicans, Japanese and South African Zulus—all played by white actors and actresses made up for the parts. But his working-class people and members of racial minorities were from the beginning endowed with a humanity that set them apart from the stock caricatures. Often minority figures were the heroes of his films, exhibiting moral strength superior to their white antagonists.

As he became more familiar with the filmmaking process, Griffith gradually began to alter the traditional Biograph techniques to enhance his developing storytelling style. The Biograph camera was mounted on a rolling platform in the studio so that it could be moved closer to the set, eliminating the wide stretch of open floor which generally filled the bottom third of the frame. He also borrowed a technique from comedy chases and began cutting back and forth between two scenes of action. Camera takes were cut up into shorter sections as the stage convention of scene-by-scene continuity was abandoned. The individual shot began to replace the complete scene as the basic unit of construction in a Griffith film. He started to change camera placements within a scene and take multiple shots. Before the end of 1908 he made a ten-minute film, *The Guerrilla*, a Civil War melodrama, with the unheard-of total of more than forty separate shots.

Griffith later made large claims for himself as the creator of basic cinema techniques. Assiduous students of the early film have worked hard to prove him wrong. In fact, Edwin S. Porter preceded Griffith on almost every specific innovation. Though Griffith asserted that the close-up was his own discovery, he had himself appeared in a head-and-shoulders shot, wearing a clown costume, in a spring 1908 Biograph comedy. But to clear away Griffith's exaggerations only makes his significance easier to grasp. Unlike his predecessors, he understood that each new technique was not merely an attention-getting device but a sign, a special way of communicating, a link in a chain of cinematic discourse. He was the first to forge them into a complete and original style of moving images.

Thanks to the Library of Congress Paper Print Collection, nearly all of Griffith's more than four hundred and fifty Biograph films have been recovered and restored for viewing. Not all of them, of course, contributed to the growth of his style: he worked too quickly for that. But if one looks at his Biograph output, week by week and month by month over the years from 1908 to 1913, his development becomes strikingly clear. Gradually he moved the camera closer and closer to the players, so that by 1912, indoors or outdoors, he shot primarily in medium close-ups, completely eliminating any feeling of a theatrical stage. Gradually he increased the number of shots in his one-reel films so that by 1912 many of his ten-minute films were made up of more than one hundred separate shots. Gradually he increased the complexity and variety of movements within his frame, so that the hallmark of Griffith films became the rich texture and detail of his settings and his direction of acting—in the French term, of his *mise en scène.* Gradually he took over from his cameramen the responsibility of setting up camera placements, so that the lines of composition and movement in each shot became more carefully chosen and aesthetically significant.

Year after year he gave more detailed attention to natural and artificial lighting, using side lighting for the effect of firelight, backlighting with reflectors to soften facial features, changing light within a shot, using fades and focused lighting on individuals. By 1912 he had become a master of the effects of chiaroscuro, of light and dark shading, in a motion-picture frame. He improved his skill as a director of actors, slowing down the movements of his players, creating a quieter yet more intense acting style commensurate with a close camera and a larger figure on the screen.

Each year he found new ways to increase the tempo and build the tension of his dramatic chase and rescue films: he mounted a camera on the back of a car to shoot another car speeding behind it, and another time shot a racing train from a moving car; from parallel action he moved to multiple crosscut action, using three separate story lines instead of two. He developed a rudimentary rhythm in his suspense sequences with shorter and shorter shots and cuts not only from action to action—from the pursued to the pursuer to the rescuer—but also from medium shots to long panorama shots to close-ups. In *A Beast At Bay* (1912), one of the most effective of his chase melodramas, he used a radical shift in spatial perspective, showing a man running toward the camera and then cutting to a shot of the same running man moving away from the camera.

This could be respectable work for a man with creative ambitions: in 1910, when he received his third annual contract, Griffith crossed out "Lawrence" and inked in "David." Henceforward he would be one man rather than two; he would be a filmmaker only. But ambition soon began to clash with management conservatism.

Biograph's officers doubled as administrators of the Motion Picture Patents Company, and they strictly adhered to the Trust's cautious production policies. None of their pictures could be longer than two reels; Griffith and his players could receive neither screen credit nor personal publicity. As his skill and self-confidence grew, Griffith began to chafe under these restrictions. He had built up an acting company of extraordinary quality, including Mary Pickford, Lionel Barrymore, Mae Marsh, Lillian and Dorothy Gish, Blanche Sweet and Henry B. Walthall. Most of them had opportunities to defect to the independents for more money and recognition, but they all remained with Griffith except Pickford, who went over to Imp, came back, then left again.

Griffith became even more annoyed at Biograph's restrictions when feature pictures began to draw the attention and acclaim of critics and middle-class audiences. Early in 1913, the third consecutive year the Biograph production unit wintered in Southern California, he went to work on a four-reel picture without informing the company's managers in New York. He planned a Biblical epic based on the story of Judith and Holofernes, adapted from Thomas Bailey Aldrich's 1904 stage melodrama, *Judith of Bethulia.* In the open, rocky terrain of western San Fernando Valley he constructed a large set of a walled city. There he made his first feature, the film that brought to fruition the motion-picture style he had developed over the past five years.

The keynote of Griffith's approach to his epic was spectacle. Seeking to outdo the Italians and to turn the attention of the new middle-class audience to the special qualities of movies that drama could not match, he created opulent settings and filled them with people, striving for a varied choreography of motion in shot after shot: lines of starving people inside the gates of Bethulia, the driving power of massed and charging Assyrian cavalry, the clashing together of hundreds of foot soldiers, the serpentine dancing of houris in Holofernes' tent.

More significant, Griffith discovered a temporal spaciousness in the longer film he had not experienced before. Unlike the directors of *Queen Elizabeth* and *The Prisoner of Zenda*, who simply used the expanded running time for lengthier takes of stock stage shots, Griffith saw the opportunity to try new ways of cutting and assembling separate shots—to try, indeed, a new way of conceiving the space and time of the succession of moving images. It was not until more than a decade later that anyone adequately described what Griffith was doing here. In the 1920s Sergei Eisenstein, the Soviet filmmaker and theorist who had repeatedly screened and studied Griffith's films at the start of his own career, used the French word *montage* to describe a type of film editing and assembling. *Montage* meant the building up of impressions through the juxtaposition of separate shots, in order to create a single, complete mental image or emotional state. Essentially *montage*, like any other aesthetic style, was a means of attaining a specific response from an audience, and this is what Griffith worked toward with greater freedom in the longer film.

In the first big scene, the siege of Bethulia by the Assyrians, Griffith triumphantly unveiled his *montage* style. The camera's range of vision shifts rapidly from one place to another, then another and yet another: now we see the beleaguered people behind the city walls; now their defenders atop the wall; now their attackers on the ground outside; now Judith in her chamber; now Holofernes in his camp. Back and forth the camera moves, from attackers to attacked, from crowd to solitude, from close to far, from the ground looking up to the wall looking down. Here is no simple "cutback" technique; here the eye seems free to rove anywhere, be everywhere at the same time. Every spot is accessible; every action knowable. All of life can come before the viewer's eye. Time and space are conquered; sitting in our theater seat, we are the unseen witness of every act, every gesture, every secret.

With *Judith of Bethulia*, Griffith completed what *Mary, Queen of Scots* and *The Great Train Robbery* had begun—a style that expressed the unique resources of motion pictures. It was more than the applied principles of cinema, the serial images of *Nude Descending a Staircase* or the continuous successions of Gertrude Stein's prose. It was a movie style, and it was like nothing but itself. Griffith was the first artist of the moving image, the first to reproduce on the screen a complete world, the likes of which no one had seen before.

The Biograph management was angered by Griffith's flouting of their rules. For a time they refused to release *Judith of Bethulia*. Meanwhile, in a belated attempt to copy Adolph Zukor's success, they decided to produce feature films of stage plays. The popularity of Griffith's two-reelers with a working-class audience did not qualify him, in their eyes, to make films that might capture the patronage of the middle classes. In September 1913 he resigned, announcing in a full-page ad in the *New York Dramatic Mirror* that "D. W. GRIFFITH, Producer of all great Biograph successes, revolutionizing Motion Picture drama and founding the modern technique of the art," was now at large.[9]

He had already turned down lucrative offers from Zukor and from Samuel Goldwyn, judging that their emphasis on filmed drama would not allow room for his new cinematic style. A more congenial opportunity was offered him by Harry E. Aitken, head of Mutual distributors, who was moving into production to keep his exchanges supplied. Griffith agreed to become supervisor of production at Aitken's Reliance and Majestic companies, and Aitken in turn promised to finance two of

[9] The ad is reproduced in Robert M. Henderson, *D. W. Griffith: The Years at Biograph* (1970), facing p. 113.

Griffith's own "special" films a year. Griffith was now thirty-eight years old. He had made more than four hundred films, but not one of them had displayed his name on the screen. For all he knew, the public might never see his only feature; Biograph held back *Judith of Bethulia* another six months, until March 1914, just before the release of Griffith's first Mutual feature. He wanted the chance to show what he could do, unfettered and independent, on his own.

Despite the undoubted ability he had demonstrated in many of his Biograph films, Griffith had functioned essentially as a mass-entertainment worker. His nearest equivalents in his own time were writers of Western, detective and love stories for the pulp magazines that had sprung up about the same time as movies; in our time a similar figure would be the director of a television series. Griffith was required to produce about a half-hour of screen time each week, equal over a year to a series of hour-long television shows today. His great need was for stories, and he got them where he could: from the theater, fiction, poetry, newspapers, plots submitted by outsiders. He tried to give everything the stamp of his personal style, sometimes with success, sometimes not.

Under these circumstances only a partial and selective view of Griffith's Biograph films could produce a coherent set of themes and points of view. For every *A Corner in Wheat*, a 1909 film adapted from the Frank Norris novel *The Pit*, showing the death of an evil grain speculator, there was another Griffith film that sentimentalized the rich; for every *Ramona*, a 1910 film from the Helen Hunt Jackson novel, there was one that portrayed Indians as murderous savages. Eventually, however, Griffith moved toward a more consistent imagery depicting the extremes of life, the extravagant ostentation of the rich and the daily struggle of the poor. In 1912, when free-lance writers began to deluge studios with unsolicited scenarios, Biograph informed them that it was seeking "plots contrasting the rich and poor."[10] But soon afterward Griffith shifted to feature production, and social realism was subsumed as a minor theme beside his predilections for the other extremes of sentiment and spectacle.

During the winter of 1913–1914 he quickly made four feature films for Mutual. They were well received and exhibited some of his most imaginative visual devices, but essentially they were intended to clear away his obligations, for he had at last found the subject he was looking for, the one theme that could bear his unmistakable personal signature: he would make a film about the American Civil War. He would spend more money than had ever been put into a film before, and create a motion picture so long, so powerful and so significant that people of culture would stop wondering whether movies could ever be as good as live drama: they would say, like working-class people before them, that they had never seen anything so marvelous as this.

---

[10] "How to Write and Market Moving Picture Plays" (1912), p. 98.

The genesis of the film was Thomas W. Dixon's novel and stage melodrama *The Clansman*, a work that glorified the hooded Klan of the post–Civil War South, ridiculing Black Reconstruction and the desire of Negroes to attain political rights. Its plot rested on fervid racism and fear of sexual relations between blacks and whites. Griffith the Kentuckian, son of a Confederate officer, swallowed it whole. He added, however, themes of his own: he broadened the canvas, showing the war as well as the aftermath, the sacrifices of the North as well as the South, the desire among the victors for moderation and reconciliation, represented in the film by the martyred Lincoln. At the film's Los Angeles premiere in February 1915, the author Dixon graciously and justly said it was Griffith's story more than his own, and Griffith thereupon changed the title from *The Clansman* to *The Birth of a Nation.* For that was what his film was about: the creation of a new nation after years of struggle and division, a nation of Northern and Southern whites united "in common defence of their Aryan birthright," with the vigilante riders of the Klan as their symbol.[11]

The Birth of a Nation cost nearly $60,000 to produce and an equal amount to promote; in later years, after movie costs went soaring, press agents would say that Griffith had spent millions. The movie ran for twelve reels, or two-and-one-half hours' screen time, the longest film ever made up to that time, as well as the most expensive. Ticket prices were set at a minimum of $2. In theme, form and price it was meant to appeal to the American elite, to community leaders and opinion makers, to tell them something about their own culture and also something about the movies, about the epic power and grandeur of cinematic expression.

Both messages came through loud and clear. Describing the famous Klan ride at the climax of the film, especially the silhouetted shot of riders galloping along a hillside, a *New Republic* writer reported that "every audience spontaneously applauds when it flashes upon the screen."[12] Griffith convinced thousands of wealthy and educated Americans that movies could appeal to their emotions and please their aesthetic tastes. As an entrepreneur as well as a director he completed what others had begun: at last the movie audience came from every segment of American society.

Not everyone, however, saw the film or wanted to see it. Ohio banned it. The National Association for the Advancement of Colored People vigorously fought it in Boston and elsewhere. The crux of their complaint was the film's racism. The Cameron family of South Carolina, focus of the plot, is continually the tragic victim of black rapine. After losing two sons in the Civil War and having a third saved from execution

---

[11] Quoted from a screen title, reproduced in Seymour Stern, "Griffith: I–*The Birth of a Nation*," *Film Culture*, No. 36 (Spring–Summer 1965), between pp. 202–3.

[12] Harold Stearns, "Art in Moving Pictures," *New Republic*, Vol. 4 (September 25, 1915), p. 207.

THE MUSEUM OF MODERN ART/FILM STILLS ARCHIVE

D. W. Griffith's epic of white supremacy, *The Birth of a Nation* (1915), went over well with white audiences almost everywhere. A building at 322 S. Adams Street, Peoria, Illinois, is covered with posters advertising the film (bottom); the Klan rides to the rescue of endangered white womanhood in a frame enlargement from the famous sequence that made audiences cheer (top).

THE MUSEUM OF MODERN ART/FILM STILLS ARCHIVE

by a pardon from the "Great Heart," Lincoln, they have their home looted by vicious black soldiers; a daughter, Flora, leaps to her death resisting the advances of a black man; the father is dragged away by black troops for harboring a Klansman; mother, father and the last remaining daughter are about to be wiped out by blacks when they are rescued by the Klan; the Klan's leader, their pardoned son, has just saved his Northern sweetheart, the daughter of a notorious Radical politician, from rape by an evil mulatto. Few people could resist responding to the plight of this white family, continually wounded and threatened by cruel and lustful blacks. Audiences cheered when the Klan riders gathered and swept to the rescue, as Vachel Lindsay wrote, "as powerfully as Niagara pours over the cliff."[13]

Herein lies the issue about *The Birth of a Nation*: is it a work of racist propaganda or of consummate artistic skill? Would we cheer as much if, with the same sequence of shots, Griffith had shown us hooded black riders dashing to the rescue of their loved ones endangered by villainous whites? We must grant that an exceptional artist can make a world, any world, and convince us of its truth. But as the didactic purpose of a film becomes more evident, its artistry is undeniably compromised.

In fictional films—as opposed to documentaries like the Nazi *Triumph of the Will*—didacticism usually appears in characterization. *The Birth of a Nation*; Melvin Van Peebles' 1971 film of black struggle and resistance, *Sweet Sweetback's Baadasssss Song*; and a film from the People's Republic of China, *Tunnel Warfare* (1965), are examples of fiction films with exceptional visual qualities and obviously simplistic, one-dimensional caricatures of their villains. Ultimately this detracts from their impact. A more convincing propaganda may be seen in films like Gilles Pontecorvo's *The Battle of Algiers* (1967) and *Queimada* (1968; American title, *Burn!*), in which the antagonists are treated not as dunces and fools but as complex, intelligent persons whose perspectives and policies are dramatically shown to be inadequate or wrong.

Defenders of *The Birth of a Nation* follow the tactic of ignoring its depiction of blacks and concentrating on its visual qualities, its separate sequences and shots: the incomparable battle scenes, the assassination of Lincoln, the homecoming scene, the sentry who moons over Lillian Gish. But even here Griffith undercut his artistry to make didactic points. Many of the shots are slower and more static than usual in Griffith films; his omnipresent use of iris and vignette techniques to highlight faces or actions sometimes proves enormously effective but often simply curtails the space and movement of the shot. Even the famous Klan ride is compromised—as art, if not as propaganda—by intercut tableaux of young white girls awaiting ravishment. The acting is strong and memorable, but most of the whites as well as the blacks are carica-

---

[13] Vachel Lindsay, *The Art of the Moving Picture* (1915; Liveright ed., 1970), p. 75.

tures. Insofar as aesthetic judgments can ever be separated from moral choices, *The Birth of a Nation* seems as remarkable, and as flawed, in its art as in its theme of white supremacy.

In the controversy that arose over the picture after its release, Griffith left most of the defense to the author, Thomas Dixon, who spent considerable energy on it; the director said simply that the film was accurate and asserted his right to free expression. But he could not conceal the bitter resentment he felt against his critics. He published a pamphlet, "The Rise and Fall of Free Speech in America," contending that demands for censorship of motion pictures were merely the opening wedge of an effort to impose restraints on all forms of free expression. And he began to plan a movie that would be an epic counterattack.

He originally planned to follow *The Birth of a Nation* with a feature about contemporary industrial life, but as his appetite to strike back against his critics grew he decided on a far more ambitious design. The modern story would become one strand of a larger theme linked to three other episodes in the same film: the fall of Babylon, Christ's life and crucifixion, and the sixteenth-century massacre of the Huguenots in Paris on St. Bartholomew's Day. Each was to illustrate the universal history of bigotry and prejudice, attitudes Griffith seemed principally to associate with people who disliked *The Birth of a Nation.* The film would be called *Intolerance* and would show, as an opening title proclaimed, "how hatred and intolerance, through all the ages, have battled against love and charity."

Griffith spared no expense. *Intolerance* was the most spectacular and ambitious silent film ever made. He built as a set a Babylonian city a mile wide and three hundred feet high, towering in lavish splendor over the bungalows of Hollywood. He filled it with thousands of exquisitely costumed extras. All the considerable profit he had made from *The Birth of a Nation* went into the new film: he budgeted *Intolerance* at ten times the cost of the earlier film and probably spent a million dollars to produce it. It ran to forty-eight reels, and Griffith planned to release it in two parts, each four hours long, to be screened on consecutive nights. But since he could not find exhibitors willing to handle such a long film, he cut it to just over three hours; surviving prints are about twenty minutes shorter.

What remains is one of the greatest visual experiences in the history of movies. Decades of Hollywood costume spectacles have dulled our eyes to merely colossal display, but nothing in Cecil B. DeMille's florid imagination, backed by Technicolor, CinemaScope and multimillion-dollar budgets, can compare with Griffith's original spectacular conception of architectural form and crowd movement, and above all, of the emotional power and beauty of screen imagery. Many directors have copied its settings and battles, its cruelty and sensuality, but few have been able to combine with them Griffith's sure touch for comic gesture or his extraordinary ability to compose shots for the maximum effect of movement and spatial form in the frame.

ACADEMY OF MOTION PICTURE ARTS AND SCIENCES

This publicity shot shows the master, D. W. Griffith, surveying his make-believe domain, the huge Babylonian set for *Intolerance* (1916) that towered over Hollywood. The balloon was used to take aerial shots of orgies and battles in the Babylonian sequence, and the words on the banner advertise *The Mother and the Law*, the title given the modern sequence from *Intolerance* when it was released separately.

Griffith's strike sequence in the modern story is one of the classic examples of dynamic *montage* in American movies. It cuts rapidly, with shorter and shorter shots, from the strikers to their anxious families to the factory owner, shown in a brilliant long shot as a tiny figure behind a huge desk stranded in a sea of floor space, to the militia with their rifles and machine guns. It culminates with a sudden change of tempo and remarkable use of open space as the factory guards begin shooting and the camera pans slowly in a long shot across the battleground separating the retreating strikers and the firing guards.

Another remarkable brief sequence, "the hangman's test," dramatically repeats a single moment in time. It is composed of five short shots: semi–close-up of three guards with knives, close-ups of strings the men cut, close-up of weight falling, close-up of trap door in floor opening, and then, time resumed, a long shot of a dummy weight hanging below the gallows platform. Sergei Eisenstein was to copy and elaborate this technique in the *montage* of such films as *Ten Days That Shook the World*.

But Griffith had difficulty putting his individual sequences and vast historical panorama together as a coherent whole. When *Intolerance* was released in September 1916, audiences watched the film with awe but also with confusion. The four separate episodes are intermingled, connected by a repeated shot of a woman rocking a cradle, after Whitman's "Out of the cradle endlessly rocking," used as a bridge. The stories were not difficult to follow, but their message was harder to grasp. Despite the references to intolerance, the film seemed to express only inchoate and contradictory sentiment.

Its unifying theme appeared to be religious persecution. This was clear in the Judean and French episodes, but these were the briefest and least developed sections of the film. Religious conflict also lay behind the betrayal and fall of Babylon, a struggle between adherents of male and female gods, but sequences which develop the rivalry are missing from many extant prints. One may need several viewings to understand that a vengeful or Spartan god is competing with a goddess of pleasure. Religion barely plays a part in the modern story, however; observant viewers will note that the workers are Roman Catholics, but reformers and uplifters seem to harass them out of motives other than religious prejudice, chiefly hypocrisy and personal inadequacy.

Here Griffith made his greatest miscalculation: he misjudged the predilections of his audience. He assumed that the elite who responded to the vision of national unity through white racial solidarity in *The Birth of a Nation* also condemned what he believed were a small but noisy minority of censors and moral uplifters. He failed completely to understand that his elite audience gave financial support and social power to middle-class reformers, that they endorsed the words his villains spoke—"We must have laws to make people good"—and backed the reforms he ridiculed, like prohibition and the suppression of prostitution.

If this error were not serious enough, he compounded it by affronting respectable sensibilities with unparalleled scenes of Babylonian sensuality, scarcely clad women sprawled with open legs, and, in one shot, the bare breasts of a bathing woman. Moreover, he offended prevailing views on law and order by calling a prison a "sometimes House of Intolerance" and questioning the legal system that condemns an innocent youth to death. The film ended with an epilogue proclaiming a vision of battlefields and prisons turned to flowering meadows and the advent of love and peace forevermore. This sentiment helped to kill the film as the war spirit mounted in America early in 1917, but *Intolerance* had already suffered mortal wounds at the box office.

What happened to Griffith after 1917 was shaped by the commercial failure of *Intolerance*. He was thereafter continually in need of outside financing to support his productions, and the intricacies of business absorbed an increasing amount of his time and energy. Early in 1919 a print of *Intolerance* appeared in revolutionary Moscow, where audiences were enthralled by it, and young Soviet filmmakers screened it again and again, absorbing the tempo and tensions of Griffith's editing. Legend even has it that Lenin cabled Griffith an offer to head the new Soviet film industry. By 1919, however, Griffith was too far ensnared in the nets of capital to escape, even if he had wanted to.

His difficulties were exacerbated by what appears to have been a quixotic attitude of hostility toward the motion-picture industry. He had demonstrated that movies could be art; he had attracted upper-class Americans to movie theaters for the first time; more than Laemmle, Fox or Zukor, he deserved credit for the significant achievements that made the movies respectable, powerful and successful. But as soon as he could, he removed himself from the new center of motion-picture production in Southern California; he returned to the East Coast in 1919 and stayed there until 1927, important years of growth and development in Hollywood. For a year after *Intolerance* was finished, the Babylonian set remained, dominating the Hollywood skyline. Then, in the fall of 1917, it came down, and sections of it found their way into the back lots of other studios. Along with the directors and players he had trained, and the techniques and styles he had developed, they served to carry on the Griffith influence as Hollywood became a source of entertainment, mores and culture throughout the world.

THE MOVIES IN THE AGE OF MASS CULTURE

5

HOLLYWOOD AND THE DAWNING OF THE AQUARIAN AGE

The moviemakers, like people in most American success stories, were often vague about their past. The rags-to-riches tradition required only that origins be humble; too many details exposed roots one had tried to leave behind. By World War I, as the movies became respectable, it was increasingly a source of embarrassment for the new entertainment industry to have been nurtured in the ethnic ghettos of Chicago, the steel mills of Pittsburgh and the tenements of New York. The moviemakers refused to accept so plain and poor a heritage. They fled westward to Los Angeles, of all large American cities at the time the one least resembling the teeming industrial centers they had escaped. There, on the far shores of the continent, they gave form to a platonic conception of themselves called Hollywood.

In the myth of Hollywood that has come down to us, beginnings have almost no place. The most frequently repeated story about Hollywood's origins is that independent producers set up there so that they could beat it across the Mexican border when agents of the Motion Picture Patents Company came serving subpoenas. A moment's reflection reveals the absurdity of this. Mexico was a five-hour drive from Los Angeles in those days; to make the trip would have cost at least a day's production, while the legal papers could be served at the business offices in New York. The independents, in fact, stood their ground to fight the Trust. There is evidence of only one occasion when a film company retreated below the border, and that was to escape a possible morals charge.

Actually, the first motion pictures produced in Southern California were made by members of the Trust. The Selig company of Chicago is credited with originating production in Los Angeles in 1907, while Biograph began sending D. W. Griffith and his cast and crew out west for the winter in 1909–1910. Selig set up a studio in the Edendale section, near Silver Lake Reservoir and not far from a modern landmark of downtown Los Angeles, Dodger Stadium. The New York Motion Picture Company, first of the independents to go west, located down the block from Selig in 1909.

Southern California's attractions for moviemakers were obvious. The area offered nearly year-round sunshine and warm weather for outdoor shooting without the humidity and tropical storms of Cuba and Florida, which production companies also visited in the early years. Even better, it provided a unique physical environment: in close proximity to one another were mountains, desert, a city and the sea. Within an hour or two of downtown Los Angeles one could find a location resembling almost any conceivable scene one might want to use—factory or farm, jungle or snowy peak. Land was inexpensive and available. Carl Laemmle purchased a large tract in the San Fernando Valley near the Cahuenga Pass, on the other side of the mountains from Hollywood, and there built a studio which he called Universal City and incorporated as a town. The New York Motion Picture Company acquired land in a canyon north of Santa Monica where mountains ran down to the ocean, and produced Westerns there under the Kay Bee and Bronco trademarks.

And if all this were not enough to make Southern California the clear preference of motion-picture producers, Los Angeles was well known at the time—though no Hollywood memoir chooses to recall it—as the nation's leading open-shop, nonunion city. A constant inflow of new residents, buying inexpensive bungalows and seeking work, maintained a surplus of settled laborers and kept wages low, from a fifth to a third below the prevailing rates in San Francisco, and in some cases half the wage levels of New York. As the studios moved into feature production and built more elaborate and authentic sets, they needed skilled craftworkers—carpenters, electricians, dressmakers and many other specialists—and lower costs became an increasingly important factor in locating production in Los Angeles.

Gradually, as the industry expanded, production came more and more to center in Southern California. Some of the major new producers, like Zukor's Famous Players (later to merge with Lasky and finally to adopt the name of its distribution unit and become Paramount Pictures), opened studios on the West Coast while retaining production facilities in Manhattan or Long Island. The more common practice, however, was to maintain business offices in New York and concentrate production in Los Angeles. The fact that the moneymen remained on the East Coast and the creative talent moved to the West proved a source of considerable friction and new myths about moviemaking as the years went by.

In Culver City, Harry E. Aitken built an imposing studio for his short-lived Triangle Productions (the studio was later taken over by Samuel Goldwyn and eventually became famous as the MGM lot). Production facilities were also set up in Glendale, Long Beach and other outlying communities. But the favorite location for studios was the suburb of Hollywood. Nestled at the foot of the Santa Monica Mountains, it marked the westernmost expansion of urban settlement and offered easy access to the downtown business district, available lots for studios, comfortable bungalow housing for employees, and good locations nearby for Western action.

There DeMille made *The Squaw Man*, Griffith built his Babylonian set for *Intolerance*, Zukor and Fox located their studios, and after World War I, Charlie Chaplin, Mary Pickford and Douglas Fairbanks—the biggest star names in the industry—opened studios. Within a few square blocks between Sunset Boulevard on the north and Melrose on the south,

Gower Street to the west and Western Avenue to the east, a large share of the world's film production became concentrated. By the early 1920s, when people spoke of American motion pictures they began to use the name Hollywood to describe a place, a people, and as many over the years have said, a state of mind.

As far as the local residents were concerned, the motion-picture people were in Los Angeles and Hollywood, but not of them. Migrants to Southern California came preponderantly from the South and Midwest, and brought with them strong strains of the fundamentalist condemnation of popular amusements and the theater. They called the studios "camps"; it was a good name in the sense that studio life was self-contained and isolated from the community, a bad one if they thought the motion-picture interlopers would pack up and go away. The studios stayed to become, until World War II, the largest Southern California industry and a unique one in many ways, as Carey McWilliams pointed out in *Southern California Country*: it did not tear up the countryside, pollute the skies, assail the ears, yet it created thousands of jobs and poured millions of dollars into the local economy. Though they often tried over the years to maintain their distance from the surrounding city, the motion-picture studios could not help but exert a profound influence on the character of Southern California life.

There were many reasons, besides antipathy, why the movie people and the "private" people, as Colleen Moore remembers calling them, did not often mix.[1] Motion-picture work started early and ended late: casts and crews frequently worked a twelve-to-fourteen-hour day. Players sometimes had to make themselves up and be in costume before arriving at the studio, which meant rising as early as five o'clock and appearing on the morning streetcar as if coming home from an all-night costume party. Weeks at a time were spent away from home on location in the nearby mountains or desert. Studio employees had little time or energy for social life except when they were not working, and in those circumstances they stuck as close as they could to other motion-picture people, hoping to find a new assignment.

They had their compensations, of course. The early years of filmmaking in Hollywood were for many a great adventure. They were doing something new and untried, and making an incredible success of it. Their bosses, the alien moguls, remained in New York, and their day-to-day working environment was more open, free and egalitarian than it would ever be again. After working together all day, players and directors often dined together, went out on the town together, visited together. For many performers, whose theatrical work had forced them to travel and live for months at a time in hotels or boarding houses, it was their first opportunity to own a home and live year-round in the same place. Lacking the rich cultural attractions of New York, and the com-

---

[1] *Silent Star* (1968), p. 10.

QUIGLEY PHOTOGRAPHIC ARCHIVE, GEORGETOWN UNIVERSITY LIBRARY

Filmmaking was open to the sun and sometimes to the public in the early silent days. Spectators were invited to watch at Universal City (top) from platforms atop players' dressing rooms; at the Jesse L. Lasky Feature Play Company (bottom) you could sometimes see the wind gust through what were supposed to be indoor scenes.

HISTORICAL COLLECTIONS, SECURITY PACIFIC NATIONAL BANK

petition and acquaintanceship of creative workers in allied arts, they fell in upon themselves with the intensity sometimes found in isolated, specialized groups, such as diplomats in a foreign capital. They became a distinctive, self-aware, permanently settled community of entertainers.

Then, there was the further, monetary compensation. Though stage players had looked down their noses in the past at movie jobs, those who had made the shift discovered that movie work, even at basic levels of pay, could be much more lucrative. Players in the theater worked no more than thirty to forty weeks a year, though a few could augment that by appearing in summer-stock productions. It was the universal custom not to pay them during rehearsals. An actor or actress could spend six weeks rehearsing a play that closed after a fortnight, and receive two weeks' pay for two months' work. Contract players in the movies, although their initial weekly rates may have been lower than what they had been getting for stage work, were paid fifty-two weeks of the year, including rehearsals and time between films. A beginning player in the movies around 1913 could earn from $2,000 to $5,000 a year.

When the independents launched the star system of publicity and advertising, players whose names attracted audiences began to get salaries of $200 or $300 a week. How much these rates reflected a star's real worth was a question no producer was willing to answer publicly. A successful motion picture could gross anywhere from twice to four times its costs without difficulty, and often much more. If a star's name brought crowds flocking to see the movie, what was a just wage for the star? In the legitimate theater the biggest names pulled down about $500 a week. This was the weekly figure Mary Pickford—or rather, her mother—demanded when, after having worked for Biograph and Imp and then gone back to the stage to star in a Belasco production, she was asked by Adolph Zukor to repeat her stage role on film for Famous Players. Zukor met her price. It was a new high for motion-picture salaries, but it still did not reveal how much a producer thought a movie star was worth.

That became clearer within the next year or two when Harry E. Aitken took on Zukor in the latter's game of hiring stage stars. He organized a new production company, Triangle, and secured the services of the three most famous producer-directors of the time, Griffith, Mack Sennett and Thomas H. Ince. But the heart of his plan, like Zukor's several years earlier, was to put the great names of Broadway on the screen—to buy the services of established stars and famous names. Sir Herbert Beerbohm Tree, DeWolfe Hopper, and Lew Fields and Joe Weber were among the theatrical headliners who headed for the train to Culver City when Aitken made well-publicized offers of $1,500 to $3,000 a week.

Aitken didn't realize, however, that you can't repeat the past. *The Birth of a Nation* had taught the new middle-class and elite audiences to appreciate movies with close-ups, swift cutting and other advanced cinematic techniques. Zukor himself had at least partially abandoned the famous-players formula: stage stars could no longer expect merely to act their familiar parts while distant cameras cranked out long takes. They had to act by the rules of moviemaking, and a vastly different set of rules applied.

The movie player worked in an atmosphere lacking entirely the emotional setting of live theater. He had no audience, no great auditorium to command with his powerful voice, no long familiar build-up of character and mood through the acts of a play. The environment was more likely a plain, barnlike building or an outdoor lot with three or four sets working simultaneously side by side, out of one another's camera range but contributing to a common mingled din. After long periods of waiting the actor or actress might be asked to do a scene of love, rage or sorrow; to move abruptly from one to another without any regard to the consecutive development of the character, but rather because all the scenes on a particular set were to be shot at the same time; to perform the same short, disjointed scene over and over until the director was satisfied.

All of this made for a new and unfamiliar mode of acting. Indeed, one well-known player, the comedian John Bunny, one of the first to make a successful transition from stage to movie stardom, said that movie playing was not acting at all, it was being natural. This was a gross oversimplification, as many players learned. The acting style Griffith developed in his players, which was widely copied by others, was one of restraint and repression, a far cry from the open expressiveness of the stage or the exaggerated gestures of the early one-reelers. Sessue Hayakawa, the Japanese actor who starred in Thomas H. Ince Westerns, likened the style to kabuki acting—intensity of emotion was conveyed by the concentrated visible act of holding back rather than booming forth; the audience became enthralled not by large gestures and broad expressions, but by small movements of eyes, face, body and hands, an interest enhanced by the absence of voice in silent movies.

The Broadway players had not expected this. As far as most theater people were concerned, movie acting was a grosser form of pantomime in which registering emotion—almost any emotion—consisted of clutching one's hands at the chest and rolling the eyes heavenward. All of the big names Aitken brought to the West became ignominious failures at the movie box office; the only notable survivor was Douglas Fairbanks, whose natural physical grace and comic style found an outlet in comedies written by Anita Loos. Burdened suddenly with extraordinary production costs and dwindling receipts, Triangle fell as spectacularly as Babylon in the epic that Griffith was making across town in Hollywood with the last of Harry E. Aitken's money.

By then the front-office secret was out. If legitimate-stage names were worth $1,500 to $3,000 a week, audience appeal untested, the real drawing cards had a more accurate estimate of their value. Even before Triangle's fiasco, Pickford had early in 1915 pushed Zukor up to $1,000 a

THE MUSEUM OF MODERN ART/FILM STILLS ARCHIVE

Harry E. Aitken hired the three leading producer-directors of the pre–World War I period for his Triangle Film Corporation, but the company foundered when Aitken paid enormous salaries to Broadway stars who did not please the movie public. In this famous 1915 picture the producers are joined by Charles Chaplin: (from left to right) Thomas H. Ince, Chaplin, Mack Sennett and D. W. Griffith.

week, and Charlie Chaplin, who had broken into movies with Keystone in 1914 and become an overnight success, switched to Essanay early in 1915 for a salary of $1,250 a week. After Triangle, Pickford demanded and got $2,000 and half the profits from her pictures; then in 1916 Chaplin, asked to name his price by the Mutual company, said $10,000 a week, and they paid him that, plus a $150,000 bonus to sign. Suddenly, as the movies became big business, the stars, the surefire box-office moneymakers, realized they could command salaries almost, but not quite, beyond the dreams of avarice.

The wonder was that nobody knew what made a star. Stage success apparently had nothing to do with it (though Chaplin, Pickford and Fairbanks, the major movie stars of the 1910s, came from theatrical or vaudeville backgrounds). Acting ability, traditionally defined, did not indicate star potential. Previous experience or training did not necessarily play a part. Natural movement, the glow of a vital personality, perhaps one's resemblance to a type, were what seemed to count on the screen.

Even so, there was sometimes a magical transformation from a person to his or her reproduced image. One might gain in magnetism and fascination—or lose. Not even the professionals could always tell; the ultimate judge was the mysterious collective choice made by moviegoers in the dark. Potentially anyone, anywhere, possessed the special quality that made one out of thousands a star. But if one was blessed, nobody might notice in Kankakee, Illinois, or Cottage Grove, Wisconsin. The aspiring movie player had to go where the moviemakers were, to Hollywood. Around 1915 this thought began to occur to hundreds and then thousands of people, but mostly to young women. They bought one-way tickets to Union Station, Los Angeles, to find out if the wand of stardom had somehow, somewhere, touched them.

"The movie-struck girl," as anxious observers called her, was not only an American phenomenon.[2] She was reported trying to break into films in Great Britain, and there were probably few countries with movie studios that did not harbor her. But circumstances in the United States were different, and not only because America produced more than 80 percent of the world's films. When New York was the center of American production it was easy for a girl from the metropolis or beyond to commute daily to the studios to look for work as an extra or be discovered by a director. A girl could come from as far away as Chicago and still be only a day's train ride from home. But when production shifted to Hollywood, movie ambitions entailed a much more serious commitment. This was true for men as well, of course, but single men leaving home to find work were a familiar aspect of American society, and their movie ambitions did not attract the same public attention.

---

[2] William A. Page, "The Movie-Struck Girl," *Woman's Home Companion*, Vol. 45 (June 1918), p. 18.

The additional distance, time and cost to get there, as well as the added significance—there were many reasons why a young person might go to New York, but only one for going to Hollywood—eliminated the casual applicant. In the World War I era—an unsettled period when late-Victorian mores persisted side by side with an emerging image of a "new woman"—it could only have been disconcerting to respectable Americans to see photographs of determined young women in their ankle-length dresses, high-button shoes and broad-brimmed hats standing in long lines outside a Hollywood casting office. The American middle class had only just begun to regard movies as something other than immoral trash for working-class people; and suddenly their daughters were packing up and leaving home to seek their fortunes in the movies.

If they had to go, the least one could do was give them sound advice, most of it intended to be discouraging. A girl should plan to have enough money to survive for a year without additional income: authors of advice books and articles for the movie aspirant set the minimum figure at $2,000. She should have resources enough to be able to acquire her own wardrobe, since extras in those days had to supply their own outfits for scenes of contemporary life. She should consider what abilities she possessed and perhaps direct her ambitions to other interesting work in motion pictures.

Studios needed talented dress designers, set decorators, film cutters, all jobs that were open to women. In fact, the motion-picture studios in the 1910s and 1920s gave more opportunities to women than most other industries, far more than they ever did again. Many of the leading scenario writers were women, among them Anita Loos, June Mathis, Frances Marion and Jeanie Macpherson. Lois Weber was a well-known director and independent producer, and Elinor Glyn, Dorothy Arzner and other women directed films during the 1920s. Women were occasionally found in executive positions in Hollywood producing companies. And if a woman possessed none of these talents, there were always jobs as secretaries, mail clerks, film processors, and in other modest but essential roles in the making of movies.

But what the women wanted was to be actresses. They could see that other girls, many still in their teens, without acting experience, were making it. Why not they? But no one informed them that a fair share of the young girls with film contracts were "payoffs," as Colleen Moore called them: players who were hired as a favor to influential people or to pay back a favor they had done the studio.[3] Moore got her start because her uncle, a newspaper editor, gave D. W. Griffith help in getting his films approved by the Chicago censorship board, and Griffith repaid him with a contract for his niece. In *Silent Star*, Moore reports that Carmel Myers, Mildred Harris (a bride at sixteen to Charlie Chaplin) and Winifred Westover, who began acting as teen-agers, were all "payoffs" in similar ways.

---

[3] Moore, *op. cit.*, discusses "payoffs" on pp. 22, 29.

What the authors of books and articles did tell them was that the road to becoming an actress might also be the road to hell. The moguls may have won a few friends in the American middle class, but friendship ended when it came to daughters. In the more restrained approach, the girls were warned that the movie bosses were financiers who knew nothing of the theater or quality acting. They cared only for pretty faces, and with the lax standards of movie audiences, ability was not needed to become a star. Since stars were so easily created, according to this view, producers made stars of their favorites—wives, girl friends, or the wives and girl friends of those whose favor they sought for business reasons. Outsiders might as well not apply. The more sensational exposés pictured a leering foreigner with "a large nose and small ratty eyes," trying to seduce any attractive applicant who knocked on his door.[4]

The girl who could or would not get the message was warned in no uncertain terms what fate awaited her. A manual for prospective movie players claimed in the mid-1920s that some five thousand persons, mainly young and innocent women, disappeared from sight every year in Hollywood. There were tales of nice Midwestern girls who ended up in brothels and opium dens; and there was always the ever-present "menace of Mexico," that convenient border across which, it was implied, many of the missing persons had been spirited.[5] And how many were like the girl about whom another writer told, who found her way back home to Illinois, only to die there of diseases contracted in the land of movies?

Some girls, however, got a different message from these warnings. If the "casting couch" was the pathway to a film career, it might be used to advantage by the applicant as well as by the employer. If certain services were the going currency, they could be invested as well as spent. Intelligent girls learned to calculate a man's worth. Enterprising aspirants had several alternatives: they could be supported as mistresses; could marry; could divorce for the alimony; could sue for breach of promise; could blackmail. The leering mogul may have been a real figure, but so, too, was the producer who always kept his door open and never saw a young woman in his office without another person present. Smart women did not become streetwalkers on Skid Row; some of them bankrolled their charms into acting careers.

The end result of all that happened, good and bad, in those early Hollywood years left a permanent mark on Southern California. Actors and actresses could be and were discovered clerking in drugstores; the magic wand of stardom sometimes did strike any time, anywhere. And even if it didn't strike you, there were compensations if you kept yourself slim, tanned, well-groomed and -dressed, if your bearing was sure and your manner dynamic. Someone, even if it was only a tourist, might

---

[4] *The Sins of Hollywood* (1922), p. 77. This anonymous work is subtitled: "A Group of Stories of Actual Happenings Reported and Written by a Hollywood Newspaper Man."

[5] Marilynn Conners, *What Chance Have* I *in Hollywood?* (1924), chapter title.

think you were a star. At the least you were playing a role, if not in a movie, then in movieland, where the stars lived, worked and played: it was a source of vicarious pride and pleasure to dress up to and act your part.

They were a new race, these men and women of the movies, said a writer in the 1920s. They were a people dedicated more completely to the body, to beauty and health, than any the world had seen before. They marked the dawning of the Aquarian Age—nearly a full half-century before 1960s youth culture and the rock musical *Hair*.

They lived unspiritual lives, said a visiting European intellectual, lives devoted to the senses. Hollywood possessed no theater, no good bookshops, no museums, no art galleries, no institution of traditional high culture. They played golf at their country clubs and tennis on their private courts. They swam in their pools or at the beachside colony in Santa Monica. They ate and drank, they listened to the radio, they danced, they flirted. They had a wonderful time.

These, of course, were the successful ones, the top few in the happily embarrassing position of having more money than they knew what to do with. Some put their surplus into real estate and became wealthier still. Others bought land on which to build their own dream castles. They may have gotten the idea from newly rich oilmen who began to build mansions in the Beverly Hills district around 1912 and incorporated their community in 1914 as a self-governing enclave surrounded by Los Angeles. Thomas H. Ince was the first movie figure to join the oil magnates when he built a mansion in the Spanish style and inaugurated the Aquarian life style of outdoor sports, big cars and weekend parties. Others followed with bigger and costlier homes in the hills above Hollywood, and in Bel Air and Brentwood to the west.

Americans had always been of mixed minds about great wealth. They agreed it was a desirable goal, but they feared the temptations that came with the power of money—the release it gave from ordinary social restraints. They had traditionally been able to condone the accumulation of money more easily than the enjoyment of it: Commodore Cornelius Vanderbilt was a nineteenth-century hero, no matter what means he had used in seeking profit, but his granddaughter Consuelo was heavily criticized when she married an English title in a lavish wedding. The situation of the movie stars was doubly disturbing, for as far as the public was concerned the players had just as much fun making money as they did spending it.

Many people associated with the movie trade believed it would be wise to play down the stars' pleasures. They blamed public disquiet over the players' private lives on the new breed of gossip writers who had sprung up to satisfy popular interest in the stars. The industry should refrain, said one official, "from allowing silly, half-baked writers to exploit the fictitious romances that deal with imaginary, half-million-dollar Venetian gardens and palaces of stars who in reality live modestly amid wholesome family surroundings in leased homes, but who sometimes for cheap publicity purposes pose with one foot on the running board of a Rolls-Royce loaned for the occasion."[6] Others insisted that Hollywood people worked too hard to have time for amusements, that the tone of life in the movie community differed not one whit from that in any wholesome American town: they rolled up the sidewalks at 9 P.M. in Hollywood, too.

The public would not be fooled. They had a fair suspicion of what might happen when you gave the average American male fabulous wealth and power over the careers of beautiful young women; they also feared what beautiful young women would do with their own great wealth and the freedoms it provided. Their expectations were amply fulfilled in September 1921, when scandal-filled headlines hit the nation's newspapers: ACTRESS DIES AT DRUNKEN PARTY; FAMOUS MOVIE COMEDIAN CHARGED WITH MURDER.

Roscoe "Fatty" Arbuckle, a comedian second in popularity only to Chaplin during the 1910s, had with another actor and a director rented a suite in a San Francisco hotel on the Labor Day weekend, filled it with bootleg liquor and with as many friends, acquaintances and pretty girls as could be found. The party went on for days—obviously these hard workers were between assignments. One of the women, Virginia Rappe, a minor actress, became ill with stomach pains, but the merrymakers assumed she had drunk too much bad booze, like everyone else. When at last the party ended, however, she was found fatally ill in a bedroom, her clothes torn. She died in a hospital of peritonitis.

Circumstantial evidence placed Arbuckle alone with the girl in the bedroom with the door locked. He was charged with murder, eventually indicted for manslaughter and tried three times. The first two trials ended in hung juries; in the third the jury deliberated for six minutes and declared him innocent. During the trials it was testified that Miss Rappe had a long history of internal problems and had frequently screamed and torn her clothes, as she apparently had done in the hotel bedroom. The cause of her death was a ruptured bladder, but many people preferred to imagine Arbuckle's great weight crushing her in a forced embrace. Protests from pressure groups caused his films to be withdrawn from theaters, and his career was destroyed.

While Arbuckle's first trial was going on, another Hollywood scandal erupted. The director William Desmond Taylor was found murdered in his home. Mabel Normand, popular comedienne and Arbuckle's onetime partner in Keystone comedies, was known to be the last person to have seen Taylor alive; nightgowns bearing the initials MMM and love letters from the actress Mary Miles Minter were found in Taylor's house. Aided by the sensational press, many jumped to the conclusion that Normand had murdered Taylor out of jealousy. Normand was cleared of suspicion, but the mystery deepened when it was discovered

---

[6] Charles C. Pettijohn, *The Motion Picture* (1923), p. 19.

that Taylor was not his real name, that he had run away from a former life as a respectable businessman, and that he had some connection with the drug traffic. The murder was never solved, and again careers, both Normand's and Minter's, were ruined.

And these were not all. An actor was committed to a sanatorium as a drug addict. A young actress committed suicide, as did an actor in Griffith's company. There were divorces and quick remarriages. The Hollywood stars who had enjoyed such unprecedented popularity now became objects of another kind of curiosity: How sinful were their lives? What could be done about it?

"There is something about the pictures," said the anonymous author of *The Sins of Hollywood*, published in the year of Taylor's murder and Arbuckle's martyrdom, "which seems to make men and women less human, more animal-like." Their working lives subjected them to "close, unrestrained contact"; late-night shooting schedules and long location trips provided "numerous excuses and opportunities that exist in no other walk of life."[7] Temptation was everywhere, made stronger by the power of the few and the aspirations of the many. Some could indulge forbidden fantasies, others would help them to be realized. Hollywood life, according to such accounts, was an unrelieved round of nude dancing parties, strip-poker games, assignations, and dope parties where guests had their choice of opium, cocaine or heroin.

The rationale behind such exposés was always said to be the protection of American youth. Granted that this explanation was often a pious excuse for simple prurience, the assumptions behind it nevertheless mark an interesting change in attitude. In earlier years the dire warnings about the baneful effects of movies had focused on the nature of plots and individual scenes. Now the emphasis was on the stars' private lives. This was in part the first faint recognition that moviegoers responded less to stories and scenes than to the presence of actors and actresses on the screen, their inner essence of being as it came through in larger-than-life-size reproduction; the players, in other words, were more real to audiences than the characters they portrayed. Therefore, it was argued, what influenced youthful lives was the moral nature of the individual performer as it projected through the make-believe of screen roles. Any person whose private behavior did not meet respectable standards should not be allowed to contaminate youth by appearing in movies.

These arguments suffered, unfortunately, from a serious internal contradiction: they held that immoral persons should be replaced by moral persons on the screen, but they also contended that the Hollywood environment was such that it almost inevitably corrupted those who moved within its orbit. A kind of Gresham's Law operated in which moral people would stay out of movies to retain their virtue, leaving the field to the immoral. Although the concern about private behavior continued for several years, eventually the point was conceded, and moral-

---

[7] *Op cit.*, pp. 68, 69, 71.

THE MUSEUM OF MODERN ART/FILM STILLS ARCHIVE

Roscoe "Fatty" Arbuckle, the comedian, resists a bevy of bathing beauties in a publicity still (top) from the World War I period. Fatty didn't resist enough; in 1921, when a woman died after a party in his San Francisco hotel suite, the scandal rocked the movie industry and destroyed his career. To improve Hollywood's image the producers hired Postmaster General Will H. Hays (bottom, photographed March 1922) to serve as their "czar."

THE MUSEUM OF MODERN ART/FILM STILLS ARCHIVE

ists went back to condemning the plots and scenes of movies, leaving the private indiscretions of the stars in the hands of gossip columnists, press agents, sensational newspapers and an ever avid public.

The question remains, however, whether the exposés of Hollywood life were true. There are clear indications that many of the stories described real events. Some of the incidents recounted without names in *The Sins of Hollywood* are repeated with names in recent, unsensational Hollywood memoirs. Evidence comes from many sources that motion-picture work made unusual demands and provided unique opportunities that affected the way people behaved. Every field has its forms of competition, but in Hollywood the stakes were always much higher, in money and in fame, the standards often much less sure. Ultimately it was the public who decided the winners, but much had to be done before one got a chance before the public. And the most important equipment with which one played the game was one's body.

Hollywood's emphasis on the body was a matter of business as well as philosophy or pleasure. Players photographed as if they were about twenty pounds heavier than their actual weight. Physical trim had to be maintained, through exercise and massage, not only to look well but also to perform difficult tasks like riding and running, often again and again for retakes. The heightened awareness of the body was enhanced by knowledge of its worth in dollars. No matter what sentiments the stars voiced to the public through their press agents, visitors to Hollywood found that movie players spoke with extraordinary frankness among themselves about sex, money or personal likes and dislikes. It was as if they experienced so much pretense in their work and public image that the only way to keep a grip on reality was to eschew pretense completely in their private lives. Occasionally such frankness got through to the public: Joan Crawford corroborated *The Sins of Hollywood* when she told an interviewer in 1930 that "hot love scenes" often strike sparks between the players, and "you know the rest."[8]

It is difficult to resist Ben Hecht's observation that "the chief advance (or backslide) the movie people have made is freeing sexual activity from social censure."[9] He was referring to censure only within the Hollywood community, but the words have a wider application as well. During the 1920s, public interest in the stars' private affairs continued unabated while the demands for purity in individual behavior gradually declined. By the end of the decade, movie players could speak to the public about their divorces and love affairs with at least some of the frankness they used among themselves. There is no way to show a cause-and-effect relation between Hollywood's pleasure principles and the gradual unloosening of sexual restraints in American life; perhaps the two go together as symptoms of social change which affects them both. But Hollywood's sexual behavior was the most publicized frontier of a

---

[8] Harry T. Brundidge, *Twinkle, Twinkle, Movie Star!* (1930), p. 88.

[9] *A Child of the Century* (1954), p. 492.

new morality—or lack of one—during the 1920s, and there is reason to believe that the Aquarians of Hollywood were a vanguard of the increasingly larger role sexual openness has played in American public behavior during the past half-century.

The idea that their employees were harbingers of a new sexual freedom was the last thing, in the winter of 1921–1922, the movie moguls wanted to hear. Indeed, they had been listening to similar views, in the wake of the Arbuckle and Taylor affairs, but the language and interpretations were rather different: movie players were wicked, depraved, corrupt and corrupting. The movies had had a few years of comparative reprieve from hounding by moralists, who were occupied with the war and the advent of Prohibition and also somewhat taken aback by the tidal wave of middle-class accommodation to motion pictures. But they came howling back into the breach opened by the postwar scandals.

What was worse, after years of rapid, steady and apparently endless growth, attendance at motion-picture exhibitions began suddenly to fall in 1922. A drop in moviegoing would not have been unexpected during the brief depression following the war, but the industry had been agreeably surprised by the continuing upsurge in attendance. Then, as the economy emerged from its downturn, movie patronage declined.

The factors behind this were many. The total number of theaters had reached a saturation point, and many of the older neighborhood storefronts were closing; meanwhile, the declining practice of daily changes meant that there were fewer programs to see. More significantly, the movies were encountering new forms of competition for leisure time and money. Commercial radio broadcasting began late in 1920, and people were buying sets and staying home to enjoy the novelty of what Edison and Bellamy had long before promised—direct transmission of live entertainment into the home. Automobiles were available to working people through installment plans, and many were spending their weekends on the road instead of at the movies. But moralists and reformers could claim the drop in attendance during 1922 as a sign of public discontent with movie-star behavior and salacious films.

After Arbuckle's fatal party, the moguls began looking for a can of whitewash with which to cover themselves. A precedent they probably had in mind was the action of major-league-baseball owners in hiring a conservative federal judge to serve as commissioner of the sport after the Black Sox bribery scandal of 1919. They formed a new trade organization, the Motion Picture Producers and Distributors Association (MPPDA), superseding earlier, weaker efforts at unity, and sought as its president an outsider with credentials that could serve as defenses against their enemies: political influence, active Christian convictions, ties to the American heartland. To the person who could fulfill these requirements they offered a salary of $150,000 a year, a figure that might have attracted the President of the United States; as it was, they settled for a member of his Cabinet.

The man who took the job and began work in March 1922, during the Arbuckle trials and the investigations of Taylor's murder, was Will H. Hays, former chairman of the Republic National Committee and Presbyterian elder from Indiana. He resigned as Postmaster General in Warren G. Harding's Administration to serve as frontman for the movie industry; for Hays, though no one knew it at the time, it was a little like jumping from the fire into the frying pan. It was not until after Harding's sudden death in 1923 that a Senate investigation unearthed a scandal that dwarfed Fatty Arbuckle's drunken indiscretions: Harding's Secretary of the Interior had contravened federal law by leasing government oil at Teapot Dome, Wyoming, for private drilling and sale; he was later convicted of accepting a bribe and sentenced to a year in jail. Other Cabinet members were implicated, and Hays later testified before a Senate committee that in his capacity as Republican campaign chairman he had accepted questionable loans to the party treasury from an oilman who profited from the "Teapot Dome" concessions.

Hays functioned for the movie industry as a glorified public relations man. His visible role was as speechmaker, author of articles, sponsor of books, studies and committees to placate the movies' critics. The official line of the Hays Office, as the MPPDA came to be called, was that the movies had left behind the restless past and were beginning to fulfill their infinite promise as the "Esperanto of the Eye," the silent voice that broke down all barriers of language, spoke to all nations and peoples, and eventually would lead to the clearing up of misunderstandings among nations and thus to the abolition of war.[10] Hays and his writers branded censorship as nothing less than an un-American attack on the principles of democracy. Hays's invisible role as a lobbyist in Washington and state capitals we can only guess at.

Unexpectedly he discovered he had tasks of negotiation and reconciliation cut out for him in Hollywood as well. His office, as the first central administration for the movie industry, swiftly became the focus of organized grievances that had rarely been heard in the carefree pioneer days of democratic good fellowship and shared hard work. The panicky and punitive response of the producers to the Taylor and Arbuckle scandals, the drop in attendance, the founding of the Hays Office itself, all coming together in the winter of 1921–1922, sharply brought home to movie workers how much their trade had changed. In its rise to international success the industry had shifted from individual to corporate enterprise, as we shall see later, with new constraining ties to banks and brokers. Hierarchies of salary, billing and job classification had replaced the old open camaraderie. The pressure of aspirants and fans had caused studios and stars to build walls of privacy against the outside world. In the space of three or four years the movie trade had recapitulated the evolution of industry from small- to large-scale organization, and many people had been distressed by its sudden new impersonality,

---

[10] Edward S. Van Zile, *That Marvel—The Movie* (1923), p. 10, and passim.

rigidity and bureaucracy. Their complaints found an obvious target in the new "czar" of the movies.

Performers were the most publicized of the dissidents. The Actors' Equity Association, having won an agreement with Broadway producers after a successful strike in 1919, sought to organize movie players by appealing to Hays. Clearly, the producers had introduced new forms of exploitation. Noncontract players who were paid by the day were often forced to work a fifteen-to-twenty-hour day, from nine in the morning until well past midnight on their flat daily wage, or to work seven consecutive days for a week's salary. Some companies did not pay players on days they were not photographed, even though they spent a full day in make-up and costume, or were with a production unit on location. Extras also had grievances, particularly the payment of wages in scrip that could be redeemed only by the employment agencies that had placed them.

In addition, the studio craftworkers were attempting to organize. There had been strikes by the craftworkers in 1918 and 1921, but they had been unsuccessful in gaining union recognition. The producers wished to maintain an open shop, and they were aided by jurisdictional rivalry between the International Alliance of Theatrical Stage Employees and Moving Picture Machine Operators (IATSE), which hoped to forge an industry-wide union of all backstage workers, and the individual craft unions that wanted to represent their own specialties. Competing to get their members into the studios, the unions sometimes accepted lower wages and less favorable working conditions than prevailed in Los Angeles, already a poor town for unions. By the mid-1920s, however, the rival unions agreed to cooperate and divide the jurisdiction, and they finally approached Hays and the producers in one body.

Hays proved as adept an organizer as he was a publicity man. Under his leadership the producers came to terms with the unions and set up their own institutions to handle the problems of extras and performers. In 1926 the Studio Basic Agreement was signed between producers and unions. Through its provisions, studio craftsmen reversed their position relative to similar workers in other Los Angeles trades, gaining higher wages and better working conditions, while the producers retained the open shop. That same year the producers created the Central Casting Corporation, a jointly owned subsidiary firm which was given exclusive right to furnish extras to the studios. This eliminated the long lines of aspirants outside studio gates and the futile rushing from one studio to another looking for work; it also, by regulating the employment of extras, made clear what many already knew, that almost no one could make a living as an extra player, and it was no longer a path to stardom.

Finally, as a response to Equity's drive to organize actors, the producers' association in 1927 set up the Academy of Motion Picture Arts and Sciences to function more or less as a company union. It had five branches for various production personnel—producers, writers, directors, actors and technicians—and was open to membership by invitation only. Studio managers made clear that they would gladly negotiate with Academy committees, and for a time most of the creative workers were content to let the Academy represent them in labor relations with studios.

All of these arrangements had to be counted as triumphs for Will H. Hays. He neither silenced Hollywood's critics nor put an end to dissent within the industry, which would, of course, have been asking too much of him, but he did forge imposing façades of moral purpose and labor amity that enabled the private lives of the stars and the personal prerogatives of the producers to continue much as they had before. The Academy, Central Casting and the Studio Basic Agreement, though not immune to controversy and alteration, continued to function for years to come, even though shortly after their founding the industry went through a fundamental change. In 1926 Will Hays presided over the first public performance of sound motion pictures. The silent era of American movies, which in three decades had moved from a tar-paper shed in West Orange, New Jersey, to vast studio complexes, palatial mansions and a new Hollywood life style, was rapidly coming to an end.

6

THE SILENT FILM AND THE PASSIONATE LIFE

The silent feature film as a medium of art and mass commercial entertainment was born, flourished and died within a span of less than twenty years. Of more than ten thousand silent features produced in the United States between 1912 and 1929, only a handful remain in circulation for screening on television, at museums or by university film societies—the tip of an uncharted iceberg of surviving prints in archives, studio vaults and private collections. Though they date back little more than half a century, well within memory for many, they are, no less than Etruscan vases, artifacts of a departed culture, an irrecoverable past.

Who can re-create the experience of going to the pictures in the radiant dawn of popular mass culture? By the late 1920s every large city and most medium-sized towns boasted at least one brand-new sumptuous picture palace. Outside on the sidewalk stood a doorman, attired in frock coat with white gloves, waiting to open your car door and direct you to the ticket booth. If it was raining, he held an umbrella over your head; if snowing, an usher in the lobby rushed forward to brush off your coat.

You passed from usher to usher as you moved through ornate lobby corridors, hushed by the atmosphere of an Egyptian temple or a baroque palace that had provided the inspiration for architectural imitation. (A *New Yorker* cartoon of the period shows a child in a picture-palace lobby, asking, "Mama—does God live here?")[1] Eventually you came to the auditorium itself, or one of its serried balconies, where additional ushers stood, poised beside automatic seating boards that indicated which seats, if any, were empty. One, holding a flashlight to direct your steps, personally escorted you to your seat. There, after live stage performances, musical interludes played by an orchestra numbering up to thirty pieces, a newsreel and a travelogue, you saw what you had come for—a feature film, accompanied by its own especially arranged musical score.

Of the feature films exhibited in such picture palaces, and at every other movie theater large or small throughout the country, no more than a tiny number were produced without the expectation or at least the strong hope of reaping a profit. This made the movies unique among the arts. Among the creators and disseminators of literature, painting, sculpture, the graphic arts, music, dance, even theater, there were some who

---

[1] Reproduced in Ben M. Hall, *The Best Remaining Seats: The Story of the Golden Age of the Movie Palace* (1961), p. 123.

made their work available for public sale or performance with the hope of no more than breaking even, or of making a profit on a few products that would cover the costs of many less popular. The almost undiluted commercialism of motion-picture production was a constant source of exasperation to critics and reviewers in the silent era, who looked, most often vainly, for redeeming aesthetic value in the stream of feature films pouring out of Hollywood at the rate of nearly two a day.

Posterity, however, has found it easier to recognize enduring artistry in American silent films. In a world-wide poll of critics published in 1972 by the British Film Institute in its quarterly, *Sight and Sound*, some twenty American silent features were named at least once on the various critics' lists of the top ten motion pictures in the history of world cinema. One, Buster Keaton's *The General* (1926), ranked among the ten leading films; it was surpassed by only two other silents, Sergei Eisenstein's *The Battleship Potemkin* (USSR, 1925) and Carl Th. Dreyer's *The Passion of Joan of Arc* (France, 1928). Two more, Chaplin's *The Gold Rush* (1925) and F. W. Murnau's *Sunrise* (1927), were the only other silents to place in the top-twenty selections. In all, thirty-five silent films received mention.

The value of such listings can obviously be exaggerated. The predominance of American films becomes less impressive when one recalls that the United States produced more than 80 percent of all silent films; twenty significant movies works out to be little more than one a year.

Still, the movies need not suffer in comparison with other arts. Out of the thousands of American novels published between 1915 and 1928, twenty works of major significance would be a considerable number, and the same may be said for American plays or American paintings. It would be as false, however, to tell the story of moviemaking in the silent era on the basis of a few artistic achievements as it would be to leave art out of it. For producers, movie workers, audiences and observers alike, the meaning of American movies lay in the multiple and cumulative messages of the more than ten thousand good, bad and indifferent films that played selectively across the vision and consciousness of their viewers.

To speculate about the cultural messages of movies en masse is to display one's skill at fantasy, philosophy or metaphor. Yet there are also ways to root such speculation in history. The German critic Walter Benjamin demonstrated one important approach in an essay called "The Work of Art in the Age of Mechanical Reproduction."[2] In it he put forward the view that techniques of mechanical reproduction acted as decisive forces in shattering cultural tradition and creating new cultural forms. One hallmark of traditional elite culture was scarcity of product—the individual painting, the hand-lettered manuscript, the live performance. Mechanical reproduction created an abundance of copies. Another hall-

---

[2] From his book *Illuminations* (1955; translated by Harry Zohn, 1968). This essay first appeared in 1936.

mark of traditional culture was control over the cultural environment—the museum, the theater, the private home. Mechanical reproduction spawned a multiplicity of environments where cultural products could be experienced.

Though the cultural impact of mechanical reproduction had been felt as early as the fifteenth century with the invention of the printing press, the motion picture brought significant new factors into play: its appeal was universal, overcoming language differences and even illiteracy; it offered the power of the moving image, easy access in terms of time and money, and a group experience. The social significance of film, said Benjamin, "particularly in its most positive form, is inconceivable without its destructive, cathartic aspect, that is, the liquidation of the traditional value of the cultural heritage."[3]

It remains to ask more specifically what role the movies played in destroying old cultural forms and building new ones as part of the social and cultural conflicts that marked America in the first three decades of the twentieth century.

The movies' place as instruments of social transformation may be clarified by asking three separate questions: What were the subjects of American movies, and in what way did their contents change? Did the changes in movies coincide with, precede or follow similar changes in the culture itself? How were the movies themselves involved in the cultural struggles of the period?

The overwhelming difficulty standing in the way of a comprehensive knowledge of movie content is the paucity of surviving films, particularly from before 1920. Every claim to originality or innovation is suspect when one does not know for certain what came before; and the more we learn about early movies, the more it becomes clear that few things are new under the Southern California sun.

Unfortunately, the efforts now under way at systematic cataloging of American motion pictures are not likely to provide solutions to the problem. The American Film Institute, for example, has begun a complete listing of motion pictures produced in the United States; its first two volumes, covering feature films from 1921 to 1930, have been published. They list some seven thousand films with production data and brief plot synopses. Each film is categorized by its major themes, and one entire volume is given over to an index of themes with relevant films listed below each one (*marriage*, for example, has over five hundred films listed; there is one entry for *sex*, in the category of *sex instruction*).

When one samples the plot synopses, one discovers a number of inaccuracies in both summary and categorization, which is scarcely surprising, since the sources were plot descriptions prepared by studios and synopses printed in contemporary newspaper reviews. Both these are

---

[3] *Ibid.*, p. 221.

well known to be unreliable, because of last-minute changes in the film, or inattention or indifference on the part of the writer.

We are like the people in Plato's cave. The flickering movement of light and shadow we see may not be the reality of silent motion pictures at all. In an old book one comes across a still of "the 'great' strike scene" from William C. DeMille's *The Ragamuffin* (1915).[4] Young women are poised at their sewing machines in a crowded sweatshop, listening intently to an older woman exhorting them—presumably to strike. What did this film tell its audiences about labor struggles, unions, the conditions of women workers? How many others were there like it?

One screens a print of a rare surviving episode from the Kalem company's early serial *The Hazards of Helen.* Helen Holmes, the heroine, drives a car at high speed around mountain curves, outraces a speeding train, leaps from her moving car to the locomotive and brakes it to a halt. She rescues the detective strapped to the engine and captures the gang of counterfeiters. How often did the early movies portray such courageous, competent, resourceful women? When did they disappear from the screen, and why? Each glimpse into unexplored aspects of the movies' past opens the tantalizing prospect of unforeseen perspectives.

Nevertheless, it is possible to exaggerate what we do not know. All the evidence suggests that the vast majority of silent films fell into well-defined categories of subject and treatment: the crime story, the Western story, the historical costume story, the domestic melodrama, the romance. Overwhelmingly, films of contemporary life, crime movies, melodramas and love stories centered on men and women from the upper-middle and wealthy classes: people who lived in large spacious houses, kept servants, owned cars and earned their money from business, finance or the professions.

This was as true before World War I as after. But the dramatic changes in American cultural styles and values in the war years and after have sometimes confused historians of motion pictures, who, like other historians of the arts, sometimes oversimplify about the larger culture in which their medium was shaped. In his brief survey *Hollywood in the Twenties*, for example, David Robinson suggests that producers made a deliberate choice after the war to change the class emphasis of motion-picture content—from the working-class appeal of the prewar Victorian drawing-room melodramas to the postwar leisured upper- and upper-middle-class image of country-club and cabaret society dramas. He claims, in fact, that moviemakers "conspired" with conservative businessmen and a supine and hedonistic public to create a false image of American life in the 1920s, to make it appear as if nearly everyone (who was not a cowboy or a cross-eyed comedian) dressed in evening clothes, lived in an elegant home and passed the time in cabarets.[5]

What this viewpoint ignores is that in this period American society

---

[4] William C. DeMille, *Hollywood Saga* (1939), opposite p. 145.

[5] *Hollywood in the Twenties* (1968; Paperback Library ed.) pp. 39–40.

and culture were changing faster and more fundamentally than the movies themselves. Contemporary audiences and moviemakers were fully aware, as Robinson was not, that the inhabitants of Victorian drawing rooms in 1914 movies belonged to the same classes that flocked to cabarets a decade later. Members of the urban leisure and professional classes indeed led the way in discarding the social code symbolized by that Victorian drawing-room scene. The traditional middle-class moral order had, even before the war, been losing ground in its effort to maintain small-town values in an increasingly urban, industrial and ethnically heterogeneous society. Its drive to recover dominance during the war through excessive patriotism, moralism and repression, though leading to impressive victories with the enactment of Prohibition and immigration restriction, also drove segments of the culturally influential urban elites away from adherence to traditional beliefs and behavior.

The targets of the campaign for conformity—the recently arrived immigrants and their children, the "hyphenated Americans"—related in a more confused and ambiguous way to the dominant social order. They sought success, comfort, status on the same terms as other Americans; many newcomers were quite willing to adhere to American standards because they marked the path to the American rewards they had come for. Yet they were told in painfully explicit ways, from discrimination and restrictive legislation to Klan violence, that their character and traits, their religions, languages, dress styles, complexions, features, cuisines, mores and habits were barriers to full admission into American life. And the fact that they had provided the original audience for movies and the dynamic leaders of the motion-picture business was also held against them.

To the spokesmen and spokeswomen of the dominant order, the movies stood in direct opposition to respectable American values and institutions: power over movies rested largely in the hands of foreign-born producers; even native-born movie workers came from marginal and disreputable subsocieties of vaudeville and stock company theater; and the movies were full of incitements to crime and salacious behavior.

Movies thus came to play a central role in the cultural conflicts that followed World War I. On both sides of the struggle, movies came to be seen as offering values distinctly different from those of the older middle-class culture, and providing greater opportunities for ethnic minorities than other economic sectors. Immigrants and their children were attracted to movie culture not merely because movies were cheap, ubiquitous and appealing as fantasy or entertainment; their preference became a conscious, one might almost say a political, choice.

In American society, movies became a major factor in the reorientation of traditional values—Walter Benjamin's word "liquidation" in the American context would be too strong. For no matter how despised they were by defenders of traditional middle-class culture, movies were, after all, made by men deeply committed to the capitalist values, attitudes and ambitions that were part of the dominant social order. Any new options they offered would clearly avoid breaking away from the fundamental economic and social mold.

On the level of culture preferences and standards, however, the escalation of cultural division after the war greatly reduced the range of public agreement. More subjects became controversial; groups adhered more firmly to their own interests and images. Novelists and poets found in the disintegration of general norms a release from stultifying conventions, which created the setting for one of the glorious eras of American literature. The situation for workers in the mass media was different. The mandate from their employers was to generate profit by appealing to the largest possible audience. In the prewar atmosphere of confidence, order and limited pluralism, they had found it possible within this framework occasionally to explore political, religious, economic and ethnic themes. After the war it became much more difficult.

Faced with an audience more divided, more defensive, and yet increasingly avid for visions of alternative styles and behavior, moviemakers not unnaturally sought the subjects and treatments that pleased the most and alienated the fewest. The noisy and well-organized opposition and their own settled beliefs and filmmaking practices kept them from straying too far beyond the remaining stereotypes and formulas of the middle-class order. What they became adept at was reformulating older conventions; only when the need was obvious and overwhelming did they dare generate a new formula.

The results were not so different from traditional culture as reformers and censors sometimes made it appear. The overall effect of the movie version of reality was as always to place audiences at a distance from direct contact with their social environment. To choose between movies and traditional culture was essentially to choose one highly elaborated social code over another—a fact of which movie patrons were never totally unaware.

The tactics of moviemakers in transforming social codes were nowhere more successful than in the films of Cecil B. DeMille. He became notorious early in 1918 when he unveiled the first in a series of spicy morality tales of extramarital temptation, *Old Wives for New.* His audacity has since become a centerpiece of the Hollywood legend, but like many such stories, the facts are much more interesting.

The DeMille legend focuses especially on the most controversial of his early postwar films, *Male and Female* (1919). Moralists grew outraged as soon as they learned of DeMille's suggestive change of title from its source, James M. Barrie's play *The Admirable Crichton*, and the picture disappointed no one's expectations. In its famous bathroom scene Gloria Swanson, as Lady Mary, steps into a sunken bath the size of a small swimming pool, revealing a momentary glimpse of her breasts. Later DeMille introduced a lavish Babylonian fantasy sequence not to be found in the original, taking his inspiration from a poem by William Ernest Henley, whose lines the butler Crichton quotes in the play: "I was a king in Babylon/And you were a Christian slave."

By all accounts, *Male and Female* could never have been made before World War I. It was "a highly moral picture," Adolph Zukor, whose Famous Players-Lasky company produced the film, recalled in his autobiography, "yet its emotional theme—the noble lady falling in love with the butler—would probably not have been acceptable to prewar audiences."[6] In Lewis Jacobs' classic study, *Male and Female* is called "more daring in its subject matter than any other picture Hollywood had produced."[7]

Is it merely the narrow moral climate in which movies have been judged that has led such commentators to ignore the relation of DeMille's films to their sources? Barrie's satire on the British aristocracy and its servants had been a stage favorite for nearly twenty years before *Male and Female* was produced (its original performances took place in London in 1902 and on Broadway in 1903). Similarly, David Graham Phillips' novel *Old Wives for New*, the source of DeMille's film of the same title, had been published back in 1908 and had aroused considerable controversy over its portraits of plutocratic American women. Perhaps the point is that before the war, playwrights and novelists, with smaller and higher status audiences, had been permitted more freedom of expression than filmmakers.

The more we learn of early motion-picture history, however, the more difficult it is to validate such judgments. Glimpses of nudity did not originate with *Male and Female*; not only were women with bare breasts shown in the Babylonian sequence of *Intolerance*, but Annette Kellerman, the champion swimmer, appeared nude in *A Daughter of the Gods* (1916). Nor was infidelity a novel topic—indeed, the attraction and danger of dalliance was the constant theme of Theda Bara's many "vampire" films, beginning in 1914 with *A Fool There Was*. (Long before *Dracula*, the term "vampire" described a predatory woman whose sexual desires, if fulfilled, were sure to drain a man's life blood; after World War I, as American society became more relaxed about sex, it was shortened to "vamp" and described a woman whose sexual forwardness was, though ambiguous, a great deal less harmful.) Nor was the subject of romance across the master-servant barrier so daring in DeMille. As far back as 1903, Biograph had made a comic film on that theme, *With a Kodak*. Filmmakers before the war explored nearly all the aspects of the subjects and the images that were to occupy their successors for half a century more; only in our own era have innovations gone further, with the display of male and female genitals and the performance of sex acts in commercial movies.

DeMille's daring lay not in subject matter, theme or revelation of the

---

[6] *The Public Is Never Wrong* (1953), pp. 202–3.

[7] *The Rise of the American Film* (1939), p. 400.

THE MUSEUM OF MODERN ART/FILM STILLS ARCHIVE

Natural leadership asserts itself over class prerogative in Cecil B. DeMille's controversial *Male and Female* (1919). Shipwrecked on an island, the butler Crichton (Thomas Meighan) takes command and orders Tweeny (Lila Lee) to stop tending Lady Mary (Gloria Swanson) and watch the fire; Lady Agatha (Mildred Reardon) looks on aghast.

human form; what he did was give familiar topics a treatment that precisely suited audience desires in the immediate aftermath of the war. He was able to free the subject of marriage from the overstuffed parlors of Victorian melodrama, to infuse it with wit, style, vicarious pleasures, and above all, practical hints on contemporary ways to behave. DeMille's triumph was one of manner, not matter. Though his films suggested new attitudes, none challenged moral order. DeMille's films angered moralists largely because they were popular with respectable middle-class audiences; and they would not have been so popular had they not been so conservative.

Indeed, DeMille's original reluctance to make such films was one of the themes of his autobiography. As chief director at the Hollywood studios of Famous Players-Lasky, he had devoted his efforts principally to Westerns and historical costume dramas. Early in 1917, however, he received new instructions from the company's New York business office. "What the public demands today," said a memo, "is modern stuff with plenty of clothes, rich sets, and action."[8] DeMille ignored this. During 1917 he made more costume spectacles, featuring former opera star Geraldine Farrar; the only new step he took was to direct Mary Pickford in two patriotic and sentimental melodramas, *A Romance of the Redwoods* and *The Little American.*

The messages from New York to DeMille became more insistent. From their metropolitan vantage point, the business managers were directly experiencing the changing moods of urban elites and ethnic minorities in ways unavailable to their production workers, surrounded by retired Midwesterners living in the low frame bungalows of early Hollywood. At the end of 1917 Jesse Lasky informed DeMille that he had purchased the rights to the David Graham Phillips novel *Old Wives for New.* He challenged DeMille to make the picture, to "become commercial" and "try to do modern stories of great human interest."[9]

So at last DeMille did the job his superiors asked of him; and his success demonstrated the obverse side of Hollywood's distance from the ferment of the East. Separated as they were from the realities of cultural change and conflict, Hollywood filmmakers found themselves less constrained by social fact, more capable of inventing a frame of fantasy or formula for contemporary life. DeMille reports that Zukor did not want to release *Old Wives for New.* The grounds for his opposition are not stated; perhaps, as the entrepreneur principally responsible for attracting middle-class audiences to movies, he was fearful of their reaction to a film that even gently satirized their traditional moralisms. If so, he need not have worried; DeMille was hardly even a Phillips, and far from being a realist, muckraker or impassioned critic of the upper bourgeoisie. In Phillips' novel, "modern" marriage ends in adultery and divorce; in DeMille's movie, in temptation and reconciliation.

---

[8] *The Autobiography of Cecil B. DeMille* (1959), p. 212.

[9] *Ibid.*

DeMille, was, above all, a consummate sentimentalist. He had the knack of titillating audiences while at the same time reinforcing their conventional standards—of letting them eat their cake and have it too. A few years later he discovered the most congenial form for his particular skills, the religious epic, which proved the perfect vehicle for his deft combination of moral didacticism and orgiastic fantasy. His "modern stories" in the early postwar period were preliminary expressions of this long-enduring formula. They told moviegoers of the necessity for, and the boundaries of, social change that would not disturb the inherited moral order; and in dream sequences of opulent sensuality, set in ancient times, they provided a voyeuristic glimpse of forbidden pleasures and desires.

There was one serious difficulty about eating one's cake and having it too: as a steady diet it quickly led to undernourishment. DeMille's modern dramas of temptation could gratify middle-class ideological expectations only when they insisted that adult men and women would not let lures and desires override their fundamental morality. Yet the films also frustrated a basic emotional expectation American audiences had traditionally brought to their popular arts—the wish to experience vicariously the sweet succumbing to temptation, and the guilt and retribution of those who step beyond the boundaries of the social code. Ultimately DeMille's formula narrowed the range of behavior too much. Of its kind it was superior, but alone it was not a strong enough base for Hollywood popularity and profits. In a period of cultural change, moviemakers could never feel certain that their conventions and stereotypes would last beyond a season. The longings of postwar audiences set them on a perpetual quest for more commercially and emotionally satisfying entertainment formulas.

The extent of alternative human behavior was, of course, never limitless. The vast majority of the world's nonwhite peoples were not considered subjects for the movies, any more than they were treated as other than stereotypes in the fiction, travel books, social sciences and political rhetoric of the time. An artist could rise above the barriers of his own culture and carry an audience with him, as Robert Flaherty proved with his classic silent documentaries *Nanook of the North* (1922), about Eskimo people on Canada's Hudson Bay, and *Moana* (1926), about the people of the western Samoan island Safune. But the audience for Samoans was smaller and did not go to movies so frequently as those who preferred to see Gloria Swanson on a tropical island, and Flaherty had few followers in the documentary field.

There were, however, Caucasian people known to behave very differently from Americans. These exotics inhabited such countries as France, Italy, Germany, Russia, Sweden, even Great Britain. Natives of these countries, though much on American minds during the European war of 1914–1918, did not often appear on the screens of American movie theaters, since the war had diverted European film industries from making fiction feature films. American moviemakers were thus given a free hand to perpetuate their own versions of the character of European nationalities, which generally did not rise above the gross stereotypes of blacks or American Indians, though normally they were more favorable.

Europeans were more sensual, decadent, emotional, sinful than Americans, and also more calculating, rational and willful. They dared what the innocent American flirts in a DeMille movie would never dare—to be direct and clear in their intentions, to express themselves emotionally, to seek fulfillment of their desires. They were charming, fascinating, beguiling, dangerous and possibly evil.

They could do so many things forbidden to Americans! In one of the most interesting sexual dramas of the 1920s, Herbert Brenon's *Dancing Mothers* (1926), a married woman begins her flirtation with a single man (for the highly moral purpose, in the beginning at least, of distracting him from her frivolous flapper daughter) by posing as a Frenchwoman and speaking to him in French. One of the memorable scenes of romantic pathos in silent films is in the long tracking sequence in King Vidor's war epic *The Big Parade* (1925), when Renée Adorée, as the French peasant girl, runs frantically along the dusty line of marching American soldiers to carry his boots to her departing doughboy lover. The silent movies would not have risked depicting an American woman acting in the same open, vulnerable, loving way.

As a ground for sexual expressiveness, the stereotyped European had already become a familiar figure in American movies by the time of World War I. The war, however, infused even the most mundane European caricatures in the popular arts with a new intensity. It was the most emotional of America's overseas conflicts; the fate of civilization itself seemed to rest on combating the despicable Hun and supporting the brave French and British. The waves of popular sentiment engulfing the country gave new life to the settled forms of the movies.

Erich von Stroheim was among the first to experience the changed audience response to stock European figures. The war gave him a chance, after several years of hand-to-mouth work as a bit player and production assistant, to use his Austrian military background and play a series of villainous German officers. His personal appearance in public could set off angry murmurs and threats of violence. He had superseded the old stereotypes and become himself an archetype, the cruel, overbearing Prussian aristocrat, "the man you love to hate."[10] When the war ended he was able to capitalize on this infamous characterization to launch a new career as a director, with himself as star of his own films.

In Von Stroheim's early postwar films his warrior is transformed into a seducer, and the struggle between America and the Central Powers becomes a battle of the sexes. He is Von Stuben in *Blind Husbands* (1919), vacationing at the same Alpine resort as a young American couple; in *Foolish Wives* (1921) he is Count Sergius Karamazin, an

---

[10] Thomas Quinn Curtiss, *Von Stroheim* (1971), p. 91.

adventurer in Monte Carlo who seeks to take advantage of an American diplomat and his wife. Both films follow a basically similar format: the suave and graceful European beguiles the idle American wife; he very nearly seduces her, but in each case her own feeble will and timely outside intervention save her from violation; in the end the European is unmasked as evil and meets a just death at the hands of someone he has wronged. American husband and wife are strengthened in their loyalty.

Though such a brief summary hardly does justice to Von Stroheim's qualities as a director, his skill in characterization, the rich detail of his social settings, his talent for macabre violence that was to reach a peak in his classic of motion-picture naturalism, *Greed* (1924), it does suggest how little his formula varied from the sentimental conventions developed by DeMille. No marriage vows are breached; the American man learns a trim little lesson about not neglecting his wife, the woman learns to beware of continental lovers; and the European reveals how weak and miserable he is before meeting an ignominious death. Compared to DeMille, Von Stroheim adhered far more strictly to traditional American morals. He did allow audiences more of a chance to flex some larger emotions, but these were mainly negative: revenge, retribution and relief that the moral order was not seriously breached. Where were the warm, outgoing cathartic emotions to come from, love and sympathy, admiration and awe, pity and sorrow?

They were not to be found in the leading postwar films about contemporary American men and women, nor in Von Stroheim's films about Americans encountering Europeans. Only one possible alternative form of human interaction remained, and moviemakers were not required to think of it themselves, because the American reading public gave them the idea: for more than a year after the Armistice, book buyers and readers had clamored to get Vicente Blasco Ibáñez's *The Four Horsemen of the Apocalypse*, a romantic novel about an Argentine playboy in Europe who at first disdains the struggle, then converts to the cause of civilization, enlists in the French army and dies a hero's death in battle. The answer had been on the tip of every Hollywood tongue all along: if you were used to putting Europeans in your movies to hike up the emotion, think of the emotion you could generate by making *all* your characters European.

Metro got the chance to pioneer this new conception by buying the rights to the Ibáñez novel. For the part of Julio, the playboy, they assigned a young Italian, a former tango dancer who had been biding his time in movies playing bit parts as a south-of-the-border villain. His name was Rudolph Valentino. The rest, one is tempted to say, is history. In the brief span of years before Valentino's sudden death in 1926 at the age of thirty-one, Metro as well as Valentino's subsequent employers and the women and men of America got considerably more emotion than they had bargained for.

Valentino was a presence the silver screen had never seen before. He had passion; he loved, openly and fully; his love was strong but could be

© PARAMOUNT PICTURES CORPORATION

Silent-movie versions of upper-class and middle-class felicity: Noël Coward (standing, in overcoat) visits the lavish night club set (top) of Herbert Brenon's *Dancing Mothers* (1926); among the players shown are Conway Tearle (in formal attire, at left), Alice Joyce (seated, center), Clara Bow (standing) and Norman Trevor (right). The champagne flows at the wedding dinner in Erich von Stroheim's 1924 film *Greed*; the newlyweds (center, facing camera) are ZaSu Pitts and Gibson Gowland.

FROM THE MGM RELEASE *Greed* © 1925 METRO-GOLDWYN PICTURES CORPORATION. COPYRIGHT RENEWED 1952 BY LOEW'S INCORPORATED

tragic weakness, too, as in *Blood and Sand* (1922), based on another Ibáñez novel, where he plays a famous matador whose desire for a "vamp" leads to self-destruction and death in the bull ring. Valentino's remarkable screen persona was not mere happy accident; he was also a skillful actor. "He is not a great actor," Robert E. Sherwood wrote of him in *Blood and Sand*, "because he lacks both the necessary abandon and the requisite range of expression. But he is no mere tailor's dummy. He has great poise, lithe grace and a considerable amount of power."[11]

It is instructive to compare Valentino with the most popular American male star of the period, Douglas Fairbanks. Valentino's character in Clarence Brown's *The Eagle* (1925) was clearly patterned after the carefree adventurer Fairbanks had so successfully portrayed in such films as *The Mark of Zorro* (1920), *Robin Hood* (1922) and *The Thief of Baghdad* (1925). Valentino demonstrated skill in horsemanship, sufficient athletic prowess—though nothing equal to Fairbanks' gymnastic feats—and a surprising capacity for wit and self-irony in his semicomic role as a Russian Robin Hood. The telling difference between the two men was that Valentino always projected himself in a way that Fairbanks, the smiling, clean-cut, genteel American hero, rarely did, if ever—as a sexual being.

In the as yet unwritten history of the revolution in modern American sexual attitudes and behavior, Valentino must play a considerable part. It was not only that he seemed to fulfill the fantasies of millions of American women—a collective dream that received its quintessential embodiment in his performance in *The Sheik* (1921), the film version of E. M. Hull's sensational novel, where, as an Arab chieftain, he ravishes an Englishwoman, then reveals himself an Anglo-Saxon aristocrat—there was also the tangled resentment and emulation he aroused in American men.

His grace, his ease with his body, his skill as a dancer, all clearly attractive to women, seemed to cause some men considerable unease. For a man to make himself appealing to women they considered a certain sign of his effeminacy. Valentino's masculinity was questioned because, among other things, he wore a bracelet, given him by his second wife. His deviance from the "cave man" ethic of male sexual behavior was particularly galling to the Chicago *Tribune*, which several times attacked him editorially; one such diatribe, published only a few weeks before Valentino's fatal illness, was blamed by Valentino's business manager for hastening the actor's death.

The equation Europe=passion was not, however, a discovery Americans made wholly through the screen image of Rudolph Valentino. It was a time-honored theme of American fiction, in the works of, among others, Henry James; and Europeans, using the logical calculating side of their natures, had long before figured out the value of passion as a means of achieving rational ends. The Germans, for example, deliberately

[11] *The Best Moving Pictures of 1922–23*, edited by Sherwood (1923), p. 16.

turned to the theme of passion as a way of reviving their film industry after the war.

Burdened with their nation's defeat and the accumulated odium of Allied anti-German propaganda, the UFA studios and director Ernst Lubitsch planned to regain their international audience by a tour de force, making intimate sexual dramas about great figures in the histories of their conquerers. Curiosity and outrage would persuade British and French exhibitors to book their films, and their quality would win over hostile audiences—so it was plotted, and so, by and large, it occurred. The first of these films, *Madame Dubarry*, appeared in 1919, with Pola Negri in the title role and Emil Jannings as Louis XV, and was hailed as a classic. It was taken up by American distributors and opened a year later in New York, the first postwar German film to be shown in the United States (*The Cabinet of Dr. Caligari*, also made in 1919, was not imported until 1921), although its origins were described vaguely as Central European. *Madame Dubarry* also was given a new name for its American run—*Passion*.

The alternative to traditional American behavior that movie audiences most clearly demanded was passionate behavior. And as the food industry turned to Latin America for its bananas, the movie industry looked to Europe for its supplies of passion. Passionate actresses, actors, directors and writers answered the call, and passionate philosophers as well. Foremost among the latter was the British novelist Elinor Glyn, who propagated the philosophy of "It," a form of personal magnetism not to be confused with sexual attraction—though everyone managed to, anyway.

The list of Europeans who came to Hollywood reads like the guest list of Gatsby's parties. Lubitsch, Negri and Jannings all came, the first two to stay, and the director continued his brilliant career, bringing an altogether new kind of sophistication and wit to Hollywood comedy. From Germany also came Conrad Veidt, the leading actor of *Dr. Caligari*, and directors Paul Leni, E. A. Dupont and F. W. Murnau. Murnau's first American film, *Sunrise* (1927), was ranked in the *Sight and Sound* poll mentioned earlier as one of the half-dozen greatest silent films of world cinema.

Hungary gave the American movies director Paul Fejos and actress Vilma Banky, whose blond beauty made an attractive contrast to Valentino's dark good looks when she played opposite him in *The Eagle* and *Son of the Sheik*. France contributed director Jacques Feyder, and the Swedish film industry lost its two leading directors, Mauritz Stiller and Victor Sjöström (known as Seastrom in Hollywood). Sjöström (who was an outstanding actor and matinée idol in Sweden) directed Lillian Gish in *The Scarlet Letter* (1926) and an extraordinary work of cinema naturalism, *The Wind* (1928). With Stiller to Hollywood came his protégée, Greta Garbo, a young actress who became the new embodiment of European passion in the same year Valentino died.

There is an uncanny lesson to be learned from Garbo's Hollywood

The dream lovers of the 1920s at their most ardent: Rudolph Valentino (top), playing a British aristocrat disguised as an Arab, overcomes Agnes Ayres in *The Sheik* (1921); Greta Garbo (bottom), in an uncharacteristic pose, gazes adoringly at Lars Hanson in *The Divine Woman* (1928).

debut: American moviemakers, then and for decades after, held fast to their formulas as faithfully as a newborn duckling adheres to the first moving thing it sees. Garbo was cast in her first two American films, *The Torrent* and *The Temptress* (both 1926), as a female Valentino, a sultry Spanish siren drawn from novels by none other than Vicente Blasco Ibáñez. If these were tests of her skill as an actress, she passed with flying colors, for as the *Variety* reviewer wrote of her first American performance, when a Scandinavian "can put over a Latin characterization with sufficient power to make it most convincing, need there be any more said regarding her ability?"[12]

As it turned out, much more needed to be said, and was—no one doubted Garbo's appeal, but everyone seemed puzzled as to its nature. Though she was obviously a fine actress, her studio, MGM, gave her little chance to show it. Her ten American silent films were not exactly alike in their plots, but to all intents and purposes they were the same; following the first two came *Flesh and the Devil*, *Love*, *The Divine Woman*, *The Mysterious Lady*, *A Woman of Affairs*, *Wild Orchids*, *The Single Standard* and *The Kiss*. Garbo's principal challenge was to show how a passionate Russian woman differed from a passionate Austrian, French or English woman (and because everyone knew she was European, she was even allowed to portray passionate American women).

On the screen Garbo shone with an inner intensity few other performers in motion pictures came even close to. Director Fred Niblo demonstrated Garbo's power with a clever opening sequence in *The Mysterious Lady* (1928). The film begins at a party. The camera moves among the guests. Then a woman appears at the top of a staircase. You see parts of her, her legs, her arms, you see her from the back, she moves downstairs among the others, and still you have not seen her face. It does not matter. She has created an excitement in the audience, an emotional quickening, that makes the other players appear mere mannequins. This was Garbo: if her career had any major flaw, it was that she made Hollywood's most romantic male stars look callow and inadequate beside her.

It is pertinent to ask how European audiences reacted to all the passion committed in their name. Overseas exhibition accounted for more than a third of the American movie industry's total income during the 1920s and provided the vital margin for the high profits, high salaries and extravagant life style of the moguls and stars. Clearly, then, they did not mind it. But it would be fair to say that Europeans did not go to American movies to see themselves, nor did they consider Gloria Swanson or John Gilbert "Europeans" no matter what nationality they were presumably portraying. They wanted to see Americans, the wild raw new

---

[12] Quoted in Michael Conway, Dion McGregor and Mark Ricci, *The Films of Greta Garbo* (1963), p. 47.

people of the Western world, doing what Americans do, in characteristically American ways.

To Europeans, what epitomized American life was movement. Compared to themselves—encrusted with traditions, weighted down by forms, customs, habits, procedures; measured, lugubrious, drained of life—American motion, and therefore American motion pictures, possessed an enchanting, irresistible allure. "There were long sequences of action—without a single dull passage—portraying sensational abductions," Philippe Soupault wrote of the early postwar American movies in France; "there were the pictures of Douglas Fairbanks, of Rio Jim, and of Tom Mix; there were complicated stories ending in the robbing of banks, in violent deaths, in discoveries of gold mines. . . . Doors open and close; bronzed men, strong men, terribly refined or terribly frivolous women come and go with happiness or unhappiness in their hands."[13] Americans had physical genius; they held the secret of action, and Europeans went to American movies to learn the secret.

There was a time after the war when the arrival of the latest American Western was an exciting cultural event in European cities. With its tough, lean men, spectacular riding and blazing guns, the Western seemed to represent American action at its purest. But the novelty of Western stereotypes quickly paled. American producers began sending over films that combined a more refined, supple, versatile kind of physical genius. After a time Westerns came to seem unintentionally comic; these new films were comic by design. European audiences were among the first to recognize that the silent comedians were artists as well as funny men, and that in their antics the heritage of cultural values was more thoroughly explored and exploded than anywhere else in American movies.

---

[13] *The American Influence in France* (1930), pp. 16–17.

7

CHAOS, MAGIC, PHYSICAL GENIUS AND THE ART OF SILENT COMEDY

The American comic tradition and American movies were made for each other. Theirs was a foreordained, defiantly unconventional love affair that even Hollywood's ripest imagination would have found it difficult to match. They were both black sheep, outcasts from and embarrassments to respectable American society. Alone, each was pressed to conform to upright, moral, four-square genteel American standards and was for long periods confused as to how properly to reform and behave. But when they found each other, they found support for their freest and wildest natures, for the crudity and bawdiness which the middle-class social code tried so persistently to suppress. Together they gave expression to the underside of American values and behavior, the opposite pole from order and decorum. Together they projected their grotesque exaggeration, their extravagance, violence and sexual license, on a screen as large as the world.

Better yet, they were the offspring of vastly different classes, one rich, well-born and clever, the other humble and poor but full of creative energy. The movies, of course, began as bottom dogs; it may come as more of a surprise to learn that the American comic tradition originated with conservative elites.

The first extensive writing and publishing of humor in America was done by members of the conservative Southern gentry in the early nineteenth century. They wrote about the common men and women of the South and West, and pictured them as cruel, violent, deceitful, inept —and funny. Their aim was to ridicule and thereby contain the rising spirit of democracy: such comic louts and slatterns were clearly incapable of controlling themselves and therefore required the continued leadership of the traditional ruling class.

The writers' means of putting this point across marked their significant contribution to the forms and styles of American expression. They masked themselves, writing in a vernacular prose as if their voices were the voices of the plain-spoken men and women whom they feared. Had their attack been direct, it would have been taken for what it was—an act of political and social aggression. But by letting the comic mask do the talking in an appropriately homely style, they made it appear as if a common person were ridiculing himself and his class. The success of their endeavor—as humorists if not as politicians—was demonstrated by the widespread popularity of their comic stereotypes. Their victims were willing to recognize themselves in their unflattering portraits and took pride, ironically, in the very traits that were meant to make them look foolish and unworthy. Yes, they were licentious, braggart, and prone to violence—and do you want to make something of it? Stories written by conservative humorists in books and national magazines found their way into local newspapers, oral tales, and finally, into folklore.

Thus the roots of the American comic tradition lie not in popular imagination, as has sometimes been assumed, but in political and social imperatives and the commercial necessities of writing and publishing. As America changed, so did its humor, though the forms devised by the Southern humorists remained largely intact. After the Civil War, newspapermen took over the comic tradition as writers and platform speakers, retaining the vernacular style and the mask of the frontier oaf and bumbler, but in a cleaned-up, more genteel fashion. Later the growth of urban society fostered a group of sophisticated writers who transformed the comic mask into the little man or woman, the middle-class city dweller or suburbanite harassed by a powerful, complex, unfeeling system. The Southern conservatives' creation remained intact as a legacy into the twentieth century, a comic persona who directs ridicule principally inward upon himself and his peers rather than outward against the forces arrayed against him in the world.

By the end of the nineteenth century, the mainstream of written, spoken, theatrical and vaudeville humor that carried on the American comic tradition had almost entirely purged its raucous, lascivious core when the advent of movies came propitiously to its rescue. The movies appealed to a large audience untouched by the established media of entertainment; moreover, they provided visual techniques ideally suited to a new and expanded expression of the old comic violence, exaggeration and grotesque imagination. In the movies, audience taste and media form came together in what may have been the one genuine expression of popular feelings in the history of American commercial humor.

The crux of the difference between movie comedy and mainstream American humor lies in the fact that movies direct their comic ridicule and aggression outward as well as inward—against wealth and power as well as against themselves. In the early movies, wit and satire could be used as means not of preserving but of subverting authority and social control. Cops, schools, marriage, middle-class manners, all the fundamental institutions of the social order, were made to look as foolish and inane as the lowlife characters.

No wonder working-class audiences found movies so much to their liking—among all the other good reasons, movies gave palpable expression to their feelings of hostility and resentment against those who brought misery into their lives. Order was invariably restored, of course, but not before authority and respectability had had their pretenses unmasked. As soon as moviemakers realized how popular such comedies were with their audiences, they produced more and more. Nearly a third of the pre-1912 motion pictures recovered from the Library of Congress Paper Print Collection are comic films, and since newsreel films were almost the only kind made until 1900, the proportion of comedies after 1900 in the nickel-theater era was considerably higher.

One might even argue that the serious dramatic film played a decidedly minor role in American movies until Griffith began his ambitious efforts at Biograph in 1908. At first, however, comedy production was a significant part of his regular responsibility. He proved as capable as any other director at making police seem like bumblers, authority look ludicrous, and marriage turn into a farce. Early in his Biograph days he began a series of situation comedies about a middle-class couple, Mr. and Mrs. Jones, who fought, flirted with others' spouses and generally behaved foolishly in more than half a dozen films made in 1908 and 1909. One Griffith protégé was Mack Sennett, who worked at Biograph as an actor and comedy director until 1912, when he left to become production head of his own comedy studio, Keystone. It has been said that the golden age of American movie comedy begins with Mack Sennett at Keystone, but it might equally be said that the golden age of American comedy begins with the movies themselves.

The four films advertised in Keystone's first announcement ran the gamut of subject matter Sennett was to use in silent comedy: the buffoonery of plain folks (*Cohen Collects a Debt*); girl in bathing suit (*The Water Nymph*); the incompetent cop (*Riley and Schultze*); sexual competition (*The New Neighbor*). Ridicule the poor, ridicule the powerful, ridicule romance, ridicule the prevailing standards of propriety in female dress; Sennett's comic aggression made its debut cutting a wider swath through society and its values than any previous expression of the comic tradition in America, with the single exception of that nineteenth-century masterpiece of comic prose, *The Adventures of Huckleberry Finn.*

Years later, in his ghostwritten autobiography, Sennett struck a humble pose about his contribution to screen comedy. "It was those Frenchmen who invented slapstick and I imitated them," he said. "I stole my first ideas from the Pathés."[1] Pathé films, of course, dominated the nickel theaters and featured the first famous comic star, Max Linder. Yet Sennett's debt to France for slapstick might be compared to T. S. Eliot's debt to France for symbolism: both were drawn to the power, prestige and artistry of the foreign form, unable to see as clearly the deep American roots of their traditions. Though he obviously drew his techniques and concepts from many sources—burlesque theater is another influence he mentioned—Sennett's vulgar and violent energy immediately gave his films a recognizable stamp of their own.

Indeed, Sennett's greatest debt for his particular slapstick style was probably to Griffith. From Griffith he learned, as he wrote, to "cut our

---

1 *King of Comedy* (1954), p. 65.

pictures sharply . . . and we did get 'pace' into them."[2] Without comparisons one tends to forget what Sennett meant by "pace." Griffith's developed sense of motion-picture timing emphasized swift cutting back and forth among multiple lines of action; he cut his films into as many as three to five times more separate shots than other contemporary filmmakers. Sennett accelerated Griffith's rapid timing even more: the weaker the acting or story line, the easier it became to conceal the fact by stepping up the pace. In some comedies he cut the shots twice as swiftly as even his earlier fast tempo, and with his cameramen cranking slowly in order to increase the speed of movement on the screen, Keystone comedies are sometimes little more than a blur of frantic action. Sennett's style of split-second cutting was unique in motion pictures until avant-garde noncommercial filmmakers developed it anew after World War II.

Sennett made comedies under the Keystone trademark for five years, distributing first through Mutual and then as part of Harry Aitken's Triangle organization. He relinquished the Keystone name in 1917 in order to rescue his other resources from the collapsing Triangle empire, and continued producing comedies under his own name into the sound era. In the early days at Keystone's Edendale studio he often played minor comic parts while sharing directorial duties with Henry Lehrman, but by mid-1914 he had given up directing and begun to function as overall production supervisor, copying the studio organization first developed by Thomas H. Ince. Under this system, his star performers were allowed considerable independent authority to direct and write, or more precisely, to improvise their own films. Yet Sennett retained final approval, and it was difficult for performers to deviate from the Keystone formulas. Many of them—most notably, of course, Charlie Chaplin—perfected their own personal styles only after leaving Keystone.

The remarkable flowering of silent-movie comedy in the 1920s makes it difficult to assess Sennett's achievement fairly. Chaplin and Keaton relied on grace, precision, nuance, gesture and surprise in their famous comedies, while Sennett's style was rough, blunt, gross, broad and obvious. Ford Sterling, the leading Keystone comic during the first year and a half of the studio's operation, was a grimacing, frenetic performer whose most subtle movement was to jump two feet in the air, and in the Keystone comedies that survive, Roscoe "Fatty" Arbuckle appears to have been misused; only rarely does one see the deft, light movements, so incongruous with his bulk, that led contemporary observers to rate Arbuckle second only to Chaplin.

Nor did Sennett later refine his style. Vulgar and violent he began, and vulgar and violent he remained. The sum total of vulgarity and violence through hundreds of films can only be described as awesome. Reel after reel, week after week, year after year, Sennett's audiences were privileged to observe a society in total disorder. The vast majority in Sen-

[2] *Ibid.*, p. 90.

Mack Sennett himself joined in the early Keystone chaos. He's in the straw hat (top) with his arm around Mabel Normand, while Ford Sterling looks miffed, at the right; the frame enlargement, possibly from *The Beach Flirt*, dates from 1912 or 1913. Mabel and Fatty Arbuckle are caught (bottom) in a frequent Keystone dilemma, the flooded bedroom, in *Fatty and Mabel Adrift* (1916). The production shot shows how it was done.

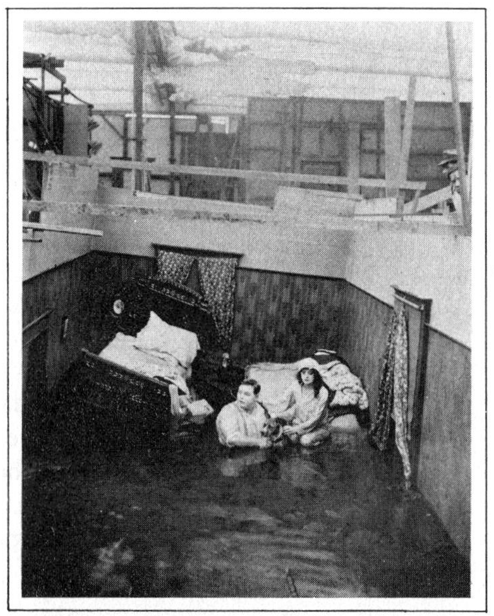

nett's world were motivated by greed and lust; they cheated, lied, stole and committed casual acts of violence against others. The few who wished to be honest and loyal found themselves desperately in need of authority to control the chaos constantly threatening them. Authority always arrived more or less promptly, in the persons of the Keystone Kops, but proved to be, if anything, more disordered than the world that whirled outside the precinct station's door.

Sennett knew he was debunking dignity and pretension, but dignity and pretension are merely the branches of the tree whose trunk is authority and whose roots are the very structure of the social order. Other American filmmakers had occasionally dug around those roots: Edwin S. Porter had made *The Kleptomaniac* (1905), showing how differently the political system treats a rich and a poor woman who steal; D. W. Griffith had produced a few socially analytical films like *One Is Business, the Other Crime* (1912), which equates payoffs among the wealthy with thievery by the poor. But no one before Sennett had so consistently created a society chaotic, disorderly and violent from bottom to top. It is not too much to say that Sennett's comedies, appearing in an era of strife and official violence, gave audiences their first glimpses of a social perspective that was to become one of the most emotionally powerful of Hollywood formulas—the anarchic individual pitted against disordered violent authority—which re-emerged in later periods of upheaval in the early 1930s and the late 1960s.

Curiously, the Keystone comedies agitated the ever-censorious moralists and reformers hardly at all. They were on the lookout for "serious" deprecations of society, and comedy was a central weapon in their arsenal of social control. They saw comedy as a means of relaxing tensions and poking fun at the everyday cares of work and family life, and it seems never to have occurred to them that Sennett's comedies were something more. The British, with their sharper sense of social distinction, were not as easily taken in. More than once British cinema critics insisted that vulgar comedies could not persistently lampoon respectability and shatter class divisions without having an effect on audience consciousness.

One could argue that because people in real life do not often throw pies in others' faces or drive cars off piers into oceans, Keystone tomfoolery was too far removed from reality to give audiences suggestive ideas about social behavior. But it does not take more than an occasionally effective image to implant the idea of disorder with great force. One such image occurs in *A Hash House Fraud* (1915). Louise Fazenda, playing a restaurant cashier, idly pulls her chewing gum out through her teeth, making a long string of it. A nearby customer deftly snares the string with his cane, wads it and pops the wad into his mouth. Such inventive, resourceful vulgarity opens whole vistas of social chaos for the imaginative moviegoer and serves as Mack Sennett's principal legacy.

* * *

In a narrow sense, Charlie Chaplin was another Sennett legacy. The Keystone producer "discovered" Chaplin, hired him, stimulated the development of his comic style during their struggles over conflicting philosophies of humor, and over the span of a year featured him in thirty-five films, almost precisely half of Chaplin's total film performances during the silent era. Chaplin's screen persona at Keystone, as Sennett was later to insist, was motivated by "cruelty, venality, treachery, larceny, and lechery" like any other Keystone character, and Chaplin was never to turn his back completely on the slapstick tradition.[3] Yet, while giving Sennett his full share of credit, one should bear in mind that Chaplin's sensibility was nurtured in the slums of turn-of-the-century London.

When one understands that Chaplin's consciousness was English—and working-class English—before it was American, some essential elements of his comic repertoire begin to fall into place. No comedian before or after him has spent more energy depicting people in their working lives: his first motion picture was the prophetically titled *Making a Living*. Chaplin's class settings differ visibly from Sennett's. Though the Keystone comedians were lowlife characters with no visible, or legal, sources of income, their behavior marks them as belonging within the great middle range of the American class system, even if often at the lower end. In the comedies Chaplin made at Keystone and later, the characters were concentrated at the extreme ends of the social scale more easily encompassed by English than by American ideology, the extremes of wealth and more often of poverty.

This difference in social perception between Chaplin and Sennett marks a critical difference in the nature of their comedy. Chaplin's recognition of social extremes led him not in Sennett's direction, to a liberating kind of comic disorder, but to an understanding that the only alternative to the faults of the social order was radical change. This viewpoint enabled him as a comic artist to subvert the social order and put in its place not Keystone chaos, but a powerful new imaginative order founded on the creative possibilities of magical transformations.

There is unusual consistency as well as immense variety in Chaplin's films of the silent era, but his genius did not spring full-grown onto the screen, and there are several significant moments of self-discovery and elaboration of his comic persona. After his active first year of work with Keystone in 1914, Chaplin directed and acted in fourteen films for Essanay in 1915; twelve for Mutual in 1916–1917; eight for First National between 1918 and 1922, including one feature, *The Kid* (1921); and two for United Artists distribution, *The Gold Rush* (1925) and *The Circus* (1928). The first moment of self-discovery came at the very beginning of his movie career, when he realized that although Sennett had hired him, he did not care for his style of comedy.

In his autobiography Sennett gives a curiously revealing account of his decision to sign Chaplin on. With Ford Sterling planning to leave and

---

[3] *Ibid.*, p. 180.

form his own company, Keystone needed a new leading comedian. Arbuckle, Chester Conklin and other comics on the lot were all "specialists" with established comic stereotypes; rather than disrupt their images with audiences, Sennett wanted to find a new personality to play Sterling's role. Mabel Normand, Sennett's leading comedienne, suggested the English pantomimist they had seen doing a comic turn, "A Night in an English Music Hall," with the touring British Fred Karno company. A telegram was dispatched, and in December 1913 Chaplin became a Keystone comic.

But Chaplin already had his own ideas about making people laugh. Dressed for his movie debut in the frock coat, top hat, monocle and walrus mustache of his stage act, from his first moment on the screen in *Making a Living* he moved more slowly, subtly and gracefully than anyone yet seen under the Keystone trademark. He displayed his skill at quiet comic gestures in the way he tipped his hat and took a little skipping sidestep, in the movement of kissing Virginia Kirtley's hand and then continuing up her arm. Chaplin's style did not prevail, however, in *Making a Living*. The entire second half of the film is the usual Keystone high-speed chase. A scene Chaplin considered one of his best in the film, his job interview with a newspaper editor, was sliced up in the cutting room from one unified action into many separate disjointed shots.

Sennett immediately announced that the persona of a foppish Englishman would not do for his leading comedian. Chaplin faced a difficult decision. Once stuck with a persona, a Keystone performer had little chance to change or grow in the role. Chaplin's choice of a character might shape his career for years to come. It was a stroke of genius that he hit upon the figure of the Tramp, who was incarnated in Chaplin's body not merely as a comic mask but as an inventor of masks, seeking ever to surpass and redefine his limits.

In oversize shoes, baggy pants, tight coat, bowler hat, wearing a mustache and sporting a cane, the Tramp appeared in Chaplin's second Keystone picture, *Kid Auto Races at Venice*. Chaplin did not, of course, invent the figure; among its many appearances in popular comic media, the tramp was a familiar type in British, French and Italian film comedies at the time. But Chaplin gives himself credit for seeing more in the figure than anyone had yet realized. "You know this fellow is many-sided," he told Sennett, "a tramp, a gentleman, a poet, a dreamer, a lonely fellow, always hopeful of romance and adventure. He would have you believe he is a scientist, a musician, a duke, a polo player."[4] The Tramp was a masquerader. He possessed mysterious pasts and unknown futures. He could pose as anyone: could he be, or become, that person too?

According to Chaplin, Sennett continued to dispute him over proper comic methods; it was only when Chaplin's films proved considerably more popular than other Keystones that the producer gave way, eventually letting Chaplin direct his own pictures. Significantly, the masquer-

---

[4] Chaplin, *My Autobiography* (1964), p. 144.

ader, Chaplin's original mode of magical transformation, made his initial appearance the first time Chaplin had a hand in directing, in his twelfth Keystone picture, *Caught in a Cabaret*, which was credited jointly to him and Mabel Normand as directors.

In the film, the Tramp works as a waiter in a cabaret. On his lunch break, after rescuing a society girl (Mabel) from a park robber, he introduces himself as Doobugle, a baronet. Mabel is infatuated by his aristocratic manners, but he excuses himself, having to return to his job. Their parting leads to one of the earliest moments of pathos for the masquerader: after the title "Tender Memories," first the girl is shown dreaming of the aristocrat; then the Tramp, amid the raucous din of the cabaret, dreaming of her. The masquerade is revealed when the girl's thwarted suitor takes her to the cabaret on a "slumming" expedition. She knocks the Tramp out, and the film ends in a donnybrook.

The masquerader reappears several times in Keystone films—twice as a woman—and often again in Chaplin's maturing art: in *The Count*, *The Rink* and *The Adventurer* from the Mutual period, in *The Idle Class*, and most notably perhaps, in *The Pilgrim* (1923), in which the Tramp masquerades not as an English aristocrat, but as a small-town preacher who is called upon to deliver a sermon and perform his everyday ministerial duties. The Tramp was an uncomplicated comic figure—a charlatan, a fraud, who showed that the low *could* become high, *could* win the heart of the society girl; it was only temporary, of course, but the Tramp expected nothing else, and he could always escape with an air of magnanimity and triumph, as in *The Adventurer*, when, revealed as an escaped convict, he pauses in flight to plant a kiss on his discoverer, the big man whose head he has caught between sliding doors.

In two films made during 1915 at Essanay, *The Tramp* and *The Bank*, Chaplin developed the pathos of his screen persona. The pathos lies in the Tramp's hope for a more permanent transformation through love, and his failure to achieve this. In the end the Tramp manages to shake off disappointment and resume his carefree ways, but in a more profound and complex manner—with the sad comic joy that was to become the indelible stamp of Chaplin's art.

The Tramp again has Charlie saving a girl from robbers, three of them this time, and protecting her home from their subsequent raid. In the confusion her father shoots and wounds him, and the girl nurses him back to health. The Tramp mistakes her kindness for love; when he learns his error, he limps off dejectedly down the road, leaning heavily on his frail cane. Then suddenly the cane twirls in the air, and he begins his insouciant bouncy walk. His disappointment at the denial of transformation into a new life falls away as he is magically transformed back to his own essential self: it is the first poignantly happy moment in Chaplin's screen career.

The comic device of misinterpretation as a haven of hope and ground for disappointment, only briefly sketched in *The Tramp*, is fully elaborated in *The Bank*; in addition, the film introduces a new technique—

fantasy wish fulfillment. Charlie, a bank janitor, reads a secretary's gift card to a cashier—"To Charles With Love"—and thinks it is meant for him. He gives her flowers; she throws them away. Robbers come, and the cowardly cashier hides, but Charlie routs them and rescues the girl from their clutches—alas, it's "Only a Dream," as the title baldly states, and Charlie wakes up kissing not the girl but his wet floor mop. He shrugs and returns to work.

During this period at Essanay, Chaplin introduced yet another form of magical transformation, extended from the Tramp to the animate and inanimate world. Material objects and even living things become magically adaptable in his hands. The technique was first demonstrated in *His Night Out*, when Charlie, a drunk, tries to get water out of a telephone receiver and shines his shoes with his toothbrush and paste. Later, in *The Tramp*, unable to figure out how to milk a cow, he works its tail like a pump and comes back with a full bucket; in *A Woman*, impersonating a woman, he sits down on a feather hat, the hat pins stick in his pants and he jumps around looking like a rooster; in *Work* he turns a lampshade into a skirt for a nude statuette and sets it dancing; and in the famous scene in *The Gold Rush*, he cooks and eats his boots, devouring the shoelaces as if they were spaghetti.

Chaplin's magical transformation of creatures and things was carried out entirely by the human imagination and through human movement, assisted by no camera manipulation or laboratory processing: it lifted cinema fantasy for the first time beyond the realm of trick photography.

His remarkable period of concentrated productivity reached its climax at Mutual, particularly in two films, *Easy Street* and *The Immigrant* (both 1917), which serve as both tributes and farewells to the symbiotic relationship between the early movies and their working-class audience. Though there had been films depicting the lives of immigrants and urban workers, no filmmaker before Chaplin had created their experience so humanly and lovingly. Chaplin gave up the Tramp's lonely solipsism to place him unabashedly in a social matrix as a member of a group, a community, a society. This provided valuable new sources for humor, especially the comedy of dissonance or juxtaposition, the funny and serious united in one gesture, of which *The Immigrant* is a classic example, as, for instance, the scene when Charlie discovers Edna sitting across from him in the restaurant and gives her his soul look of love, while simultaneously spilling a knifeload of beans into his coffee.

In *Easy Street*, Chaplin gives us a microcosm of the lives of the poor and then presents perhaps the supreme metamorphosis of the Tramp. Converted by reformers, the Tramp becomes a policeman, and then, irony on irony, he defeats the neighborhood bully after he has accidently sat on a hypodermic needle containing heroin and the narcotic gives him superhuman powers. At the end the Tramp is the cop on the beat, arm in arm with the lovely young woman who converted him, leading the Easy Streeters into the mission—"Love Backed by Force," reads the title.

These two films established a pattern Chaplin was to elaborate upon in his most famous features of the silent period, *The Kid* and *The Gold Rush*: the comedy about poor people with a sentimental happy ending. The happiness of *The Immigrant* and *Easy Street*, it is true, consists of survival, love and harmony within the continued framework of working-class life, while in the later pictures the Tramp has the promise or the reality of material riches and class transformation. At the end of *The Kid* he joins the foundling in the home where the boy has been united with his now wealthy mother; in *The Gold Rush*, sharing the millions of Big Jim McKay's lode, he is fortuitously reunited with Georgia, the Klondike dance-hall girl.

Some of Chaplin's critics have questioned the value of these improbably sweet endings, without, to my mind, paying sufficient attention to the social realism of the body of the films. Very few directors were interested in or capable of depicting the lives of the poor; and though Chaplin's settings often seem exotic and stylized, his subjects are invariably essential ones: how to survive, how to find food, shelter, safety, companionship, love. One might argue that the extremes of his sentimental endings are compensations for the extremes of his social realism. Significantly, his two major films of this period which end in pathos, *The Pilgrim* and *The Circus*, are not so directly films of lower-class life. *The Pilgrim* takes place in a bourgeois setting, *The Circus* in the special world of that entertainment medium.

Chaplin early adopted a working method the very opposite of the slapdash haste of Keystone. Where his films for Sennett were put together in three days to a week, for Mutual he took six weeks or more for a two-reel film, and his painstaking efforts increased as he moved into feature-film production after the war. He shot 90,000 feet of film for *The Immigrant*, the final running length of which was 1,809 feet—the same amount of exposed footage for a twenty-six-minute film, according to the film scholar Theodore Huff, that Griffith used to produce his two-and-one-half-hour epic *The Birth of a Nation*. In later years Chaplin's ratio of exposed to final-print footage increased slightly, so that he was taking half a million feet for a feature film, an unprecedented amount made possible only by his independence and his expectation that high costs would be made up by high profits. The scene in *The Kid* where the urchin is making pancakes and Charlie rises from bed, turning his blanket into a lounging robe, is reported to have taken two weeks and consumed 50,000 feet to produce 75 feet of screen time.

Given this extraordinary care in getting the acting and movement exactly as he wanted, critics have often noted an anomaly in the crudeness of other essential aspects in Chaplin's films—ranging from lighting and sets to characterization and plotting. He seemed content with simplicity in the exterior elements of cinematic style in order to keep the viewer's focus on the complex nature of his own comic persona. In this he succeeded far beyond any other figure in the history of twentieth-century mass media.

THE MUSEUM OF MODERN ART/FILM STILLS ARCHIVE

The Tramp can't pay and the headwaiter knows it, in Charlie Chaplin's *The Immigrant* (1917). Eric Campbell, Charlie's frequent nemesis in the short films made for Mutual, is the headwaiter, Edna Purviance is the immigrant girl with whom Charlie has been reunited, and James T. Kelley is the coffee drinker at left.

British soliders sang "The moon shines bright on Charlie Chaplin" as they marched off to World War I, and the song remained popular with British children at least until the 1950s. On both sides of the Atlantic, children jumped rope and bounced balls to the chant of "Charlie Chaplin went to France/to teach the ladies how to dance." His legend had spread throughout the world before he was thirty years old; the Tramp was a universal character. In recent years, reacting against the effusive adulation Chaplin received, some critics have insisted he was only one of many exceptional silent comedians, and that he borrowed techniques and ideas from others as well as they from him. Undoubtedly this is true. Yet it misses the essential Chaplin, the inimitable Chaplin—the man who made comedy and pathos out of working-class people's lives and dreams.

Three times in the early postwar years Chaplin ventured into the bourgeois world—in *A Day's Pleasure* (1919), *The Idle Class* (1921) and *The Pilgrim* (1923). These are the most obvious examples of Chaplin as a borrower, even though *The Pilgrim* is one of his superior films. The times, however, seemed to call for a new middle-class orientation in motion-picture comedy.

Neither Sennett nor Chaplin was capable of taking the lead in satisfying new audience needs. The Keystone credo proclaimed that all men and women, regardless of class or status, were equal in vulgarity, venality and licentiousness; Sennett simply carried his slapstick style over into the 1920s, when he produced films for distribution by Paramount and then by Pathé, making his characters more obviously middle-class in appearance but in behavior as chaotic and amoral as ever. Chaplin, after his relatively unsuccessful fling at middle-class comic masks, returned to his familiar portrayal of lowlife with magical transformations into wealth. The field was open for performers who could create a comic style specifically tailored to American middle-class values; and so a new group of bourgeois comedians emerged in the 1920s, with Harold Lloyd and Harry Langdon among its stars, and Buster Keaton its consummate artist.

At the core of the difference between prewar slapstick and postwar bourgeois comedy lies their respective treatments of that most sensitive area of middle-class behavior and belief—sex. In Keystone comedies, sex was all buffoonery and conflict: villains kidnapped young maidens; lovers thwarted censorious parents; wives and husbands schemed against each other and flirted with every available member of the opposite sex. Sexual attraction in Chaplin's films, whether the Tramp loved and won or loved and lost, was imbued with romance and sentiment, with tender glances and spontaneous emotion.

In contrast, bourgeois comedy steered a middle way between Sennett's chaotic sexual struggles and Chaplin's sweet, unrestrained expression of love. Sex in the middle-class comedies was rigidly structured, and linked with preservation of the social order. Sexual attraction occurred only between unmarried youth, and marriage was its goal. It was a goal, however, to be attained not through the intimate attention of the prospective lovers, but rather through separation and action in the world—through challenge by the young woman, and in response, achievement by the young man in the face of obstacles placed in his way.

This was a familiar theme in American novels and stories of earlier days, but what marked the movie comedians as special was their firm roots in the comic tradition of extravagance and grotesque exaggeration. Their physical skills, and the vividness of their visual medium, pushed the young man's imagination to new heights of foolhardiness, danger and absurd complications. In the films of Lloyd and Keaton the traditional social order was never breached (that, it turned out, was one of their strengths), but within the bourgeois framework, comic formulas were carried to such extremes that they became parodies of themselves and struck at the roots of the cultural heritage no less powerfully than the films of Chaplin and Sennett.

Harold Lloyd's *Safety Last* (1923), directed by Fred Newmeyer and Sam Taylor, is a classic example of what happens to the aspiring young man in silent-movie comedy. Harold is a small-town boy going off to the city to start his career and earn wealth and status sufficient to enable him to marry his small-town girl. He takes a job in a department store and writes glowing but false letters home telling of rapid advancement. When the girl comes to visit he must go through elaborate comic byplay to demonstrate his exalted position without being caught.

Meanwhile, in an effort to promote himself, he arranges a publicity stunt for the store, a climb up its outside walls by a "human fly." An earlier joke played on a policeman backfires, however, and the cop chases the human fly, so that as the crowd gathers Harold has lost his performer. To save his idea Harold goes up the wall himself, in one of the superb comic stunts in the history of motion pictures. His climb is impeded successively by pigeons, a tennis net, a painter's board, a clock, a mouse and a weather gauge. Each new encounter throws him into graver danger. After one harrowing comic escape after another, he finally reaches the roof and falls into his girl friend's arms. One could hardly ask for more graphic satire on the theme of "upward mobility."

Keaton, the greatest of the comedians to emerge in the 1920s, derived his comic persona from the same stereotype, but he created an entirely different figure out of it. Lloyd was the quintessential middle-class climber, brash and knowing, caught up in a comedy of excess and panic; Keaton was stoic and naïve, an impassive inventor of solutions to life's bizarre challenges. Their differences resembled the earlier contrast between Sennett's style and Chaplin's: one was haste and tension, the other grace and subtle motion; one fixed and permanent in character, the other mobile and utilizing many social masks. Where Lloyd accepted middle-class order and made comedy from the foolish antics of the man on the make, Keaton's existence within the same social setting was predicated

THE MUSEUM OF MODERN ART/FILM STILLS ARCHIVE

Two famous shots from classic silent comedies of the 1920s: Harold Lloyd (top) hangs on by the minute hand in his precarious climb to success and the girl, in *Safety Last* (1923); Buster Keaton (bottom) is so occupied with chopping wood to stoke the engine of his train he doesn't notice the Union troops marching past, in *The General* (1926).

THE MUSEUM OF MODERN ART/FILM STILLS ARCHIVE

on a recognition of not his but *its* absurdities. His comedy always had as its goal the restoration of order in the face of society's errors and false judgments.

After a career in vaudeville that began virtually in his infancy, Keaton began making movies in 1917 with Fatty Arbuckle. In 1920 he went into production for himself, making five to seven two-reelers a year over a three-year period. Beginning in 1923 he made features, ten in five years, of which no fewer than six received at least one vote in the *Sight and Sound* poll—recognition of one of the most concentrated periods of high creativity of any motion-picture artist. Of these, four are considered the classic examples of Keaton's comic art: *The General* (1926), *Sherlock Jr.* and *The Navigator* (both 1924), and the earlier two-reeler, *Cops* (1922).

In each of these four films Keaton is cast in the familiar role of a young man courting a young woman of more respectable position than his own. Each film opens with a rebuff—"I won't marry you until you become a big businessman," says the girl bluntly in *Cops*, in straightforward parody of the middle-class formula; while in *Sherlock Jr.* and *The General* the spurning is motivated by accusations of theft or cowardice. The stage is thus set for Buster, a perfect blend of ineptitude and ingenuity, to stand up to the challenge, perform feats of daring and imagination, right wrongs, clear his name and win back the woman. *Cops* is the only one of these films where the rebuff is repeated at the end; this utterly destroys his reason for being and he voluntarily submits himself to the police he has been eluding.

More than any other silent comedian, Keaton developed mechanical ingenuity and contrivance as basics of his comic style; they served, among other things, as counterpoints to his astounding acrobatic skill, an ability that always made his triumphs over machinery the result of neither brains nor blind luck but of his full comic persona. He locked himself in struggle and alliance with a wide range of the nineteenth-century's machinery of motion: a locomotive in *The General*, a steamship in *The Navigator*, a motorcycle and a motion-picture projector in *Sherlock Jr.*

Keaton's dream encounter with the movies in *Sherlock Jr.* is one of the greatest parodies of the medium ever made. Keaton plays a projectionist who falls asleep. In his dream, a double arises from his sleeping form, sees his girl friend threatened on the screen and rushes forward to rescue her. He steps into the screen, is pushed away, re-enters, and then the scenes begin to change. Over and over again in mid-movement Keaton is shifted from one setting to another, each more fraught with danger: from a doorstep he finds himself in a garden; sitting down, he is suddenly in the midst of traffic; beginning to walk, he finds himself on the edge of a cliff; and so on, through a lion's den, a desert, a hill, an island, a snowbank and back to the garden again. Ironically, the motion-picture projector is the only machine over which he cannot assert control. In the end he becomes its pupil: reunited with his girl in the projection booth, he courts her by following each move of the celluloid lovers, until a shot shows the screen couple with three babies.

If Chaplin's comic fantasy rested on an underlying realism of class distinctions, Keaton's was firmly anchored in the outer world of American mechanical civilization in its encounter with nature. In a Chaplin film the locus of movement was always the Tramp; movement was a principle of the entire Keaton motion-picture universe, emanating from machinery, from the natural setting and from the camera, as well as from Buster himself. Keaton was a master of outdoor action, in part because he refused to stint the money, time or detail necessary to achieve authentic action shots: in *The General* a real bridge is blown up, and a real locomotive, not a miniature, plunges into the water; in *Steamboat Bill Jr.*, a real frame wall falls on Keaton, who is spared because he is standing in a space corresponding to an open window frame, and neither a double nor trick shots were used. The physical genius that Europeans regarded as the hallmark of American silent movies found its embodiment in one man, Buster Keaton, and in his struggle to wrest order from the recalcitrant machinery, natural environment and moral values of the American landscape.

Few of the silent comedians made the transition successfully to talkies. Stan Laurel and Oliver Hardy were two who did, in a partnership that began in 1927 and moved into sound comedy as early as 1929. From his position of financial independence, Chaplin held out against the tide and made two more silent features, *City Lights* (1931) and *Modern Times* (1936), adding only musical sound tracks; in 1940 he made his first sound comedy, *The Great Dictator*. Keaton, Lloyd and other comic stars of the 1920s began their fall from prominence almost at once.

One wonders if the qualities of silent comedy would have survived the 1920s had sound not come in at all. The comic styles of bourgeois figures like Keaton and Lloyd were nurtured in a particular social setting, where the loosening of the bonds of the old cultural system made space for comic exaggeration and alternative modes of order. The silent comedians of the 1920s—Keaton in particular—used the forms of bourgeois culture to build a critique of traditional values within the framework of an imaginative vision of human values restored. This produced some of the great works of twentieth-century American art, but it could not survive the impact of the Depression without reassessment and sharp reorientations.

In motion-picture comedy, a medium close to popular moods and tastes, the pendulum in the early years of Depression and sound swung back to the rough-and-tumble chaos of the Keystone style, this time in a highly verbal form with a more pointed antibourgeois animus. It was appropriate that W. C. Fields, the supreme nihilist of sound comedy, made his sound debut in two-reel talkies produced by Mack Sennett.

One of the unintended consequences of the shift from visual to verbal comedy was the spoken word's greater vulnerability to censorship. In a culture traditionally attuned to communication through aural rather than visual or kinetic signs, the motion-picture image was potentially more threatening than the printed or spoken word, but its nuances were often less clearly understood. The long-term effort of reformers and cultural traditionalists to comprehend the impact of movies on consciousness and behavior came to a climax in the early 1930s, and the free spirit of verbal comedy was a principal target of proscription. Comedy, of course, survived, but the rich comic tradition, with its roots in social conflict, ridicule, exaggeration and license, largely vanished from the commercial screen.

8

MOVIE-MADE CHILDREN

On a summer evening a few years before World War I, the economist and social critic Simon N. Patten went strolling on the main street of a provincial Eastern city. He noticed that one side of the street was dark and the other brightly lighted, and on the dark side—the forsaken side, he called it—were located "the very Institutions of Civilization itself," the library, the high school and the church, all locked, closed for the evening or the season.[1] Across the street were people, noise, enthusiasm, life—clustered around soda fountains, fruit stands, popcorn wagons, penny shows and the nickel theaters.

To Patten, the symbolism was all too clear: when the institutions of civilization lock their doors, then people—in this case laboring men and women who worked all day, without summer holidays in the mountains or at the shore—look elsewhere for their knowledge and gratification.

It is possible to view a culture in much the same terms as Patten viewed his main street—as a marketplace of intangible commodities. The intangibles Patten saw working-class people buying with their pennies and nickels were happiness and pleasure; one could name many others in the inventory of cultural commodities. Patten's essential point was that the institutions of traditional culture were not competing effectively in the market; they needed to reform and revitalize themselves if they were to become sources of strength and sustenance for workers and their families.

The response of traditional cultural institutions was that *they* were the marketplace, for, after all, they were American culture, were they not? Their rules required new customers or new products to enter the market only on terms and conditions laid down by those who held title to the deeds. The guardians of tradition did not, however, set a strong enough guard against technology on the one hand, and the urban working-class districts and immigrant ghettos on the other. At the confluence of these two unappealing cultural zones, the movies thrived. The American elite classes, once they discovered the fact, recognized intuitively that this new medium threatened the liquidation of their heritage.

That much is obvious from the vast array of books and articles by educators, clergymen, academics, reformers, intellectuals, clubwomen, penal workers and politicians deploring the baneful influence of movies. But there was a curious quality in this tidal wave of protest and accusa-

---

[1] *Product and Climax* (1909), p. 13.

tion. The writers rarely said what was on their minds. They dealt, often deliberately, with symptoms rather than causes, surfaces rather than depths. Only a person of great naïveté or unusual candor was willing to state the issue openly.

One who dared was Donald Young, a sociologist at the University of Pennsylvania who in 1926 contributed an article to a special motion-picture issue of *The Annals*, a political-science journal. Young placed movies in the context of those many forms of recreation—he named the stage, books, magazines, newspapers, fraternal organizations, hotels, clubs and dance halls—that create "a reckless lack of appreciation of true values" and "introduce and spread personal and social standards far beyond the reach of most of us." Because they were ubiquitous, inexpensive, and above all, easy to understand, the movies more than any other form presented "impossible standards most frequently to the most people with the most personal and enticing appeal."[2]

Young's perspective, of course, clashed with certain central myths of American social ideology, among them mobility and the dream of success. He implied there ought to be no flow of information in American society that might tempt individuals to desire a change in their class, status, income, appearance or place of residence. No wonder others with less courage than he cloaked the real nature of their desire, which was to control access to information so as to limit the ability of the lower classes to gain knowledge about the social system in which they lived.

In the same issue of *The Annals*, Wilton A. Barrett, executive secretary of the National Board of Review, made the point succinctly: ". . . it is to be feared that the privileged in life were beginning to see a menace to their safety and their monopoly of more expensive entertainment and to resent this encroachment on their domain of control and enjoyment of the arts." The motion picture, he said, was a "purveyor of ideas and symbols and secrets," and "it could narrate facts to the great majority and offer suggestions which the jealous minority did not intend, as it never has intended, the humble servants of humanity and an exploiting civilization to know."[3]

The struggle over movies, in short, was an aspect of the struggle between the classes. Taking place, as it did, in the realm of leisure and amusements, and in a society where to speak of class conflict was a breach of good taste, it was almost invariably masked. The passage of a Pure Food and Drugs Act and of meat-inspection legislation during Theodore Roosevelt's Administration, for example, gave the guardians of traditional culture an apt analogy to which they often pointed: the state had the obligation to protect the general welfare by prohibiting the circulation of any product that might cause people harm; therefore, just as inspectors entered stockyards and certified meat as fit for consump-

---

[2] "Social Standards and the Motion Picture," *The Annals of the American Academy of Political and Social Science*, Vol. 128 (November 1926), p. 147.

[3] "The Work of the National Board of Review," *ibid.*, p. 176.

tion, they should also inspect movies before people were allowed to consume them, so that any idea or image harmful to the moral, social or political health of the state could be suppressed.

If the traditional elites were really concerned about the general welfare rather than about preserving their social and economic status, there were other aspects of industrial civilization more harmful to health and happiness than the movies, as Horace M. Kallen pointed out. "The fact is," he wrote, "that crowded slums, machine labor, subway transportation, barren lives, starved emotions, and unreasoning minds are far more dangerous to morals, property and life than any art, any science or any gospel—certainly than any motion picture."[4]

Kallen even suggested that the protectors of the cultural heritage were blind to the possibility that movies were their ally rather than their enemy: movies pacified and sublimated grievances, built dreams and diversions in otherwise oppressed lives and thus served as "safeguard and insurance" of a stable social order.[5] But for "Patriotic Gentile Americans" (as one foe of movies identified his cohorts) it was far too unpalatable to accept the Jewish moguls of Hollywood, with their tawdry romances and dime-novel adventures, as the bulwarks of their safety and privilege.[6]

Since the enemies of movies could deal only indirectly or covertly with the issue of class conflict, they made their case on the ground of protecting the young. In the first three decades of the twentieth century the movies were what "permissiveness" became to a later generation—the prime cause and explanation for the perennial adult complaint that children were not behaving the way they should. A professional could rattle off any number of deleterious effects of moviegoing on children. "There seems to be a great deal more of nervousness among the children," a physician testified before the Chicago Motion Picture Commission hearings in 1919; "there seems to be a greater tendency to produce neurosis or St. Vitus dance." Questioned by members of the commission, he added that movies harmed vision and had "very decidedly" increased the use of glasses; that late-night moviegoing took away needed sleep and led to injurious physical consequences; and that prolonged attendance at movies over a period of years would turn neuroses into organic disturbances, and "then you could not do anything for them."[7]

Moreover, the doctor noted what any lay adult could readily have attested—that movies were making young people mentally lazy. This was as close as most critics dared to come to the question of information

---

[4] *Indecency and the Seven Arts* (1930), p. 51.

[5] *Ibid.*

[6] William Sheafe Chase, *Catechism on Motion Pictures in Inter-State Commerce* (1922), p. 116.

[7] Chicago Motion Picture Commission, *Report* (1920), testimony of Dr. Fred C. Zapffe, pp. 121, 122, 126.

control. Since movies presented information in a compact and rapid fashion that youngsters found easy and enjoyable, they had no incentive to pursue established modes of learning, like schoolwork or reading books, which in comparison seemed too tame or arduous. "Our children," said another alarmed guardian of culture, "are rapidly becoming what they see in the movies."[8]

This litany of concern and accusation was repeated in dozens of books and scores of articles; it filled the religious press, the genteel magazines, the halls of Congress, where periodic efforts were made, beginning in 1915, to put through legislation establishing federal censorship of movies. But all these statements shared one damaging flaw—they completely lacked any trustworthy evidence for their assertions. No one *knew* anything about the actual impact of movies on children, the psyche or the social fabric; no systematic research and hardly any systematic thinking had been done on the subject.

During the first quarter century of the motion-picture phenomenon, only one work in English made a significant effort to understand the nature of the moviegoing experience, and neither its title nor its author, as the film scholar Richard Griffith has pointed out, commended the book to persons with axes to grind on the subject of movies and society. The author, Hugo Münsterberg, was a German-born Harvard professor of psychology whose considerable popular reputation was swept away by the virulent anti-Germanism of the war period. His book, published in 1916 just before he died of a heart attack, raised a question central to an understanding of twentieth-century cultural change: What happens in our heads and nervous systems when we go to the movies, and what are the social consequences?

We have to engage our minds actively in moviegoing, according to Münsterberg, because the actual form of movie images is different from our perceptual expectations and desires. The projector flashes before our eyes a series of two-dimensional still pictures. We learn to make the mental and visual adjustments so that what we see accords with our notions of reality; we give to the movie image what in technical fact is not there, and we experience depth and movement because our mind requires them. "Depth and movement alike come to us in the moving picture world, not as hard facts but as a mixture of fact and symbol," Münsterberg wrote. "They are present and yet they are not in the things. We invest the impressions with them."[9]

On the other hand, a whole range of mental tasks that other media require of us are superfluous to the movie experience. Elsewhere, in the theater or at a lecture, the mind must create its own spatial or temporal impressions. If we are asked to remember the past or imagine the future

---

[8] Norman E. Richardson, editor's introduction, in Minnie E. Kennedy, *The Home and Moving Pictures* (1921), p. 3.

[9] Münsterberg, *The Photoplay: A Psychological Study* (1916; Dover ed., retitled *The Film*, 1970), p. 30. Italicized in the original.

we have to make our own mental images. Movies do that work for us by the devices of cutbacks or flash-forwards. In fact, Münsterberg said, movies obey "the laws of the mind," where a variety of spatial and temporal images can co-exist, "rather than those of the outer world," where we experience only one space and time dimension. Münsterberg was the first writer to observe what has now become a commonplace of movie aesthetics and psychology—that "the soul longs for the whole interplay" of many spatial and temporal dimensions, and the motion picture "alone gives us our chance for such omnipresence."[10]

Movies create new forms of visual experience, forms that overcome the limitations of the outer world and do the work of the inner world. And this essential nature of the medium is enhanced, according to Münsterberg, by the characteristic features of the silent film: speeding up of action and simplification of social conflicts. Such power, energy and correspondence between mind and image, such sharp lines of social drama, all combine to excite the viewer, "to intensify the personal feeling of life and to stir the depths of the human mind." The senses are receptive, the mind is merged with the image, the larger-than-life picture transmits to spectators the feeling that their lives are heightened, concentrated, enlarged. "The high degree of their suggestibility during those hours in the dark house," Münsterberg concluded, "may be taken for granted."[11]

Münsterberg asked his readers to imagine the social potential of such psychic force. Conceding that the susceptibility movies engendered might lead some viewers to emulate their glamorous depictions of crime and vice, he nevertheless stressed their capacity for good. "Any wholesome influence emanating from the photoplay," he declared, "must have an incomparable power for the remolding and upbuilding of the national soul."[12] But this was precisely the ground of conflict, and in 1916 it seemed an outright alien threat. Let a cheap, popular form of entertainment, controlled by foreigners, hold sway over the national soul? Not without all the controls alert defenders of traditional culture could get the state to muster.

The exercise of civil authority over motion-picture content had begun in a formal way in Chicago with the censorship ordinance of 1907, which empowered the police chief to cut or to prohibit any film prior to its first public screening. The law appears to have been ignored until 1909, when the Juvenile Protective Association made a survey of nickel theaters and generated a demand from civic reformers that it be enforced. Police officials thereupon took up the role of censors, eliminating scenes of murder, robbery and abduction, and occasionally rejecting entire films.

---

[10] *Ibid.*, pp. 41, 45.

[11] *Ibid.*, pp. 95, 96.

[12] *Ibid.*

Two such films were *The James Gang* and *Night Riders.* Jake Block, an exhibitor who had planned to show the films, challenged the censorship law in a court suit. His case went to the Illinois Supreme Court before the end of 1909, and the ordinance was unanimously upheld. "The ordinance applies to five-and-ten-cent theatres such as the complainants operate," Chief Justice James H. Cartwright said for the court, "and which, on account of the low price of admission, are frequented and patronized by a large number of children, as well as by those of limited means who do not attend the productions of plays and dramas given in the regular theatres. The audiences include those classes whose age, education and situation in life specially entitle them to protection against the evil influence of obscene and immoral representations."[13]

Block's counsel had argued that the statute's definitions were too vague; the court rejected the contention. "The average person of healthy and wholesome mind," Chief Justice Cartwright wrote, "knows well enough what the words 'immoral' and 'obscene' mean and can intelligently apply the test to any picture presented to him."[14]

Censorship of films at the state level began as the independent producers rose to prominence. Pennsylvania passed the first state law in 1911, followed by Ohio and Kansas in 1913. Harry E. Aitken's Mutual distributors took the latter two states to court, and both cases eventually reached the United States Supreme Court, where they were heard simultanously in 1915. The Court unanimously held that prior censorship of motion pictures was within the constitutional powers of the individual states. Justice Joseph McKenna, speaking for the Court, repeated the by then familiar arguments about the dangers of exciting prurient interests among children and added, for good measure, audiences of mixed sexes. "There are some things," he wrote, "which should not have pictorial representation in public places and to all audiences."[15] The central constitutional issue the case raised, however, had to do not with whether the states' police power could be exercised over movies (the complainant did not contest that), but when.

Mutual asserted that motion pictures fell under the protection of the First Amendment: they were expressions of speech and opinion and therefore could not be constitutionally restrained prior to their public utterance. Justice McKenna, for the Court, rebuffed the idea. "We immediately feel," he said, "that the argument is wrong or strained which extends the guaranties of free opinion and speech to the multitudinous shows which are advertised on the billboards of our cities and towns. . . . It cannot be put out of view that the exhibition of moving pictures is a business pure and simple, originated and conducted for profit, like other spectacles, not to be regarded, nor intended to be regarded by the Ohio

---

[13] *Block v. City of Chicago,* 239 Ill. 251 (1909), at 258.

[14] *Ibid.,* at 264.

[15] *Mutual Film Corporation v. Industrial Commission of Ohio,* 236 U.S. 230 (1915), at 242.

constitution, we think, as part of the press of the country or as organs of public opinion."[16] As the Court saw it, the movies' power for evil outweighed all other considerations. Thus the state was within its right in preventing such evil from reaching the public.

The Supreme Court's decision stood for nearly four decades as one of the few instances when that august body upheld the power of civil government to censor expression prior to its public circulation. Its significance for civil liberties and constitutional law, however, turned out to be considerably greater than its impact on the struggle over motion-picture censorship. The fact that the Court declared prior censorship of motion pictures constitutional was rarely stressed in later years by advocates or practitioners of censorship; they had to convince their opponents on social or moral rather than legal grounds. And their opponents were not constrained by the Court's decision when they argued that the exercise of the constitutional power of censorship was "un-American."[17]

One obvious reason why Justice McKenna's opinion was so universally ignored was that it completely lacked intellectual force; if anything, it was even more *ad hominem* than the typical case for censorship. Even the most avid censor would not have cited, as Justice McKenna did, the dangers movies posed to mixed audiences; persons with experience in the field were more worried about films whose content attracted all-male audiences. His reliance on the threat to children was, of course, standard, but by the time of his decision the censors of Chicago, who had had the most experience with censorship, had decided that they did not have to make all films conform to the hypothetical mental and emotional limitations of children.

Chicago amended its censorship ordinance in 1914, setting up a category of films approved for showing only to persons over twenty-one—the first example of a rating system in motion-picture exhibition. The police were authorized to give such films "pink permits." According to testimony before the Chicago Motion Picture Commission, the plan took shape following an incident over a film based on Hawthorne's novel *The Scarlet Letter*.

A delegation of women, having seen the film, requested the police to allow it to be shown. The official in charge replied that he did not know how he could explain to his fifteen-year-old daughter what the scarlet "A" meant, therefore he could not pass the film—an interesting instance of conflict between men and women over female sexuality in public media. Nevertheless, he was troubled, since clearly murder and robbery, the usual censorship taboos, were not at issue. He entered into a "man's agreement" with the producer, allowing the film to be shown publicly,

---

[16] *Ibid.*, at 243, 244.

[17] Will H. Hays, "The Motion Picture Industry," *American Review of Reviews*, Vol. 67 (January 1923), p. 75.

THE MUSEUM OF MODERN ART/FILM STILLS ARCHIVE

About the time of World War I, censorship groups regarded advertising posters like those (top) on a Union Square theater—in the same building as the Automatic One-Cent Vaudeville, (p. 15)—as more detrimental to youthful morals than the pictures themselves. They even considered Charlie Chaplin vulgar, but Charlie, Mary Pickford and Douglas Fairbanks (clowning, bottom) won over people of all ages on their Liberty Bond tours during the war.

THE MUSEUM OF MODERN ART/FILM STILLS ARCHIVE

provided no one under twenty-one was allowed in.[18] After several similar dilemmas over films based on literary classics, the "pink permit" policy became law.

By 1919 the police official who had instigated the "pink permit" was at pains to tell the Chicago commission that it had failed and that he opposed it. Instead of using the easing of restrictions as an opportunity to film mature works of literature, he said, unscrupulous producers found it a wedge for "white slave and sex pictures making a travesty of marriage and women's virtue."[19] These were featured in a small number of theaters in Chicago's downtown Loop, where the words "pink permit" were prominently advertised as a code signal for a salacious film.

Good or bad, clean or dirty, the movies rolled over censorship barriers like waves over castles in the sand. Despite the decision authorizing state censorship, within the next several years only one other state, Maryland, established a censorship board. Efforts to push a federal censorship bill through Congress met with even less success. The lengthy hearings of the Chicago Motion Picture Commission in 1918 and 1919 brought into focus the frustration and annoyance of clergymen, clubwomen and politicians (who principally made up its membership) over their failure to contain the flow of information to workers and their children through the movies.

One contrast tells the story in a nutshell. The witness who received perhaps the most respectful attention from the commission was Ellis Paxton Oberholtzer, historian, secretary of the Pennsylvania censorship board and one of the nation's most vocal advocates of censorship. His testimony contained the following pronouncement: "I do think that the motion picture comedy is the most vulgar thing we have ever seen in the history of the world."[20] A few sessions later the commission heard firsthand of the power of one of those vulgar comedians, Charlie Chaplin.

Along with Mary Pickford and Douglas Fairbanks, Chaplin had paid a surprise visit to a Chicago school when the three performers were touring the country during the war promoting the sale of Liberty bonds. The principal told the commission what happened. "I never have in all my life seen the electrical, wonderful grasp that those people had over a school," he said. "Why, they seemed to take it right out of our hands. We were nothing when those people came along. Their power was marvelous. It broke our school up completely. Everybody was as light as though they had inhaled some laughing gas."[21] Teachers, too? Yes.

The principal went on to describe how, when the movie stars arrived

---

18 Chicago Motion Picture Commission, *Report* (1920), testimony of Major M. L. C. Funkhouser, p. 87.

19 *Ibid.*

20 *Ibid.*, testimony of Ellis P. Oberholtzer, p. 106.

21 *Ibid.*, testimony of Mr. Stephenson, p. 136.

without advance notice, he quickly assembled everyone and announced there was to be a special treat. "The children's faces were dull," he said, "as people's faces usually are when no real treat is in store for them. But I had the pleasure of introducing Charlie Chaplin. From that time on everything was out of our hands at once. The lesson that came to us from it was that if we could only by some method utilize their wonderful power, the making over of this country would be greatly facilitated, indeed."[22]

There it was again, as in Münsterberg: the allure of movie power; the capacity of the medium to influence people for good; its promise as an instrument to make over, remold, uplift the country. Few members of the traditional cultural elite spoke such thoughts aloud; why indulge such fantasies? Except for a brief period before 1910, cultural leaders had been more interested in policing someone else's movies than in making their own, and as each year passed, movie power slipped farther and farther from their reach, no matter what tactics of control they tried. No cultural force as strong as movies had ever established itself so independently of the proprietors of American culture.

Throughout its hearings the Chicago commission was acutely aware it was playing with shadows, listening to censors and physicians and school principals while its real antagonists were thousands of miles away, in New York and California. At last, near the end of the hearings, a delegation of the enemy came to palaver. Three hundred spectators packed the chambers. Five movie executives from New York filled the witness chairs. At their head was William A. Brady, the one-time theatrical impresario and early partner of Adolph Zukor, acting in his role as president of the National Association of the Motion Picture Industry, the New York-based trade organization which was soon to be supplanted by the more powerful Motion Picture Producers and Distributors Association (MPPDA). He was also a Catholic family man and churchgoer, as he made clear.

The movie powers had the floor first. They attacked censorship, claiming that the criminal laws were adequate protection against the occasionally obscene film. They called the commissioners a minority group trying to force the majority of Americans to conform to their views. They accused censors of political bias, ignorance and inconsistency. The commissioners did not flinch; they gave as good as they got.

An exasperated Brady finally told the commissioners they were applying harsher standards to movies than to other media. Magazines and newspapers were just as guilty of indecency as motion pictures, he said, but censorship advocates knowingly ignored the fact. Why? "The reason you will not attempt this thing [censorship] with the newspapers," he challenged the commission, "is because you are afraid of them." Perhaps it was time for the movies to throw their weight around a little, too.

---

[22] *Ibid.*

"Up to date the motion picture business of the United States has had no religion and no politics, and I will issue to you now a warning from the motion picture industry of the United States, that they propose to use the wonderful power in their hands and they are going into politics, and perhaps you will pay a little heed to them after they get into politics."[23]

There is evidence suggesting that at the time of Brady's remarks, producers were already entering into discussions with leaders of the Republican party about mutually advantageous ways of working together during the 1920 elections. If this is true, it is likely that the selection of Will Hays as "czar" of the motion picture industry in December 1921 was not a sudden response to the Arbuckle and Taylor scandals of that year, but the end result of a collaboration over several years.

No fewer than thirty-two state legislatures debated censorship bills in the aftermath of the Arbuckle and Taylor scandals; during 1921, New York and Florida had swiftly passed new laws establishing movie censorship (though Florida's law was weak and confusing, requiring only that films shown in Florida previously be approved by the New York censors or the National Board of Review). Hays's arrival on the scene stopped the tide in full flow; of the thirty censorship bills pending at the end of 1921, only one, in Virginia, became law. Censorship advocates loudly decried Hays's lobbying skills.

In Massachusetts a censorship bill passed the legislature but was subject to approval by popular referendum on the November 1922 ballot. It was one of three amendments up for popular vote in the state, and observers reported that movie theaters were flashing slide cards on the screen asking patrons to "Vote NO on the amendments"—on the theory that voters would not be intelligent enough to remember which one of the three applied to censorship.[24] All three amendments were indeed defeated, the censorship bill by a landslide margin of five to two.

With Hays firmly at the helm, and the crisis of 1921–1922 weathered, the movie industry began taking a more cavalier attitude toward its old antagonists. "The day of the professional reformer, as far as his energies may be applied to the motion picture business, is over," a spokesman for theater owners proclaimed in 1924. ". . . No group of malcontents with antiquated mentalities can secure an audience now when they assail motion picture."[25] "Malcontents with antiquated mentalities" was a harsh way of describing traditional cultural elites, but it was true that their audiences were sharply reduced. Some continued to agitate, turning their attention to the remote possibility of federal censorship legislation. But many others recognized they had been effectively disarmed.

Their essential dilemma was that they were sure movies were dangerous, yet they had no way of convincingly analyzing the danger. Con-

---

[23] *Ibid.*, p. 176.

[24] "The Screen in Politics," *The Independent*, Vol. 110 (January 6, 1923), p. 6.

[25] M. J. O'Toole, *How to Build Up and Protect the Business of the Motion Picture Theatre* (1924), p. 32.

trary to all expectations, as the Reverend Charles N. Lathrop candidly admitted in a pamphlet, reformers simply could not agree on standards for judging movies. Despite what Chief Justice Cartwright of Illinois had said, "high-minded," respectable and cultured people in fact held sharply different opinions about what was immoral or obscene. Having discovered that no uniform world view about movies existed in his own class, Lathrop made a daring leap into cultural relativism. "The critic who carries to the motion picture theatre the preconceptions of a refined home life," he wrote, "is likely to be shocked and depressed by scenes that are much less degrading than many that are daily enacted in real life before the eyes of a large part of the audience."[26] It was a very ambiguous effort to imagine the needs and consciousness of the lower orders, but it was undeniably a step away from total nonconcern.

Hostile attitudes and coercive actions against motion pictures, Lathrop concluded, were no longer productive. Already clergy and lay-organization leaders had begun to discover they could put movies to work for their own purposes, raising funds or attracting members through nontheatrical screenings of suitable films. Reformers were learning to thread a projector.

By the mid-1920s the efforts of traditional cultural groups to exert direct control over movie content had come to a standstill. It is possible, however, that influence over the flow of information through movies was exercised in quieter, more subtle ways. How often did Will Hays pass the word that a certain subject should not be tackled, a certain book or play not filmed, a certain actor or director not hired, because of real pressures or anticipation of controversy? The self-regulation that Hays proclaimed as the one true way to improve the movies was regarded by reformers as a sham; it took an entirely new interest group, made up of civil libertarians, intellectuals and artists, to question whether informal internal controls were not as pernicious as police censorship.

For the movie industry, civil libertarians were hardly worth the trouble of swatting at; censors and reformers had always been the clear and present danger, but they had grown weak and toothless. One could hardly resist a little playful revenge on the old, now harmless antagonist. In a 1926 article Charles C. Pettijohn, Will Hays's right-hand man, expansively asked: What did censorship accomplish? Take Chicago, he suggested, possessor of the first municipal censorship law, scene of the widely quoted commission hearings, vigorous censor of movies in the mid-1920s at a time when other localities were slacking off. Everyone could see the beneficial results for Chicago, Pettijohn said: movie censorship had made it "the nicest, cleanest, most orderly, crime-less city in the world to-day."[27]

* * *

[26] "The Motion Picture Problem" (1922), pp. 9–10.

[27] "How the Motion Picture Governs Itself," *The Annals*, p. 160.

In 1928 William H. Short, director of the National Committee for Study of Social Values in Motion Pictures, a euphemistically named pro-censorship group, put together a confidential four-hundred-page *vade mecum* of citations attesting to the horrible influence of movies on American society. He had pored over the sermons, editorials, transcribed testimonies, books, articles and pamphlets of two decades and extracted the pith of every negative opinion about the movies ever uttered. It was a dazzling array of erudition, versatility and precept, of indignation and high moral tone. But it was hardly worth the paper it was printed on, as Short well knew. "It has been recognized," Short lamented, "that the absence of an adequate and well-authenticated basis of fact has probably had much to do, hitherto, with preventing agreement of the civic-minded forces of the country on policies and programs of action for dealing with the problems of the screen."[28]

It was a humbling experience for the traditional cultural elite to learn, as they did in the 1920s, that their healthy and wholesome minds did not infallibly arrive at unanimity, even on what seemed so clear-cut an issue as obscenity in motion pictures. This recognition was part of a process of the devaluation of what may be called "literary" forms of opinion, in contrast to "social-scientific." In the previous generation, the beliefs and judgments of professors, clergymen, essayists and other cultural figures were regarded by their peers as sufficient to define and explain social reality; during the cultural crises and transitions of the war period, social-science practitioners had emerged as equals, if not superiors, in the field of social fact and as guides to right conduct. Social-science methods may have been no less subjective, opinionated and classbound than the explanatory modes of lay and clerical essayists, but in the 1920s their aura of modest self-confidence, precision and careful procedure seemed to offer a clarity and persuasiveness that all competing forms of social explanation lacked.

But the social scientists rarely paid attention to the movies. In the decade before Short's compendium, the number of social-science forays into movie research could almost be counted on the fingers of one hand. The field was virtually clear, therefore, for exploration, ordering and definition: whoever was first in gathering and interpreting the essential data might determine the issues of public debate on motion pictures for years to come. It was to precisely such a project that William H. Short turned when he collected his volume of quotes and realized how completely ineffective they were. What he lacked, as he said, were facts, but he obviously sought no facts that would hinder "civic-minded forces" in their campaign against the movies.[29] The monumental social-sciences research project that grew out of Short's initiative was thus shaped from the beginning by his special needs and goals: to get the goods on the movies, to nail them to the wall.

---

[28] *A Generation of Motion Pictures* (1928), pp. 69–70.

[29] *Ibid.*

On behalf of his committee, reincarnated as the Motion Picture Research Council, Short obtained a grant from the Payne Study and Experiment Fund, a private foundation, for a scholarly investigation of motion pictures and youth. Nineteen psychologists, sociologists and educational researchers from seven universities joined the project and divided among themselves twelve different research tasks. Their work took four years, from 1929 to 1932; nine of the research reports were published in 1933, two came out two years later, another for unknown reasons never appeared in print, and separate scholarly and popular summaries interpreted the significance of the total body of work. Nowhere before had such factual information ever been gathered about the behavior and values of young people in response to motion pictures. But how far could one trust it?

The slant of the project—one might even say its bias—was made clear in the common preface to each volume, written by the chairman of the research group, W. W. Charters, director of the Bureau of Educational Research at Ohio State University. All its assumptions about motion pictures were negative. "Motion pictures are not understood by the present generation of adults," he began. "They are new; they make an enormous appeal to children; and they present ideas and situations which parents may not like."[30] Do children understand scenes which are objectionable to adults? he asked. Can they grow superior to motion pictures? Are their emotions harmfully excited? The motion pictures stood accused: they could be found innocent or guilty of the charges against them, but it was clear that the scholarly investigators were working for the prosecution.

Several of the Payne Fund studies were based on laboratory or systematic-testing methods. Two University of Iowa psychologists researched the emotional responses of children to motion pictures by attaching electrodes to the bodies of subjects and recording their psychogalvanic responses. They concluded that children responded more emotionally to movies than adults, and no one reacted more emotionally than adolescents to scenes of love-making. Two scholars from the University of Chicago tested young people to see if movies brought about changes in their attitudes toward social types and national groups, and found the answer a decided yes. Three psychologists studied the sleeping habits of children in an Ohio youth facility, with and without moviegoing, and asserted that movie-viewing disturbs healthy sleeping patterns.

Another research team investigated how much information children retained from motion pictures they saw, and discovered not only that retention was good but that months after seeing a movie they could remember even more than before. Two Yale researchers sought to find out how the conduct and values of young movie fans differed from those of nonmoviegoers (or, since few of the latter could be found, of infrequent moviegoers). Their conclusion, the most modest of any of the

---

[30] *Motion Pictures and Youth* (1933), p. v.

studies, was that there were differences, but whether they arose out of prior circumstances or movie attendance was impossible to tell.

Other studies were more impressionistic, statistical or aesthetic. Edgar Dale of Ohio State University wrote no fewer than three of the eleven published monographs: a textbook of motion-picture criticism and appreciation for young people, a survey to discover the actual number of children attending motion pictures, and a statistical analysis of motion-picture content—types of plots, themes, characterizations, settings, costumes—based on a survey of feature films from 1920, 1925 and 1930. A Pennsylvania State College professor of education made an elaborate effort to ascertain the moral standards of several social groups and tested them to see if certain motion-picture situations met or fell below those standards. His premise was that movies ought to reflect the prevailing mores of the community and not challenge or deviate from them. Some of the most provocative data collected came in the form of students' autobiographies about their motion-picture experiences, utilized by University of Chicago sociologist Herbert Blumer in two reports, one on how movies affect conduct, the other (co-authored with Philip M. Hauser) on motion-picture influence on delinquency and crime.

The Blumer volumes, which put forward the most far-reaching hypotheses about the impact of movies on American society and culture, also presented in starkest form the central weakness of all the Payne Fund studies—their almost total lack of perspective. The essential comparisons were universally, and sometimes candidly, ignored: How does the influence of movies compare with that of other stimuli in the environment? Before there were movies, did other sources provide similar kinds of experiences?

Would the psychogalvanic response meter, for example, have recorded the same quickening pulse beat in an adolescent reading a romantic novel in 1880 as at a romantic movie in 1930? Would a bedtime story have disturbed children's sleep as much as a movie? Would dime novels, melodramas or Walter Scott adventures have dominated children's imaginations in the nineteenth century as much as movie plots in the early twentieth? Would reading an article in the *Saturday Evening Post* influence young people's attitudes as greatly as seeing a movie on the same subject? The exclusion of all such data from the Payne Fund studies seemed chiefly intended to dramatize the effect of movies by treating them in isolation. One wonders how the pulse rates of the "civic-minded forces" leapt when they read the revelations in students' motion-picture autobiographies.

The narrow focus of the research design limited the comprehensiveness of the scholarly conclusions. Several of the researchers found generalization difficult: they stressed that their subjects responded in highly different ways to the same movie scene, and reacted to whole films individualistically and idiosyncratically. Movie influence is undoubtedly strong, wrote one research team, but it "is specific for a given child and a given movie."[31] Among the broader generalizations about the social significance of movies was Blumer and Hauser's point, in their work on movies and delinquency, that movie influence looms large in communities where traditional cultural institutions (the family, school, church and neighborhood) are relatively weak—an observation hardly different from Simon Patten's description of a provincial main street a quarter century before.

The Payne Fund project was designed to be a weapon in the cultural struggle Patten first illuminated, and ultimately the restraints of the social-scientific method were not allowed to dilute the fervor and conviction of traditional elite beliefs. It was left to Henry James Forman, the journalist who wrote the popular summary volume *Our Movie Made Children*, to resolve all hesitations, dramatize dry research findings and place the scholars' data firmly within the structure of familiar moral and social ideologies.

"What the screen becomes," Forman wrote, "is a gigantic educational system with an instruction possibly more successful than the present text-book variety."[32] Therefore it is of no less importance to citizens than the schools their taxes pay for, and the milk and water their children drink. "The vast haphazard, promiscuous, so frequently ill-chosen, output of pictures to which we expose our children's minds for influence and imprint, is not this at least of equal importance? For, as we cannot but conclude, if unwatched, it is extremely likely to create a haphazard, promiscuous and undesirable national consciousness."[33]

There was one subject, above all, for which the Payne Fund methods and cultural perspective were particularly suited: the sexual behavior of the young. This was an area of social conduct in which movie influence may have been pristine. Where in American culture could one learn about love-making techniques? Not from the daily newspapers, certainly, nor from magazines and books, and rarely from watching others do it, as one might learn some other sport or skill. Before the movies, the art of love played almost no part in the culture's public curriculum. In movies, however, it became the major course of study.

The sociologist Edward Alsworth Ross, writing in the 1920s, was one of many guardians of traditional culture who placed the blame for America's changing sexual mores squarely on the movies. In a lecture, "What the Films Are Doing to Young America," he claimed that "more of the young people who were town children sixteen years ago or less are sex-wise, sex-excited, and sex-absorbed than of any generation of which we have knowledge. Thanks to their premature exposure to stimulating films, their sex instincts were stirred into life years sooner than

---

[31] Frank K. Shuttlesworth and Mark A. May, *The Social Conduct and Attitudes of Movie Fans* (1933), pp. 92–93.

[32] *Our Movie Made Children* (1933), pp. 64–65.

[33] *Ibid.*, p. 140.

used to be the case with boys and girls from good homes, and as a result in many the 'love chase' has come to be the master interest in life."[34]

Ross went on to make the movies responsible for less-concealing women's fashions, pornographic literature, provocative dances and briefer bathing suits—and fell just short of accusing the movies of having invented the automobile so that young people could have a place where their sex-excitement could be expressed. Such blanket indictments, of course, raise certain doubts. One would like to know more, for example, about the role of the upper classes in introducing European fashions, dances and ideas into American private and public social life; about the urban environment; about advertising, leisure and habits of consumption; about changing ideas of religion, health, the human body; and much else. But Ross was content with his simple explanation: "This is not the place to cite evidence," he said, "and I am not going to cite any."[35]

The motion-picture autobiographies that Herbert Blumer collected from students for his Payne Fund study, *Movies and Conduct*, provide the evidence Ross lacked. They are filled with testimonials to the movies as a training ground for lovers. Blumer's idea of letting young people speak in their own voices was much more effective than giving the opinions of experts or gathering survey data. Over and over again young men and women described how they avidly watched their favorite stars for lessons in gesture, expression, movement, technique. ". . . it was directly through the movies that I learned to kiss a girl on her ears, neck, and cheeks, as well as on the mouth," wrote one boy.[36] A girl noticed that actresses closed their eyes when kissing, and imitated them. Moreover, the rapid pace of silent movies, of which Münsterberg had spoken, convinced some young people that romance is something that happens quickly: it seems to have led to kissing and necking at an earlier point in relationships between young men and women.

The deep psychological identification that movies drew out of their viewers had the effect of preparing some young people emotionally for love. "I've been thrilled and deeply stirred by love pictures and love scenes," wrote a sixteen-year-old girl, a high school sophomore. "Usually when I see them, it seems that I'm a looker-on and one of the lovers at the same time. I don't know how to describe it. I know love pictures have made me more receptive to love-making because I always thought it rather silly until these pictures, where there is always so much love and everything turns out all right in the end, and I kiss and pet much more than I would otherwise."[37]

In addition to having a direct influence on behavior, the movies also

---

[34] In *World Drift* (1928), p. 179.

[35] *Ibid.*

[36] *Movies and Conduct* (1933), p. 47.

[37] *Ibid.*, p. 109.

appeared to have a profound effect upon fantasy life. They provided rich materials for dreams about sexual partners, settings or passions far removed from the realities of one's environment. Many young men and women wrote of imagining experiences they were unable or unwilling to seek in their actual lives. Blumer claimed, in fact, that it was "inexpedient" for him to reprint the full range of fantasies derived from motion pictures, and he offered only "milder" examples. "Fantasy," he solemnly reported, "is largely monopolized by kinds of experiences which are tabooed by the moral standards of community life."[38]

Movies and Conduct, among all the specialized Payne Fund studies, provided the most effective propaganda against the movies. Blumer placed the rich stores of emotional and imaginative data gathered from young people in a traditional cultural frame: he assumed that the middle-class social ideology was the only appropriate system of values for American culture, and that people actually practiced what they preached.

"It is perhaps of some social significance," Blumer wrote, "to observe that the impulses which are brought into play in witnessing passionate love pictures or scenes are those which our conventions and standards seek in some measure to check. In this sense, without attempting to evaluate the matter, it seems that emotional possession induced by passionate love pictures represents an attack on the mores of our contemporary life."[39] If we took Blumer at his word, we would never know that men and women experienced sexual passion before there were movies, or that social values in America had always been in a state of conflict, confusion and change.

Despite their vast array of scientific procedures, the Payne Fund studies hardly advanced an understanding of the impact of movies on American society beyond the Chicago physician who claimed they caused St. Vitus dance, for the physician in 1919 and the researchers a decade later were operating from the same social perspective and worried about the same challenge: the movies provided information; they were sources of knowledge that took people outside the boundaries of their class, status and setting; they fueled social movement. To those who wished only to preserve the status quo, movement of any sort was bad; but it was true, as William A. Brady said, that it was easier to attack movies for causing social movement than to condemn newspapers (or books, magazines, fraternities, clubs and hotels) for doing the same thing.

From a later perspective it may seem absurd that virtually the entire body of writing on motion-picture influence during this period assumes that movies were tearing down American culture rather than representing and reinforcing it. It may be, however, that few late-twentieth-century Americans are capable of grasping the changes in American culture that movies wrought. Are we not all members or offspring of that first rising generation of movie-made children whose critical emo-

---

[38] *Ibid.*, pp. 70–71.

[39] *Ibid.*, p. 116.

tional and cognitive experiences did in fact occur in movie theaters? American culture for us, may be movie culture.

Could it be true, after all, that a couple of hundred hours a year of movie attendance—most children in the 1920s went once or twice a week—might have had a stronger influence on a child's cultural attitudes and growth than his or her daily experience of family, peers, school, neighborhood, work, religion? By the end of the 1920s nearly everyone in America recognized the powerful suggestibility engendered in the movie experience, the way, as Blumer said, movies took possession of one's emotions. But no one was really certain, no matter how many research studies were made, what that power consisted of or what effect it had on individuals and on the culture. As a result, it remained easier to focus on something tangible, graspable, human: who controlled the movies. The power of the movies seemed too vast, elusive, awesome; one could understand, and wrestle over, the power of their producers.

9

THE HOUSE THAT ADOLPH ZUKOR BUILT

To outsiders, the question of who held power over movies was a simple one: it was the men who made them, the balding little men in dark double-breasted suits—Laemmle, Fox, Zukor, Goldwyn, Louis B. Mayer and a few others—who peered mildly at the camera in photographs from the 1920s, hardly noticeable alongside visiting royalty or one of their stars. No one who feared or contested their power, however, would have been fooled by such diffident poses. Behind those affable masks, they were convinced, lurked ruthless calculating minds, vast ambitions and imperial life styles; palatial mansions, chauffeured limousines, private tennis courts, million-dollar incomes. These men were the moguls whose daily commands shaped the national consciousness.

The leaders saw themselves in quite another light. Their power was real, but it was not something they could hold and keep like money in the bank. It was like quicksilver, constantly changing shape, shifting here and there, never the same one year to the next. To get and maintain power required daily struggle, struggle that possessed their dreams and their waking hours, filled their calendars far into the future. Power was something they continually had to rediscover, guessing under which walnut shell it lay in a never-ending game of choice and chance. Power was something they always had to reshape, like a clay model for a sculpture that would never be satisfactorily finished, and it was constantly being challenged.

Before World War I, with few exceptions, expansion of the motion-picture industry was financed through resources generated internally, from profits of production, distribution and exhibition, from investments in theaters, exchanges and studios. From the war to the onset of the Great Depression, however, continued development required the assistance and intervention of outside capital: from investment bankers, commercial banks and corporations in the period of rapid growth, consolidation and vertical integration of the industry's three branches between 1917 and the early 1920s, and from the communications, electronic and radio industries at the time of the changeover from silent to talking pictures in the mid- and late-1920s.

Dependence on outside funding meant dependence on stockholders, creditors and financial experts, whose sense of economic order sometimes clashed with methods in the motion-picture world. In the 1920s it already meant occasional usurpation of power by representatives of outside financial investors, a tactic that was to be directed against the mightiest moguls in the depths of the Depression. And even at the height of prosperity in the 1920s, the motion-picture leaders most invulnerable to the inroads of private capital found themselves set upon by the federal government, which sought to break up the very concentrations of power that seemed to guarantee their independence.

Power abhors a vacuum, and the rapid weakening of the Motion Picture Patents Company (the Trust) in the years between 1912 and 1915 left an empty spot at the center of the industry into which many aspirants rushed. The question was not only who would come out on top in the struggle to dominate the field, but from what branch of the motion-picture business the leader or leaders would emerge.

It was not merely an academic issue. The Trust had been formed principally by producers who sought to control both production and distribution, and by a system of royalties, to redirect a higher share of theater profits into their own pockets. The independent challenge to the Trust had come from men like Laemmle, Fox and Zukor, who had begun as exhibitors and used their box-office profits to expand into distribution and then production. To ambitious men on both the Trust and the independent side, it had seemed clear that not enough of the nickels and dimes taken in at the door had trickled up from those who merely showed movies to those who distributed and made them. The stage was set for a contest to alter this imbalance.

The first grasp for power, however, came from the ranks of the distributors, or exchange owners. After all, they were the middlemen without whom neither the manufacturers nor the retailers could operate. In the period around World War I, even the large theaters that had switched to feature pictures still changed their programs twice a week and thus required a minimum of 104 feature films a year. The largest of the independent producers, Zukor's Famous Players, was equipped to supply only half that many. Moreover, the feature producers had already adopted the practice of selling or leasing their films to exchanges on a "states' rights" basis, receiving a fixed amount of profit while the distributor took the risk. Rapid popular acceptance of features had meant unexpectedly high profits for exchange owners. Several of them undertook to reorganize the industry with themselves at the center.

The idea, in essence, was that distributors would serve the motion-picture business much like traders in the commodity market, contracting to deliver at a specified time and price feature movies they did not yet possess, that did not, in fact, yet exist. To fulfill this commitment they would underwrite the production of the required number of features, providing capital out of their own accumulated profits or from advance payments by exhibitors. Since the existing producers were too small in number to meet the expanding need for features, the exchanges established new production units of their own. In this way they hoped to hold the pivotal position in the motion-picture world, guaranteeing product to theaters and financing to producers, and for their trouble they would take a hefty fixed percentage of box-office receipts.

Two enterprising nonimmigrant businessmen, Harry E. Aitken of Wisconsin and William W. Hodkinson of Utah and San Francisco, tried to put this system into practice. Their differing tactics are instructive, as are their separate fates.

In 1913 Aitken put together a nationwide exchange, the Mutual Film Corporation, for the distribution of independent films. Among his first acts was to set up D. W. Griffith as a producer-director in charge of several Mutual-financed production companies; later he raised the money for Griffith to begin shooting *The Birth of a Nation.* Aitken lacked sufficient funds of his own, however, for all the advance financing he was committed to. But he did not lack persuasiveness and convinced Wall Street acquaintances to support him with influence and cash. Their names opened doors at several commercial banks which supplied him with loans to maintain his operation. This was the first significant venture by finance capital into the movie trade.

Aitken's willingness to take risks, with his own power and with others' money, proved his downfall. A cautious board of directors, aghast at his heavy expenditures on Griffith's costly epics, among other things, removed him as president of Mutual. Then Aitken formed his own production company, Triangle, built a huge studio in Culver City, hired Griffith, Ince and Sennett as directors and offered enormous salaries to famous stage players. To finance this grandiose plan he sold shares in his new company, the first time a motion-picture firm went public. When this proved insufficient he borrowed heavily from investment banks, ceding power over the company to his creditors. As soon as it became clear that films with theatrical stars were failing dismally at the movie box office, they liquidated Triangle and sent Aitken back to premature oblivion in Wisconsin.

The lesson of Aitken's brief flight and spectacular crash served to confirm Hodkinson in the fundamental precepts he began with when he formed Paramount Pictures Corporation in 1914: Don't let power out of your own hands, and don't lose sight of your winning strategy—to stick primarily to distributing and financing films, and to stay away from the problematic areas of production and exhibition. Four other major "states' rights" distributors came together with Hodkinson in Paramount, each getting an equal number of shares and a seat on the board. Hodkinson then contracted with Adoph Zukor to distribute the entire production of the Famous Players studio, fifty-two pictures a year, and obtained the other half of his 104-picture commitment from independent producers and Paramount's own production companies.

Paramount profited handsomely from Hodkinson's system, yet the plan had one small but significant flaw. It did not take into account Adolph Zukor's discontent at being relegated to a mere subcontractor's role in another man's business enterprise. In the swiftly changing structure of the motion-picture industry, too many assets were available, too many deals offered, too many schemes concocted, for power to remain stable, safe, entrenched. Hodkinson had made a logical plan, carried it through with skill and brought great benefits to everyone associated with him. But he refused to budge from the status quo, and it disappeared around him. Specifically, he rejected Zukor's demand that producers be allowed to become shareholders in Paramount. Zukor thereupon bought out three of the five partners and took control.

Now it was Zukor's turn to grasp for the ring of power. At first glance his path seemed a simple one. Everyone concerned now realized that distribution was the pivot of the motion-picture trade. To restore the producer to a dominant role one had merely to make distribution a part of the producer's business. The Patents Company had taken this step when it founded its own distribution company and tried to buy or force out its affiliated exchanges, but it had failed because the independents had offered exhibitors a more desirable product. Zukor had been one of the independents who thwarted the Trust by producing feature pictures with star performers, and they continued to be his greatest asset. In 1916 he merged his own Famous Players Film Company with the Lasky Feature Play Company and added several smaller Paramount production subsidiaries, forming the Famous Players-Lasky Corporation, a production-distribution firm large enough to meet or exceed the output of competing distributors.

But no path to power in the motion-picture world was ever simple. Zukor could no more than Hodkinson afford to rest with the existing structure of control, even in the unlikely case that he had been so inclined. By 1916 the once predominant European films had all but disappeared from American theaters, and the sudden absence of foreign competition created a demand and an opportunity for the swift expansion of American production. At the same time, the rapid construction of larger and more richly appointed theaters made necessary a rationalization of the chaotic rules and procedures of renting movies to exhibitors. Zukor would have to formulate policies to deal with both these new challenges.

Before Zukor took command at Paramount, the transformation of the film-rental system was already well under way, begun by innovative distributors and theater owners like Hodkinson. It made no commercial sense to retain the old practice of renting a picture simultaneously to as many houses as wanted it so long as the prints held out. That meant in essence that you were competing with yourself, and the result was likely to be brief runs at low prices in half-filled theaters. With the opening of sumptuous, comfortable theaters it was absurd to proceed on the assumption that all theaters were equal, especially since the "states' rights" distributors of individual features had immediately begun to classify theaters by quality and profitability.

The result, particularly after the emergence of a few powerful distributors in the 1914–1916 period, was the establishment of an elaborate class system for motion-picture theaters. Its categories ranged from the handsome new palaces down through older, downtown, neighborhood and small-town theaters. The premise was that the run of a picture could be extended and its gross rentals increased if it was first released for exclusive showing at the most prestigious theater with the highest prices, then after a suitable time made available to smaller, less expensive theaters. Exhibitors would pay more for the chance to get a popular picture first if they knew that no other theater in their locality could show it until weeks or months later. Zones were established covering theaters in competition with one another, and a schedule of staggered release dates was set up. The time between a first- and a second-run opening date was called "clearance," and the overall system was given the appropriate but somewhat ominous name "protection."

Zukor's coup at Paramount was in some respects a response to the growing protection system. If someone was going to assign pictures to theaters at different rental rates, a producer might drive a harder bargain for his own pictures than a distributor would. Once in control of the distribution of his own pictures, Zukor hit on a way to use the new protection system to increase his profits and provide a guaranteed source of revenue: he insisted that any exhibitor who wanted any picture made by Famous Players-Lasky would have to take them all.

This method, known as "block-booking," did not differ much in theory from the earlier system of selling a whole's year's package of films, but in practice it was almost as ominous an innovation as the Trust. Famous Players-Lasky made more than enough pictures for a first-run house to show in a year. When Zukor's salesmen insisted that major theaters take only their pictures, other producers were effectively cut off from those theaters. Some theaters were powerful enough to bargain with Zukor for a smaller number, but they then had to cope with Famous Players-Lasky's demands for preferential dates and higher rentals. Exhibitors found Zukor's new policy infuriating but almost unassailable; he had too many of the most popular stars.

In 1917 the motion-picture industry had just concluded eight years of war over the Trust; now it faced a new conqueror. Peace meant capitulation to Adolph Zukor. The strongest exhibitors chose renewed war.

The catalyst for the exhibitors' counteroffensive was Thomas Tally, the Los Angeles theater owner whose "electric" theater had shown Edwin S. Porter films in the antediluvian days before *The Great Train Robbery*. Under his leadership some two dozen of the most powerful showmen from all sections of the country met in April 1917 and agreed to form an alliance, the First National Exhibitors Circuit. With a large percentage of the first-run houses under their control, and several hundred smaller theaters quickly affiliated, the shoe was on the other foot: if First National theaters closed their doors to Zukor's pictures, he would have a hard time finding decent outlets. And since exhibition was still the most profitable branch of the motion-picture trade, First National was wealthy enough to buy big-name stars and go into distribution on its own. Charlie Chaplin was its first big catch; he signed up in 1917 as an independent producer, with First National advancing him production costs.

To hear Adolph Zukor tell it, his life as a motion-picture magnate was a bland, simple affair, punctuated here and there with obvious, clear-eyed, inevitable decisions. On one occasion, however, the genial mask could not contain his anger over the retaliatory tactics of exhibitors. Addressing a group of Harvard Business School students, he described meeting with First National's leaders and warning them to stay on their side of the fence. If they persisted in moving into distribution and production, he had no choice but to strike back in kind: he would buy and build first-run theaters of his own.

With the limited capital at his disposal, Zukor was able to acquire several first-run houses, the Rialto and the Rivoli on Times Square in New York, and another in Los Angeles, ensuring himself prestige outlets for his films in the two centers of the motion-picture trade. The central question then became: How far could he go?

His strongest ally was Otto Kahn, investment banker with Kuhn, Loeb & Company. Kahn's firm issued and sold $10 million worth of preferred stock in Famous Players-Lasky, providing Zukor with the funds to reach for the top. Zukor was never the first to do anything, but he was invariably the most thorough, resourceful and successful. As with feature pictures and the linking of distribution and production, so it was with vertical integration of the movie industry. William Fox had brought together exhibition, distribution and production in one company four or five years before. The scale, however, was in no way comparable. Fox's modest endeavor was hardly noticed; Zukor once again shook the industry to its foundations.

In a span of less than three years, from 1919 to 1921, Zukor's agents bought, built or gained an interest in some six hundred theaters for Paramount—the name Zukor had retained for his distribution wing and now gave to his venture in exhibition. This was less than 5 percent of all theaters in the United States, hardly to be called a monopoly in the sense of the Patents Trust, but it served admirably for purposes of control and profit.

Paramount could now set up its own program of pictures, ballyhoo its own stars, advertise and promote its special films, with the assurance that they would play in prominent theaters in every major city, daily newspapers would review them, and popular national magazines like the *Literary Digest* cover them. Naturally, moviegoers would want to see the films they had read about. Independent theater owners had little choice but to accede to an expanded block-booking system, giving up more of their autonomy and more of their receipts, if they wanted to hold their audiences.

Meanwhile, the other motion-picture companies were forced to emulate Zukor. First National completed vertical integration in the reverse

THE MUSEUM OF MODERN ART/FILM STILLS ARCHIVE

Executives of Metro-Goldwyn-Mayer and United Artists team up to escort naval officers on a studio tour in the 1920s. At the left are Harry Rapf, Irving Thalberg and Louis B. Mayer of MGM; at the right is Joseph M. Schenck of United Artists.

direction by adding production studios to its exhibition and distribution arms. Fox, already integrated, strengthened all three of its branches. Carl Laemmle's Universal company began acquiring theaters. Marcus Loew, the vaudeville tycoon with whom Zukor had once been a junior partner, went into motion-picture exhibition and quickly acquired Metro studios. Samuel Goldwyn obtained financing from the Du Pont family and purchased theaters. Many other companies with names long forgotten followed suit.

The independent producer was no less threatened than the independent exhibitor. In the years immediately following World War I, independent production had flourished. Several dozen male and female stars with proven box-office appeal and several prestigious directors set up production companies, confident they could place their pictures with distributors. Four of the most famous names in motion pictures, Charlie Chaplin, Douglas Fairbanks, Mary Pickford and D. W. Griffith, were even persuaded to pool their independent productions and create their own distributing firm, United Artists. As it turned out, the formation of United Artists protected them from the sudden integration of the industry that swiftly followed. Other independent producers were neither so powerful nor so lucky.

As the industry took on the structure it was to retain over the next generation, until after World War II, the power of the major companies became apparent most quickly in their role as distributors. Independent producers could not find theaters on their own; independent exhibitors could not find movies on their own. More and more independents at both ends came under the sway of the studios, with stars and producers becoming employees and theaters becoming affiliates of one or another large company.

The studio system was the house that Adolph Zukor built. As a structure designed to concentrate power and as a profit-making enterprise it was without flaw, as long as one essential condition was met: that the people of the United States continued to put out their dimes and quarters, and increasingly, their half dollars and dollar bills at the box office.

One reads with skepticism the many works written by movie-industry insiders that claim the moviegoing public holds the real power over motion pictures. Yet there is some truth in it; at times when people have withdrawn their patronage from motion pictures, the government has shown no inclination, as it has for railroads and aircraft companies, to protect the owners from the consequences of their errors and excesses, to defend them against the laws of the marketplace. Awesome as the power and profit of the movie moguls became in the 1920s, they never ceased to depend on their ability to please the public.

In the glorious adolescence of mass commercial entertainment, the years between the war and the Great Depression, the movie business invited city dwellers and visitors to take their pleasure in glorious monuments to audience sovereignty. The Roxy formula for fantasy environments was developed before the war, it's true, but the boom period for movie palaces came in the mid-1920s, after the studios had made their move into theater ownership.

For prestige purposes, all the big companies wanted their name on one of these theaters. It was said of Loew's movie theaters that you would pay your way in just to use the rest rooms, since they were more richly appointed than any other lavatory you were likely to see in your life. Was it surcease from daily cares that you sought, a chance to lose yourself in voluptuous surroundings, the attention of courteous and impeccable servants? Then take yourself down to the Paramount, the Fox or the Loew's, the Keith, the Orpheum or the Stanley, the Majestic, or most aptly named of all, the Paradise (of the Bronx, Chicago, and among others, Fairbault, Minnesota).

Such was the experience of picture palaces and such is the surviving myth, as lovingly chronicled in the pages of Ben M. Hall's illustrated book of wonders, *The Best Remaining Seats: The Story of the Golden Age of the Movie Palace* (1961). But the theaters caused their managers and owners more gall than contentment. The shocking fact, so disruptive of the myth that no historian of the movies seems ever to have uttered it, appears to be that the picture palaces were economic white elephants. Their financial weakness was obvious not merely in the hard times of the Depression but in the good years, during the boom. The crisis of the picture palace is the unmentionable skeleton in the closet of the motion-picture industry in the 1920s, and one of the major causes of revolutionary changes in movie production and ownership.

The basic truth about the picture palaces was that movies alone could not bring in enough revenue to meet their heavy expenses. In a rare burst of candor Sam Katz, the Chicago exhibitor who in the mid-1920s took charge of Paramount's theater operations, admitted to Harvard Business School students that the average motion picture did not have sufficient drawing power to fill the major theaters. And there were not enough above-average films to go around.

Since the early part of the decade the studio system was geared to mass production of so-called program pictures: inexpensive genre and formula films—Westerns, romances, comedy and crime. The major studios each turned out from 40 to 80 movies a year; the industry total ran to nearly 700 annually, to service the thousands of theaters in neighborhoods and small towns which still changed program three or even four times a week and required 150 to 200 films a year. Only a handful of these, the specials, were worthy of a picture-palace first run. Only the best and most popular pictures, like *The Big Parade* and *Ben Hur*, could consistently draw crowds large enough to keep the palaces in the black.

Theater owners turned to live performers, vaudeville and variety acts, and gave more time on the program to orchestra numbers; it was a reversion to the old days, when movies began to crowd onto vaudeville programs, only now it was happening in reverse. And the increased costs of stage performers cut into the added revenue they generated.

THE MUSEUM OF MODERN ART/FILM STILLS ARCHIVE

MUSEUM OF THE CITY OF NEW YORK

One of the great picture palaces of the 1920s, the Paramount in Times Square, New York, interior (top) and its much-admired curved marquee (bottom).

In his text on *Motion Picture Theater Management* (1927), Harold E. Franklin, manager of a West Coast chain of theaters, gave some insight into the costs of running a picture palace. The California Theatre in Los Angeles, for which he analyzed expenses, produced a profit of only 5.4 percent. (In a Depression-era handbook on management a 15 percent profit from gross revenues is recommended for deluxe theaters.) Its particularly high expenses included rent (30 percent of gross receipts) and advertising (nearly 13 percent). Almost 40 percent of gross intake went to program expenses, and the breakdown is revealing: nearly 15 percent for orchestra, a little more than 7 percent for stage performers, and less than 15 percent for the movie.

There are two especially important figures here. The first is the low cost of film rental. A few years earlier, in 1919, Adolph Zukor had demanded that producers receive a larger share of box-office receipts, and named 22 to 25 percent as the figure he desired; in part his movement into theater ownership was a means to force up the producer's portion of the take. A few years later, in the Depression era, theaters generally paid 30 to 35 percent of gross revenue for the films they showed. How did the picture palace chosen as a typical example get away with spending only 15 percent?

It seems likely that the answer lies in a significant policy change that the major companies initiated in the late 1920s to protect their investments in the palaces. The old practice of paying distributors a stipulated share of the gross was dropped in favor of a new system in which theaters paid a much larger percentage of their net income. But the costs of running a picture palace were so high that many bookings, after operating expenses were deducted, produced no profit at all. In those cases, producers and distributors received not one cent for the showing of their films. The crisis of the palaces thus lowered the earnings of the principal producing studios, and seriously weakened the independent companies who sought to produce and market first-run features.

The second important figure reveals the basic cause of the situation: more than twenty cents out of every dollar taken in by the California Theatre was paid out for nonmovie segments of its entertainment program. The picture palace could not survive unless it downgraded the importance of the picture. This galling fact led a number of commentators to sound the death knell for movies, latest victim of the primal show-business law: the public bores easily and craves incessant novelty.

That, of course, was exaggeration. The program picture was doing fine in small, inexpensive theaters, and every year a few big-hit films brought out huge crowds. The problem was a very specific one, having to do with the expense of operating first-run theaters and with the quality of first-run films: the former was too high, the latter too low.

It would have been impossible, for reasons of prestige, investor confidence, debt obligations and the block-booking system, to solve the problem by getting rid of the picture palaces. Nor, given the established method of quantity motion-picture production, could the situation be overcome by an effort to make more satisfactory first-run features. Why not, however, test out the theory that people were tired of the old black-and-white silents and wanted something new?

Ever since Edison had forecast that motion pictures would be lifelike, inventors, scientists and engineers had been working on schemes to bring sound, color and three-dimensionality to movies. By 1926 the first two techniques, sound and color, had advanced to the point where they could be successfully demonstrated in experimental efforts. Sound apparatus in particular, backed by the resources of major radio, telephone and electrical companies, was ready for commercial exploitation. Talking pictures would be no mere novelty; they would be the culmination of a generation of labor and the fulfillment of one persistent strand in motion-picture consciousness—the desire for heightened realism.

Yet the major studios, with the exception of William Fox, were reluctant to tamper with the status quo. Already burdened with heavy investments in real estate, they would face extensive remodeling costs for theaters and production facilities if sound was successful. A major government investigation, directed against Paramount but with implications for all the big companies, was nearing completion, and in 1927 the Federal Trade Commission ordered Zukor's firm to disband the block-booking system (Paramount eventually got a federal court to overturn the FTC ruling). Thus preoccupied, the reigning powers of the industry left the new risk and opportunity to others.

This time there was not one gambler but four: Harry, Albert, Sam and Jack Warner, yet more Jewish immigrant entrepreneurs, whose careers as exhibitors and producers had been indifferent, and whose status as independent producers was jeopardized by the weakening of the picture palaces. They put together financing, made the first feature talking picture, *The Jazz Singer*, with Al Jolson, and opened it in October 1927 at their only theater, at Fifty-second Street and Broadway in New York. Later, after *The Jazz Singer*'s momentous success and the subsequent rush to bring the clamoring public talking movies, Harry Warner recalled his motives. "I saw the salvation of the cinemas," he was quoted as saying in Great Britain, "and the defeat of the vaudeville invasion that was seeking to dominate the cinema theatres."[1]

Overnight Warner Bros. leaped from nowhere to the front rank of the industry. From one theater in 1927 they gained control over seven hundred by 1930. Acquiring the Stanley Company of America, one of the nation's largest theater chains, they also took over Stanley's dominant position as principal stockholder in First National, and quickly absorbed that unique endeavor of a major studio owned by exhibitors. Their assets rose in value from $5 million in 1927 to $160 million two years later; their net profit for 1929 was more than $17 million, a record high for the industry, and nearly 900 percent greater than the previous year.

---

[1] Quoted in Garry Allighan, *The Romance of the Talkies* (1929), p. 7.

Meanwhile Fox, the other talkie pioneer, set in motion a plan to purchase a controlling interest in Loew's, Inc. (following the death of Marcus Loew in 1927), in an attempt to get power over two major studios—Loew's producing subsidiary, Metro-Goldwyn-Mayer, as well as his own. Zukor's Paramount, formerly the leading studio, made a complete turnaround: while in 1928 it persisted in making only silent pictures, by 1930 its feature production was exclusively devoted to talkies.

Surveying these remarkable financial and technological transformations, *Fortune* magazine in 1930 heralded the advent of American talking movies as "beyond comparison the fastest and most amazing revolution in the whole history of industrial revolutions."[2] But without questioning that the transition from silence to sound in American movies was one of the great success stories of American capitalism, it must be understood not only as a revolution but as a counterrevolution, and also as a coup.

The talkies provided in an instant the solution to the crisis of the picture palace. Moviegoers who had disdained the average first-run silents flocked to see any kind of talking film, even at jacked-up prices. With packed houses, theater owners no longer needed to depend on live performers and orchestras. Indeed, the real losers in the talkie revolution were musicians, several thousand of whom lost their jobs when recorded sound took over movie theaters.

Theater owners, however, saw little of the money they saved when they ceased to pay salaries for nonmovie entertainment. The producers demanded higher rental rates for talkies and captured most of the money that had previously gone to performers. Between 1927 and 1929, net profits for exhibition companies went up 25 percent; for producers they rose nearly 400 percent.

An interesting change also occurred in the behavior of movie patrons. During the silent era it was considered acceptable for members of the audience to express audibly their views about the action on the screen. Sometimes this might cause disruption or annoyance, but it also had a potential for forging a rapport of shared responses, a sense of community with surrounding strangers; naturally, such comments were made most openly in neighborhood and small-town theaters, where a large number of moviegoers were likely to be acquainted. (The use of canned laughter in television comedies is a device to create this comfortable group feeling in a setting where people are spatially as well as psychically isolated.) With talkies, however, people who talked aloud were peremptorily hushed by others in the audience who didn't want to miss any spoken dialogue. The talking audience for silent pictures became a silent audience for talking pictures.

The talkies cast the whole issue of censorship in a different light as well. The Vitaphone sound system used by Warner Bros. involved separate recorded disks for the sound, synchronized to movements on the screen (Fox Movietone used an optical sound process recorded directly

[2] "Color and Sound on Film," *Fortune*, Vol. 2 (October 1930), p. 33.

onto film, of the type later to become standard for the industry). It was impossible for state and local censors to tamper with Vitaphone talkies: the disk itself could not be cut or altered, and any changes they might wish to make in the film would throw the sound out of synchronization. Moreover, with the coming of sound, civil libertarians were ready to reopen the question of whether movies were protected from prior censorship by the First Amendment. Under all these circumstances the procedures of internal self-censorship set up by Will Hays became increasingly important. A new Production Code was promulgated in 1930, and the influence of the Hays Office over scripts and personnel grew stronger.

In the studios themselves, the impact of the talkie revolution was even more obvious. Everyone knows an apocryphal story or two about silent stars with squeaky voices, immortalized by Hollywood's memorable self-satire *Singin' in the Rain* (1952). But the problem of speech was a real one: elocution coaches made a killing; actors with clipped British accents hastened to Hollywood; observers predicted that the foreign players who had become so significant in Hollywood silents would be packed off back to Sweden, Germany or Czechoslovakia; and others feared that uncouth, uneducated movie writers and performers would corrupt the American idiom. Some stars did fall out of favor or retire prematurely, but that had been happening before the coming of sound as well. The more important changes caused by the spoken word had to do not with the players but with the technology of moviemaking.

The requirements of sound recording brought to an end what seemed, in retrospect, the simple, casual, almost primitive manner of silent-film production: the director calling out instructions while the camera turned. There had been a time, in fact, when studios permitted the public to watch, from discreet distances, while scenes were shot on open-air stages. Sound, however, required the absence of interfering noise. Studios moved quickly to construct elaborate, expensive soundproof stages. Cameras had to be housed in stationary padded booths to keep the noise of their whirring gears from reaching recording microphones, until quieter cameras could be developed, and the old sputtery stage lights had to be replaced by soundless new ones.

For a time, the high cost of rebuilding studios for sound seemed almost self-destructive. Fully 30 to 40 percent of gross revenues from production had derived from foreign markets, yet many industry executives feared that non-English-speaking peoples would not pay to see films in languages other than their own. One solution, a boon to the European players in Hollywood, was to shoot a film with different casts speaking different languages. But as it turned out, not even the language barrier could dim the appeal of Hollywood in foreign lands: the problem was disposed of through the development of dubbing techniques or the use of subtitles.

Despite such challenges, the talkie revolution was smooth, progressive and generally beneficial. Where, then, is the evidence that it was also a counterrevolution or a coup?

One clue lies in the very smoothness of the transition in the central aspect of filmmaking: the way the pictures looked. Granted that at the beginning of sound production many talking pictures were crudely shot, woodenly acted, poorly lighted and immobile, these difficulties were ironed out rapidly and by 1930—even as early as 1929 in such films as Roland West's *Alibi* and King Vidor's *Hallelujah*—the outstanding talkies demonstrated the same mobility, pace, action or atmosphere as their counterparts in silent films. Furthermore, the switch to talkies had almost no effect on directors.

To be sure, some directors gained and others lost, but it is not clear that these alterations had much to do with sound. The Swedish director Victor Sjöström's departure from Hollywood does indeed seem to have been precipitated by the arrival of sound, but it is the outstanding case; and the only significant directors who entered movies because of sound were Rouben Mamoulian and George Cukor. The stability of directorial personnel reflects an important but neglected fact—the visual aesthetics of Hollywood movies, the way shots were taken and assembled into a whole, changed little if at all from silents to sound.

This fact might not be worth remarking upon were it not for the fact that the reigning aesthetic of American commercial movies experienced its first major challenge in the mid-1920s when an alternative motion-picture aesthetic came to the fore from the Soviet Union. Its film theories, emphasizing a calculated effort in the juxtaposition and assembling of shots, aimed at a visual effect that would evoke in audiences a Marxist perspective on social reality. One could hardly expect that theoretical statements about Soviet filmmaking would attract much interest in the world center of capitalist filmmaking, but the films produced by Soviet directors compelled Hollywood's attention because their astonishing visual power outclassed all but the very best that American filmmakers had ever created. Late in 1926, after seeing Eisenstein's *Potemkin*, a young MGM producer, David O. Selznick, wrote an associate to acclaim the film for "a technique entirely new to the screen," and suggested that the studio study it "in the same way that a group of artists might view and study a Rubens or a Raphael."[3]

With Eisenstein's *Strike*, *Potemkin* and *October* (*Ten Days That Shook the World*), with V. I. Pudovkin's *Mother* and *The End of St. Petersburg*, the Soviet cinema took over the vanguard of silent-film aesthetics. Its impact on intellectuals in the United States and Western Europe was exhilarating. Theretofore they had had to temper their disdain of Hollywood with the recognition that no other country produced more skillful or effective films. Now that the Soviet standard had been raised, American movies could be judged by political and aesthetic measures

---

[3] Rudy Behlmer, ed., *Memo From: David O. Selznick* (1972; Avon ed., 1973), p. 36.

that revealed how clearly their form and content were shaped by capitalist ideology and commercial goals. Hollywood was no longer synonymous with filmmaking at its best, only with filmmaking of a particular and limited kind.

It is instructive to place the talkie revolution within this context. Hollywood switched to sound at precisely the same period that Soviet silents captured world-wide attention. Along with the financial and industrial imperatives that made the shift necessary and desirable there may also have been aesthetic imperatives: to recapture the center stage by a technological counterrevolution that reformulated the elements of cinema expression and gave new vitality and validity to the familiar mode of capitalist commercial cinema.

Hollywood had a more intimate opportunity to get even with the Soviets. With the Soviet cinema unable to move quickly into sound production (partly because of American monopolies on sound processes), Eisenstein traveled to the West and ended up obtaining a six-month contract in 1930 to make a sound film for Paramount. Improbably quartered in a handsome Spanish-style villa in Coldwater Canyon, he and his associates produced two scripts, one on the California gold rush, the other based on Theodore Dreiser's novel *An American Tragedy*. The first was rejected as too expensive; the second was lavishly praised, whereat Paramount abruptly fired Eisenstein, on the ground that the public would be outraged if Paramount let a Soviet director make so critical a film about America.

David O. Selznick, then working for Paramount, wrote a memo stating the issues in an archetypal way: he called Eisenstein's adaptation of *An American Tragedy* "the most moving script I have ever read," but argued against making the film as a bad capitalist commercial risk.[4] The Paramount disappointment, and a subsequent debacle over a Mexican film project financed by Upton Sinclair, had a devastating effect upon Eisenstein's morale.

Hollywood's capitalists appeared to have triumphed over socialist filmmakers, but the talkie revolution thrust them into alliances among their own kind that were ultimately more destructive of their power than any foreign competition. Throughout the silent era, moviemaking had remained largely a business for individual entrepreneurs, assisted by private investors and sympathetic bankers. The talkie revolution immediately forced the moguls into a new realm of industrial and financial enterprise. Sound, first of all, came from outside the industry: Warner Bros. got its Vitaphone sound system from Western Electric, a subsidiary of American Telephone and Telegraph. Radio Corporation of America put a sound system on the market and took over control of a studio and an exhibition company, merging them into a new firm, RKO. The struggle over sound patents threatened to become as acrimonious as the earlier Edison-directed conflict over cameras and projectors until AT&T

---

[4] *Ibid.*, pp. 55–56.

asserted its power and forced an agreement among the competing sound companies.

While they coped with the arrival of giant communications corporations in their midst, the studio executives also took on the burden of tremendous costs in converting their theaters and production facilities to sound. With profits soaring from the introduction of talkies, they found avid friends among Wall Street investment bankers anxious to share in the booming industry through loans and stock issues. During 1928 and 1929 Paramount, Fox, Loew's (MGM) and Warner Bros., the four largest film companies, acquired the funds for their rapid changeover with the aid of Wall Street banking firms.

It would have taken prescience beyond the imagination of man, particularly when their own business was growing so boundlessly, to imagine the reckoning to come with the stock-market crash of October 1929. Within a short period, each mogul knew who his friends were: himself. The bankers to whom the studios were in debt felt no compunction about calling in their loans and setting in motion the coup that gave them control over those studios that could not meet their obligations.

MASS CULTURE IN THE AGE OF MOVIES

10

THE MOGULS AT BAY AND THE CENSORS' TRIUMPH

From particular angles and in certain lights, the stock-market crash of 1929 and the Great Depression of the 1930s can be made to appear as marvelous good fortune for American moviemakers. For a generation they had been rebuked and vilified as subverters of middle-class values. Then, as if by an act of Providence, came sudden social and economic disaster, confounding and scattering their enemies, the defenders of the American cultural heritage. The heavenly gates swung open, and American motion pictures, so their chroniclers have universally proclaimed, entered their golden age: Hollywood took center stage in the culture and consciousness of the United States, making movies with a power and élan never known before or seen again. Not only did the movies amuse and entertain the nation through its most severe economic and social disorder, holding it together by their capacity to create unifying myths and dreams, but movie culture in the 1930s became a dominant culture for many Americans, providing new values and social ideals to replace shattered old traditions.

There are tempting morsels of truth in so momentous a view of Hollywood's cultural significance in the Depression years. Yet any real understanding of the role movies played in the culture of that era must begin by recognizing that Hollywood was not an enclave, a few square miles of untroubled prosperity in sunny Southern California, cordoned off from the clouded world of economic travail and social conflict outside. Even the movies could not escape the impact of the Great Depression.

The movies did indeed attain the zenith of their popularity and influence in the 1930s and 1940s, culminating in 1946, when motion-picture attendance reached its all-time peak; but at the same time the industry became more enmeshed in the struggles over power and purpose in American society than ever before. The form that movie culture assumed grew out of interrelations with other social and economic institutions and with the state. Behind the dream world on the screen loomed the very real world of the American economy and society.

At first the novelty of talkies postponed the impact of hard times on the movies: theater attendance was up in 1930 over 1929, and theater corporations actually cleared higher profits that year. In 1931, though profits dropped precipitously from the previous year, both studio and theater operations remained, overall, in the black. But by 1932 no one claimed that the movie industry was "depressionproof." The total deficit that year for all studios and exhibition companies was more than $85 million. The following year the studios lost even more money, although the theaters' losses were considerably cut back—probably because thousands of theaters had closed, so that the losses became not corporate but personal, through loss of jobs and income.

In 1933 the movies reached the nadir of their economic fortunes. Nearly a third of all theaters were shut down. Admission prices had also fallen, by a third, to an average of twenty cents from thirty, the figure three years earlier. (Perhaps because of lower prices, or because the closed theaters had been unprofitable anyway, overall attendance held up better than other indices: the low point in attendance in 1933 was only 25 percent less than the high of 1930.) Four of the eight major motion-picture companies were in financial disarray: Paramount, the industry's leader during the silent period, in bankruptcy; RKO and Universal in receivership; Fox in the process of reorganization and within two years to be taken over by a much smaller company, Twentieth Century.

The following year, however, the movie business began to revive. Attendance climbed, theaters reopened, many studios turned modest profits. But a crisis of even so short a duration was bound to leave its mark in every area of operations and relations—with stockholders and creditors, with the government, with employees and with the public. In some cases it was the sudden vulnerability of the major companies that led these groups to act, in others it was the imperviousness of the motion-picture power structure to change. In either event, the stock-market crash set the stage for a new round of struggles over issues that had agitated American culture ever since movies first appeared: Who makes the product? Who runs the show? Who decides what the show should say?

The question of who held power over the movies became for some observers in the 1930s like a Chinese puzzle: as each box was opened, they found another box inside. In a 1937 study, *Money behind the Screen*, two British writers provided charts to show how control over the motion-picture industry had been seized by "the most powerful financial groups in the United States, if not the capitalist world," the Morgans and the Rockefellers.[1]

Their conclusion was founded on two separate aspects of motion-picture financing in the Depression years: the control of sound recording systems, and the ownership of the major studios. Although two producing companies, Fox and Warner Bros., had been instrumental in pioneering the sound processes, by the mid-1930s they had been forced, after acrimonious struggle and litigation, to yield the power over sound to such outside communications companies as American Telephone and Telegraph (through its subsidiary, Western Electric) and Radio Corporation of America (through its RCA-Photophone Company), which were linked to Morgan and Rockefeller interests, respectively. Then,

[1] F. D. Klingender and Stuart Legg, *Money behind the Screen* (1937), p. 79.

MUSEUM OF THE CITY OF NEW YORK

How to lure customers in the Great Depression: the Lyric Theatre (top) at 100 Third Avenue, New York—formerly the Comet, (p. 15)—did it with double features and a Charlie Chaplin comedy; the photographer Berenice Abbott took this picture in 1936 for the Federal Art Project "Changing New York." An RKO theater on S. Hill Street in Los Angeles (bottom) did it with cardboard figures of scantily clad women as enticement to see *Moonlight and Pretzels*, a Universal musical of 1933.

ACADEMY OF MOTION PICTURE ARTS AND SCIENCES

during the financial crisis of the early 1930s, Wall Street banking firms owned by Morgan, and the Chase National Bank, which belonged to Rockefeller, temporarily took over several studios in trusteeship or receivership. Since they held large blocks of stock, they continued to exert influence on the companies throughout the decade.

Lewis Jacobs accepted without modification the Britishers' argument in his standard history of American movies, *The Rise of the American Film* (1939). "Competition in the motion picture industry today," he wrote, "has narrowed down to a fight between the two major financial interests of the country for the balance of power within the eight major studios and their affiliated theatre and distribution channels."[2]

It would be equally foolish not to take such assertions seriously or to let them stand without question. In the history of American business enterprise, there is no great novelty in the big fish swallowing the little fish. At the very beginning of motion pictures, Thomas Edison set the precedent for making movie production merely one aspect of a conglomerate-style research and manufacturing concern, and the subsequent development of the industry was marked by integration and consolidation of smaller into larger. It should come as no surprise, then, that the electronic communications industry decided it wanted a hand in one of the major forms of communication, or that moneylenders and money manipulators took a share in one of the nation's most attractive moneymaking industries. That, one assumes, is what capitalism is all about.

The question is rather what difference it made to moviemaking when control was wrested from middle-sized capitalists with offices in Times Square to giant-sized capitalists with offices in Wall Street. "Whether the movies will regain their former financial success," the authors of *Money behind the Screen* concluded, "ultimately depends on whether the Morgans and Rockefellers will find it to their interest in the unceasing change of American life to provide the masses with the type of pictures that alone will induce them to flock to their cinemas."[3] The unstated premise of this *non sequitur* was that the Morgans and Rockefellers might have found it to their interest to make movies that the masses wouldn't touch with a ten-foot pole. But *Money behind the Screen* offers no evidence that high finance acquired a voice in the movie business in order to lose money, while there is every indication that Wall Street's interest coincided with that of Hollywood's old hands—to make as much money as possible.

The ultimate issue is not who owns the movie companies but who manages them. When several studios began to founder in the early Depression years, the outside interests who took them over were determined to play a direct role in running them, to demonstrate how practical business and financial minds could make money where mere movie men could not. By the end of the 1930s, however, all the studios

---

[2] P. 421.

[3] Klingender and Legg, *op. cit.*, p. 79.

were back under the management, if not the ownership, of men experienced in the world of entertainment.

Of the eight major motion picture companies that produced two thirds of all Hollywood feature films and nearly all the first-run movies, four weathered the Depression with no significant alterations of management or control: Warner Bros., MGM, Columbia and United Artists. After several years of losses and a period in receivership, Carl Laemmle of Universal sold his holdings in 1935 to a group of financiers who quickly replaced the old management with men experienced at running theaters, hoping to regain their footing, as the *Film Daily* put it, by getting "as close as possible to the demands of the theater-going public."[4] RKO went first into receivership and then bankruptcy and was taken over by the Irving Trust Company, which divided ownership among several outside groups, including Atlas Corporation, an investment trust; Rockefeller Center and Time, Inc., and the former majority stockholder, RCA.

But it was Paramount and Fox that endured the bitterest contests for power. Each involved a man whose show-business career had begun a quarter century before in the immigrant neighborhoods of Brooklyn or Manhattan, and whose name was synonymous with power and change in the motion-picture field—Adolph Zukor at Paramount, William Fox at the studio bearing his name.

In essence the stage was set when Zukor and his associates, kingpins of the industry for more than a decade, were caught flat-footed as Warner Bros. and Fox leaped ahead by being first in the talking-picture field. The two successful sound pioneers clambered over each other in their efforts to expand their empires; each acquired hundreds of theaters, and in the process both made a bid for the exhibitor-owned studio, First National, which Warner Bros. managed to get. At precisely this time the death of Marcus Loew suggested that Loew's, Inc., his theater-management company, which also owned MGM, might be ripe for plucking.

Zukor and Loew had been old-time vaudeville partners, and according to Fox's later assertion, had had an understanding whereby their Paramount and Loew's theaters would show only their own films. If Fox could acquire Loew's, he could put his own pictures into Loew's theaters and keep Paramount out, knocking Zukor off the throne and grasping the crown for himself.

He would also have control over Loew's producing subsidiary, MGM, emerging in the late 1920s, under the leadership of Louis B. Mayer and Irving Thalberg, as the number-one studio for stars and successful pictures. From all indications, Fox did not plan to run two studios simultaneously but rather to merge MGM with his own company. To do this, however, he had to persuade Nicholas Schenck, president of Loew's, to assemble a sufficient block of available shares to give Fox control and at the same time keep the deal secret from the MGM executives. Schenck's

---

[4] The *Film Daily, Cavalcade* (1939), p. 137.

price for delivering Loew's was $10 million, a full 25 percent over and above what Fox was to pay for the shares.

Fox did manage to pull off his deal with Schenck, but he never wore the crown he sought. His creditors, who had advanced him more than $50 million for the Loew's purchase—and additional millions to buy the Gaumont theater chain in Great Britain—became, in his eyes, inexplicably unreasonable and demanding. The Justice Department, which Fox believed had informally given its blessing to the Fox-Loew's merger, unexpectedly brought antitrust action against him. In mid-summer 1929, in the midst of his rising difficulties, Fox was injured in an auto accident and laid up for weeks. And then the market crashed.

Within a year Fox was forced to sell his personal holdings in his own company. A few years later he declared bankruptcy, and in 1941 pleaded guilty to and served a short prison term on a charge of attempting to bribe a judge during bankruptcy proceedings. The Fox Film Corporation, meanwhile, suffered heavy losses under its new ownership, barely escaped receivership, and in 1935 merged with the up-and-coming Twentieth Century Film Corporation.

Fox persuaded the muckraking author Upton Sinclair to write a book about his losing struggle. Sinclair spent five weeks interviewing him and produced a remarkable and curious volume, *Upton Sinclair Presents William Fox* (1933). It gave Fox the opportunity to present in monumental detail his contention that his Wall Street bankers, Halsey Stuart & Company, and AT&T had deliberately conspired to gain control of his assets, loot them and abandon them, with the connivance of numerous attorneys, financiers, government officials and many of his own trusted executives. What it neglects entirely is Fox's propensity to play precisely the same game against others as his opponents played against him—he describes the deal to acquire Loew's with bland innocence.

It is likely that Fox's ambitions suffered their fatal blow not in Wall Street but in the corridors of the Justice Department. He knew he could not swallow Loew's unless the government agreed to look the other way, and much of his energy went into political machinations to secure a favorable attitude in the antitrust division. But the Justice Department brought suit against him, and he was caught in a cross fire of challenges, owing money in a rapidly declining market for stocks the government did not want him to keep.

In comparison to the Fox saga, Adolph Zukor's tale is simple. When the crash came, Paramount, like Fox, was greatly overextended in debts and commitments, in Paramount's case through the acquisition of theaters. There was considerable pressure on Zukor, just as there was on Fox, to sell out. It is possible that Zukor was able to hold on solely because he retained the backing of his Wall Street bankers, Kuhn, Loeb & Company. (Upton Sinclair later speculated that Fox's fate might have been different had he been associated with Jewish rather than gentile bankers.) As Paramount went into receivership and then declared bankruptcy, Zukor remained.

In 1935 the company was reorganized under new ownership, which included several financiers who had played a role in Fox's demise. Kuhn, Loeb was pushed out of the picture, but miraculously, Zukor was kept on as chairman of the board. When the new management team of East Coast businessmen failed to get the company on its feet, an experienced Chicago showman, Barney Balaban, was brought in as president, and Adolph Zukor returned to power as head of production. In 1973, having survived many more changes in ownership and management at Paramount, Adolph Zukor celebrated his 100th birthday and still retained an office at the company's studios.

If Justice Department opposition was the major factor in William Fox's downfall, it marked the first time that action by any branch of the federal government played a decisive role in the fortunes of the motion-picture trade. Congress, the executive departments and the federal courts had tried persistently over the years to influence the policies and practices of the industry without marked success. Even the antitrust suit against the Patents Company, though clearly important, was not begun until the independents had effectively broken the monopoly. The unanimous Supreme Court decision upholding state censorship had little impact on the practice of censorship or the debate over it; and though at the time of Fox's troubles Adolph Zukor was facing a stiff challenge from the Federal Trade Commission, which in 1927 had ordered Paramount to cease and desist from its block-booking practices, Zukor fought back in federal court and five years later won a reversal.

Why was William Fox the first movie tycoon to suffer harm at the hands of the federal government? The answer is that other, more powerful movie tycoons did not want Fox to acquire Loew's, and their wishes carried greater weight than his in Washington. Fox discovered as much when the Justice Department seemed to change its views abruptly on the merger. He had enough muscle to take his problem directly to President Hoover, and still the Justice Department would not accommodate him. Then a political ally whispered to him that the source of his troubles was Louis B. Mayer, an influential voice in California Republican politics and head of MGM.

Fox had already earned Mayer's enmity by leaving the MGM executives out in the cold during the merger negotiations and payoffs. It proved to be a fatal mistake, though Fox tried to rectify it quickly by promising Mayer $2 million for him and his associates if he would remove the roadblocks he had set up to the deal. According to Fox's account, Mayer agreed; Bosley Crowther, Mayer's biographer, talked to a top Justice Department official who remembered his astonishment when Mayer dropped his opposition to the merger; but Mayer steadfastly denied that he did anything but fight Fox all the way. These conflicting accounts cannot be reconciled, but it is useful to remember that Mayer had nothing to gain and much to lose by becoming Fox's subordinate. As it turned out, Mayer went on in the next decade to take over Adolph Zukor's role as the industry's most powerful mogul.

For a dozen years, ever since Will Hays's appointment in 1921, the predominantly Republican tycoons of Hollywood had enjoyed a cozy relationship with the Republican officeholders in Washington. With the advent of a Democratic Administration in March 1933, they might have expected a burst of hostility against movie-industry mergers and controversial trade practices like block-booking. However, the Great Depression was at its most severe point, and Roosevelt's initial plan for reviving the economy rested on cooperation rather than conflict between government and industry. The National Industrial Recovery Act (NIRA), which passed Congress in July 1933, in effect suspended antitrust efforts by the government and placed power in the hands of businessmen to regulate and coordinate their own industries, through written codes of trade practices to be set up under the National Recovery Administration (NRA).

The motion-picture industry was chosen for one of the boldest experiments within the NRA framework. Although the general procedure was to write separate codes for buyers and sellers within a trade, the government decided to propose a single code for the entire motion-picture industry, the only code among more than six hundred that combined manufacturing, wholesaling and retailing within one structure. Thus the government seemed to give its overt blessing to the domination of the industry by a few major studios, which controlled production, distribution and nearly all first-run theaters. By accepting the status quo in the movie industry, the New Deal Administration apparently hoped to make it a model for the successful resolution of problems general to American industry—discriminatory pricing by wholesalers and manufacturers, and price cutting by retailers.

But the Roosevelt Administration's surprising benevolence toward the motion-picture moguls did not produce the results either of them anticipated. The honeymoon that big business and big government hoped to embark upon in the NRA's movie code was rudely disrupted by the little men of the industry—the owners of second-run, independent small-town and neighborhood theaters.

Organized primarily in the Allied States Association of Motion Picture Exhibitors, the independent theater owners fought many of the provisions of the code, beginning with the very way the NRA defined the interest groups within the industry. The NRA established the basic division of interest as between affiliated producers, distributors and exhibitors (those owned by or associated with major studios) and nonaffiliated (the independents in all three branches of the trade). The independent exhibitors protested, unsuccessfully, that the division ought to be between sellers and buyers.

One central aim of the NRA codes was to encourage big businessmen to rationalize the trade practices in their industry; the movies' big businessmen, the major studios, wanted their code to approve one trade practice and outlaw another. They sought the government's official acquiescence in the practice of block-booking, on the grounds that it stabilized production and led to savings they could pass on to exhibitors. At the same time they tried to put a stop to a new retailing practice of exhibitors—double features—because it effectively cut the producer's share of box-office revenue in half.

The small theater owners mounted an intensive lobbying campaign against the studios' proposals and won on both counts. After NRA received fifteen thousand protests against the plan to prohibit double features—a remarkable figure considering that fewer than fourteen thousand theaters were operating in 1933—the code writers decided to omit any reference to double features, in effect allowing the practice to continue. Meanwhile, in the face of exhibitor counterdemands that block-booking be stopped, the code arrived at what was described as a compromise but was in fact more like a concession: no mention of block-booking was made in the code, and exhibitors were given the right, under certain circumstances, to cancel up to 10 percent of the films they contracted for.

The code for the motion-picture industry ended up strengthening the small businessman at the expense of the major producer-distributors. Most of the complaints that came before the grievance boards set up by the code were filed by independent exhibitors. One practice they protested was overbuying, whereby big theaters bought the rights to more pictures than they could use, or changed their programs more frequently than usual, in order to prevent competitors from gaining access to popular films. The other principal grievance had to do with the allegedly excessive time and area differentials prior-run theaters were allowed against competing houses. Overwhelmingly, decisions were made in favor of the complainant.

One of the few areas in which the code went against the practices of small exhibitors was in the elimination of most rebate schemes that theaters had resorted to in the economic crisis to entice customers. Producers and distributors contended that gimmicks like lotteries, free gifts and two admissions for the price of one constituted price cutting. The code outlawed such giveaway schemes and games as Bank Night, Race Night and Screeno—all variations of drawings for cash prizes—but a vigorous protest from pottery manufacturers led to a compromise on premium gifts; thrifty housekeepers could continue to stock their china closets by going to the movies.

When the Supreme Court declared NRA unconstitutional in 1935, lotteries and drawings immediately began to proliferate. Theaters struggled to survive by any means at hand. In the days of silent pictures, theaters with pretensions to class had disdained installations like candy and popcorn machines; in hard times they discovered that candy machines returned a 45 percent profit on gross sales and that popcorn, which had therefore been synonymous with a cheap show, could earn profits three or four times its cost. Food and drink sales became for many theaters the difference between making money or closing their doors.

In 1938 the Justice Department filed an antitrust suit against all eight major movie companies, charging them with combination and conspiracy to restrain trade and monopolize interstate trade and commerce in violation of the Sherman Act. It was fitting, in a way, that the case was called *United States v. Paramount Pictures, Inc.*, since Adolph Zukor at Paramount was the last remaining movie mogul who had stood up to the earlier motion picture trust: the wheel had come full circle; now the old independent companies and their successors stood before the bar of judgment.

Two years later the government attained a consent decree against five companies—Paramount, Loew's, RKO, Warner Bros. and Twentieth Century-Fox—whereby the companies, without admitting guilt, agreed to change their trade practices, in exchange for which the Justice Department would drop its suit. The companies accepted four stipulations: they could not offer for rental to exhibitors more than five films in a block; they could not rent a film without first giving it a trade showing, which was to end the practice of "blind-booking," offering films in a block even before production began; they could not require theaters to rent shorts as a condition of obtaining features; and they were to stop acquiring theaters for a specified time. The government retained the right to reinstitute the suit if it was dissatisfied with results of the consent decree, and in 1944 it did so. Four decades after the dissolution of the Patents Company, the studio system, which had supplanted it, went on trial.

The producers suffered yet another setback on the labor provisions of the NRA code, and this time the blow was struck by President Roosevelt himself.

The root of the struggle that attracted Roosevelt's personal attention was the ability of the most popular performers to demand enormous salaries on the grounds of their box-office appeal and their importance to studio income. When the President, immediately after taking office in March 1933, declared a four-day bank holiday, several studios declared that they could not meet their payrolls, and some executives advocated closing down movie production entirely. To avoid suspending studio operations, industry leaders, working through the Academy of Motion Picture Arts and Sciences, devised a plan to reduce expenditures by cutting salaries for an eight-week period. Low-paid employees would lose no income, but for higher-paid workers the reductions would begin at 25 percent and go up to 50 percent. At the end of the salary-waiver period, however, several studios, most prominent among them Warner Bros., refused to return to earlier salary levels, neatly demonstrating the powerlessness of the Academy.

Shortly afterward the National Industrial Recovery Act was passed, and code writers went to work analyzing the labor structure of the movie industry. One of the aims of the act was to stimulate recovery by raising wages and reducing hours. This was easily accomplished for theater employees and skilled studio workers, but the salaries, as one NRA document put it, paid to "child, animal, and adult stars" and executives, presented a contradictory problem.[5] They seemed to be earning too much, and not even a depression had changed this. According to NRA statistics, production costs were cut 35 percent in the studios between 1929 and 1933, but salaries went down only by 16 percent. The wages of nearly 11,000 hourly studio workers amounted to 15.4 percent of total production costs, while the incomes of 8,000 salaried employees comprised a full 44 percent. Studio managers argued that salaries for stars and production executives were exorbitant and prevented the hiring of additional workers as the New Deal desired.

At the instructions of the major studios, solutions to the salary problem were written into the code, which strictly regulated the freedom of production companies to bid for the services of employees under contract to another studio, and at the same time similarly regulated the activities of employees' agents. In addition, the code authority was empowered to investigate any "unreasonable excess payment" of salary to individuals and to assess fines against companies they found had done so.[6]

The implications of the NIRA struck some of Hollywood's elite at once. They feared the Academy would be certified as the official bargaining agent for movie performers, permanently tipping the balance of power in favor of their employers. In April 1933, screen writers revived the Screen Writers Guild, which had existed briefly in the 1920s before the Academy was formed, and in October, a large number of performers left the Academy and formed the Screen Actors Guild, threatening to strike if the code was not altered.

It was then that President Roosevelt entered the scene. At the request of the Actors Guild he invited its representative, Eddie Cantor, to Warm Springs, his Georgia retreat. Perhaps he foresaw popular protest and upheaval or a dangerous decline in morale if the nation was deprived of its favorite movie stars. In any case, a few days later he ordered the code provisions regarding excessive salaries and employee negotiations suspended, and they were never enforced. Firmly established by this triumph, the Actors Guild continued to grow and in 1937 was recognized as a guild union in the studios.

The passage of the famous Section 7A in the NIRA, which gave employees the right to organize and bargain collectively, also reopened old jurisdictional disputes among Hollywood's skilled workers, and labor strife disrupted the studios throughout the rest of the decade. For seven years, ever since the signing of the Studio Basic Agreement in 1926, an uneasy truce had kept peace between the separate craftworkers and the

---

[5] Daniel Bertrand, *Work Materials No. 34—The Motion Picture Industry* (1936), p. 149. A publication of the National Recovery Administration, Division of Review.

[6] Code of Fair Competition for the Motion Picture Industry, quoted in Louis Nizer, *New Courts of Industry* (1935), p. 273. The full text of the code appears in this work.

union that had sought to organize all motion-picture workers, the International Alliance of Theatrical Stage Employees and Motion Picture Machine Operators (IATSE). With the talkie revolution, the old disputes had begun to smolder again as the Alliance competed with an electrical workers union over jurisdiction to organize the new sound technicians. IATSE put pressure on Columbia, a new major studio that had not yet signed the Studio Basic Agreement, to recognize it as the bargaining agent for the sound men. When the NIRA was passed, IATSE saw an advantage in its umbrella structure and took the offensive, hoping to seize dominance over the motion-picture field. In July 1933 it called its Columbia workers out on strike.

The tactic proved disastrous for the Alliance. When Columbia held out, the union escalated the strike to the entire industry. But the studios brought in scabs, and the competing craft unions decided to take the studios' side. The electrical workers union supplied members to replace the striking Alliance workers, and the strike petered out. IATSE members jumped at the chance to join the competing unions so they would not be frozen out of their jobs. IATSE suffered a complete eclipse in the Hollywood studios.

At the same time, however, it retained and even enhanced its position as the union of motion-picture projectionists, and in 1935 it launched a new campaign to gain control over Hollywood's skilled workers, under the leadership of two Chicago men who took over in 1934—William B. Browne, the new president, and William Bioff, the international representative. The latter was a veteran of Chicago's gang rivalries of the 1920s, and he brought tactics to his union activities which the underworld had perfected in Prohibition days. IATSE threatened to take its projectionists out on strike and shut down most movie houses in the country unless the studios agreed to make it sole bargaining agent for studio technicians. Early in 1936 it won a closed-shop agreement with the producers, who ordered their skilled employees to join the Alliance; overnight IATSE membership jumped from 100 to more than 12,000.

From that auspicious beginning, as court proceedings later revealed, Browne and Bioff extended their power by Chicago gangland methods. Once they had control over studio workers, they extorted hundreds of thousands of dollars from studio executives by threatening selective strikes against individual studios unless they came across with secret payments. Special dues assessments against members brought more than a million additional dollars into the union leadership's hands, and neither membership meetings nor elections for local officers were permitted. A rank-and-file rebellion led to state investigations, an industry-wide election supervised by the National Labor Relations Board, and intricate maneuvering among Hollywood labor organizations. Browne and Bioff retained control, however, until newspaper exposés in 1939 revealed that Bioff was a fugitive from an Illinois prison sentence for pandering. Bioff was extradited from California to Illinois, and shortly thereafter a series of indictments was handed down, charging him and Browne with extortion.

They were convicted and sentenced to ten- and eight-year terms, respectively, in federal prison. Joseph M. Schenck, head of Twentieth Century-Fox and president of the Motion Picture Producers and Distributors Association, was indicted for perjury in connection with his testimony concerning a $100,000 payment to the union racketeers, and after trial and conviction was sentenced to a year and a day in prison.

In the early 1930s the Payne Fund studies and Forman's *Our Movie Made Children* gave compelling new ammunition to the lagging censorship struggle. This time leadership was taken over by Roman Catholic clergymen who possessed precisely what the Protestant effort had always lacked—unity of ideology and organization. With an impetus apparently coming from the Vatican, American bishops in 1933 set up a committee on motion pictures which devised a strategy to replace the demands for state and federal censorship with a nationwide organization, the Legion of Decency, to coordinate a campaign to boycott movies that the Catholic Church considered indecent.

Beginning in April 1934, the Legion distributed pledge forms throughout Catholic dioceses calling upon the signers to observe the boycott; it was claimed that within ten weeks eleven million people signed, including many Protestants and Jews whose organizations rallied behind the Legion effort. What could the studios do? Having lost millions of dollars in 1933, with attendance dropping to a five-year low, they found themselves in no position to ignore so massive a threat of box-office desertion. Quickly they communicated their willingness to sue for peace.

Will Hays, speaking for the producers, offered their victorious foes a new instrument of enforcement, the Production Code Administration, headed by one of his employees, an Irish-Catholic one-time Philadelphia newsman, Joseph I. Breen. Breen would have absolute power to approve, censor or reject movies made or distributed by the Hollywood studios. The Catholic bishops' committee interrogated Breen, who was supported by an influential Catholic layman and motion-picture trade publisher, Martin I. Quigley, and were convinced he would serve as their surrogate. Self-regulation by the movie industry was at last accepted by the censorship forces, which could not have attained more effective control over movie content in any other way.

The movie producers already possessed a code of moral standards, the Production Code of 1930, which went about as far as it could toward expressing the Catholic bishops' viewpoint without converting the movies from entertainment to popular theology. It was written with the precise aim of uniting religious morality with box-office necessity by none other than Quigley himself in collaboration with a Jesuit priest and teacher at St. Louis University, Daniel A. Lord. The immediate occasion for a new code at the end of the 1920s had come from the censorship problems posed by talking pictures, but Quigley and Father Lord went beyond the moment to prepare a document that attempted to establish once and for all a standard for moral values in a popular mass medium.

For sound political reasons, Will Hays had sponsored the Quigley-Lord code and secured its adoption by a committee of producers in 1930, but the studios proved as adept at ignoring the new standards as they had been with previous ones. From the early one-minute pictures of ladies in the corset shop, American commercial movies had always tried to give their public as much sexual titillation as contemporary morals would allow, and in the early Depression period, with attendance dropping rapidly, the producers had no qualms about tossing aside the code and hanging on to their audiences by offering more sex stories, risqué language and glimpses of nudity than they had ever dared before. One reason why the Legion of Decency campaign proved so quickly effective in mobilizing support was that the general run of movies had never before been so clearly in opposition to traditional middle-class morality. But when Joseph I. Breen assumed his tasks as Production Code Administrator, he had only to make sure the producers lived up to standards they themselves had already proclaimed.

The code at least faced up to a fact which previous moral regulators had cloaked in ambiguity: without sex and crime pictures, there wouldn't be enough patrons to sustain a movie business. Granting this, Quigley and Father Lord sought to devise a formula that would keep sex and crime pictures within moral bounds. Their solution allowed for a fairly wide leeway in depicting behavior considered immoral by traditional standards—adultery or murder, for example—so long as some element of "good" in the story balanced what the code defined as evil. This was the formula of "compensating moral value": if "bad" acts are committed, they must be counteracted by punishment and retribution, or reform and regeneration, of the sinful one. "*Evil and good are never to be confused* throughout the presentation," the code said.[7] The guilty must be punished; the audience must not be allowed to sympathize with crime or sin.

The code went on to prohibit a vast range of human expression and experience—homosexuality, which it described as "sex perversion," interracial sex, abortion, incest, drugs, most forms of profanity (permitting, however, such vivid moments as Virgil Adams' vehemently repeated colloquial "dang" in *Alice Adams* in 1935), and scores of words defined as vulgar, including s-e-x itself. It is unnecessary to belabor the obvious point that the code cut the movies off from many of the most important moral and social themes of the contemporary world. What is more interesting to speculate about is not what the code prevented Hollywood from doing, but what it enabled it to do. If there was a golden age of Hollywood film production in the 1930s—the creation of a glamorous, appealing, mythical world of satisfying values in life and on the screen—it is important to know what role the Production Code played in its creation.

---

[7] Olga J. Martin, *Hollywood's Movie Commandments* (1937), p. 99; the quote from the Motion Picture Production Code appears on p. 102.

11

THE GOLDEN AGE OF TURBULENCE AND THE GOLDEN AGE OF ORDER

In the first half decade of the Great Depression, Hollywood's moviemakers perpetrated one of the most remarkable challenges to traditional values in the history of mass commercial entertainment. The movies called into question sexual propriety, social decorum and the institutions of law and order. The founding of the Breen Office in 1934 seriously curtailed the permissible range and depth of Hollywood films for years to come, but it would be a mistake to imagine that the movie industry's new moral watchdogs smashed a successful and prosperous filmmaking style like Carrie Nation chopping up a saloon. The movie moguls gave up their adversary stance because they suddenly found greater opportunities for profit and prestige in supporting traditional American culture, in themselves becoming its guardians.

The months of agitation over movie morals in 1933–1934 were also a watershed period in mid-Depression American society and culture. The New Deal Administration was seeking to boost the morale of a confused and anxious people by fostering a spirit of patriotism, unity and commitment to national values, a political goal that coincided with similar tendencies within the movie industry.

A new generation of studio managers and producers was coming to power. Their leaders were young men—Irving Thalberg was thirty-four when Roosevelt was elected, David O. Selznick and Darryl F. Zanuck both thirty. Born in the United States around the turn of the century, they had had little or no experience of the vaudeville, peep-show and nickelodeon antecedents of feature motion pictures. As opportunists they could, and did, produce any kind of film that gave promise of turning a profit. But they felt that even greater profits could be made producing pictures that appealed to the ideals, ambitions and sentiments of moviegoers. Like the politicians, they recognized how much their audience longed to be released from its tension, fear and insecurity. They had no difficulty in turning away, in their own self-interest, from divisive and controversial topics and giving new energy to old-fashioned themes.

So in 1933–1934, spurred by the changes in national mood brought about by the New Deal and prodded by the Legion of Decency, Hollywood directed its enormous powers of persuasion to preserving the basic moral, social and economic tenets of traditional American culture. This inaugurated a period of peace that was to last, by force of circumstance, until the end of World War II.

* * *

There were not one but two separate golden ages of Hollywood filmmaking in the 1930s, and the first, from 1930 to 1934, was at heart an aberration, a surprise even to Hollywood itself. The sudden turn to social realism in the early sound era, to cycles of gangster and sex and even political melodramas, was shaped by the crassest expediency: the search began for whatever forms of shock or titillation would lure audiences into theaters as economic conditions worsened and patronage began to fall away.

In a way, the secret of the moviemakers' social bravado may be that subject matter was not their principal concern. What they gave attention to was settings—settings that provided the fullest opportunity to raise the pitch of excitement on the screen, to amaze, frighten and even sexually arouse. Though they carried over their silent-era visual styles intact, they quickly discovered the resources of sound for attaining sensational effects.

At its most basic level, sound was noise, and noise itself could be a source of thrills. Hollywood did not tear down its boudoir sets overnight, but the possibilities of sound attracted filmmakers more and more to noisy settings. War was one, and Lewis Milestone's *All Quiet on the Western Front* became the big hit of 1930. Two world-war air spectacles—Howard Hughes's *Hell's Angels* and Howard Hawks's *The Dawn Patrol*—were also popular that year.

But if shock was what one was after, few things were more unsettling than disorder and the threat of death on familiar city streets. From their beginnings the movies had thrived on crime films, yet as the film scholar Richard Griffith has pointed out, sound added a whole new physical jolt—blasts of gunfire, shattering glass, squealing tires, wailing sirens, screaming victims. The silent crime picture relied on artful development of suspense and tension; the early sound gangster movies abruptly and repeatedly exploded them.

Sound was also language, and the introduction of dialogue pushed moviemakers toward contemporary urban settings as strongly as did noise effects. Words could shock and arouse audiences as well as stuttering machine guns—even as well at times as pictures, since dialogue writers could often be more subtle than cameramen, could make their point more swiftly. From Broadway and newspaper city rooms, Hollywood imported writers who could turn double entendres and slip risqué phrases into swift exchanges of repartee. Stories of everyday life gave writers a chance to write a blunter, more direct colloquial dialogue.

For example, Garbo, after playing sophisticated socialites in all her American silent films, made her talkie debut as a prostitute in MGM's adaptation of Eugene O'Neill's *Anna Christie* (1930). Her long-awaited first movie words were spoken to a waiter in a waterfront dive: "Gimme a visky. Ginger ale on the side. And don' be stingy, ba-bee."

No director had a keener sense of mass tastes than Cecil B. DeMille, and he put so many elements of potential audience appeal into his first sound picture, *Dynamite* (1929), it was as if he were compiling an anthology of what the microphone could do. The improbable story concerns an heiress who must marry in order to receive her legacy. In desperation she arranges a wedding with a coal miner condemned to death for murder, on the day before his execution. Naturally, the real killer confesses at the last minute, and the miner is set free.

The film begins with astonishingly risqué dialogue about adultery and divorce. It shows the heiress' rich friends dancing and singing, drunk and dissolute, the women with their skirts awry and thighs exposed. Then it moves to the miner's town, where sharp language is exchanged about class differences, and the rich girl's car runs over a child. Finally it ends underground with a mine cave-in and an explosion in which the rich girl's socialite lover kills himself so she may be saved to unite with her true love, her coal-miner husband. *Dynamite* laid out many of the ways sound could be used to shock and excite audiences well before the onset of Depression forced other filmmakers to follow DeMille's path.

Sound was, of course, also music. With the coming of talkies, studios put as many operettas and musical romances on their shooting schedules as they thought the audience would tolerate. The same economic conditions that dictated the shift to contemporary urban and lowlife settings for more advantageous noise effects and dialogue also applied to music. If a producer could sneak a little sexual titillation into musicals set in old Vienna or modern Paris, think how much more he could get away with by making the location a back-street cabaret or sleazy burlesque show.

Song and dance could also enliven crime and gangster melodramas. Roland West's *Alibi* (1929), a superior early sound gangster film, contains several scenes of scantily clad chorus girls performing in a night club; one shot shows the chorus line in tight short pants, close-up from the waist down. Melodramas of show-business lowlife like Rouben Mamoulian's *Applause* (1929) and Josef von Sternberg's *The Blue Angel* (1930) displayed female performers in skimpy costumes or partially disrobed in their dressing rooms, and had many imitators. Gradually the contemporary musical evolved into a more genial vehicle for sexual display, where the plot line served mainly as time filler between lascivious production numbers like Busby Berkeley's elaborate erotic creations or the nearly nude chorus line in Mitchell Leisen's *Murder at the Vanities* (1934).

Hollywood had other strings to its bow as well during the first golden age of 1930s movies. A Western, *Cimarron*, was voted the best picture of 1931 in the *Film Daily* poll of newspaper critics and also won the statuette (later to be named Oscar) of the Academy of Motion Picture Arts and Sciences; MGM's all-star production of Vicki Baum's novel *Grand Hotel* was another double winner in 1932; and the movie version of Noël Coward's British historical drama *Cavalcade* took both awards in 1933. Other important historical pictures included D. W. Griffith's first sound film, *Abraham Lincoln* (1930). George Cukor made several fine adaptations from Broadway and novels, including *A Bill of*

Divorcement (1932), *Dinner at Eight* and *Little Women* (both 1933). With five hundred features a year coming out of Hollywood, one could find a veritable encyclopedia of entertainment styles and subjects.

Yet the trend was unmistakably toward more sex and violence. Any churchgoer or clubwoman would have said there had been far too much of both in silent films already. Though producers certainly hoped to avoid further antagonizing their genteel critics if they could help it, they had a more pressing need to fill the empty seats in their theaters. Gilbert Seldes, the pioneer critic of popular culture, suggested in *The Movies Come from America* (1937) that studios began to tailor their pictures deliberately to men, hoping to win them back into an audience that had become increasingly composed of women and children (an insight which assumes that women and children were less interested than men in sex and violence).

For women, there was little comfort in the way early sound films treated relations between the sexes. The classic man-woman shot of the period brought sex and violence together in the same gesture: James Cagney at the breakfast table shoving a grapefruit in Mae Clarke's face in *The Public Enemy*. Talking pictures, in comparison to silents, gave women a certain superficial boldness and freedom of action, if only because dialogue was a richer and more varied medium than printed titles. In keeping with the general movement of movie morals, women spoke more openly about sexual topics. But their control over their own bodies and lives was, if anything, reduced in the films of the early Depression era.

Besides Garbo, a number of women stars portrayed prostitutes or kept women, among them Marlene Dietrich in *Blonde Venus*, Jean Harlow in *Red Dust*, Irene Dunne in *Back Street* (all 1932). It is unlikely that moviemakers had any more coherent purpose in the "fallen woman" cycle than catering to prurient interest. These movies did imply, however, that there was no room in the marketplace for women other than on stage or in bed.

Even as sunny a film as *Gold Diggers of 1933*—the picture Bonnie Parker and Clyde Barrow step in to watch in Arthur Penn's 1967 film romantically evoking the violent 1930s—jokes that the working girls who sing and dance will have to give up hoofing and turn to hooking if their show doesn't succeed. There's a double meaning in the film's feature song:

We're in the money
We're in the money
We've got a lot of what it takes to get along.

The sense of fear early Depression movies increasingly communicated—which stemmed, no doubt, from the anxieties of moviemakers as well as from calculated box-office sensationalism—found expression even more directly in a flourishing genre of horror films. Like sex and violence, horror had been a part of movies since peep-show days, yet again, sound provided a whole new milieu to make terror more real: creaking doors, mysterious howls, wild screams.

Universal became the studio specializing in horror during the early sound period. In 1931 it produced *Dracula* and *Frankenstein*, in 1932 *The Mummy*, *Murders in the Rue Morgue* and *Old Dark House*, all featuring either Boris Karloff or Bela Lugosi. Yet Hollywood's commercial necessities in the early 1930s also led the two producers who believed most strongly in maintaining upper-bourgeois tone and taste, Irving Thalberg at MGM and David O. Selznick, then at RKO, to make the two most unusual horror films of the period.

Over great opposition Thalberg supported Tod Browning's startling film *Freaks* (1932), made with dwarfs, a human torso and other monstrosities normally seen only in circus side shows. Selznick served as executive producer on the classic *King Kong* (1933): the great gorilla trampling New York pedestrians, tearing up elevated tracks and scaling the Empire State Building may have given audiences precisely the proper combination of fear for the survival of their society and pleasure at seeing someone, even if only a doomed gorilla, vent his rage at it.

More than any other genre, gangster films set the character of the first golden age of Depression-era movies, and fear and pleasure form their emotional core. Hollywood's gangsters stood at the very center of their society's disorder—they were created by it, took their revenge on it, and ended finally as its victims. Mervyn LeRoy's *Little Caesar* (1930) began the controversial cycle. It was different from early gangster films because it focused unblinkingly on the gangster himself. Josef von Sternberg's silent classic *Underworld* (1927) and his sound movie *Thunderbolt* (1929) were rich with psychological and visual complexity; Roland West's *Alibi* (1929) was skillfully plotted. In *Little Caesar* and its successors, all these elements were subordinated to the character and destiny of the central figure.

With *Little Caesar*, the criminal became a public man. In Sternberg's gangster films and in *Alibi* the criminals had no obvious social backgrounds or class origins; their violence was stylized, contained in a closed world against one another and the police. The early-1930s movie gangsters were poor and stemmed from immigrant stock. They became criminals to make money. Their world impinged on the respectable world, and respectable people who wanted to gamble or get a drink during Prohibition entered into theirs.

The classic gangster films were *Little Caesar, The Public Enemy* (1931) and *Smart Money* (also 1931), all from Warner Bros., and the Howard Hughes production, *Scarface* (1932), directed by Howard Hawks. They all centered on individuals who reached out to alter their relation to society. By training, ideology and inclination, Americans seek to understand the nature of their society by pondering the fate of lone men, and sometimes women. The gangster films condensed social conflicts and disorders into the ambitions and dreams of their heroes. Society's values and institutions revealed themselves in the way they formed

COURTESY OF UNIVERSAL PICTURES

Victorious leaders of the Freedonian army pose amid the rubble in this production still from *Duck Soup* (1933). From the left: Chico, Zeppo, Groucho and Harpo Marx.

the gangster's life, and in how they reacted to what he had become.

The early-1930s gangster films were not, however, overtly sociological, providing reasons and explanations for behavior—that was to come later in the decade. They never tried to clarify whether the chaotic lives of their heroes were idiosyncratic or socially inspired. If anything, they implied that gangsters were aberrant types: Paul Muni played the Al Capone figure in *Scarface* as a bizarre, demented, dangerously comic lout; Cagney's Tommy Powers in *The Public Enemy* could not be blamed on society, because his brother turned out all right.

Nonetheless, the classic gangster films did have a message: their heroes' chaotic lives were more than matched by the chaos in society around them. Their friends, their rivals, the police, all seemed capable of greater dishonesty and disloyalty than they. A stunning example of this social disorder occurs in *Smart Money* when the Greek gambler, Nick Venizelos (played by Edward G. Robinson) is betrayed and arrested. The district attorney, calling Nick a "little greaseball," declares that the end justifies the means. Thereupon he tricks Nick into killing his best friend (played by Cagney) and hauls him off to jail.

No wonder audiences identified with the movie gangsters, despite printed prologues in *Scarface* and *The Public Enemy* reminding viewers of how evil the characters were. The gangster movies were not Depression success stories, as one recent interpretation has argued; they were films of social pathos. If a disordered society led an individual to lawlessness, his strength could not compare with the deviousness and force available to a lawless society.

The message was most explicit in Mervyn LeRoy's daring exposé of ruthless public authority, *I Am a Fugitive from a Chain Gang* (1932). It tells the story of an unemployed war veteran, implicated in a restaurant robbery and sentenced to hard labor on the prison rock pile of an unnamed Southern state. He makes a daring escape and prospers as a respectable engineer, but his identity is revealed and he is betrayed back into chains. Escaping a second time, he is last seen in nighttime shadows, unshaven and desperate, saying good-bye to the woman he loves. "How do you live?" she asks the fugitive. He answers, "I steal."

Social disorder could be fun, too. Moviegoers who remembered back before the war already knew it from Mack Sennett's Keystone comedies. Sennett's films established a formula of social struggle—the anarchic individual battling disordered society—that re-emerged in the Depression era as gangster melodrama. But gangsters did not preempt the field; there was still room to laugh when the pillars of social order trembled, and even to give them a little push besides. Sound and the Depression brought vulgarity, lechery and the upsetting of values back to the movies again, after a decade dominated by middle-class forms of comedy.

Two extraordinary kinds of comic subversion came to the screen with the introduction of sound—one from the Marx Brothers, the other from

Mae West. They had significantly similar pre-movie backgrounds: both were seasoned vaudeville, variety and Broadway-stage performers; West was forty years old when she made her movie debut; the three important Marxes, Groucho, Harpo and Chico, were in their mid-to-late thirties; their styles had matured in the sophisticated atmosphere of New York theatrical and literary life of the mid-1920s. When the movie public turned a cynical eye on the old bourgeois myths in the early Depression years, West and the Marxes were well ahead of the game. More than any other movie comedians, before or since, they turned traditional culture on its head. After 1934, the Production Code and changing audience tastes forced them to set the old values right side up again, but fortunately, the evidence of their topsy-turvy moral worlds—most notably in two 1933 films, the Marxes' *Duck Soup* and West's *She Done Him Wrong*—was not erased.

Though the full flavor of their bite and effrontery came through their verbal wit, their memorable lines and language styles, it is important to remember how distinctively physical both the Marx Brothers and Mae West were. Many of the best scenes in *Duck Soup*—the running battle between the sidewalk vendors (Chico, Harpo and Edgar Kennedy, the latter one of the original Keystone Kops); Groucho and Harpo in the classic mirror mimicry scene—would be just as pointed and funny as silent comedy. Harpo, of course, was a mute comedian, though his horn and whistle gave him more than visual powers of communication. West used her eyebrows, smile, shoulders and hips, her walk, the way she turned her head, to make her message clearer than words. Neither the Marxes nor West attained the agility or grace of the great silent comics; indeed, their physical stance was deliberately more crude. But their appeal to eye as well as ear was as complete as any other comedians the movies produced.

The Marx Brothers entered the movies at Paramount's studios in Astoria, Long Island, where they made films of their two popular Broadway musicals, *The Coconuts* (filmed in 1929) and *Animal Crackers* (1930). Moving to Hollywood, they made *Monkey Business* in 1931 and *Horse Feathers* in 1932. These four films established the personae of the four brothers: Zeppo, young, handsome and subordinate; Harpo, romantic, thief, mischief-maker; Chico, the only brother ethnically distinctive, as an Italian, scheming and clever in a stolid, single-minded way; and Groucho, outrageous wit, climber and charlatan. The first two films were the most pointedly sarcastic about the rich and would-be-rich; *Monkey Business* made fun of gangsters, and *Horse Feathers* took on higher education. It remained for *Duck Soup* to tackle the very fount of social order itself, the state.

Duck Soup is as thorough a satire on politics and patriotism as any film before *Dr. Strangelove*. Its target is not directly the United States, as in Stanley Kubrick's film, but audiences were welcome to make their own connections and had plenty of hints later in the film, when Harpo parodies Paul Revere, and Groucho, as his nation's commander in chief,

THE MUSEUM OF MODERN ART/FILM STILLS ARCHIVE

Paul Muni as perpetrator of criminal violence and victim of state violence in two films from the early Depression period. He plays Tony Camonte (top, center), the Al Capone figure in Howard Hawks's *Scarface* (1932), with George Raft at his right hand and Vince Barnett peering out between them; C. Henry Gordon is at right. In Mervyn LeRoy's *I Am a Fugitive from a Chain Gang* of the same year (bottom) he is James Allen, a down-on-his-luck World War I veteran who twice escapes from a brutal chain gang and is doomed to a shadowy life on the run.

THE MUSEUM OF MODERN ART/FILM STILLS ARCHIVE

wears successively a Confederate uniform, a coonskin cap and other symbols of American military glory and/or defeat. The most direct analogy in the early Depression years was the nation's need for a leader. It was too bad the film was released half a year after Roosevelt took office; if it had arrived on the scene earlier, Groucho's inept leadership of Freedonia might have made it as black a comedy as Kubrick's, with its nuclear-holocaust finale, seemed to the early 1960s.

The people of Freedonia are restless; the government has been mismanaged. Mrs. Teasdale, the rich widow, will lend money only if Rufus T. Firefly (Groucho) is appointed leader. In his musical state-of-the-union number Groucho outlines perhaps the bleakest political program ever uttered: neither moral nor immoral behavior will be permitted; marriage and honesty are forbidden, but so too are smiles, dirty jokes and all forms of pleasure. His firmest promise is that things will get worse. And he knows how to implement his goals. When the idea is proposed at a Cabinet meeting that workers be given shorter hours, Groucho suggests beginning by cutting down lunch hours.

No wonder Freedonians are happy to go to war over a slight to Groucho's dignity, proclaiming their joy in an inspired production number in which the Marx Brothers and the chorus parody patriotism in a takeoff on a spiritual ("We got guns, all God's children got guns") in various musical styles. Since they can't be either moral or immoral, at war they can be amoral, and Groucho again leads the way. Told that he's shooting his own man, he says, "Here's five dollars—keep it under your hat." On second thought he prefers the money under his own hat.

Meanwhile, Chico and Harpo, spies for Sylvania, are busy parodying the spirit of economic competition, among other things. As peanut vendors they sabotage and are in turn sabotaged by a drink vendor. Their energy and ingenuity go into destroying each other's property. When customers gather around his rival, Harpo scares them off by jumping barefoot into the drink vat. So much for free enterprise.

Freedonia manages to win the war, but it seems clear that the Marx Brothers will remain unreconstructed—in the final scene they are throwing fruit at the nation's benefactress, Mrs. Teasdale. The only thing they could substitute for serious social disorder was comic social disorder. In his backhand way Groucho was more effective than most politicians: he knew how to make things worse, and he did. The movie didn't even hold out the promise of aesthetic apocalpyse, as did Kubrick, only more and better chaos. Unfortunately, audiences were ready by late 1933, when *Duck Soup* came out, for uplift. It was one of the less popular Marx films. The brothers left Paramount for MGM, where Irving Thalberg integrated their comedy into his own concept of audience values, and they made one more exceptional film, *A Night at the Opera* (1935). Thereafter they became more genial, more considerate, more positive, and increasingly, in seven more pictures between 1937 and 1949, shadows of their former selves.

Mae West's most noteworthy film, *She Done Him Wrong*, came out in March 1933, in time to catch the movie public in its disenchantment with traditional values, before the New Deal turned the tide. *Variety*, the show-business weekly, warned that the film would offend neighborhood and small-town audiences, but the prediction proved startlingly wrong: *She Done Him Wrong* was greeted enthusiastically everywhere and catapulted West nearly to the top in lists of box-office favorites. In retrospect it is not difficult to see the film's drawing power: the story of Lady Lou, a Bowery saloon *chanteuse* in the Gay Nineties, it offered sex and violence, the smashing of corruption and a moral ending, a near-perfect combination of titillating humor and uplift, sin and redemption. Amid all the melodrama, wit and spectacle it is easy to overlook the most daring aspect of the movie, West's revolution in sex roles.

West's comedy is the comedy of turnabout, making people laugh by saying exactly the opposite of what they are accustomed to hearing. Small wonder her flamboyance and brazen sensuality have led some commentators to connect her with the stage tradition of female impersonators: women in American society had not been permitted to behave that way, though male performers in women's dress had acted out men's anxieties and fantasies about women. Yet here was West, unmistakably female, stating her sexual tactics explicitly: "Men are alike—married or single, it's their game. I'm smart enough to play it their way." Her title therefore takes on new significance: it wasn't merely that she had done a man wrong, as women presumably had done since Eve, it was that she did it in the same way as men, as an aggressive, free, independent sexual being.

There are contradictions in West's sexual philosophy, to be sure. Sex is the only game she can play, and though she disclaims dependence on any man, she depends on her capacity to attract men for her livelihood. What's most astonishing is her lack of sentiment and cant. If sex is her economic necessity, she never forgets that her desire and pleasure are the grounds of her behavior. Her most striking line in the film is not meant as a joke: to Cary Grant, playing a missionary (actually a federal agent in disguise), she says bluntly, "You can be had." That puts a certain hard edge of truth on her sexual repartee elsewhere in the film, of which the following is perhaps the most notorious example: Grant: "Haven't you ever met a man who could make you happy?" West: "Sure, lots of times."

But marriage is to be her fate—perhaps a concession to the boundaries American moral precepts still imposed. Grant takes her ill-gotten jewelry off her fingers and slips on a wedding ring instead. It's true he was the man she was aiming for (though not exclusively) all the time; it's also true he will have no easy time changing her ways. "Surely you don't mind me holding your hand?" he says. "It ain't heavy," she answers. "I can hold it myself."

West's popularity continued for several more years, though her light-hearted approach to sexual satisfaction immediately became a focus of agitation among censorship groups, and after 1934 the Breen Office effectively tied her down. She could still make jokes, but she was not

Gold diggers of 1933, individual and collective: Busby Berkeley's spectacular finale production number, "We're in the Money," (top) from Mervyn LeRoy's *Gold Diggers of 1933,* with Ruby Keeler at stage center. A more solitary gold digger was Mae West, Lady Lou of *She Done Him Wrong* (1933), shown (bottom) on the set with director Lowell Sherman. West's capital was not in coin but in jewelry, and even more in her daring repartee and sexual independence.

THE MUSEUM OF MODERN ART/FILM STILLS ARCHIVE

allowed to express independent attitudes toward women's sexual freedom or pleasure. She became merely a self-deprecating, comic bad girl on her way to redemption. By 1940 she was reduced, not unlike the Marx Brothers, to trading limp one-liners with W. C. Fields in *My Little Chickadee*, in which the filmmakers merely traded on her reputation and audience memories.

Fields belongs with West and the Marx Brothers as a master of 1930s verbal comedy, but his comic role differed significantly from either of the others. He was the screen's most extreme misanthrope (outside of horror movies), and such consistent naysaying took its toll in bite and meaning. When everything, including one's self, is a target for destructive wit, there's no room left for alternative social visions. The Marx Brothers were at least committed to being charlatans and disrupters; West, despite her self-mockery, meant what she said about sex. Fields's verbal style distributed comic aggression toward the world and toward himself so evenly that it often carried no resonance. There was no way audiences could see the world in a different light, and his formula, like that of later TV comics, gave plenty of laughs and a sense of daring but in no way affected the status quo.

Fields was at his best on the few occasions when his animus was focused and directed outward, as in *The Man on a Flying Trapeze* (1935) and the first part of *The Bank Dick* (1940): his targets in these films were shrewish wives and mean-spirited children, and no sharper satires of family life exist in the movies. Fields's fame rests on his starring vehicles just before World War II: *You Can't Cheat an Honest Man* (1939), *The Bank Dick* and *Never Give a Sucker an Even Break* (1941), made at a time when comedy that more effectively challenged cultural values was in eclipse.

One didn't, of course, have to be a social critic to be a comedian. During the brilliant quarter century of classic movie comedy, from Mack Sennett through Chaplin, Keaton and Lloyd to the Marx Brothers and Mae West, American moviemakers also produced scores of formula comedies every year whose humor was intended to reaffirm social values. When the Breen Office and Hollywood's new self-conscious role as upholder of the cultural heritage nipped off the last buds of iconoclastic humor in the mid-1930s, the strong current of tried-and-true comic conventions kept the laughs rolling in. What is remarkable about Hollywood's second 1930s golden age—from 1935 to 1941—is the verve and self-confidence that created a new comic style from the old trite formulas: the style of "screwball" comedy.

Screwball comedies were the last refuge of the satire, self-mockery and sexual candor of early 1930s filmmaking, but their iconoclasm was used, overtly at least, to support the status quo. They belonged firmly to the tradition of romantic comedies whose purpose was to show how imagination, curiosity and cleverness—those dangerous levers of social change—could be channeled into support of things as they are. The screwball comedies by and large celebrated the sanctity of marriage, class distinction and the domination of women by men.

There were perhaps two dozen screwball comedies in the late 1930s, and other comedy genres, including musicals and dramas, which contained screwball-comedy elements. Most of them came in the years 1937 to 1940, though the list might begin as early as 1933 with Ernst Lubitsch's *Design for Living.* A partial list of outstanding examples includes *Twentieth Century* (1934), *Ruggles of Red Gap* (1935), *My Man Godfrey* (1936), *The Awful Truth, Nothing Sacred, Easy Living* and *Topper* (all 1937), *Bringing up Baby, Holiday* and *Joy of Living* (all 1938), *Midnight* (1939), *The Philadelphia Story, His Girl Friday, My Favorite Wife, Too Many Husbands* (all 1940) and *The Lady Eve* (1941).

Certain players and directors seemed particularly suited to the screwball style: Cary Grant starred in half a dozen of the best, and Carole Lombard, Katharine Hepburn and Irene Dunne were among the most effective comediennes. Leo McCarey (who also directed *Duck Soup* and a Mae West film), Howard Hawks, George Cukor, Mitchell Leisen, Tay Garnett and Gregory La Cava directed nearly all the best screwball comedies. They all possessed a flair for the inspired unselfconscious idiosyncratic moment and the ability to build tight, fast plots that leaped from improbability to incongruity to reassuring resolution.

That was the point: improbability and incongruity were never allowed to disturb the social order but, rather, to show how well it worked. More often than not, the characters in screwball comedies were wealthy, and their wacky behavior showed audiences how funny and lovable and harmless the rich could be. Who could hold anything against Irene Dunne or Cary Grant after the hilarious last half-hour of *The Awful Truth,* which included Dunne playing a drunk at a posh social gathering, throwing away the knob on a blaring car radio, releasing the handbrake so the car crashes, and the two of them riding on the handlebars of police motorcycles? Or dislike Katharine Hepburn and Grant after the somersaults and games in the playroom in *Holiday*? Or find anything but charming Dunne's romance with Douglas Fairbanks, Jr., in *Joy of Living* after they go roller-skating together?

For women, especially, the messages were persistent: romantic love is better than gold digging, marriage better than a career or divorce. The screwball comedies were in essence funny versions of Cecil B. DeMille's post–World War I domestic melodramas: they carried their characters to the brink of social disorder, but they always stopped just in time.

And yet, though they never challenged the social order, the pictures gave audiences a whole new vision of social style, a different image of how to be a person: it was okay to be pleasure-loving, even if it made you look sexy or odd; it was good to puncture stuffed shirts and be lively, gay and carefree; it was good to throw decorum to the wind. There's no question but that they made their contribution to cultural change, just by repeating over and over again how attractive it was to be a person who liked to have fun.

* * *

This second golden age, like its screwball comedies, was a revival of the past, but with a difference. Beginning in 1934 and for the remainder of the decade, the majority of important moneymaking pictures had little to do with contemporary life, and nothing at all with sex or violence. No doubt the Breen Office had a great deal to do with the shift in values; the change has also been seen as a deliberate turning away from reality and controversy, a shunning of social responsibility. The essential fact is, however, that studio managers never varied in their responsibility to their pocketbooks. Their pictures changed because audience tastes changed, because American society changed. Only, this time a few producers were not simply followers, they were also leaders; and the culture they revived in their movies they considered their own.

It took no more than two or three ambitious men to transform the outlook of an industry. Half the major studios, Paramount, RKO, Universal and Fox, were in economic distress and managerial upheaval, and many of the new managers had no previous production experience; none of the independent producers who distributed through United Artists made enough movies to spark any trends; Columbia's new prestige rested largely on the work of one inimitable director, Frank Capra; and Warner Bros. went into a brief creative slump after 1933, when Darryl F. Zanuck left in the aftermath of the salary-waiver controversy. MGM was the only studio with the stability, organization and talent to take the lead, and in Irving Thalberg and David O. Selznick it possessed two of the vanguard of the second generation of movie moguls. Zanuck was the third.

Thalberg, born in Brooklyn, became the "boy wonder" of the industry. After his untimely death in 1936 Scott Fitzgerald made him the prototype of his producer hero, Monroe Stahr, in his unfinished Hollywood novel *The Last Tycoon.* Starting at Universal while still in his teens, Thalberg became production head at Metro Pictures—later MGM—in his early twenties, and led that studio to the front rank as manufacturer of financially and critically successful pictures. In the early 1930s, in good part out of jealousy, his boss Louis B. Mayer deposed Thalberg and took over the top spot himself, retaining Thalberg as an independent producer with responsibility for a smaller number of special features. Ironically, this defeat gave Thalberg a chance to concentrate on making expensive prestigious films.

Selznick was the son of Lewis J. Selznick, a pioneer producer who had been forced out during the industry's consolidation in the early 1920s; the son joined MGM in the late 1920s, moved to Paramount, headed production at RKO in 1932–1933, and then, in 1933, rejoined MGM as an independent producer. In 1936 he founded his own company, Selznick International, releasing through United Artists. Zanuck, a Midwestern Protestant, formed Twentieth Century after leaving Warner Bros., and in 1935 his company took over Fox.

Together these three men shifted Hollywood's style toward dignified,

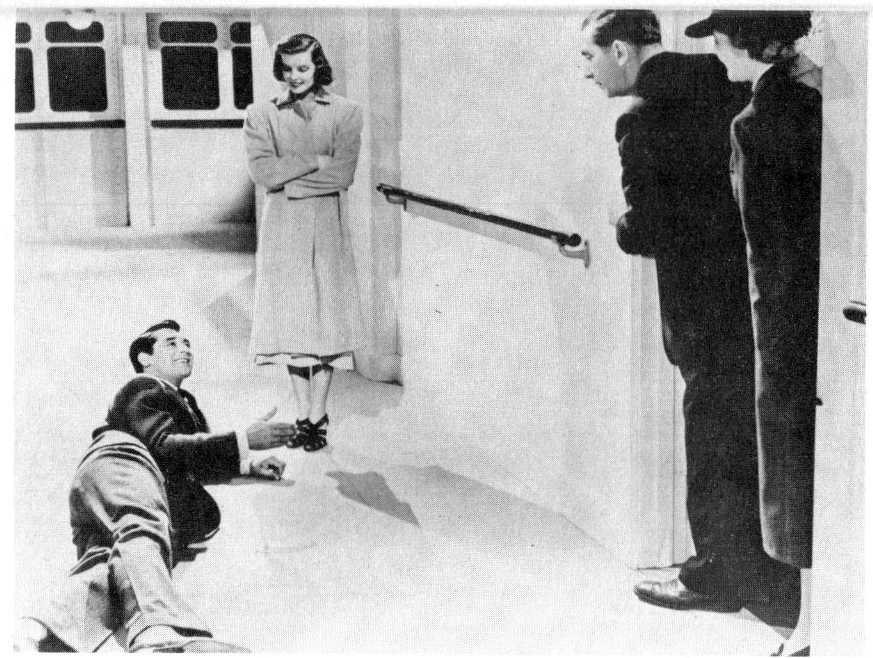

THE MUSEUM OF MODERN ART/FILM STILLS ARCHIVE

In the cycle of "screwball" comedies in the late 1930s, Depression-era audiences were entertained by portrayals of the rich playing, laughing, behaving foolishly and enjoying themselves immensely. Cary Grant smiles after turning a cartwheel (top) in *Holiday* (1938), directed by George Cukor, while Katharine Hepburn, Edward Everett Horton and Jean Dixon look on; Irene Dunne and Douglas Fairbanks, Jr., collapse in a heap (bottom) after a roller-skating escapade in *Joy of Living* (also 1938), directed by Tay Garnett; Dunne at least is laughing.

THE MUSEUM OF MODERN ART/FILM STILLS ARCHIVE

elevated, respectable pictures set in the past and usually drawn from the classics or current best sellers. Their achievement as trend setters was remarkable. In 1934 Thalberg produced *The Barretts of Wimpole Street*; Zanuck, *The House of Rothschild*. In 1935 Selznick made *David Copperfield* and *Anna Karenina*; Zanuck, *Les Misérables*. Thalberg released *Mutiny on the Bounty* in 1936 and had under way before his death productions of *The Good Earth* and *Romeo and Juliet* (both 1937) and *Marie Antoinette* (1938); Selznick made *A Tale of Two Cities*. By that time Warner Bros. had entered the field with its film biographies of Louis Pasteur and Émile Zola (1936 and 1937, respectively). These films dominated the *Film Daily* "ten best" polls from 1934 through 1937, along with a number of other historical dramas or adaptations from literature.

What attracted these men to Dickens and Tolstoy and Shakespeare, to Captain Bligh and Jean Valjean? And why, in many cases, did they have to fight to make movies from classics their associates claimed could not be filmed or would not attract an audience?

To begin with, they had sound financial reasons. When Selznick left MGM to found his own company he wrote his treasurer: "There are only two kinds of merchandise that can be made profitably in this business—either the very cheap pictures or the expensive pictures."[1] This dictum may have reflected ambition as much as observation, for there were numerous exceptions to it, but as a rule of thumb it was not far from the mark: most medium-priced pictures, in the 1930s as in the 1920s, simply were not good enough to attract sufficient customers in the first-run market, and they could not make up their expenses in the neighborhood and small-town theaters. If a picture was expensively produced, with handsome sets and costumes, big-name stars and plenty of ballyhoo, it was likely to make out all right even if it was mediocre—and if it was good, it could make a fortune. Famous novels and historical themes lent themselves well to the big-budget treatment.

There were obvious personal motivations as well. Selznick felt compelled to vindicate the family name among the moguls who had fought and defeated his father. Lewis J. Selznick, a Russian Jew who had emigrated as an adolescent to England and then to Pittsburgh, was a largely self-taught man who loved the classics with the fervor of one who has discovered them for himself. He gave his son Dickens and Tolstoy to read when, as David recalled, other boys his age were reading Frank Merriwell. When Selznick made *David Copperfield*, he carried with him the copy of the novel his father had given him.

Of his Thalberg-like figure, Monroe Stahr, Fitzgerald wrote that "he cherished the parvenu's passionate loyalty to an imaginary past."[2] Unlike the earlier moviemakers—the immigrant ex-furriers and haberdashers and glovemakers—the second generation was more deeply entwined

---

[1] Rudy Behlmer, ed., *Memo From: David O. Selznick* (1972; Avon ed., 1973), p. 134.

[2] *The Last Tycoon* (1941; in *Three Novels of F. Scott Fitzgerald*), p. 118.

with the values not of the American marketplace, but of traditional American culture. In Fitzgerald's vision they were like Lincoln, men of humble origins whose power at a certain moment gave them responsibility over the nation's destiny. In their own eyes, however, they saw themselves more as eighteenth-century gentlemen, Jefferson's natural aristocrats, leaders of their culture through their talent and earned wealth.

There is a fascinating symbol of the moguls' changing self-image in two David O. Selznick productions about Hollywood, one made in 1932, the other five years later. The first, *What Price Hollywood*, directed by George Cukor, is in the characteristic style of the first 1930s golden age—swift, brash, a little sensational, risqué, cynical, satirical. It shows people really working at making movies. The producer is a hearty ethnic type named Saxe, played by Gregory Ratoff, who shouts at his babbling assistants, "One yes at a time!"—which suggests that the famous line later attributed to Darryl F. Zanuck, "Don't say yes until I finish talking," may be a case of life imitating art.[3]

The second, *A Star Is Born* (1937), directed by William Wellman in the newly perfected Technicolor process, is far more self-conscious: the movie game has become a cultural institution. The film shows all the paraphernalia of moviemaking, the preparation for a screen test, make-up, costuming, night life and private life, sneak previews and gala opening nights, but never the thing itself. And the producer, with the blue-blood name of Oliver Niles, was acted by the epitome of Hollywood elegance, sophistication and polish, Adolphe Menjou.

An English writer, R. J. Minney, who worked with Zanuck on the script of one historical epic that made nobody's ten-best list, *Clive of India* (1935), described how he turned in the first draft after six on a Friday evening and planned to take a few days' holiday in Mexico. By ten the next morning, however, "Zanuck had read it, made elaborate marginal comments, and discussed it with all the departments concerned." All day Saturday they spent in conference on the script, "Zanuck talking all the time."[4]

At one such conference, Zanuck spoke of "a milestone round the neck"; someone laughed, and according to Minney, was fired instantly.[5] Perhaps moguls like Selznick and Zanuck wanted to think they looked and talked like Adolphe Menjou, but Gregory Ratoff was still the more accurate casting.

At the end of the prewar period, Selznick and Zanuck were at the zenith of their power and prestige. Their pictures swept the Academy awards for three consecutive years—Selznick's *Gone With the Wind* won the Oscar for the best movie in 1939, and his *Rebecca* made it two

---

[3] Mel Gussow, *Don't Say Yes Until I Finish Talking* (1971). Zanuck attributes the line to himself in the book's epigraph.

[4] *Hollywood by Starlight* (1935), pp. 150–51.

[5] *Ibid.*, p. 86.

THE MUSEUM OF MODERN ART/FILM STILLS ARCHIVE

David O. Selznick presented a self-conscious image of Hollywood as a cultural institution in *A Star Is Born* (1937), directed by William Wellman; and the most obvious wish-fulfillment aspect of it was the suave, debonair, aristocratic producer, Oliver Niles, played by Adolphe Menjou (center). From the left: Janet Gaynor, Fredric March, Menjou, Lionel Stander, Vince Barnett. Hollywood's later political conflicts are prefigured in this still: March was a liberal who was attacked for allegedly supporting Communist causes; Menjou, a conservative who testified as a "friendly" witness before the House Un-American Activities Committee in 1947; and Stander, a radical who was blacklisted.

in a row in 1940; Zanuck took the prize with *How Green Was My Valley* in 1941. Yet all that ambition and elevation were beginning to take their toll.

Film subjects had shifted from the classics to recent best-selling novels. Selznick's respect for the prose of Margaret Mitchell and Daphne du Maurier turned out to be even greater than for Dickens and Tolstoy. He insisted that the scripts follow the plot and language of the novels as closely as possible, declaring that readers of the books would be annoyed by any changes in the movie version (a reversal of his views on *David Copperfield*, *Anna Karenina* and *A Tale of Two Cities*). This faithfulness to the text made the Civil War epic nearly four hours long, and *Rebecca*, though just over two hours, seems twice that. While *Gone With the Wind* was redeemed by the scale of epic splendor, Selznick's literary deference constrained his filmmaking vitality.

Zanuck was more cavalier in rewriting his two best-seller adaptations, *The Grapes of Wrath* (1940) and *How Green Was My Valley*. He was aided by the fact that they were about poor or working families, and that they were both directed by John Ford, a director with unusual feeling for common life. Nevertheless, Zanuck also had difficulties putting the large canvas of the novels into film form.

Although filmed best sellers continued to dominate the box-office, genre pictures began to make a comeback in the last years before the war. They were as much a commentary on the second golden age as a continuation of it. They sought to restore some of the vulgar energy of the early sound era, to regain some of the old shock and fear and titillation without the obvious excesses of sex and violence that the Production Code now forbade. Among the outstanding movies of the period were an action melodrama, Howard Hawks's *Only Angels Have Wings* (1939); a Western, Ford's *Stagecoach* (1939); a gangster film, Raoul Walsh's *High Sierra* (1941); and a detective story, John Huston's *The Maltese Falcon* (1941).

And then a brash young newcomer arrived to remind Hollywood of how culturally and emotionally powerful movie images could be. For his debut as a film director, the *enfant terrible* of theater and radio, Orson Welles, began to make a satire on the historical biography, a film about a megalomaniac publisher modeled on the career of William Randolph Hearst. But in his hands *Citizen Kane* (1941) turned into an apotheosis of the form—bawdy, insolent, deliberately scandalous, and superbly constructed, designed, acted and photographed. A world-wide consensus of film critics in both the 1962 and 1972 *Sight and Sound* polls voted it the greatest of all motion pictures. By the sensationalism of its style and the controversy over its content, *Citizen Kane* made obvious to everyone what intellectuals and critics had begun to speculate about more and more, Hollywood's role in the forging of the nation's cultural myths.

12

THE MAKING OF CULTURAL MYTHS: WALT DISNEY AND FRANK CAPRA

In the late 1930s, public discussion about Hollywood changed. Clergymen in backwater towns could still raise a crowd by railing against sin on the silver screen, and judges and reformers here and there continued to maintain that movies led impressionable youth to crime. Among academics and in literary circles, however, and in the principal newspapers and magazines, the moviemakers were regarded with considerably more respect, awe and even envy, as the possessors of the power to create the nation's myths and dreams.

"Dreams hung in fragments at the far end of the room," Scott Fitzgerald wrote, describing a producer's projection room in *The Last Tycoon*, "suffered analysis, passed—to be dreamed in crowds, or else discarded."[1] This evocative image and its counterparts in other fiction and social science of the period were not simply imaginative or analytical efforts to grasp the nature of the Hollywood phenomenon. They were observations on the possession and use of cultural power. Whether they wrote in indignation or scholarly detachment, these writers were explicitly or implicitly acknowledging that movies had taken over cultural functions they themselves had exercised, or aspired to, in the past.

In traditional American society the task of describing the world and communicating that vision to its members had belonged, with different emphasis at different times, to the clergy, political statesmen, educators, businessmen, essayists, poets and novelists. There had never been a totally uniform cultural expression in the United States, there had always been schisms and struggles, alternatives and counterviews, but in general the combatants had come from similar ethnic and class backgrounds and had utilized the same means—the written and spoken word. Now for the first time power to influence the culture had been grasped by a group of men whose origins and whose means were different.

This is the principal reason why the message of the movie image was described as myth or dream. In ordinary language, myths and dreams are falsehoods—fantasies, fictions, imaginary tales. In the strict sense, this was a political choice of words. It implied that other forms of cultural communications spoke more truly about human experience than the movies.

What was different about the movies in the 1930s was not that they

[1] P. 56.

were beginning to communicate myths and dreams—they had done that from the beginning—but that the moviemakers were aware in a more sophisticated way of their mythmaking powers, responsibilities and opportunities. Among intellectuals and in centers of political power, the importance of cultural myths to social stability was a seriously debated topic. The Depression had shaken some of the oldest and strongest of American cultural myths, particularly the middle-class homilies about the virtues of deferred gratification and the assurance that hard work and perseverance would bring success.

This loss of cultural certitudes had created a mood of shame and self-reproach in American society, as the historian Warren Susman has pointed out, and a sense of foreboding about the future. With the rise of Nazi Germany and the aggressive challenge to democratic ideals, the widespread doubt about traditional American myths threatened to become a dangerous political weakness. In politics, industry and the media there were men and women, as often of liberal as of conservative persuasion, who saw the necessity, almost as a patriotic duty, to revitalize and refashion a cultural mythology.

The high priority the nation's leaders placed on recementing the foundations of public morale was not lost on those producers and directors whose goal was enhanced prestige, respectability and cultural power. Moreover, they were quickly gaining considerable skill at communicating their messages with subtle nuances beneath the surface of overt content. More and more effort in motion-picture production was given over to the service of cultural mythmaking.

A generation later in time, uncounted generations later in consciousness, it is almost impossible to recapture the sense of discovery, wonder and loss which writers like Fitzgerald felt when they observed the Hollywood dream machine. Their concern was not simply that movie producers had usurped their ability to command the attention and allegiance of a larger public. A deeper, more impersonal cultural issue was at stake.

The media of written and spoken words had been various enough, flexible enough, inexpensive enough to accommodate critics and naysayers. Men and women who wanted to expose the dreams and myths of cultural elites—to pull away the veil of mystification that made it seem as if the parochial values of the American middle class were universal fact—had been able to make themselves heard. Behind such works as Fitzgerald's portrait of a doomed producer was the foreboding that Hollywood moviemaking was too costly, too single-minded in its quest for profits and therefore too narrowly conceived, to permit deviation from familiar cultural norms.

Even satirical movies like the screwball comedies, or socially aware films like *The Grapes of Wrath*, were carefully constructed to stay within the bounds of essential American cultural and political myths. It was feared, with considerable justification, that whatever challenge movies presented to the more straightlaced traditional norms, Hollywood's contribution to American culture was essentially one of affirmation.

Such perspectives seem a little naïve and old-fashioned today. After living a quarter century with television, witnessing the rise and fall of the prophet McLuhan and experiencing annual revolutions in media technology, one is all too likely to assume a superior knowledge of media power and an immunity from its effects, without quite comprehending the process of media influence. The youth culture of the 1960s exhibited the tragicomic contradiction of proclaiming its liberation from the bourgeois culture of its parents while at the same time uncritically embracing the bourgeois myths of movies past and present—an up-to-date version of the old middle-class American desire to have it both ways.

The fact is that the careful analysis of movie dreams and myths has barely begun. As the French critic Roland Barthes said of mass-culture messages, or as he called them, "collective representations," the task now is "to go further than the pious show of unmasking them and account *in detail* [his italics] for the mystification which transforms petit-bourgeois culture into a universal nature."[2] This new stage of discovery properly begins with Hollywood movies in the golden ages of the 1930s, the first fully conscious era of cultural mythmaking; and it requires not a sweeping overview but a close-up look at significant examples of the dream creators' art.

No Hollywood filmmakers of the 1930s were more consistent or coherent in their efforts at cultural mythmaking than two men whose careers offer striking similarities—the producer of animated cartoons, Walt Disney, and the director of comedy and drama, Frank Capra. Though their work hardly exhausts the variety of movie dreams in the Depression era or the subtlety of relationships between movies and cultural norms, it does offer a clearly marked path along the major lines of development during the decade. In an exploration of Hollywood's myths and dreams in the 1930s their movies serve almost as touchstones by which to compare the elaborations of others, and therefore as the essential place to begin.

Almost alone among moviemakers of the period, Disney and Capra shared the acclaim of all three significant audiences for movies: the ticket-buying public, the critics and commentators on films, and their Hollywood co-workers. Disney won every Academy award for cartoon shorts from 1932 to 1939; his first animated feature, *Snow White and the Seven Dwarfs* (1937), was voted the best picture of 1938 by critics in the *Film Daily* poll. In the same span of years Capra was awarded the Oscar as best director three times, while no other director was honored more than once. *It Happened One Night* was named the best movie of 1934 by the Academy, and *You Can't Take It With You* won again for him in 1938.

---

[2] *Mythologies* (1957; English translation, 1972), p. 9.

Not since Chaplin's early comedy shorts had any filmmaker succeeded so completely in capturing both a popular and a highbrow audience. Capra and Disney each possessed the knack of providing mass entertainment in which intellectuals could find both pleasure and significance. They managed, as did no other of their peers—again, Chaplin excepted, although Chaplin made only three films during the entire decade—to create comic images of heroes cast in a popular mold who could embody a full range of fantasies and nightmares, who were so likable precisely because they could be simultaneously loved and ridiculed.

Another aspect of their work that set them apart was their independence. Disney, a producer with his own studio, retained sole control over his films; Capra attained such commercial success and prestige as a director that he gained the power, after long struggle, to pick his own projects at Columbia and oversee every element of film production—he even demanded and won the fight to have his name appear above the title of his pictures.

Both men were closely attuned to shifts in public tastes and cultural moods, and their independence gave them an opportunity to take full advantage of their audience sense. Their individual developments remarkably reflected—may, indeed, have prefigured—the basic transformations in Hollywood's relation to American culture in the 1930s. Disney's animations, particularly his short cartoons, which will be the focus here, and Capra's comedies and dramas demonstrated the way movie myths and dreams changed from the first years of the decade to the end.

Disney and his fellow animators were heirs to Méliès, trick photography, Chaplin's pre–World War I comedy shorts and the tradition of magical metamorphoses in movies. They faced, however, a different challenge and a different opportunity than did filmmakers who worked with human subjects: the very premise of their art was fantasy. They could draw worlds different from any experienced world, lead audiences into uncharted realms as far as imagination or daring could carry them. Blank paper gave them a chance to reinvent the world.

There are scant signs among the few surviving films of the silent period that animators were able to grasp the power in their pens. A 1924 *Felix the Cat*, drawn by Pat Sullivan, in the Museum of Modern Art collection shows a considerable gift for magical transformation: needing a way to get to the Yukon, Felix buys hot dogs in a butcher shop and attaches them to a sled; needing to see a distant object, he takes off his tail and uses it for a telescope. Animators who later became famous in the sound era mixed photographed live action with their drawings during the 1920s. Max and Dave Fleischer, creators of Betty Boop and Popeye the Sailorman, in silent days produced the *Out of the Inkwell* series, putting boundaries on fantasy by its very title. In a charming film from the series, *Modelling* (1921), the animators appear in the film along with their cartoon character, Koko the Clown. The youthful Disney also limited the fantasy in the title of his series *Alice in Cartoonland*, in which a teen-age girl encounters drawn characters. In both cases the photographed segments indicated that human life took precedence over the animated world—it brought fantasy into being and then put it away out of reach, back in the inkwell.

What was so astonishing about the Mickey Mouse films Disney began to make in 1928 was how completely they formed a world of their own. It was Disney's brilliant use of sound that immediately caught the public's attention and catapulted him to success and leadership in the animation field: the first Mickey Mouse release, *Steamboat Willie* (1928), came at a critical moment in the industry's transition from silence to sound, and Disney's bold inventiveness with integrated visual and sound effects gave animated shorts a popularity and aesthetic significance they had never had before. But his triumph with sound should not obscure the rich and complex pictorial world thus made audible.

Disney's interpreters invariably described the early Mickey Mouse films, and the Silly Symphony series that followed in 1929, as crude—in drawing, story and the behavior of their characters. The basic thrust of such criticism is technical: as the years went by, Disney and his animators became increasingly proficient, elaborating their drawings, adding color (again, as with sound, ingeniously integrated with the drawings and story and perfected well in advance of the larger studios), and even producing the effects of three-dimensional depth through another technical achievement, the multiplane camera.

This argument from technical growth describes a clear-cut process of advancement: when the mouse series was inaugurated, Disney was capable only of primitive and simple animation, but he and his staff swiftly got better and better—more sophisticated and more complex. To say that later is better than earlier, however, is to ignore a more fundamental kind of change. In the early Mickey Mouse and Silly Symphony films, Disney and his animators created one kind of fantasy world. Then they gave it up, putting in its place not a fantasy but an idealized world. A preference for the later over the earlier cartoon shorts should be recognized as an aesthetic and cultural as well as a technological judgment.

In his classic anthropological work, *The Savage Mind*, Claude Lévi-Strauss attacks the common notion that modern civilization is necessarily higher, or better, than "savage" societies. Modern life is not a sophisticated version of a simple life; it is an altogether *different* life, based on an entirely separate understanding of the world. Indeed, according to Lévi-Strauss, "savage" peoples with their highly elaborated knowledge of terrain, flora, fauna, kinship and ritual, may live a more complex life than we do. Somewhat the same distinction applies to Disney's cartoons. The two worlds, the fantasy of the early period and the idealization of the later, stand in direct contrast to each other, and both possess their separate kinds of sophistication and complexity.

The early Mickey Mouse and Silly Symphony cartoons are magical. Freed from the burdens of time and responsibility, events are open-ended, reversible, episodic, without obvious point. Outlandish events occur without fear of consequence. There is no fixed order of things: the world is plastic to imagination and will. Yet its pliant nature also renders it immune to fundamental change. Almost presciently, this comic fantasy world portrays the cultural mood, the exhilarating, initially liberating, then finally frightening disorder of the early Depression years.

Around 1932 the Disney cartoons began to change; by 1933 a whole new world view had emerged. The later cartoons are tales, many of them moral tales. They rejoin the straight and narrow path of time. They have beginnings and endings, and everything that happens in between has consequences. The world has rules, and you'd better learn them or watch out. Don't be too imaginative, don't be too inquisitive, don't be too willful, or you'll get into trouble—though there's always time to learn your lesson and come out all right. This idealized world was a full year or two ahead of feature films—perhaps because the features took longer to plan, produce and market—in expressing the spirit of social purpose, the re-enforcing of old values, in the culture of the later 1930s.

Mickey Mouse survived in both these worlds. He personified each in turn, though not without some major changes. Like no other twentieth-century motion-picture character except Chaplin (on whom some say the mouse was modeled), Mickey possessed the world's imagination. He, too, was a creature of many masks, expressing what we all like to think are the best traits of our humanity: sweet sentiment, unfeigned pleasure, saucy impudence. Mickey was all heart, but in the beginning he did not wear it on his sleeve.

At first he was very much a rodent. His limbs were thinner and his features smaller than the later, anthropomorphic version. In *Plane Crazy* (his first film, made as a silent, then released with sound after *Steamboat Willie*) he went barefoot and barehanded, but by *Steamboat Willie* he wore shoes and soon acquired white four-fingered gloves. He was unselfconscious and egocentric, wearing the same confident, self-satisfied grin Edward G. Robinson was to flash a couple of years later as the immigrant gangster Rico in *Little Caesar*. Unlike Rico, however, Mickey had no end. Success eroded him in other ways. "Mickey's our problem child," Disney said later. "He's so much of an institution that we're limited in what we can do with him."[3] He became respectable, bland, gentle, responsible, moral. Donald Duck was added to the Disney cast to provide the old vinegar and bile.

The first four Mickey shorts were made in 1928. The next year the Disney studio produced sixteen cartoons, including a handful of Silly Symphony films. Thereafter they completed a cartoon short about once every three weeks—a total of 198 from *Steamboat Willie* to the end of

[3] Quoted in Leonard Maltin, *The Disney Films* (1973), p. 8.

1939. About half were in the Mickey series, the other half in the Silly Symphony series, the name for all the shorts without the mouse.

In *Plane Crazy*, Mickey is an inventive, willful aviator, a barnyard Lindbergh. He builds his craft from any material at hand, live or inanimate; to provide power for the plane he twists a dachshund like a rubber band, and for its tail he plucks a turkey feather. Once constructed, the airplane also becomes a living thing, as must the objects in its determined path: a church steeple folds itself down to avoid being hit.

It turns out that Mickey's goal is not fame or heroic achievement, it's lechery. He has built the plane to impress his girl friend, Minnie, and get her up in the air where she won't be able to run away from his advances. Instead of submitting, however, she jumps from the plane, pulls a cord on her bloomers, and they billow out to float her safely down.

The public first saw Mickey and Minnie in *Steamboat Willie*, in which the brilliant fusion of music with visual images adds immeasurably to the magic possibilities of plastic forms. A goat eats up Minnie's sheet music. She swiftly twists its tail into a crank, turns it, and the notes come pouring out of the goat's mouth as "Turkey in the Straw" (a scene reminiscent of Chaplin in *The Tramp* pumping a cow's tail and filling his pail with milk). Mickey also made music by playing animals for different sounds—he got melody from, among others, the tails of suckling piglets and then from the teats of the sow.

Disney's early films had their share of raunchy scenes and outhouse humor. Some official responses, however, were even more ludicrous. Ohio was reported to have banned a cartoon showing a cow reading Elinor Glyn's novel of adultery, *Three Weeks*—perhaps because the Buckeye State thought it safe to drink milk only from monogamous cows. Then the Hays Office ordered Disney to take the udders off his cows: thereafter, no matter what they read, their milk at least would not harm anyone.

A taste for the macabre was another strong element in Disney's style, and in early 1929 he launched the Silly Symphony series to express the grisly humor that was out of place in Mickey's sunny world. The first Silly Symphony, *The Skeleton Dance*, depicted a nighttime outing of skeletons in a graveyard, dancing and cavorting to music. One skeleton makes music on another, like a xylophone. *Hell's Bells* (also 1929) was even more grotesque: it takes place in hell, whose inhabitants include a three-headed dog and a dragon cow that gives the devil fiery milk (even Hades has its barnyard aspects).

Disney and his animators knew the value of shock and titillation before the feature producers, and though he often borrowed ideas from popular features, it is as likely that his cartoons fertilized the imaginations of other filmmakers in the early Depression years. In a 1930 Mickey Mouse comedy, *Traffic Troubles*, Mickey and Minnie crash into a truck loaded with chickens and end up covered with feathers, clucking and crowing—a comic fate Tod Browning transmuted into horror for Olga Baclanova two years later in *Freaks*.

Living and inanimate things reverse their roles. In *The Opry House* (1929) Mickey begins to play the piano, but the piano and its stool kick him out. The instrument plays its own keyboard with its front legs, and the stool dances. When it's over, Mickey comes back out and all three take a bow. Mickey's taxicab in *Traffic Troubles* bites a car to grab a parking place, licks a flat tire and goes crazy after drinking "Dr. Pep's Oil." What have those fantasies to do with a culture's myths and dreams?

It would be easy to claim too much for these cartoons, yet their immediate and steadfast popularity makes them of prime interest. In the long-standing style of American humor their extravagance, exaggeration and grotesque imagination serve as mythic constructs of their society. Moreover, as animations they stand at an even further remove from the requirements of verisimilitude. Their fantasy nature frees the viewer's mind from normal expectations of what the world is like, and the simplicity of the drawings, far from signaling stylistic crudity, is a necessary aspect of opening up the imagination. (Disney's press agents later coined the term "imagineering," which is an accurate description of what the later cartoons do—structure all effects so there is no room for the viewer's imagination to operate.)

The early fantasy cartoons are deeply committed to the old American tradition of individual initiative and enterprise. Yet the extreme of their fantastic possibilities, the ease and plenitude of their magical metamorphoses, puts the viewer at a distance from the usual motifs of individualism—hard work, self-denial, upward striving—and throws some of its deeper meanings into bold relief. In the real world, people do indeed turn themselves into instruments and machines to pursue their goals; and machines do in fact take on a life of their own, directing and dominating their supposed masters, taking them places they did not want to go. In a profound way these fantasies do not create myths so much as expose them.

The first signs of the dissolution of the fantasy style came with the increased tempo of violence in Disney's cartoons. By 1932, even in such superbly inventive films as *Touchdown Mickey* and *Building a Building*, the fantasy elements have been almost completely replaced by a spirit of physical and material violence. Pain and injury cause no permanent damage, but that is no longer magical, it is merely a convention.

At the same time, the emotional range of the characters and plots begins to expand. There are more joys and sorrows, pleasures and terrors, but they are cast in a sentimental formula mold. Creatures become more anthropomorphic and less versatile. These changes are prominently exhibited in the first Technicolor cartoon short, *Flowers and Trees* (1932), about a villainous old tree who tries to stop a romance between a boy tree and a girl tree, which won Disney his first Academy award. Mickey Mouse, too, begins to succumb to the pattern of conventional melodrama, heroes and villains and happy endings, in such films as *The Mail Pilot* (1933), which ends with a clinch between Mickey and Min-

Magical transformation in Walt Disney's first sound cartoon and the first Mickey Mouse film to be released, *Steamboat Willie* (1928). Note that Mickey and Minnie are shod but don't yet wear gloves.

nie, instead of the old Chaplinesque impermanence of relations (though it should be said that Chaplin's endings in his silent features, like *The Kid* and *The Gold Rush*, had become more sentimental, too).

Disney's most popular and influential cartoon short, *Three Little Pigs*, came at the climax of his stylistic transition and unites essential aspects of the old and new. It was drawn in the new style of full-color idealization, and it told a familiar moral tale, but by an uncanny prescience Disney picked a story that was open-ended, that left the individual imagination free to decide what it all meant.

Three Little Pigs was released in May 1933, in the midst of Roosevelt's "hundred days" campaign of legislation to combat the Depression and raise public morale. Its upbeat theme song, "Who's Afraid of the Big Bad Wolf?," became a nationwide hit, and Disney could not supply enough prints of the film to meet popular demand. Richard Schickel, in *The Disney Version*, argues that Disney's retelling of the fairy tale of the home-building pigs and the hungry wolf had a basically conservative point, in keeping with the producer's conservative political allegiance: the pig who exhibits old-fashioned virtues, hard work, self-reliance, self-denial, is the successful one. It's just as plausible, however, that the most effective pig is the one who does not minimize the fact of crisis and builds with modern material and tools. No doubt there were some contemporary viewers who, like Schickel, saw the film as a paean to Herbert Hoover, but the film's extraordinary popularity appears to have stemmed, whatever Disney's intentions, from its apparent expression of the confident, purposeful spirit of the early New Deal.

Three Little Pigs was among the last of Disney's cartoons open to multiple interpretation. Thereafter there was no mistaking the films' moral messages. In *Lullaby Land*, made later in 1933, a baby with his toy dog wanders in a dream through a world where nature has been transformed into inanimate household objects. He enters a "Forbidden Garden" filled with plants and trees made of knives, clippers, scissors, pens, hammers, razors, matches and pins. "Baby mustn't touch," watches growing on a tree sing out, "they'll hurt you very much." He gets burned by matches and chased by bogeymen before the sandman rescues him.

This is a message of survival, not by old-fashioned initiative and self-reliance, but by sticking to society's rules, a very different kind of conservatism. The hare in *The Tortoise and the Hare* (1934) is the clever, ambitious one—the preening male who can run so fast that he can pitch a ball and bat it himself, shoot an arrow and be waiting for it like William Tell's son with an apple on his head—and we all know who won the race. The mouse who wanted to fly in *The Flying Mouse* (1934) also learns the hard way: he frightens off the birds he wants to play with and scares his own family by the shadow of his wings, but he doesn't fool the evil bats, who sing, "You're nothin' but a nothin'." The good fairy who gave him his wings rescues him with the admonition: "You've learned your lesson. Do your best. Be yourself. And life will smile on you."

Even Mickey is recruited to the new morality. In *Pluto's Judgement Day* (1935) he's so anthropomorphic that he's an owner of domesticated animals. He rebukes Pluto for chasing the cat, and the dog settles into a troubled sleep near the fire, dreaming of punishment in hell for his misdeeds. The underworld scenes have interesting affinities with *Hell's Bells* (1929) that illuminate the transformation of Disney's style. In the earlier film they are a fantasy, in the later, a dream, carefully bounded by waking reality: they are not magic, not out of time, they are part of Pluto's imagination, not accessible to the viewer's.

No account of Disney's later 1930s cartoon shorts would be complete without paying tribute to their remarkable feats of sound, color and animation, their sustained inventiveness, their frequent brilliance of design and conception. Such films as *The Band Concert*, *Music Land* (both 1935) and *The Old Mill* (1937) are tours de force of tight construction, pace and the steady building of effects to a spectacular and satisfying climax. But one should not lose sight of what their style signifies; there is one right way to imagine (as elsewhere there is one right way to behave). The borders to fantasy are closed now. The time has come to lay aside one's own imagination, and together all shall dream Walt Disney's dreams.

There is not quite so dramatic a shift in the style and message of Frank Capra's movies during the 1930s, yet in mid-decade the comedy director basically reoriented his work in remarkably similar ways. His early films of the Depression era were fantasies of social relationships, his later movies idealizations. The mythic structure of the earlier films encouraged viewers to exercise their imaginations, though it constructed a world they could never enter. The later movies provided an integrated prepackaged network of myths and dreams and invited viewers to join in.

When Disney was having distribution difficulties in 1930 it was Capra who persuaded Harry Cohn, head of Columbia Pictures, to take over the distribution of cartoon shorts; though the arrangement lasted only two years, it assured Disney of independent control over his own production and set him on the road to financial success. Considering how different their origins were, surprising affinities existed between Capra, a Sicilian-born Catholic, and Disney, a Kansas Congregationalist. They both knew the rural and small-town heartland of America. Their comic talents veered toward sentimentality and they were imbued with social purpose, a desire to revitalize the nation's old communal myths.

Capra had got his schooling in American folkways when he spent three years after World War I roaming through the Western states, making a living, among other things, as a door-to-door salesman and cardsharp. (He had immigrated with his family to Los Angeles at the age of six, earned an engineering degree at Cal Tech, and served in the Army during the war.) He started out in Hollywood writing comedy shorts for Hal Roach and Mack Sennett. When the comedian Harry Langdon left Sennett, he took Capra with him to direct his independent productions.

Capra succeeded too well: the features he directed for Langdon—*Tramp, Tramp, Tramp*, *The Strong Man* (both 1926) and *Long Pants* (1927)—propelled the baby-faced comedian into the forefront of silent comedy with Chaplin, Keaton and Lloyd, and Langdon thereupon fired him, resenting the Hollywood gossip that Capra was principally responsible for his success. Thereafter Langdon swiftly faded from prominence while Capra began a comeback at Columbia, a marginal, "Poverty Row" independent studio, where his popular, profitable films helped keep the studio solvent through the Depression and enhanced its reputation as it rose to become a major producing company.

At Columbia, Capra started out as a jack-of-all-trades, making military spectacles, drawing-room melodramas and romances as well as comedies—fifteen pictures in his first four years with the company. He re-established his comic métier when he began, in 1931, to collaborate with Robert Riskin, a New York playwright scooped up in the Hollywood dragnet for screen writers after the coming of sound. Capra and Riskin first worked together on *Platinum Blonde*, and thereafter Riskin wrote scripts for eight of the director's eleven films over the next decade.

Neither the screen writer nor the comedy genre was essential, however, to Capra's fantasy style. Fantasy, as the word is used here, is meant to apply not only to supernatural illusions (flying nuns or Clarence the Apprentice Angel in Capra's 1946 film, *It's a Wonderful Life*) but to formula constructions in popular entertainment, a way of depicting the issues and conflicts of human relations so that everything comes out all right in the end—a way of pleasing audiences with glimpses of the forbidden or impossible without upsetting conventional values or beliefs: in short, the finely honed mass-media skill of having it both ways.

Capra presented a remarkable example of it in *The Bitter Tea of General Yen* (1933). Its subject was miscegenation, sexual relations between an Oriental man and a Caucasian woman. An extremely well made package, the film achieved the basic Hollywood goal of satisfaction without transgression. The very idea that a white woman might be interested in an Asian man, however, was enough to make Great Britain ban *The Bitter Tea* both in the United Kingdom and throughout the empire.

In the film Barbara Stanwyck is an American missionary, Megan Davis, in China during the civil war in the early 1920s. She is rescued from a riot and carried away to the estate of warlord General Yen (played by a Swede, Nils Asther). Her racist superiority conflicts with her Christian principle that "we're all of one flesh and blood." His refinement and sensuality conflict with his brutal military leadership. They are drawn to each other, Yen willfully ("I am going to convert a missionary"), Megan in spite of herself: sleeping in a sumptuous Oriental bedroom, she dreams of sex with Yen.

In the end each comes over to the other's point of view, but the film demonstrates how impossible this is. His lust turned to love, Yen succumbs to her morality, suffers military defeat and then prefers death to violating her virgin purity. As he prepares his poisoned tea he doesn't know she has fallen in love with him. She enters his room as he fades into death and says to him, weeping, "I'll never leave you." The film offers a fantasy of interracial sex without the consummation; it proclaims the superiority of Western morals—Yen accepts death as a punishment for his evil designs on a white woman, and she, having avoided her transgression but realizing its moral implications, promises posthumous faithfulness. It's nice to dream of interracial sex, the film says, but you better not try it.

Following *The Bitter Tea of General Yen*, Capra made his two most successful fantasy comedies, *Lady for a Day* (1933) and *It Happened One Night* (1934). These two films, particularly the latter, have mistakenly been described as "screwball" comedies, and it is useful to distinguish Capra's fantasy world from the wacky style that became prevalent several years later. In screwball comedies the screwballs are the rich: sometimes they enlist the less well-to-do (as in *Easy Living* or *My Man Godfrey*, where the poor man is actually a rich man in disguise), and sometimes they inspire common folk to beat them at their own game (as in *Midnight*). In Capra's comic fantasies, imagination comes from below and requires recognition and participation by the rich or powerful to make one's dreams come true.

It Happened One Night is the classic motion-picture expression of an important sub-genre in American popular entertainment—the genteel comedy-romance. The formula begins with a bored, headstrong rich girl looking for adventure and mixes in an imaginative, aspiring poor man. Fate throws them together. She finds she's in adventure over her head, but the young man's cleverness saves her. He is entranced by her will, she by his imagination, and before you know it they've fallen in love. It's a fantasy of upward social mobility and romantic love, a comedy of submission and reward. The rich girl gives up her freedom for the hero, the poor boy weds his vitality and vision to the dominant social class.

Capra and Riskin made their version of this formula fresh and distinctive by taking it out of the narrow social setting of the rich and endowing it with commonplace scenes of everyday life. The rich girl, Ellie Andrews, played by Claudette Colbert, dives off her father's yacht along the Florida Gulf Coast and takes a night bus to New York, where she plans to elope with a rich aviator. On the bus she encounters Peter Warne (Clark Gable), a newspaper reporter just dismissed from his job who discovers her identity and figures he can get his job back by writing an exclusive story on her escapade. But first he has to protect her from her father's detectives. Their common pleasures and their masquerades—singing "The Daring Young Man on the Flying Trapeze" with their fellow bus passengers; posing as a sparring married couple in a motor court; trying to hitch a ride—demonstrate Capra's extraordinary inventiveness at creating warm incisive humor out of simple moments.

THE MUSEUM OF MODERN ART/FILM STILLS ARCHIVE

Bedroom scenes from Frank Capra's fantasies of the early 1930s: Barbara Stanwyck (top) in *The Bitter Tea of General Yen* (1933); Claudette Colbert and Clark Gable (bottom) in *It Happened One Night* (1934). Unmarried and sharing the same bedroom, they've put up a blanket on a clothesline, a "Wall of Jericho," between them. At the end of the movie, the wall comes tumbling down.

THE MUSEUM OF MODERN ART/FILM STILLS ARCHIVE

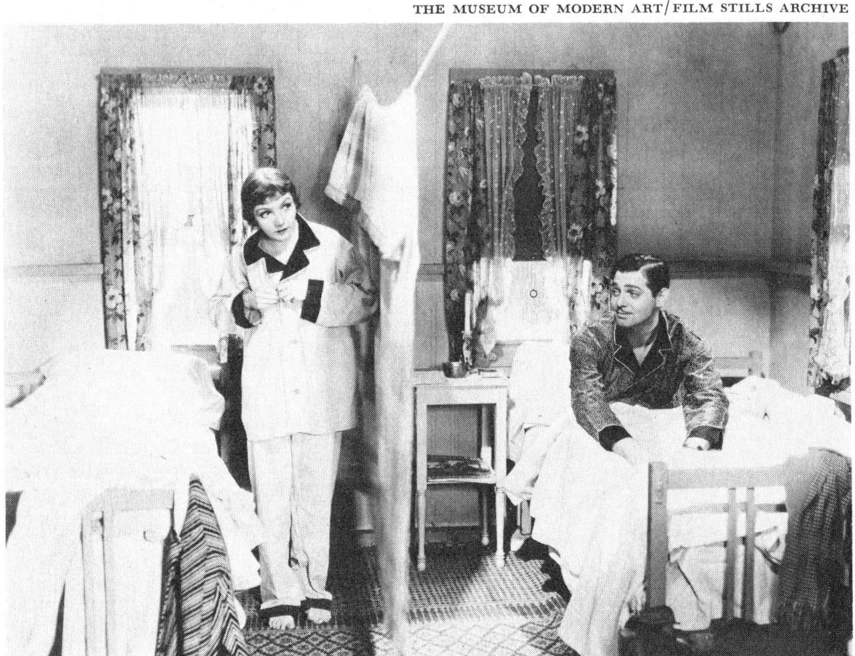

The brilliant complication of *It Happened One Night* is that the two have fallen in love and neither knows the other's feeling. Naturally, misunderstandings occur and they separate, he to his job, she to marry her aviator. It takes the kind and knowing heart of a rich man, her father, to bring them together again. The final fantasy touch is for Ellie's father, as they walk to the altar at her sumptuous outdoor wedding, to whisper that Warne is waiting for her in a car. Instead of saying "I do," she runs across the lawn to go off with the man who had kept her, as she said, "thoroughly entertained."

"Say, look, you believe in fairy tales, don't you?" gangster Dave the Dude says to the governor and mayor of New York in *Lady for a Day* (based on the Damon Runyon story "Madame La Gimp"), inviting them to help him carry out a masquerade for the apple-seller Annie and marry off her daughter to a Spanish nobleman. Of course they do, and once again people in power and authority make the fairy-tale ending come true. These interventions are magical in a sense quite similar to Disney's early cartoons: one believes them in the context of the image on the screen, one is stimulated and satisfied by all that transpires, yet in the end it is fantasy pure and simple. Eventually Capra, like Disney, wanted to attain more socially purposeful effects.

Capra tells his own fantasy of the intervention that brought about his change: a bald man wearing thick glasses came to his house when he lay ill and rebuked him for not using his creative talents more to God's and humanity's purposes. That presumably was the turning point that led him to make five social-message films in the next half-dozen years: *Mr. Deeds Goes to Town* (1936), *Lost Horizon* (1937), *You Can't Take It With You* (1938), *Mr. Smith Goes to Washington* (1939) and *Meet John Doe* (1941).

Capra was not alone in continuing to make films on contemporary social themes when other filmmakers increasingly turned to genre or historical subjects. But the tendency of Hollywood's social films in the late 1930s was to focus on narrow "problems" or aberrant behavior: slum conditions, as in William Wyler's *Dead End* (1937); the lynch mob, as in Fritz Lang's *Fury* (1936); the plight of the ex-convict, in Lang's *You Only Live Once* (1937). Capra was the only Hollywood director who tried to construct a large-scale model of American society in his films.

When he shifted from fantasy to an idealized version of social relations, Capra did not need to alter his approach radically; instead he rearranged and re-emphasized the elements of his earlier style. The imaginative hero remained central to his formula, though he became more folksy and bucolic—Gary Cooper playing Longfellow Deeds and Long John Willoughby (John Doe), James Stewart as Jefferson Smith—rather than a sharp-tongued reporter like Clark Gable's Peter Warne or Robert Williams' Stew Smith in *Platinum Blonde*. The role of the press and publicity continued to be important, and authority figures continued to take a significant part in validating the fairy tale: judges in *Mr. Deeds* and *You Can't Take It With You*, the Vice-President of the United States in *Mr. Smith*. The major changes concerned the wealthy: rich young women became unsuitable for the hero, and the power of wealthy men, sinister rather than benign, a subject for redemption, or failing that, opposition.

In the heart of the hero the rich girl's place is taken by a working woman; instead of wealth and power giving aid to the hero's dreams, it's "the people" who rally behind him. Capra's social myth requires the recognition and participation of common people to make it come true; it's a myth in which audiences are assured they, too, have a part to play.

These later films have often been attacked for their "Populist" ideology—for sentimentality, demagoguery, anti-intellectualism, a belief in tyranny of the majority; for idealizing small-town and "middle" Americans who think they can do no wrong because their motives are pure and who hate lawyers, bankers, artists, intellectuals and urbanites. In any precise sense of the word Populist, this is clearly a misnomer. Capra's social myth, it's true, required turning back the clock to an imagined past social stability founded upon an image of the American small town, with comfortable homes, close-knit families, friendly neighbors—a modest but prosperous community with bountiful farms and a benign wilderness nearby. Unlike actual Populists in the American past, he was not making a critique of the American social and economic system, did not even want a redistribution of wealth and power. He simply wanted more neighborly and responsible people to be at the top of the social and economic hierarchy. It is closer to the truth to describe him as a Jeffersonian agrarian, or more simply, a pastoralist.

Capra's late-1930s films are myths about false leaders and true. The false leaders are tycoons, media barons, political bosses, kept politicians. The true leaders are idealistic, gentle young men who can articulate the pastoral dream, as in Longfellow Deeds's plan to spend his inherited millions on small plots for destitute farmers, Jefferson Smith's boys' camp in the Western outdoors, John Doe's network of clubs where people can practice Capra's social ethic, which Jefferson Smith described as "plain, ordinary, everyday kindness, a little looking out for the other fella, loving thy neighbor."

The false leaders have all the power; the true leaders have only moral right as their weapon. In each of Capra's idealized social fables, as the historian Warren Susman has pointed out, the hero must suffer through a ritual humiliation. The purpose of this abasement is to show that the hero is vulnerable and incomplete—he is a leader, but he needs help, the "people's" help, *our* help, to accomplish his vital task. The working girl, a reporter in *Mr. Deeds Goes to Town* and *Meet John Doe*, a senatorial secretary in *Mr. Smith Goes to Washington*, is cynical at first, then changes her mind and comes to his aid, gaining in return her femininity and a chance to lead a full emotional life. The hard-bitten reporters also change and rally to his cause. Authority figures sense his true worth and give him the smile or wink of approval. Last but not least, the people give him strength to carry on.

Nevertheless, once Capra's heroes begin their open struggles with wealth and power, they find themselves unable to triumph by asserting their strength and invoking their alliances. The false leaders are simply too wealthy and powerful. The heroes' only hope for success lies in persuading their opponents voluntarily to join the righteous side. They attempt this by demonstrating the efficacy of their social myths and then by prodding the villains to express the humane values they have suppressed during their struggle to the top. The tactic works perfectly in *You Can't Take It With You*, ambiguously in *Mr. Smith Goes to Washington*, and not at all in *Meet John Doe*.

In *You Can't Take It With You* the gift of a harmonica is the symbolic act that recalls Edward Arnold, as the tycoon Kirby, to his humanity. Kirby cancels the business deal that would have destroyed the Vanderhof house and also wrecked his son's chance for love and happiness with Alice Sycamore, Martin Vanderhof's granddaughter. In the movie's happy ending the Kirbys are sharing the human warmth and recognition of the Vanderhof household.

The conclusion of *Mr. Smith Goes to Washington* is far more equivocal. As Smith exhausts himself in an apparently futile filibuster against the crooked Taylor machine, Claude Rains, as Senator Joseph Paine, finds himself torn between his connivance with Taylor and his admiration for Smith's courageous fight in a lost cause. Paine fires a gun in the Senate cloakroom, apparently an attempted suicide, then enters the Senate to throw his support to Smith. But his change of heart does not ensure that back-room political boss and businessman Jim Taylor will change his heart, too. At the end of *Mr. Smith Goes to Washington*, the United States Senate erupts in pandemonium and the outcome of the struggle remains in doubt.

In *Meet John Doe*, Capra's last film of the prewar period, the hero is hardly imaginative in the old formula sense at all, and the villain more powerful and ambitious than ever. Long John Willoughby is merely an ex-baseball pitcher on the bum who allows himself to be put forward as a symbolic common man—*the* John Doe in a nation of John Does—as part of publisher D. B. Norton's scheme to gain national power. When called upon to speak to the public, he draws out of himself Capra's familiar social myths: everybody pull together, join the team, love your neighbor. Soon he begins to believe in his own words, but by that time he's powerless in the face of his past compromises and Norton's political and media control.

In his autobiography Capra describes the difficulties he and Riskin experienced in finishing *Meet John Doe*. He filmed four different endings and played them all in different theater previews. None was satisfactory. "I *knew* Riskin and I had written ourselves into a corner," he recalls. "We had shown the rise of two powerful, opposing movements—one good, one evil. They clashed head on—and *destroyed each other*! St.

George fought with the dragon, slew it, and was slain. What our film said to bewildered people hungry for solutions was this, 'No answers this time, ladies and gentlemen. It's back to the drawing board.' "[4] But at last they shot a fifth ending and put it on the film.

Trapped in a situation he cannot control, remorseful about his own role, Long John Willoughby determines to fulfill the original phony John Doe promise by jumping off a building in "protest against the state of civilization," a civilization in this case that has allowed his good impulses to be used falsely, has turned people against each other and against him. Capra and Riskin needed to decide—does he jump, and if not, why not? In their fifth and final ending Doe is persuaded not to jump, because their solution was to transmute the Capra hero into a modern Christ. He doesn't have to die, as the working woman who loves him says, because someone else—the first John Doe—already died in a similar cause.

The parallel between Long John Willoughby and Jesus Christ has its obvious shortcomings, but it is more of an answer than Capra is willing to admit in his autobiography. It linked the Capra hero directly to the Christian faith. Representatives of the common people confront the villain Norton atop the skyscraper from which Doe is prepared to jump, and their veneration, their need, change his mind. "There you are, Norton—the people," says the cynical reporter in the last words of the film, "try and lick that." Good and evil were not destroyed, as Capra claims, but rather had fought to a standstill, and both sides lived to fight another day.

In the process of turning John Doe into a Christ-figure, Capra transformed the myth of his American hero into a defense of Christian morality. No longer is Shangri-La, the Tibetan retreat of James Hilton's novel and Capra's 1937 movie, *Lost Horizon*, the sanctuary for the Christian ethic: it has become the United States. After Pearl Harbor, the struggle between good and evil moved from the realm of an internal conflict into the titanic battle of fascism versus Americanism. And what was Americanism? It was the rewards of social stability—wealth, success and the girl for the hero; fellowship, happiness and trustworthy leaders for the rest of us. It was a religious faith in a secular social myth that found its embodiment in patriotism and American democracy.

Capra made the point vividly in *The Negro Soldier* (1944), a film he produced for the War Department in his capacity as head of wartime film propaganda for the Armed Forces. It tells its story through the device of a worship service in a black church; while its capsule summary of black history never mentions slavery, it conveys the overwhelming impression that the black congregation gives its witness and sings its hymns in worship of America.

Earlier in the war Capra had begun production of the famous "Why We Fight" series of films explaining war aims to new soldiers and sailors.

---

[4] *The Name Above the Title* (1971), p. 305.

THE MUSEUM OF MODERN ART/FILM STILLS ARCHIVE

Capra's heroes in his late-Depression films suffer public humiliation and rejection before their ultimate moral triumph: James Stewart as Jefferson Smith (top) discovers the baskets are filled with telegrams sent by his political enemies in *Mr. Smith Goes to Washington* (1939), while Claude Rains, his challenger, looks on; Gary Cooper as "John Doe" (bottom) is hooted by his erstwhile followers at a mass political rally after a newspaper exposé by his former backer, a proto-fascist publisher, in *Meet John Doe* (1941).

THE MUSEUM OF MODERN ART/FILM STILLS ARCHIVE

Disney, too, though not in uniform, made a large number of wartime training and civilian propaganda films. The struggle against fascism transformed his bad guy, Donald Duck, into a patriotic taxpayer in a cartoon short for the Treasury Department, *Der Fuehrer's Face* (1943).

When General George C. Marshall assigned him the responsibility for the "Why We Fight" films, Capra reports in his autobiography, he asked the Chief of Staff how he would know what to say. What if no one, neither the White House nor the State Department nor the Congress, could tell him why the United States took a course of action or adopted a policy? "In those cases," replied Marshall, "make your own best estimate, and see if they don't agree with you later."[5]

The government had confidence in Capra, and in Disney as well. They had demonstrated remarkable skill at infusing social myths and dreams with humor, sentiment and a sense of shared moral precepts and responsibilities. No one in Hollywood was better equipped than they to convince wartime audiences that America was worth fighting for, that there were pleasures, satisfactions and rewards in store for those who followed their leaders.

---

[5] *Ibid.*, p. 336.

13

SELLING MOVIES OVERSEAS

American movies presented American myths and American dreams, home-grown for native audiences, yet only man-made boundaries kept them from conquering the world. The Soviet Union responded to the global popularity of Mickey Mouse by creating its own cartoon hero, a porcupine, to divert its children from Disney's bourgeois moralisms. In 1942, when the Vichy government banned American movies, a number of theaters in Nazi-occupied France ran *Mr. Smith Goes to Washington* as a symbolic political gesture.

These were conscious responses to overt social messages; what attracted foreign audiences to American movies on an everyday basis was their implicit descriptions of American values and styles, their speed, humor, brashness, glamour, their satire and violence, their open spaces and glittering cities, their cowboys and entrepreneurs. Since the eighteenth century, America had had a fascination for people in other lands. The movies carried their views of America to more people in more places than ever before. In the years between the two world wars, except where governments imposed limits, American motion pictures, and hence American images, ideals and products, almost completely dominated the world's cinema screens—a near-monopoly unprecedented in American overseas commerce, as well as one of the most remarkable hegemonies in the history of intercultural communications.

The origin of American ascendency did not lie in superior American enterprise, however, but in the ill fortunes of the other leading film producers. The 1914–1918 war had given American filmmakers their opportunity, and they held their advantage for a quarter century, until war again intervened. In the absence of foreign competition, Americans gained full control of their home market for the first time and replaced the Europeans as principal film suppliers to the nonbelligerent areas of the world, particularly Latin America and Japan.

By the end of World War I, the United States possessed well over half the world's movie theaters; twenty years later, despite a steady rise in theater construction elsewhere in the world and some contraction in the number of domestic outlets, American cinemas still comprised around 40 percent of the world-wide total. Statistics here as elsewhere in the movie field are notoriously unreliable, but the significance of even such general estimates can be readily grasped. Through their policy of theater ownership and block-booking, the major studios could budget their annual production with a fair degree of certainty that their pictures would obtain enough play dates at sufficiently high prices to return their original costs. In practice, during the interwar years, American pictures as a whole did no better than break even at the domestic box office. But with production costs already covered, every ticket sold outside the United States, less overseas distribution costs, produced profit.

American producers held an unbeatable advantage over their foreign competitors. They could pour money into "production values"—sumptuous costumes, expensive sets, crowds of extras, breath-taking location scenery—knowing that the more spectacular and expensive their pictures looked, the more they appealed to overseas audiences. For European and Asian producers, lacking guaranteed bookings and with a much smaller market, filmmaking was a far greater gamble, and capital far more difficult to find. They were forced to hold down production costs, and their movies looked it.

The moviemakers were also in an unusually favorable position in relation to other American manufacturers of exported goods. Motion-picture film was one of the very few products made to a universal world standard: every country used film of the same width with the same space between sprocket holes. In the silent period, moreover, movies had no language boundaries to cross. Printed titles could easily be replaced in non-English-speaking countries, or eliminated entirely, as in Japan, where a storyteller narrated his own version of the events on the screen.

This remarkable confluence of circumstances propelled American moviemakers to the forefront of efforts to expand the nation's overseas trade. American industry was far from being isolationist in the post–World War I years, and the motion-picture industry, as *Scientific American* wrote in 1921, became "infected with the new spirit of internationalism which has taken such firm root in the economic and industrial life of the country as the result of the seizure of war-time opportunities."[1]

Four years later the *Saturday Evening Post* altered with some pleasure a familiar cliché of world politics. "The sun, it now appears," said the *Post*, "never sets on the British Empire and the American motion picture."[2] Two decades before Henry Luce's famous *Life* editorial proclaimed the American Century, Hollywood helped lay the groundwork for America's awakening desire to assume the imperial role.

"Trade follows the film" became a favorite dictum of economic expansionists in the 1920s.[3] Though no one was able to produce more than impressionistic evidence to support the idea, it was widely accepted, with pleasure or foreboding, depending on one's point of view. In the British House of Lords a member rose to complain that Midlands fac-

---

[1] Editorial note with O. R. Geyer, "Winning Foreign Film Markets," *Scientific American*, Vol. 125 (August 20, 1921), p. 132.

[2] Edward G. Lowry, "Trade Follows the Film," *Saturday Evening Post*, Vol. 198 (November 7, 1925), p. 12.

[3] *Ibid.*

tories were forced to alter their design patterns because customers in the Middle East demanded shoes and clothes modeled after those worn by American stars. Japanese tailors were said to be attending American movies to learn how to cut the styles demanded by their Western-minded patrons. In Brazil the sale of a particular American car model was reported to have gone up 35 percent after it was featured in a newly arrived Hollywood film. Architects in the same country began building California-style bungalows.

Get the movies to foreign peoples, and orders for clothes, cars, furniture and appliances would soon come trailing back: this logic prompted Congress in 1926 to appropriate $15,000 to establish a Motion Picture Section in the Bureau of Foreign and Domestic Commerce, under the direction of Commerce Secretary Herbert Hoover. Its goal was to promote the rental of American movies and the sale of motion-picture equipment overseas. Though reformers were quick to protest government sponsorship of movie exports without any federal willingness to monitor film content, it was to no avail. The next year the Motion Picture Section began publishing frequent reports about the information it gathered on opportunities, conditions and policies in foreign countries. The first, perhaps symbolically, was on the Chinese motion-picture market. In 1927 there were only 106 theaters in all of China, with a seating capacity of 68,512, and no doubt visions were dancing in the head of many a motion-picture executive of a day when a fairer proportion of China's 400 million population would have a chance to see an American film.

In all, the Bureau circulated twenty-two reports, covering all areas of the globe, from 1927 to 1933, when it shifted to an annual review of foreign film markets in one volume. With information gathered from American consular, commercial and diplomatic representatives overseas, the Bureau's surveys are among the few available sources of data on cinema production and exhibition throughout the world.

They reveal starkly the American domination of the world's cinema screens. American studios produced around 700 feature films a year at the height of the silent period; no more than three or four other countries were able to create even a tenth as many: Germany, with 241 films in 1927; India, which made more films as a colony than did its foreign ruler, Great Britain; Japan; and France. The British produced only 44 features in 1927, and half a dozen other European countries made from 5 to 17. China produced approximately 20, and here and there, as in New Zealand or Australia, feature-length films were created.

Statistics about the number of films shown in a country can be misleading if they do not take into account the frequency of bookings and play dates. In France during the silent period, for example, American films consistently comprised more than two thirds of all films released, yet they were largely confined to a few Parisian theaters. In most countries, the United States' share of total releases ranged from 75 to 90 percent. The largest numbers of American films were taken during the

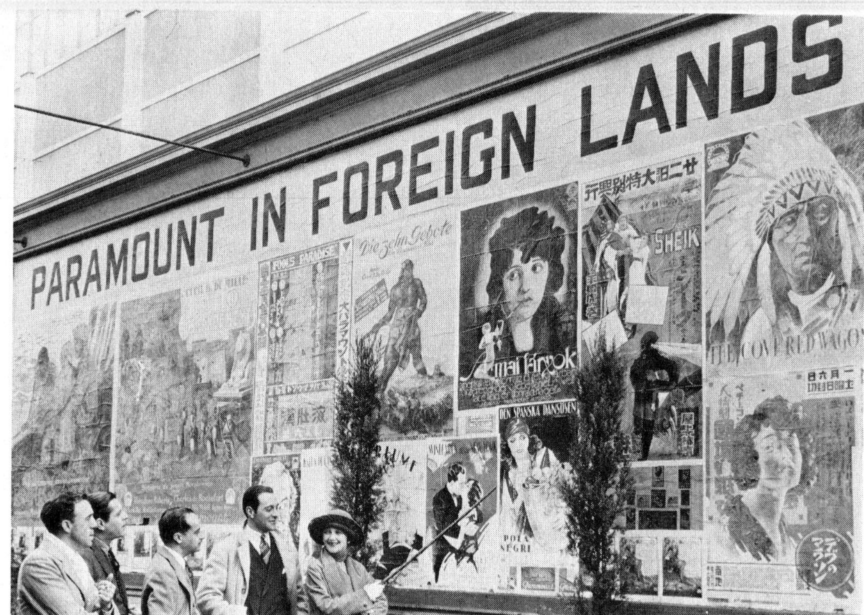

THE MUSEUM OF MODERN ART/FILM STILLS ARCHIVE

American-made movies dominated the world's motion-picture screens from World War I to the 1950s. A billboard at Paramount studios in the 1920s (top) displayed posters of its films in many languages: Jetta Goudal, at right, holds the pointer, and looking on, from left, are Raoul Walsh, Warner Baxter, Paul Bern and Ricardo Cortez. Two decades later, American movies were still packing them in at the New Elphinstone theater in Madras, India (bottom). *Tarzan and the Leopard Woman* (1946) is the feature, with *Earl Carroll Vanities* (1945) on tap.

QUIGLEY PHOTOGRAPHIC ARCHIVE, GEORGETOWN UNIVERSITY LIBRARY

1920s by Australia, Argentina and Brazil, in that order. The British Empire market was completely in the hands of American producers. More galling yet, in Great Britain more than 80 percent of the films shown were American, and British producers succeeded in claiming no more than 4 to 5 percent of their domestic market.

It did not take other nations less time than Americans to recognize the potential economic consequences of American motion-picture dominance. "If the United States abolished its diplomatic and consular services," wrote the London *Morning Post* in 1923, "kept its ships in harbour and its tourists at home, and retired from the world's markets, its citizens, its problems, its towns and countryside, its roads, motor cars, counting houses and saloons would still be familiar in the uttermost corners of the world. . . . The film is to America what the flag was once to Britain. By its means Uncle Sam may hope some day, if he be not checked in time, to Americanize the world."[4]

In the mid-1920s the more immediate problem for European countries was not whether Uncle Sam was about to Americanize the world—that they had yet to look forward to—but whether Uncle Adolph, Uncle Marcus, Uncle Carl and others could be prevented from Americanizing the world's movies. What was at stake was the survival of their film industries, or even the chance to break into film production at all. Different countries tried various plans to hold back the American tide, or regulate the flow of imports as a means of fostering domestic production. At best their efforts had negligible effect; at worst they encouraged American producers to seek power over European production as well as their own.

Germany was the first country to tilt against the American colossus. The German film industry had made a remarkable recovery after World War I: it was second to the United States in number of films produced, and in the eyes of most film observers, second to none in quality. But during Germany's period of economic instability it had not been able to attain sound financial footing, and Hollywood had frequently raided its best talent. In 1925 the German government put into effect a *Kontingent*, or quota, system: the number of films allowed to be imported would be limited to the level of domestic production; for every feature film made in Germany, a permit would be issued to bring in one foreign film.

The American uncles did not much like such restraint. Knowing the precarious financial circumstances of the German studios, several of them offered loans to keep German production afloat in return for various trade advantages—access to German studio facilities, distribution networks and theaters. Adolph Zukor and Marcus Loew put up $4 million in loans to UFA, the major German producing company; Universal and William Fox also acquired interests in German studios.

---

[4] Quoted, *ibid.*

The principal goal of these ventures was to make sure German studios produced sufficient films to provide Hollywood movies with access to the German market. As a result, a considerable share of domestic production was devoted to so-called "quota films" (later, when the practice shifted to Great Britain, they were called "quota quickies"): movies made for the primary purpose of acquiring a quota certificate permitting the importation of American films. Once such a film was recorded by the import authorities, it mattered little whether it was released to theaters or forgotten on the shelf.

These abuses of the quota system quickly became obvious, and within three years it was scrapped in favor of an import-licensing scheme with no direct link to domestic production. The quota films were not, however, an unmitigated disaster for the German film industry. They did not differ greatly from the majority of postwar German films ground out, like low-budget American program pictures, as potboilers to raise money for expensive special films, and an occasional quota film made with skill, style and talent added to the reputation of German cinema. Furthermore, as the film scholar Siegfried Kracauer points out, without the influx of American money in the 1925–1927 quota years, the German film industry might have gone under.

Austria, Italy and Hungary followed Germany's lead with the more modest aim of giving their fledgling film production a push. But no scheme managed to bring about any appreciable decline in the preponderance of American movies abroad. Great Britain observed the failure with interest. As a leading commercial nation with a great cultural heritage in literature and drama, Britain was in the embarrassing position of being barely able to get one of its own films among every twenty shown at its cinemas. Having always taken a superior attitude toward American culture, the British press and cultural guardians stood aghast at the American conquest of their movie theaters, at the insidious influence of American mannerisms, values and language habits upon moviegoers of all classes. They demanded for their anemic film industry a system of government nurture, which, unlike the continental efforts, would be sure to produce results.

Late in 1927 Parliament enacted a law providing for a long-term quota system. It required that for 1928 a minimum of 7½ percent of all films distributed, and 5 percent of all films exhibited, be of British manufacture. These percentages were to rise by increments of 2½ percent until they both reached 20 percent by 1936; the act would expire after a decade, in 1938, at which time the needs of the British film industry for government protection would be reconsidered. In addition, the act prohibited block- and blind-booking, practices the Americans had successfully imported into Great Britain which, if unchecked, virtually guaranteed Hollywood producers as large a share of the British market as they cared to claim.

The American moguls had already learned from their German experience how to get along in a country that wanted to foster its own film industry. All you needed to do was buy a share of that industry, and thereafter its prosperity was yours as well. Warner Bros. and Fox established production units in Great Britain to make quota films. In addition, William Fox bought a controlling interest in the Gaumont British Picture Corporation, the largest British production-distribution-exhibition company, and after his downfall his holdings passed to successor companies, ending up in the hands of Twentieth Century-Fox. Other American studios, functioning as distributors in Great Britain, arranged to fulfill their minimum-quota requirements by financing independent British producers to make quota films.

On paper, the consequences of the 1927 Quota Act looked good for British filmmaking; in practice, the government's efforts barely altered American control of the British market. Consistently, from 1928 on, the number of British films ran about 10 percent ahead of the minimum-quota figure: in 1936, when the 20 percent level was reached, the actual percentage of British films registered in the United Kingdom was 29.5 percent. But it is generally accepted that half that number were quota films produced by American subsidiaries in Britain or by British producers for American distributors. Since the number of Hollywood-made films imported into Great Britain in 1936 was 67 percent of all films registered, half the British total as well gave the American companies about 82 percent of the market. (Again one should recognize that, as in Germany, some worthy films were made because of the quota system.)

France still remained to take on the American giant. The French had once been the world's premier film-producing nation, and when they spoke up early in 1928, they took the startling position that the best defense is a good offense.

The French policy, put forward by a special commission and approved swiftly thereafter by the government, was this: for every seven foreign films imported into France, one French film was to be purchased and exhibited overseas. The importation of foreign films was to be divided up, four to the Americans, two to the Germans, one to the British. Thus the American film companies were to buy one French film for every four of their own shown in France. In 1926 some 444 American films had been imported into France, in 1927 some 368. In the latter year France had made 74 films, of which 10 had reached American shores. Taking the 1927 figure as a base, American companies, even if they imported the entire French output, would have to take a drastic cut of nearly 20 percent of the pictures they could send to France.

In retaliation the American producers talked of boycott: let the French government see how long it could resist its own people, aroused by the loss of Charlie Chaplin and Tom Mix. Will H. Hays set sail for France to avert an international crisis. For nearly a month he conducted arduous negotiations with French officials, taking the position that the French plan was contrary to international trade agreements to which both countries were parties. Eventually the French conceded the point. They toned down their restrictions and eliminated the provision requiring American purchase of French films. Instead, for every French film produced, seven foreign films could be imported into France, and all seven could be from one country. For each French film shown outside of France, two additional foreign films could be imported. Finally, the United States was permitted to import 60 percent of its 1927 total free of the foregoing restrictions. This triumph of Hays Office diplomacy was certain at least to maintain if not to increase the 63 percent share of the French market Americans held in 1927.

At the very moment when the Americans had thrown back the strongest challenge Europeans could offer, the coming of sound threatened to undermine the foundation of their world hegemony. Sound gave the European film industries a tremendous psychological lift and a new weapon against American domination. The British in particular were convinced their time had arrived. Who on earth would care to hear the American language—especially in Dominion countries like Australia and New Zealand—when they could hear proper English spoken? The sudden spurt of British production in 1928–1929 can be attributed as much to British optimism about sound as to the impact of the Quota Act.

Hollywood, in its turn, was racked by gloom and anxiety. The studio managers agreed with the European assessment: audiences in any particular country would prefer to see their national compatriots in talking movies, speaking the native tongue. The only saving element in the situation was the moguls' firm belief that foreign films couldn't hold a candle to American-made movies for glamour, pace, spectacle or mass-audience appeal. Hollywood decided to make its own foreign-language movies and beat the Europeans at their own game.

At the big studios like MGM and Paramount, complete foreign casts were assembled to make duplicate performances of American features, taking over the sets as soon as the English-language players were finished with them. As soon as Garbo completed *Anna Christie*, she remade it in German with a new director and, except for her, a whole new cast. The most famous dual-language production was Josef von Sternberg's *The Blue Angel* (1930), made in Berlin in English and German versions in a collaboration between UFA and Paramount.

A former production manager at Paramount, Robert T. Kane, got the idea of putting the practice of multiple-language productions into effect on an assembly-line basis. He rented studios in Paris and began producing a feature simultaneously in French, Swedish and Spanish versions, meanwhile building his own plant in Joinville and gathering an international staff of technicians, directors and players. By the time Kane was ready to begin large-scale production, Adolph Zukor and Jesse L. Lasky had hurriedly sailed to Europe and paid him a call. Kane rejoined Paramount as European production manager, and the Joinville studios became the European branch of Paramount. In 1930, its first full year, the Joinville operation produced sixty-six features in twelve different languages.

Josef von Sternberg's *The Blue Angel* (1930) was the most memorable result of the movie studios' brief efforts at dual-language production immediately after the introduction of sound. It was a joint Paramount-UFA production, filmed in Berlin simultaneously in English- and German-language versions, with Erich Pommer as producer. Marlene Dietrich played the cabaret singer Lola, and Emil Jannings was Professor

After the winter of 1930–1931, however, the rapidly worsening world depression put an end to Hollywood's foreign-language production. It turned out, in any case, that audiences were not so nationalistic as producers had thought. As the quality of sound recording improved, it was possible to synchronize dubbed sound tracks with sufficient clarity and precision so that foreign languages apparently came out of the mouths of American performers. Some films, however, seemed so quintessentially American that foreign moviegoers preferred the original sound tracks, even without subtitles: Lewis Milestone's *The Front Page* (1931), a film that left European commentators breathless with its speed, cynicism and effrontery, so completely expressed an American style that no one could have believed Pat O'Brien or Adolphe Menjou if they spoke German or French. Thereafter American studios and their European distributors adopted an eclectic approach, dubbing, adding printed subtitles or releasing the original American versions, depending on what each film required or different countries desired.

When the results were in from the sound revolution it was clear that neither European optimism nor American fears were wholly warranted. The European industries did improve their domestic positions, but not much: the American share of the German and British markets—for Hollywood-made films—dropped less than 10 percent from 1927 to 1931, of the French market less than 15 percent. Elsewhere in the world, in the Middle East, Latin America and Asia, Hollywood continued to supply anywhere from 60 to 90 percent of all the films shown, and even a third or more in such countries as India and Japan, which had their own mass-production film industries.

If one believed Hays Office publicity, the silent film had been a medium capable of breaking down all barriers of ignorance and misapprehension among nations, and its world-wide proliferation would guarantee peace for all time. Conversely, therefore, though the Hays Office never followed out this logic, sound movies would restore the boundaries of linguistic and national difference, leading to a rise in international tension. In fact, talking pictures did not cause the Japanese invasion of Manchuria or the Nazi rise to power in Germany, but they were deeply affected by the developing nationalism and international tension of the 1930s.

Until the mid-1930s, censorship of movies by foreign countries had been practiced sporadically, and generally only to express a specific moral interest of an individual country. The Japanese, for example, eliminated all scenes of kissing, and the British cut references to the Deity and religious sacraments, as well as scenes judged to depict cruelty to animals (Western stunt shots of horse and rider taking a fall were in this category). During the latter 1930s, however, nearly every foreign country began a close watch on imported films, not only for objectionable crime and sex (so many American movies were cut or banned outright after 1934 that the Production Code began to look like a license for immorality) but also for dangerous politics.

References considered derogatory to other nations were cut, as were scenes suggesting political or police corruption. Even movies that came out of MGM, where production heads Louis B. Mayer and Irving Thalberg maintained a conservative political line, were judged overseas as politically inflammatory. Several countries cut the scenes of revolutionary upheaval from MGM's *A Tale of Two Cities* (1935), and some banned outright the Academy-award winner, *Mutiny on the Bounty* (1936), because it depicted rebellion against authority.

The German government began to ban American films on a number of grounds, including the fact that they were "racially offensive" because they were produced or directed by Jews or featured Jewish players.[5] When Japan declared war against China in 1937, all imports of American films were prohibited, and the ban lasted for thirteen months. Long negotiations produced a new import agreement, which made it very difficult for American producers to gain access to their earnings in Japan. After the war broke out in Europe in 1939, the further importation of American movies was swiftly excluded from the widening arc of territory controlled by the German army. American movies had become symbols of which side you were on.

One did not have to be on the road to war with the United States, however, to dislike American movies. No sooner had Hollywood established its presence in the world in the early 1920s than the drumbeat of protest began to arise from an international brigade of critics and moralists.

In large part these editors, educators and clergymen merely restated the familiar arguments of the American guardians of cultural tradition and class prerogatives, reinforced by nationalist feelings—how outrageous that another country should make money by warping the minds of our workers! But as time went on and Hollywood showed signs of even greater international prominence, the moralists began to sound a new and more ominous theme: what mattered was not the deleterious effect of American movies on Europeans but their sinister influence on non-Europeans. Hollywood, if unchecked, would bring down the fundamental order of world civilization, the supremacy of Europe over the nonwhite peoples of the earth.

It was bad enough, these writers believed, when Hollywood lured young men into crime and women into prostitution, yet those consequences, baneful as they were, did not shake the foundations of the state. The constant emphasis on crime and sex in American movies, however, had a far different impact among Asian, African and Hispanic peoples: it brought the white race into disrepute, stripped Caucasians of their aura of rectitude and moral power, and subverted the doctrine of white superiority.

From the outposts of empire the bad news poured in (mostly from India). At a cinema in Poona an Indian turned to an Englishman (who

---

[5] John Eugene Harley, *World-Wide Influence of the Cinema* (1940), p. 130.

reported the incident to *The Spectator*) and said, "I suppose you white people would call me a nigger. I am unacquainted with other sides of Western civilization, but what I have seen to-night, and on numerous other occasions in these places, convinces me that the ordinary middle-classes in England and America are the most debased and immoral cretins any race or nation have ever produced."[6]

Lately returned from the same country, a correspondent to the *Christian Century* pointed out that wars had been fought "to uphold the sacred status of the ruling race," yet "one picture shown throughout India to the thousands who attend the cinemas in the larger cities, will do more to lower the white race in the eyes of Indians than any other influence we can imagine."[7]

An Indian student, described as "in no way wishing to be offensive but merely seeking for information," asked a British visitor, "Sir, is it possible to find a chaste woman in the West?"[8]

Everywhere the nonwhite world was torn by confusion and strife, upheaval and discontent, wrote the British authors of a full-scale anti-Hollywood polemic, *The Devil's Camera*: "And in all these countries films are being shown which depict white civilization at its most morbid and most sensual. The coloured races are gloating over pictures which reveal the white man as an unscrupulous philanderer or criminal and the white woman as a prostitute or gambler's decoy."[9]

These minor items from the treasure trove of Western imperialist racism reveal principally their authors' panic and paranoia. Outside of a narrow circle of educated persons in major cities, few subjects of European colonial domination got a chance to feast their eyes on American-made debauchery. At the end of the 1930s there were only 16 movie theaters in British East Africa, and their patronage was almost exclusively European. China had fewer than 300 theaters, with a seating capacity of little more than 100,000. In India, where moviegoing was more popular than in any other European colonial possession, only about 20 percent of the movie houses exhibited foreign films.

From a late-twentieth-century perspective, following a generation of successful struggle for national independence in Asia and Africa, it seems little short of ludicrous to imagine that screen images of Chicago gang wars or London love triangles could play any sort of role alongside the basic political, economic and psychic desires for liberation from imperialist rule. But it would be a mistake to go too far in the other direction and deny the impact of American movies on world consciousness. From the beginning, American commercial movies adopted a style that could not fail to have enormous emotional and psychological influence on their

---

[6] Quoted in R. G. Burnett and E. D. Martell, *The Devil's Camera* (1932), p. 19.

[7] Letter to the *Christian Century*, Vol. 47 (August 13, 1930), pp. 992–93.

[8] L. A. Notcutt and G. C. Latham, *The African and the Cinema* (1937), p. 238.

[9] Burnett and Martell, *op. cit.*, p. 18.

viewers. They were intimate; they opened doors through which most members of the audience had never passed: backstage at the theater, the living rooms of the rich, and then their bedrooms, and then their baths. The hallmark of American moviemaking, since before World War I, was literally and figuratively the close-up. This had nothing to do with the morals of screen characters. If they were all saints and heroes, the movies still served to overcome distance and increase familiarity, demystifying the lives of white people no matter what the theme.

It was among the middle classes (and particularly their children) that American movies were principally influential, and it was a simple matter for cultural traditionalists to confuse such popularity with a breakdown of civilization and a prelude to chaos. In the world-wide social transformations accelerated by World War I, the offspring of the affluent felt the winds of change and searched for alternative values and styles to distinguish themselves from what they saw as a stultifying past. Within the United States the postwar generation found its answer in the dances, music and language of American blacks; elsewhere in the world the culture of white Americans, as depicted in movies, played much the same role.

Clothes, hair styles, speech, gesture, all could be gleaned from American movies. In Japan, new words were coined to describe the young men and women who patterned their dress and behavior after American screen characters: "mobos" and "mogas," short for modern boys and girls. When Chinese producers began making films in the 1920s, they didn't know whether the proper way for players to behave on screen was Chinese or American. Their solution was a mixture of the two cultures: their heroes and heroines were permitted to marry for love, as in American movies (but not in China, where marriages were arranged), but they acted in proper Chinese manner to each other, bowing instead of embracing. And observers began to note the flourishing use of the slang word "gee" among young Europeans.

But it would be a mistake to conclude that the popularity of American movies overseas was based on the desire to look or talk or live like Americans. People who changed their appearance or behavior following the modes of American movies did not hope to become someone else so much as they wished to be more like their conception of themselves. Hollywood gave the world images of personal felicity that directly denied the barriers and prerogatives of class. Girls could get their boys, and boys their girls, no matter what their income or social station; right could triumph over wrong no matter what forces of power or privilege stood in its way. The happy ending was a formula invented by neither Americans nor movies, but for several decades in the first half of the twentieth century no other medium or national culture could create visions of love and social satisfaction in the glamorous, confident, compelling manner of Hollywood. Only the gates of war and tyranny could shut out American movies, and when those gates came down neither Hollywood nor the world remained the same.

14

THE HOLLYWOOD GOLD RUSH

Hollywood always changed and never changed. Even at the height of its world-wide popularity, prestige and influence, it never lost the character of a gold-rush boom town. In the 1930s its sound stages, along with (and sometimes alongside) forests of oil derricks, dominated the Los Angeles skyline; its stars and leaders filled canyons and beaches with their stately mansions; its protocol, gossip and intrigue turned much of Southern California into a sprawling, suburban Court of Versailles. Yet at its core Hollywood was still a temporary settlement, an outpost on the far fringe of the Western desert. Though no one spoke of the studios as "camps" any more, people within the industry called themselves the "movie colony." The gambling, gold-digging spirit remained fundamental to the way Hollywood went about the job of making movies. "Millions are to be grabbed out here," Herman Mankiewicz wired Ben Hecht in 1925, "and your only competition is idiots."[1] He put the thoughts of thousands into words. The twentieth-century forty-niners trekked West in Santa Fe sleeping cars.

Their sagas might have been collected under the title Bret Harte gave his stories of the California gold fields: *The Luck of Roaring Camp*. Even on the dubious proposition that one's competition was idiots, there was no guarantee that intelligence or ability would strike the mother lode. Moviemaking, at any level above the B program picture, never lost the element of gamble. Success or failure often depended on factors outside the individual's control. Producer, director, players, composer, designer, cameraman: were the proper talents for the job available when they were needed? Once assembled, would they work well together? Finding the right people, getting the right assignments, forging together or being part of an effective team, all took ability, perseverance, judgment, and an uncommon flair for understanding creative personalities and audience tastes. You had to have a gifted touch or special sense to pull it off consistently: you had to be good and also lucky.

There were so many attractive faces, so many clever pens, so much talent of every kind, with enormous rewards for a handful, and little or nothing for everyone else. Naturally, some people were more skilled at their work than others, but in few other fields was the disproportion between success and near-success so great. No matter how many years of preparation and hard work went into an individual's achievement,

---

[1] Hecht, *A Child of the Century*, p. 466.

when one was lifted so far above all others it could not be seen as other than an act of fate. The same caprice that took you to the top could pull you down again, and there were always new examples of bad luck to put beside the good.

The gold-rush atmosphere grew, if anything, more pervasive as the years went by. The easy camaraderie of the early days, the primitive democracy of equal co-workers, disappeared as the pattern emerged of the few and the many. A class system grew up based on the size of weekly pay checks. It was impolitic to be seen socializing with those who received less income, for fear one might be judged vulnerable. One false move and dozens were ready to vie for your place.

Risk-taking and competition were the daily fare of the motion-picture elite, and they spilled over into leisure time: gambling became an obsessive activity in Hollywood social life. Men and women who were earning thousands of dollars a week carried their competitive drive and their belief in their special fate into games of chance, betting on horse racing, football, cards, dice, roulette. In his sociological study, *Hollywood: The Movie Colony, the Movie Makers*, Leo Rosten reported that studio switchboards were sometimes jammed by employees calling out to place their bets with bookies.

Hollywood money founded three Southern California race tracks in the 1930s—Santa Anita and Hollywood Park, easy drives from the studios, and Del Mar, eighty miles south—and the presence of stars in the clubhouses and as stable owners served to attract movie fans to the tracks. A casino, the Clover Club, also operated for a time on Sunset Boulevard in the heart of Hollywood. For greater privacy the movie crowd crossed the border into Mexico, where Joseph Schenck had financed a resort complex at Ensenada, Baja California, with a hotel, casino, golf course, dog track and race track. Sunday racing was a feature for those whose gambler's urge could stand no day of rest.

Games of chance and the movie game required the same basic skills: one had to be good at recognizing values and manipulating symbols. World-wide audiences assigned symbolic value to a few dozen men and women stars, and they consumed the attention of everyone who wanted to strike it rich in Hollywood. To visitors from other cultural centers this narcissistic concentration often caused a jolt: filmmakers in Berlin or Paris or London or New York were unable or unwilling to separate themselves so completely from their surrounding social environments.

Crossing the continent on the way to Hollywood, wrote the English novelist J. B. Priestley, "you will have to say good-by to most of the great realities of our communal life. . . . The real roaring world will disappear behind the mountains and deserts. It will not be long before you will feel further from most of its life than if you were lounging on some South Sea Island."[2] But as world tensions mounted toward war in the 1930s, more and more men and women in Hollywood began to chafe

---

[2] *Midnight on the Desert* (1937), p. 175.

at the narrow span of their community's social vision. They did not turn their backs on Hollywood's competition or its rewards, but success gave them the motivation and means to widen the view from the studio gate. In the last years of the decade, many people struggled to make Hollywood take a stand on the world's political and ideological conflicts. Often they discovered that politics and ideology, no less than moviemaking or cardplaying, were carried forward not by attention to the great realities of common life, but by the artful manipulation of symbols.

Movie stars were a new phenomenon in world culture, human symbols who had erased all boundaries of class, nation, religion and race. Something about their larger-than-life screen image touched a universal core in the human psyche. As the motion-picture scene unfolded, audiences in darkened theaters enveloped the shadow figures with their private and shared fantasies—and naturally assumed that off-screen lives were woven of the same romance and drama. Once admitted to the intimacies of reel life, movie patrons wanted their fantasies continued unbroken into real life. The lives of movie stars became as important symbols to manipulate as their motion-picture images, and the public saw only the tip of the iceberg.

By the 1930s, the play of personalities had become the last outpost of the gambling spirit in Hollywood filmmaking. Elsewhere the once anarchic adventure of putting a movie together had become specialized, organized and as routinized as collective creative work could be. The major studios had developed departments, inventories and experts capable of producing any object, image or sound from all the world's cultures and epochs: researchers found out the right cut of a jacket or hair style; property men and women secured or made historically correct furnishings; sound men reproduced the noises of bygone machines, and stunt men the feats of ancient heroes. To manage these varied aspects of movie work, the cadre of supervisory management—producers and their associates and assistants—increased rapidly while the number of creative personnel remained about the same.

Under the circumstances, only the most obsessive and powerful producers and producer-directors could retain personal control over all the complex facets of filmmaking. A significant part of what the producer was selling the public—the "production values," costumes, sets, music, location shots—was largely determined by preliminary budget decisions. Studio specialists and craftworkers could be counted on for as high quality work as their money allowed. It was in the realm of story, direction and performance that the producer took his chances; and there the manipulation of personality became so subtle a game that it often turned into an end in itself.

Talent was Hollywood's commodity, and control over the supply was achieved by the device of the standard long-term contract. All important screen players, and many directors and writers as well, were obliged, as a condition of obtaining work, to sign contracts binding them to a studio

THE MUSEUM OF MODERN ART/FILM STILLS ARCHIVE

Control and manipulation of contract players was one of the principal activities of motion-picture producers in Hollywood's heyday. Often it was the case of older producers discovering and promoting young stars, but in this instance it's a young producer, Darryl F. Zanuck, head of production at Warner Bros. while still in his late twenties, who looks on as veteran British actor George Arliss signs a contract. Arliss won the Academy Award for best actor for his performance in Warner Bros.' *Disraeli* (1929).

for seven years. The studio's commitment, however, was for no more than six months; the contract gave it an option to renew at the end of every half-year period or to let the agreement lapse, setting the employee at liberty. Even when actors organized collectively, they did not challenge the basic structure of the contract system; they concentrated on issues of salary and working conditions.

In the flush days of the studios it was a simple matter to offer contracts to attractive movie aspirants: you could keep a beginner on the payroll half a year for the weekly salary of a star, and what better way to charm visiting journalists or public figures than to provide them with beautiful young women or handsome young men, designated "stars of the future," as studio guides? (The French writer Paul Achard was met at the train station by a Paramount starlet who presented him a bag of oranges.) It is not clear how much training in movie work they received, or how carefully their talents were assessed. Mostly their contracts were allowed to lapse after half a year; if by chance one broke through to stardom, he or she was sewed up tight for years to come.

Naturally, studio heads were willing to increase the earnings of players who went over with the public. But the question that Mary Pickford and Charlie Chaplin first opened still remained: How much was a movie star worth? If a picture cost half a million to make and took in two or three times that amount at the box office—a common enough occurrence with the star productions of the 1930s—it earned far more than the entire year's salary of several stars, and those stars generally appeared in two to four films a year. No matter how much a star was making, it was likely not to be an equitable amount, based on his or her importance as a source of studio profits.

Since they were unwilling to alter the chattel nature of their employment, the stars sought instead to arm themselves with their own experts in the art of personnel manipulation. Beginning in the late silent period, agents became a powerful force on the Hollywood scene. Their function was basically different from that of literary or theatrical agents in New York. In the book trade or legitimate theater, agents handle specific performances: a manuscript or a part in a play. In Hollywood, agents had little connection with their clients' skills and accomplishments. They concentrated on the strategy and tactics of contract writing, rewriting and breaking, the semiannual contest of guile with producers and studio heads.

Myron Selznick, the elder son of Lewis, was, like his younger brother David, bent on vindicating the Selznick name in the movie world and became the most astute, aggressive and successful agent in 1930s Hollywood. He and his peers trod a thin line on behalf of their clients. It was widely recognized that studios shared salary information in an effort to prevent stars from playing them against each other; and stars who behaved uncooperatively to force their studio into dropping its option sometimes found an informal blacklist operated to keep them out of work with other companies. But agents like Selznick had weapons on their side. Studio operations were often inefficient and complex, so that agents were able to catch studios in violations of their own contracts. And despite efforts to maintain a united front, many studio heads and producers took pleasure in snatching star properties away from the competition. Agents sent the weekly salaries of top stars soaring into the five-figure range.

Nevertheless, to be a chattel was to be a chattel, and the studios usually had the last laugh. In Hollywood's peculiar institution of gilt-edged slavery a producer never sold his property; either he emancipated—that is, fired—or leased it. The "farming out" or lending of stars became the quintessence of the manipulation game, and for some producers, more of a challenge than making pictures. In effect, producers became agents for their own employees—but instead of taking an agent's 10 percent, they kept it all.

If a producer believed he needed to use someone else's employee on a contemplated project, he could offer his own chattels in exchange, or failing that, rent the talent he required by paying its owner cash. Often studios quietly passed the word that certain of their stars were available for hire, sometimes because they had no suitable work for a high-salaried performer, sometimes as a punishment. If a star wanted more money, she might find herself loaned to another studio against her will, to appear in a mediocre production that could damage her reputation. The real fun of the game for the producers was to make a profit on the deal by obtaining a higher fee for the loan-out than the star's salary: it was easier than making pictures, and often more lucrative.

Hollywood worked hard at keeping these intense and often bitter struggles between its creative and managerial elites away from public scrutiny. Instead it gave the world substitute images of conflict and turmoil to savor, images that precisely fulfilled movie patrons' expectations that their favorites' private lives were direct extensions of their screen roles.

The first magazines about the private lives of movie players began to appear in the era of two-reelers. Then came picture books, joke books, cookbooks—many of the techniques of modern publicity and commercial exploitation were forged in the movie world. But in the early days, discussions of the players' home lives was limited to the bland and discreet. It was even feared for a time that disclosure of a star's role as a spouse or parent would destroy his or her appeal as a screen lover.

Movie fans, however, turned out to be permissive. By the 1930s, carefully managed publicity about a star's love life—not merely the spouse and kiddies at home, but affairs and divorces as well—could enhance his or her box-office appeal. Moviegoers who had assumed that stars' private lives shared the glamour of their screen roles now anticipated that their personal experiences would add a new dimension to their screen portrayals: the circle was complete.

In his survey of prewar Hollywood, Leo Rosten was careful to point out that many aspects of Hollywood's social customs and public appeal were not new to American culture: the lives of wealthy and glamorous people had fascinated the public for several generations before the advent of movie stars. Popular newspapers and magazines filled their news columns with stories of the parties and marriages of Eastern high society, and their gossip columns with rumors of their affairs and divorces.

There were fundamental differences, however, between gossip in Hollywood and on Park Avenue. Scandal or public disapproval might damage the reputations of members of the Eastern elite but would not likely affect their power or status: they still had their class standing, their wealth, the value of their family names or social connections. For a movie star, reputation was everything. Without public approval, name and wealth completely lost their power, and connections and standing rapidly disappeared. Whoever controlled Hollywood's gossip controlled Hollywood.

The studios kept a tight rein on the fan magazines and the Hollywood press corps by regulating access to the stars; without such access a reporter or a periodical was out of business. One could know precisely how the stars stood in the eyes of their employers, the strategies used to mold their public images and regulate their private behavior, by studying *Photoplay*, *Modern Screen* or any other of the many monthly magazines for fans. Nothing appeared by chance, and precious little by the independent choice of the writers.

To this monolithic management of star publicity, there was one exception—an exception that throws all generalizations into a cocked hat. One reporter had complete independence, and her freedom to say what she pleased gave her enormous power over the formation of public opinion about Hollywood. Louella Parsons controlled Hollywood gossip through most of the 1930s (her chief competitor, Hedda Hopper, began her gossip column at the end of the decade), and to a remarkable degree Louella controlled Hollywood.

Gossip may not be the stuff out of which heroines are made, but Louella Parsons' career was built out of a perseverance, shrewdness and talent for survival that gave her the power and independence few other women of her time possessed. Like so many other tycoons of the movie trade, her origins were humble. In 1910, when she moved to Chicago to seek her first job, she was a divorced woman with a small daughter whose knowledge of life was limited to the little Mississippi Valley towns of Illinois and Iowa. Through a relative's connections she found a place as story editor and scenario writer at the Essanay movie studios.

She was one of the first salaried practitioners of a new field, motion-picture scriptwriting, and she wrote one of the many books of advice for aspiring free-lancers. "The average 'movie' audience," she said, "would much rather have the heroine and her lover live happily ever after. The tragic story, with its harrowing scenes, appeals to only the few who are morbidly inclined."[3] It was a position she maintained for half a century.

---

[3] *How to Write for the "Movies"* (1915), p. 102.

In 1915 Essanay let her go; though the studio signed Charlie Chaplin that year, it was one of the conservative Trust companies that had lost business to the innovative independent producers. Using her studio experience, Parsons got a job on a Chicago paper answering readers' queries about the lives of movie players. Thus she inaugurated another new profession, the movie gossip writer. In 1918 she moved to New York; five years later she joined the New York paper of the Hearst chain, the *American*, and in 1926 Hearst named her motion-picture editor for his news syndicate, Universal Press Service. That year she switched her base to Hollywood.

Parsons emerged as a powerful figure in Hollywood at a time when opportunities for women were narrowing in the movie trade. The decline of independent production in the 1920s eliminated nearly all the independent units that had been set up for female stars. Most of the women producers and directors faded out of movie work when the sound period began, and though women continued to be employed as writers, the influx of new screen writers was almost completely male. Parsons was the only woman in Hollywood—indeed, she was almost the only person—who held power that was not delegated by the studio moguls.

It was, of course, critical to her success that she was a representative of the Hearst press at a time when his communications empire was at its zenith. Hearst's capricious temperament was itself a force in the movie world, since he never hesitated to carry on his feuds or forward his causes in his newspapers, and one of his causes was the movie career of his mistress, Marion Davies, for whom he had formed his own independent production company, Cosmopolitan Films. Hearst's backing gained Parsons a respectful attention in Hollywood she might not have gotten otherwise; it also placed her in nearly four hundred papers throughout the world by the early 1930s, with a daily readership in the millions.

From the basically chaste and almost invariably favorable tone of her New York columns, Parsons developed an approach to Hollywood that was in many ways a reflection of her boss's style. If you were her friend, millions would learn how sweet and talented you were; if you crossed her, news of your faults would swiftly circle the globe. And the friendship she demanded was in the form of exclusive news tips: tell it to Louella first, or you'll be sorry.

The struggles between studios and their contract players played directly into Parsons' hands. Agents fed her exclusive stories to break the studios' lock on the form and content of publicity about the stars. In particular she was able to overcome the studios' blackout on information about star salaries. Where pressure might be brought against one newspaper by withholding cooperation or curtailing advertising, it would have brought only retribution had it been tried against Hearst. Louella in her turn was able to play both sides against each other, exacting special treatment from studio heads and publicity men by her power to print favorable or suppress unfavorable items.

The most unusual aspect of Parsons' work was her inaccuracy. She often got names, titles, marriage partners, even sexes wrong. Half her columns were sometimes made up of corrections. She never did even the most basic research, and Hearst forbade his editors to alter her copy. They were two of a kind: the less predictable they were, the more powerful. Louella titled her autobiography *The Gay Illiterate.*

Hedda Hopper was cut from only slightly different cloth. Born in a small Pennsylvania town, she sought a theatrical career in New York and ended up as the fifth wife of the famous actor DeWolfe Hopper. The marriage lasted nine years, and when Hedda divorced her husband, she had a son to raise and a modest career in silent movies to nurture. She continued as a movie player into the sound period but made barely enough money to live on and survived by taking jobs in real estate, modeling and radio. In the late 1930s a small feature syndicate asked her to write a Hollywood gossip column; as George Eells suggests in *Hedda and Louella*, the idea probably came from Louis B. Mayer, who wanted a countervailing force to Louella. One of the dozen or so papers to take on her column was the Los Angeles *Times*, the most powerful newspaper in Southern California. The *Times* gave Hedda a foundation as strong as Hearst provided for Parsons. Hedda began as a voice of the studios' point of view, but as her power and confidence grew she gave vent to her right-wing political predilections, and in later years her enmity became more bitter and dangerous to Hollywood personalities than Louella's.

Hedda and Louella were able to outfox the studios at their own game. If the fundamental art of movie promotion was the manipulation of personalities, they brought to the play of reputation and images a set of values and styles alien to Hollywood. They retained the ability, as did few others in the motion-picture business, to speak for and to the American small-town mores that still held sway in an urbanized nation. They knew that men and women lived scandalous lives in hamlets as well as in Hollywood; what was important was not the fact but the appearance of virtue. They knew the power of outraged public opinion. They may not have known how to spell or get their facts straight, but they knew the phrases and inflections that made behavior appear moral or immoral, that made personalities liked or disliked by their vast readership and radio audiences. Like the Breen Office, they became pillars of Hollywood's superego, powerful forces of control over the movie colony's highly active egos and ids.

When sound came in, a new class entered Hollywood's struggle for prestige and power, the screen writers. From their earliest days, back when Griffith tried to break in by selling stories to Edwin S. Porter, the silent movies had employed writers of scenarios, shooting scripts and titles, and several had attained prominence and status alongside directors and stars. But with the advent of sound, studio managers were convinced they needed a whole new stable of writers with experience at dialogue. They spread their nets on Broadway and Park Row and brought in playwrights, short-story writers, novelists and journalists by the score.

The newcomers formed the nucleus of the Hollywood writing elite through the 1930s and beyond. The contrast between them and the directors was remarkable. With only two or three exceptions, all the major Hollywood directors of the 1930s had served their apprenticeship and risen to the top of their trade in the silent period. Almost the exact opposite is true for writers. Only a handful who had established themselves in silent pictures maintained a leading position after the transition to sound. Curiously, most of the significant holdovers were women—Frances Marion, Anita Loos, Sonya Levien and Jane Murfin—while only one of the recruits for talkies who made it into the front rank of screen writers was a woman, Frances Hackett, and she was a member of a male-female writing team.

The first trickle of Eastern writers arrived in 1926, just as sound was developing, and put in little time on silents. Herman J. Mankiewicz was their advance scout, and his wire to Ben Hecht expressed his sanguine estimation of the opportunities and lack of competition. Hecht, Donald Ogden Stewart and Nunnally Johnson were among the others who came soon after. The great migration took place from 1929 to 1932, when more than twenty writers who were to reach the top arrived in Hollywood. They were a remarkably youthful group: only two were over thirty-five and the oldest was forty-two.

Unlike directors and actors from the theater, they were accustomed to quite different styles from those prevalent in moviemaking; they came from writing fields where individual autonomy was the goal, and all the time they were in Hollywood they retained the option of keeping up their former roles as writers of plays, books, stories and articles. Many of them fit comfortably into Hollywood's creative modes, but more than any other movie workers they were capable of independent access to other creative outlets, and of biting the hand, in the famous *bon mot*, that fed them caviar.

Beyond the rewards of salary—even mediocre incomes for Hollywood screen writers were higher than almost any other pay scale in writing—movie writers in the 1930s were held in considerable esteem by people in other walks of life. It was widely believed that they had brought the saving grace of literature to the movies, a view fostered by critics and scholars who understood words better than images and imagined that movies would improve if they became more like filmed plays. But writers who took that attitude to heart were in for a rude awakening in Hollywood; the men of letters who cast themselves as saviors discovered that in the power games of Hollywood their most pressing task was to save themselves.

Only a small minority ever got a chance to take part in making the significant decisions about what a production would be like. The East Coast writers were of course brought to Hollywood for the stories and dialogue they could supply, but they were also enlisted as unwitting mercenaries in a battle between producers and directors for ultimate

QUIGLEY PHOTOGRAPHIC ARCHIVE, GEORGETOWN UNIVERSITY LIBRARY

The power of gossip had its perquisites for newspaper columnists Louella Parsons and Hedda Hopper, among them frequent invitations to attend motion-picture premieres. Behind Louella at a 1940 premiere (top) is a mural depicting scenes from *Gone With the Wind* (1939). Hedda wears one of the audacious hats that were her trademark (bottom) on a similar occasion; her escort is Barry Buchanan.

QUIGLEY PHOTOGRAPHIC ARCHIVE, GEORGETOWN UNIVERSITY LIBRARY

primacy over the filmmaking process. They entered the studios as employees of producers, and their arrival turned out to be the decisive final act in the producers' successful drive for control.

In the early days of filmmaking, the director was also the producer—he bought or prepared scripts, hired players, planned sets and carried out the innumerable other details of production, as well as directing the actual shooting scenes. When studios expanded, leaders like Griffith and Ince also supervised the work of other directors. In the period when independent production flourished, a star like Mary Pickford often took on basic production authority, delegating responsibilities to directors and business managers but retaining ultimate control. The intrusion of the business office into the creative side of production went, in fact, counter to the practices that had evolved in the first two decades of commercial filmmaking.

The development of the studio system was the fundamental source of change. As the large studios began to produce sixty or seventy pictures a year, the centralization of administrative procedures became essential—buying stories, reserving stage space, coordinating the working schedule of players, building sets. As what had been a craft took on some of the character of an industrial process, these tasks were assumed by managerial personnel who could oversee the whole complex operation, leaving creative people free to concentrate on the immediate effort at hand. Some prominent directors retained production responsibilities, but for the general run of pictures, studio managers assigned employees to run the production end. These could be high-paying jobs, but they were essentially concerned with materials and personnel—producers were the contractors of movies, not the architects.

Some producers had a genuine talent for conceiving effective or popular film stories and for marshaling the resources—the right writer, director and players—to realize their conception. Irving Thalberg pioneered this role, David O. Selznick and Darryl F. Zanuck emulated him. Their ambition and success became the goals for other producers to shoot for. Aspiring and romantic men whose training may have been in accounting or stenography wanted to show that they, too, possessed creative genius in a field whose product was ambiguously both commerce and art. To gain control over story and script was to have your hand on the creative pipeline and to dominate the entire filmmaking process.

The manipulation of writers therefore became as essential a part of the producers' power game as the manipulation of stars. They aimed at developing a script that belonged more to them than to any of the writers who worked on it. Often a similar assignment was given to more than one writer; writers were asked to rewrite the work of others; different writers were assigned separate segments of the same script. When a shooting script was ready, the only steady hand that had guided it along the way was more likely than not the producer's: he was the "author" whose conception the director was to put into visual images, and he retained authority to revise the director's work, either by ordering changes after seeing the daily rushes, or by taking control of the final cutting and assembling of the picture.

Not every writer and director was forced to work this way. Capra and Riskin had the ultimate responsibility for their pictures at Columbia; some writers were given the chance to direct their own scripts, some directors to produce their own films. But the manipulative style of producer control was the norm. Writers had to learn to live with it, adjust to it, or try some other line of work—after all, editors on the *New York Times* could change copy without asking reporters' permission. "If he's a pro and worth his money," as one of the more successful, John Lee Mahin put it, the writer could stay sane in Hollywood as well as any other place.[4]

There are intriguiging aspects of Hollywood movies in the 1930s that may be traceable to the producer-dominated system of filmmaking and the attitudes it generated among writers. There is an entire genre of Hollywood movies, the comedy-drama, that rarely receives critical discussion but in many ways serves as the backbone of Hollywood's box-office appeal: it has a message, but it's not too heavy and doesn't probe too deep: it's funny but doesn't question any social values. It's the genre Hollywood developed with the most solid appeal to middle-class audiences.

A prime example is MGM's *Too Hot to Handle* (1938), directed by Jack Conway, with a script by Mahin and Laurence Stallings. Clark Gable plays a newsreel correspondent, Myrna Loy a famous airplane pilot, and the movie tells the story of how he wins her love—he calls her a "comic little dame who thinks she's a man," and he's going to turn her into a woman properly dependent on a man. The film is filled with bizarre scenes. It opens in China, where Gable is covering the Sino-Japanese war, and he fires a cannon to fake a war scene. Later all the players turn up on the Amazon, where Loy is hunting her missing brother, held by a native tribe. Gable and his cameraman, played by Leo Carrillo, masquerade as medicine men and dance around dressed up as chickens in their successful effort to rescue the brother—and Gable's to woo and win the woman.

The zaniness of comedy-dramas like *Too Hot to Handle* sometimes leaves a disquieting aftertaste. They often play for laughs by exploiting racial and sexual stereotypes, and their wild plot complications frequently get resolved by casual resort to violence. The classic comedy-dramas, like Lewis Milestone's *The Front Page* (with a script by Bartlett Cormack and Charles Lederer from the Ben Hecht–Charles MacArthur play), are redeemed by the broad range of their satire and their persistent effort to shock. But in the latter 1930s the genre was more tightly confined within a restricted framework.

Too Hot to Handle bears the telltale signs of having been cooked up in one of those legendary Hollywood story conferences where writers

---

[4] "Screenwriters Symposium," *Film Comment*, Vol. 6 (Winter 1970–71), p. 96.

tried to top each other's garish plot ideas and catch the eye of the producer. Someone had the job of writing up the brainstorms into a script, and though a writer might justly deny he felt cynical about what he was doing—he was simply a pro making a living—the viewer may also with justification recognize the signs of irresponsibility and complacent indifference to consequences in what he sees on the screen.

When screen writers were given a chance in the late 1930s to comment anonymously on their industry and its product (in a questionnaire Leo Rosten circulated as part of his sociological study), three fourths of all the responses were unfavorable. Nearly half of the negative remarks focused on the type of pictures made and the stories they were asked to write, the treatment of themes and the originality and relevancy of Hollywood movies (64 percent of replies by directors and 53 percent from players were also critical). The one aspect of movies that writers approved was their artistry and technique. And the writers other writers most admired, by overwhelming vote, were two men who had succeeded, uniquely among their peers, in developing a close and sustained working relationship with a prestigious director—Dudley Nichols with John Ford, and Robert Riskin with Frank Capra.

Writing was an individual art, movie writing at best a collaboration, at worst an alien, uncreative act. "The fact that the producer can change and destroy and disregard his work," Raymond Chandler said of the screen writer, "can only operate to diminish that work in its conception and to make it mechanical and indifferent in execution."[5] Even among the most successful screen writers there was a yearning to move from the bottom nearer to the top of the collaborative hierarchy. Both Dudley Nichols and Robert Riskin directed movies during their careers, as did Ben Hecht and Nunnally Johnson. From the 1930s corps of top-flight writers, Preston Sturges, John Huston, Billy Wilder and Joseph L. Mankiewicz moved on to become prominent as directors. And some writers even joined the ranks of their adversaries, the producers.

A small minority of Hollywood writers, for whom individual craftsmanship remained the core of their self-conception, kept up their work as novelists and playwrights. Few, however, ventured into the no man's land of one of the most prolific sub-genres in twentieth-century American literature, the Hollywood novel.

Perhaps fifty novels had been written about Hollywood by the mid-1930s, not counting teen-age romances and anonymous fictional exposés of love lives of the stars, and only one, Harry Leon Wilson's gentle satire *Merton of the Movies* (1922), a work admired by Gertrude Stein, was worth remembering. Most of the remainder, as Virgil Lokke describes them in *The Literary Image of Hollywood*, were variations on the theme of literary aggression—toward movies, toward the people who made them and especially toward the moguls who ran the studios. One did not have to join the ranks of conservative clergy or middle-class

[5] "Writers in Hollywood," *Atlantic Monthly*, v. 176 (November 1945), p. 52.

guardians of culture to feel outrage that immigrant Jews had developed and held control over the nation's newest and largest medium of mass commercial entertainment.

Just before World War II, however, three quite different, and each in its own way remarkable, novels about Hollywood appeared: Nathanael West's *The Day of the Locust* (1939), Budd Schulberg's *What Makes Sammy Run?* (1941) and F. Scott Fitzgerald's unfinished and posthumously published *The Last Tycoon* (1941). They remain the most important works of fiction to have been published about Hollywood, and it was perhaps not entirely coincidence that they were written so close together. All three authors were representatives of a new class of artists and intellectuals who joined the Hollywood ranks in the latter years of the 1930s, either out of the need for money or from the conviction that movies, as the most powerful medium of communication in American society, were a form in which serious or socially conscious artists could and should work. And all three brought separate political or cultural perspectives to their fiction that raised their work above mere prejudice or spite.

West and Fitzgerald were novelists who had come to Hollywood mostly for the money and with an intermittent conviction, quickly disabused, that they could be satisfied with their work as screen writers. To their novels they brought the rich powers of observation that were unutilized in their daily tasks of script construction. West created an unforgettable portrait of movieland back streets, their pastel Spanish-style stucco apartments filled with people poor in spirit, yearning to fulfill the dreams the movies fostered, and primed to explode in rage against the frustration of their psychic longing.

Fitzgerald's novel was to have been a tragic portrait of a great producer, a Jewish parvenu who took upon himself the role of perpetuating the vital myths of national purpose, order and virtue, and who struggled to maintain himself against the powerful but visionless forces of organized capital and labor. A year after his novel was published, West was killed in an auto crash at the age of thirty-seven; only the day before, Fitzgerald had died of a heart attack at forty-four.

Schulberg was the youngest of the three novelists but the most experienced in Hollywood. He grew up in one of the movie colony's first families as the son of B. P. Schulberg, one-time head of production at Paramount. In 1936, fresh from Dartmouth, he joined Selznick International as a reader and junior writer. Five years later his first novel, *What Makes Sammy Run?*, appeared and proved, unlike most previous Hollywood fiction, a surprising commercial success.

The popular interest in Schulberg's novel came partly from the notoriety of its acid portrait of a young man who claws and pushes his way to the top, which was widely rumored to be drawn from a living Hollywood figure. Yet Schulberg, like West and Fitzgerald before him, aimed not merely at sensationalizing Hollywood but at bringing it to life as an embodiment of larger forces in American society. His Sammy Glick was meant to be more than a cold-blooded player in Hollywood's power game, certainly more than the familiar stereotype of the Hollywood Jew. In his rise from the Lower East Side, Sammy, Schulberg makes clear, cuts himself off from the values of his religious and ethnic origins. To find out what made Sammy run, one had to look at the nature of the social and economic system of his country and his time: Sammy's unbridled competitive drive is intended as "a blueprint of a way of life that was paying dividends in America in the first half of the twentieth century."[6]

Sammy Glick is the consummate individualist, a man totally lacking any sense of cooperation, consideration or social purpose beyond the self. He is a symptom of more than Hollywood, and more indeed, than America; in the end he is made to represent the fearful drive for power that led to the ultimate horrors of world conquest and war. "You had to make individualism the most frightening ism of all," Schulberg's narrator says of Sammy.[7] The point had a powerful resonance for many of Schulberg's readers in the months before the United States entered the war.

Men of greed and ambition like Sammy Glick still dominated the public imagination of Hollywood in the last years of the 1930s, but they didn't have the field to themselves in either Schulberg's novel or real life. In *What Makes Sammy Run?* the spirit of collective purpose is expressed in the struggle to gain recognition for the Screen Writers Guild; in Hollywood itself the guild issue was only the internal aspect of a much wider effort among movie workers to forge a common voice on the social and political questions of the day. Hollywood's ignorance of the world beyond America's sheltering oceans rapidly diminished in the second half of the Depression decade, more swiftly, one could argue, than in most other places in the United States. In those years the movie colony became a center for writers and performers who brought with them or adopted left-wing political views, and who saw the medium as a vehicle for mass enlightenment as well as entertainment.

The myth grew in succeeding decades—and was perpetuated even by sympathetic chroniclers—that the left-wing movie workers of the 1930s introduced the apple of political knowledge into Hollywood's Eden. The whole tenor of this book has told a different story. Long before the movie moguls hired Will H. Hays to tend their political interests, they were sensitive to the political issues that could affect their prosperity. Louis B. Mayer was Herbert Hoover's overnight guest at the White House, and when Franklin D. Roosevelt became President, Warner Bros. celebrated the occasion by filling the screen with his portrait as part of an otherwise risqué Busby Berkeley production number in *Footlight Parade* (1933).

---

[6] *What Makes Sammy Run?* (1941), p. 303.

[7] *Ibid.*

The most blatant instance of overt political action by the producers came in 1934 and may have convinced movie workers to adopt their own political stance, since they were otherwise open to political as well as career manipulation by their bosses. In the California Democratic primary for governor, Upton Sinclair scored a stunning upset victory with his proposal for a quasi-socialist recovery program for the state, EPIC (End Poverty in California). Sinclair had few friends in the party hierarchy; President Roosevelt himself was less than lukewarm about the possibility of Sinclair as California's governor challenging the New Deal with his radical schemes. The movie tycoons shared the President's antipathy: Sinclair's program included high taxes on upper income brackets and on studio profits.

They responded with an astonishing act of political propaganda. Under the direction of Irving Thalberg, MGM film crews prepared phony newsreels purportedly showing average people being interviewed about the election. A white-haired woman says she will vote for Sinclair's opponent "because I want to save my little home"; a bearded man states his preference for Sinclair because "his system worked vell in Russia, vy can't it work here?"[8] These were distributed free to theaters. Studio employees earning more than $100 a week were "asked" to give a day's pay to the Republican candidate's campaign, with veiled threats of reprisal to those who refused. Sinclair was soundly defeated, and the studio heads took credit for a job well done (though the Hearst press in California was even more virulent in its attacks on Sinclair, and there is no evidence to indicate which medium had the greater impact).

After the anti-Sinclair campaign, political opinions emerged on the surface of Hollywood life, stimulated not only by the moguls' tactics in the 1934 election but also by the increasing evidence of anti-Semitism and militarist policies in Nazi Germany and the outbreak of civil war in Spain. In 1936, a Hollywood Anti-Nazi League was formed, representing a broad coalition of antifascist opinion in the motion picture community.

At the same time, beneath the surface of overt political organizations, Communist party organizers began to form study groups and recruit movie workers. In the Popular Front period of the mid-1930s, it was neither sinister nor unusual for a man or woman of intelligence, seeking knowledge of the forces of power in the world, to turn to Marxism for understanding, or to conclude that Communism was the political affiliation that best expressed solidarity with the beleaguered loyalists in Spain and the struggle against fascist oppression in Europe and Asia.

What we think of as the Cold War mentality, however, existed even before the Cold War. Anti-Communism had played a significant role in American political rhetoric since the time of the Bolshevik revolution, and the appearance of so inflammatory a political doctrine in the heartland of so powerful a medium brought a whole new kind of outcry

---

[8] Quoted in Leo C. Rosten, *Hollywood: The Movie Colony, the Movie Makers* (1941), p. 137.

against Hollywood: the movies were being used for propaganda purposes by the ideological archenemy of American principles. Headline-seeking politicians and right-wing pamphleteers began producing lists of forty-two or forty-three or eighteen prominent movie workers who were party members or sympathizers or fellow travelers—a tactic Senator Joseph McCarthy was later to perfect. Such lists were usually dominated by famous actors who had signed their names to liberal causes—among them Humphrey Bogart, James Cagney, Melvyn Douglas and Fredric March.

In 1940 Congressman Martin Dies, Democrat of Texas and chairman of the newly formed House Committee on Un-American Activities, came to Hollywood to continue the public attack on its Communist sympathizers he had launched in articles and statements to the press. A committee of producers met with Dies and asked that hearings be held to establish the guilt or innocence of the persons accused. Dies talked privately to a number of actors, and astonishingly enough, reported that none were Communists or Communist sympathizers, and that he had never said they were. He suggested they be more careful in giving money to worthy causes.

The explanation for this curious turnabout may lie in the rapid turn of events in Europe. The Popular Front period ended abruptly with the signing of the Nazi-Soviet nonaggression pact in 1939, leaving many non-Communist opponents of fascism disillusioned about Communist tactics. In 1940 and 1941, the dominant question in American political life was whether to intervene in the European war, and the Communists for much of this period joined ranks with the right-wing isolationists. For the moment, Communism faded as a relevant issue. Hollywood turned out to be far more vulnerable on familiar, traditional grounds.

In August 1941 two isolationist senators introduced a resolution calling for a Senate investigation of what they alleged was motion-picture propaganda designed to bring about American participation in the European war. They linked the charge with the issue of monopoly in the motion-picture industry, the specter of which had again been raised by the Justice Department's antitrust suit against the major studios. Hearings were held during September 1941 by a subcommittee on interstate commerce.

The first witness, Senator Gerald P. Nye of North Dakota, a co-sponsor of the resolution, opened the hearings with an attack on movies which he considered favorable to intervention, calling them "the most vicious propaganda that has ever been unloosed upon a civilized people."[9] He took care to rebut insinuations that his opposition to intervention or to the movie industry made him an anti-Semite, but he went on to assert that the men responsible for propaganda pictures had been born overseas and come to America "with inborn hatreds and prejudices . . .

---

[9] U.S. Congress, Senate. Committee on Interstate Commerce, *Propaganda in Motion Pictures* (1942), p. 6.

quite foreign to America and her best interests and the lessons of memory and experience."[10] Some four or five men, he claimed, held monopolistic control over what millions of Americans saw in their theaters, and the three he cited by name—Harry Warner of Warner Bros., Barney Balaban of Paramount, and Nicholas Schenck of Loew's, Inc.—were all Jews. Beyond their religious and ethnic feelings about the European struggle, Nye accused them of wanting the United States to intervene so as to protect their business interests in Great Britain.

The films Nye named as propaganda pictures included *Convoy*, *Flight Command*, *Escape*, *That Hamilton Woman* and *The Great Dictator* (all 1940), and *Manhunt* and *Sergeant York* (both 1941). Under questioning, the only one he definitely remembered having seen was Charlie Chaplin's *The Great Dictator*.

The producers countered with Wendell Willkie, Republican presidential candidate in 1940, as their counsel, and papered the hearing room with a friendly audience. Schenck, Warner and Balaban all appeared as witnesses, though the most persuasive voice was that of Darryl F. Zanuck, who began by pointedly indicating his place of birth, Wahoo, Nebraska, and describing his parents and grandparents as native-born Americans, regular attenders and lifelong members of the Methodist Church. Zanuck's final statement recalled "picture after picture, pictures so strong and powerful that they sold the American way of life, not only to America but to the entire world."[11] The remainder of the testimony was anticlimactic, and the subcommittee did not meet again before Pearl Harbor rendered its work obsolete.

Nevertheless, the hearings themselves were disquieting. The movies had never been more popular or the stars more glamorous; the producers had built an industry that gave Americans—indeed, as Zanuck said, the world—their dreams and social myths. And yet the residue of animus was still strong against them; many people still resented the preponderance of foreign-born and Jews among them. They had come so far, but their enemies remained as intractable as ever, with an unerring instinct for the grounds on which the producers could least successfully protect themselves.

In a way the accusations against alleged Hollywood Communists were a useful diversion. They shifted focus away from ownership and control over the industry to the beliefs of a few employees. The movie tycoons could be called gamblers, manipulators, womanizers, destroyers of talent, but to claim that such unregenerate capitalist entrepreneurs were Reds—that was one charge, perhaps the only one, against which the producers were safe.

---

[10] *Ibid.*, p. 47.

[11] *Ibid.*, p. 423.

THE DECLINE OF MOVIE CULTURE

15

HOLLYWOOD AT WAR FOR AMERICA AND AT WAR WITH ITSELF

"I have never," said Colonel K. B. Lawton, chief of the Army Pictorial Division of the United States Signal Corps, "found such a group of wholehearted, willing, patriotic people trying to do something for the government."[1] He was speaking in 1943 about Hollywood motion-picture producers and their employees, in testimony before Harry S. Truman's Senate committee on the war effort, and of course no one on the committee believed a word of it. The committee wanted to know, among other things, how some of the moguls and their staff had wangled officers' commissions, how much the movie industry was profiting from the production of military training films, and whether the major studios exercised monopolistic control over government-contract filmmaking. No one gave a thought to the value of Betty Grable's pinup picture for GI morale or to movies like *Wake Island* (1942), the first of many to dramatize American war heroics for the home front. In war, as in peace, Hollywood served as a convenient and vulnerable villain.

Once again the motion-picture producers could not seem to do the right thing. There they were, providing essential recreation and entertainment for civilians and soldiers alike by offering feature films and live appearances by stars in Army camps and at war fronts. There they were, making dozens of skillful propaganda films depicting enemy evil and supporting the fortitude of America's British, Russian and French allies. There they were, many of them volunteering along with hundreds of their employees for military service to perform the critical tasks of battlefield and instructional filmmaking.

And to what response? Among others, the suggestion by Senator Ralph O. Brewster of the Truman Committee that "recent citizens" were not appropriate filmmakers for the war effort, that the War Department should hang out a sign saying only "seasoned citizens" may apply. His words implied a belief similar to the one Senator Gerald P. Nye had expressed in 1941: that the moviemakers were insufficiently American in origin, intellect and character.[2]

The unkindest cut came soon after the war, when the cry of Communist infiltration of Hollywood was once again raised. This time the House Un-American Activities Committee (HUAC), under new leader-

---

[1] U.S. Congress, Senate. Special Committee Investigating the National Defense Program, *Investigation of the National Defense Program* (1943), pp. 6896–97.

[2] *Ibid.*, pp. 7046–47.

ship, prepared the ground more carefully. It aimed not for a few headlines but at a thorough purge of radically oriented workers from the entertainment field.

In 1947, HUAC found the industry a surprisingly softer touch. Though their films had attained their peak of popularity, the producers—twice burned by the Senate investigations of 1941 and 1943, apprehensive about the outcome of the government's antitrust suit against them, made cautious by the advent of home television programing and lacking the experienced political leadership of the recently retired Will H. Hays—felt themselves in a peculiarly weak position. Under pressure from the congressional investigators, they devoured their own, and Hollywood began to destroy itself.

The Truman Committee had a point in its criticisms of Hollywood's relation to the war effort, though the facts were open to entirely opposite interpretations.

From Hollywood's point of view, the motion-picture studios had patriotically sacrificed their self-interest by offering to produce training films for the government without taking a profit for themselves—indeed, they were willing to absorb many of the costs. A typical film, *Safeguarding Military Information*, cost one studio \$39,000 to produce, according to Colonel Lawton, and it billed the government only \$19,600.

The committee based its skeptical attitude on the conviction that the government had been extraordinarily generous in allowing Hollywood to continue business as usual. Had the need been greater for military filmmaking, or for the raw materials of film processing, or for studio lots and equipment, the government might well have directed an end to new feature-film production, as it did, for example, with automobiles. In that case the entertainment needs of soldiers and civilians could have been met by re-releasing the best of the more than five thousand sound films stored in Hollywood's vaults.

Instead, Hollywood was able to maintain production of new features at only slightly below the peacetime level. In the three full years of war, 1942–1944, the studios averaged around four hundred and forty features a year, compared to about five hundred annually during the 1930s. With high wartime employment and limited spending options, the movies became more popular than ever: in some locations, where factories operated around the clock, theaters never closed, either, and were crowded even in predawn hours by workers getting off late-night shifts.

From this perspective, expenses for which the studios proudly refused to bill the government—salaries, overhead and use of standing sets—they had no business to charge for anyway, since these were fixed costs necessary for normal production activity. In this light, the Truman Committee could indeed imply that the movie industry's offer to produce government films without profit was motivated less by patriotism than by a desire to ensure that extraordinary wartime circumstances would not disturb the monopoly power of the major studios.

Hollywood had been channeling its relations with Washington through a body called the Research Council of the Academy of Motion Picture Arts and Sciences. Essentially this was a committee of producers, given a lofty name to mask its connection with profit-making activities. In 1930 the Research Council began sponsoring the training of a small number of U.S. Signal Corps officers in motion-picture techniques.

In November 1940 Darryl F. Zanuck, chairman of the Research Council, proposed that the industry assign it responsibility for coordinating the allocation of government film projects. The seven major production companies quickly agreed, along with Republic Studios and four independent producers—Hal Roach, Samuel Goldwyn, Walt Disney and Walter Wanger. They committed themselves not to bid competitively for government contracts, and pledged that they would perform government work on a nonprofit basis. The War Department went along with the plan.

This arrangement was one of the Truman Committee's principal targets. During the twenty-three month life of the agreement, from January 1, 1941, to December 10, 1942, the Army Pictorial Division spent slightly over $1 million in Hollywood, of which $270,682 went to Paramount, $243,515 to Zanuck's Twentieth Century-Fox, and a little more than $100,000 each to RKO and MGM—more than 70 percent of the government's business to four major studios. The Research Council's plan had been to assign filmmaking tasks equally among the twelve participating studios in alphabetical order, but exceptions were far more common than the rule, largely, according to testimony, because the big studios had the facilities, such as water tanks and submarine sets, required for government work. But the Truman Committee suggested that the work had been distributed on the ground of convenience so that big studios, with large overheads and staffs, could do government films in otherwise wasted slack time, while for other studios, government assignments need not interfere with feature-production schedules.

By 1943, the issue was moot. Smaller producers not party to the agreement had complained to committee investigators that they were frozen out of government work, and pressure from the committee had led the War Department to cancel its arrangement with the Research Council. Thenceforward, government film contracts were awarded after competitive bidding on a cost-plus basis.

Zanuck, the hero of the 1941 battle of Capitol Hill, became the goat, *in absentia*, two years later. As head of the Research Council he was attacked not only for the production agreement but also for the council's role in serving as the conduit for officers' commissions for Hollywood producers and employees. This charge was rebutted in testimony indicating that less than one fourth of the Army Pictorial Division's officers recruited from among civilian movie workers had been recommended through the Research Council. It was also argued that a large number of commissions had been necessary to match the importance of the volunteers' prior status in the industry.

Zanuck himself became a colonel (he would have required four stars to equal his Hollywood rank) and was further chastised for remaining on the studio payroll while serving on active duty, for appearing in a documentary on the North African campaign, *At the Front in North Africa* (1943), and then for requesting inactive status in the thick of war.

Though Zanuck had to endure the senators' jibes, his talents were undoubtedly more useful to the war effort in Hollywood than at the front. Once the decision was made to continue feature-film production at a nearly normal pace—or rather, in the absence of any decision to pursue an alternative course—the patterns of promotion and expectation continued as usual. GIs overseas felt dissatisfied with old movies when they knew they were missing the new pictures at home. Ultimately new films were made available for military audiences well in advance of their commercial release dates; by war's end nearly a thousand different features had been distributed to the armed forces without charge. During his several months at the front Zanuck had had an opportunity to learn what kind of movie entertainment GIs wanted, and his return to Hollywood gave him a chance to provide it.

His first major production effort for 1944 release was Alfred Hitchcock's *Lifeboat*, a film which, like *Casablanca* and a number of other wartime features, was set in the 1940–1941 period, when Europe was fighting but before Pearl Harbor. Its purpose, as Hitchcock later described it, was to tell "the democracies to put their differences aside temporarily and to gather their forces to concentrate on the common enemy."[3] However, it was attacked as antidemocratic, purportedly for showing a Nazi as far cleverer than the democrats he confronted.

Thereafter came *The Song of Bernadette*, a religious melodrama; *The Purple Heart*, a prison-camp melodrama based on a story written pseudonymously by Zanuck; *Wilson*, a biographical film on the World War I President, personally produced by Zanuck; and *Laura*, a suspense melodrama. *Wilson* was intended as Zanuck's principal contribution to social significance, to remind moviegoers there was a peace to build as well as a war to win. (He also wanted to make a film out of Wendell Willkie's book *One World*, but gave that up because of its political obsolesence.)

Wilson flopped, while *The Song of Bernadette* and *Laura* were among the big box-office hits of the war, which seemed to confirm the frequently voiced dictum that wartime audiences, GI or civilian, preferred "escape" entertainment. "Escape," however, is far too limiting a conception. From the emergence of Hollywood as a center of entertainment production, movie styles and content had subtly (and sometimes not so subtly) shifted in response to a complex variety of impulses: audience tastes, economic factors, the values and goals of movie workers, outside pressures, and the changing relationship of moviemakers to the larger culture, among others. The movies of World War II were no less products of their culture.

---

[3] François Truffaut, *Hitchcock* (1967), p. 113.

Many of Hollywood's wartime movies, particularly those with contemporary American settings, convey—to this viewer at least—an overwhelming aura of claustrophobia. They seem contained, enclosed, shadowy, explorations of an interior landscape of mind and emotion quite novel in the extroverted American cinema. Undoubtedly their dark and constricted mood derives in part from the material limitations of wartime filmmaking: restrictions on travel virtually eliminated location shooting where interior sets could serve, and stringent budgets seem to have cut down on lighting as well. Yet the gloom and constriction were not merely an accommodation to forced economies; their filmmakers intended them that way. When French critics began to see American films after the war, they identified a genre they called *film noir*: the term describes the psychology and the look not simply of a genre, but of a surprisingly pervasive tone in Hollywood films of the 1940s.

In a narrow sense, *film noir* refers to the psychological thrillers that emerged at the time of the war. Many were directed by a new generation of European expatriates on the Hollywood scene, and their cynicism and bleakness have been attributed to European sensibility. Otto Preminger contributed *Laura* and *Fallen Angel* (1945), Billy Wilder made *Double Indemnity* (1944) and *The Lost Weekend* (1945), Fritz Lang directed *Ministry of Fear*, *The Woman in the Window* and *Scarlet Street* (all 1945), Robert Siodmak made *Phantom Lady*, *Christmas Holiday*, *Cobra Woman* (all 1944) and *The Suspect* (1945); and there were even more such films after the war.

Film noir seems to have been especially nurtured by the macabre imagination of the British director Alfred Hitchcock, who made his first Hollywood film in 1940. The Hitchcock thriller, in its fascination with guilt and its ambiguous play with identities, served as a prototype for *film noir* in such movies as *Suspicion* (1941), about a young bride who suspects her husband as a murderer. Hitchcock's *Shadow of a Doubt* (1943) was one of the transcendent works of the genre, recasting its conventions as it established them, locating its intense anxiety and claustrophobic fear in a benign, sunny small-town setting (Orson Welles tried a similar approach three years later in *The Stranger*).

The hallmark of *film noir* is its sense of people trapped—trapped in webs of paranoia and fear, unable to tell guilt from innocence, true identity from false. Its villains are attractive and sympathetic, masking greed, misanthropy, malevolence. Its heroes and heroines are weak, confused, susceptible to false impressions. The environment is murky and close, the settings vaguely oppressive. In the end, evil is exposed, though often just barely, and the survival of good remains troubled and ambiguous.

Even pictures quite distinct from *film noir* share its feelings of claustrophobia and entrapment. Preston Sturges' wartime comedies, *The Miracle of Morgan's Creek* and *Hail the Conquering Hero* (both 1944), are about men trapped in false situations not of their own making. And

THE MUSEUM OF MODERN ART/FILM STILLS ARCHIVE

Commitment was a major theme of Hollywood movies during World War II. Humphrey Bogart several times played the uncommitted man for whom taking up a gun is his act of joining the struggle. That momentous time arrives (top) in Howard Hawks's *To Have and Have Not* (1944); looking on are Dolores Moran, Marcel Dalio and Lauren Bacall, and the enemy are Dan Seymour and Sheldon Leonard. More often it was the confusion and doubts about commitment that took a central role in the *film noir* genre of the period, dominated by dark, claustrophobic settings, as in the séance scene (bottom) from Fritz Lang's *Ministry of Fear* (1944), with Ray Milland.

COURTESY OF UNIVERSAL PICTURES

Warner Bros. made a series of romantic melodramas about women, played frequently by Bette Davis and Joan Crawford, who struggle against or rise stoically above the traps of circumstance and character besetting them. War itself, curiously, was less a trap than a solution to private entanglements, a means to transmute one's personal entrapment into sacrifice for a higher cause. Humphrey Bogart, as Barbara Deming has pointed out, was memorably cast several times as a man who found in commitment to war the answer to his inner dilemmas—in *Casablanca* (1942), *Passage to Marseilles* and *To Have and Have Not* (both 1944).

Deming's fascinating and curious book, *Running Away from Myself: A Dream Portrait of America Drawn from the Films of the 40's* (completed in 1950, but not published until 1969), attempts to identify the psychological predicaments depicted in films of the era. Like the French critics, she finds their message a bleak one. Unrelievedly, their landscape is nightmare. Peacetime before and after war is no less hellish than war itself. "The hero who sees nothing to fight for; the hero who despairs of making a life for himself; the hero who achieves success but finds it empty; and the malcontent who breaks with the old life, only to find himself nowhere"—these are the principal types she discovers.[4] They reveal to her a crisis of faith far deeper than the uncertainties of survival in war.

Clearly, these films were a direct response by filmmakers to the crisis of the time. One need not agree, however, with Deming's view that the psychological themes were presented by moviemakers and absorbed by audiences unconscious of their implications. Trends and cycles in commercial movie production were complex creations put together from box-office reports, developments in other popular arts (nearly all of the *films noir* were adapted from novels and heavily influenced by the hard-boiled school of thriller writers, particularly Raymond Chandler and James M. Cain), and the immersion of movie workers in the moods, values, tastes and concerns of their surrounding society. What is remarkable about 1940s movies is how much they shifted the focus of screen drama from an outer to an inner world. In Depression movies, horrible threats came from alien sources, from vampires and monsters and giant jungle beasts; by the 1940s, horror lay close to home, in the veiled malevolence of trusted intimates, in one's own innermost thoughts.

"Our films," Deming concludes, "grant us a vision of the Hell in which we are bound, but cannot grant us a vision of our better hopes."[5] Other observers of the wartime movie scene agreed with the first part of this assessment but took a more optimistic view of what films might accomplish positively. They drew their evidence from the record of wartime documentary filmmaking: propaganda films like the "Why We Fight" series produced by Frank Capra, remarkable films of war's actuality like John Huston's *The Battle of San Pietro*.

---

[4] P. 201.

[5] *Ibid.*

"These and other signposts," wrote the Editors of *Look* magazine, in a promotional picture book commemorating Hollywood's wartime endeavors, "point to a cycle of more serious, more factual motion pictures. Now Hollywood, with world-wide markets soon to be reopened, with its new documentary techniques and growing maturity of thought, is in a position to seize an exciting opportunity—the opportunity to carry abroad the message of democracy and, at home, to help American audiences preserve belief in democratic principles."[6]

These wartime sentiments very quickly came to seem indiscreet: in the postwar period they became ammunition to impugn the medium. The response to Hollywood's enemies, in Washington and elsewhere, who had demanded outside control over movies, had always been that movies were entertainment pure and simple. In proclaiming their power to mold minds, Hollywood's advocates inadvertently invited redoubled vigilance from the watchdogs who could tolerate claustrophobia and unrelieved blackness, but not one ray of informing light with which they could not agree.

The postwar attack on Hollywood could not have got off the ground had it been merely a renewal of old enmities. The familiar charges against moviemakers, although couched in moral terms, had never fully succeeded in masking ethnic, religious and class antagonisms. In the aftermath of a war against Nazism, these traditional complaints began to appear base and repugnant. When Congressman John Rankin of Mississippi denounced Hollywood in 1945, his blatant anti-Semitism was a disturbing embarrassment to the movie industry's antagonists. The more rational among them knew they had a far stronger case against the movies on ideological grounds.

Hollywood had always put up a united front against criticism, protesting that it was being used as a scapegoat by people unwilling to look honestly at other modes of communication, and least of all at themselves. This stance did not hold up before the postwar method of scrutiny. It was made clear that the investigation of Communists in Hollywood was no special harassment but only an early step in a thorough purging of "subversive" influence from every institution in the land (indeed, before the House Un-American Activities Committee got around to Hollywood, the loyalty-security program for government employees had already begun). Hollywood itself was deeply divided on the issue, and no one could say that HUAC was prejudiced against Jews or the foreign-born, since members of those categories were among its most ardent supporters.

The grounds for suspicion no longer consisted principally of wild charges by publicity seekers and right-wing cranks. In 1945 the Chamber of Commerce of the United States published a report on *Communist Infiltration in the United States*, warning that Communists were seeking

---

[6] The Editors of *Look, Movie Lot to Beachhead* (1945), p. 278.

to gain control of entertainment and information media. They already dominated the Screen Writers Guild in Hollywood, the report claimed. The way to stop this Communist plot, it suggested, was to expose it.

The new prominence of respectable businessmen among Hollywood's critics may have been the principal reason why the producers picked the Chamber's president, Eric Johnston, to succeed Will Hays as their industry's front man. Johnston was expected to influence his former colleagues on Hollywood's behalf, as Hays had influenced politicians a quarter century before.

Neither Johnston nor anyone else, however, could stop the effort to expose "un-Americans," and the movie community was the obvious place to launch the crusade. Its critics had always been able to abuse it with impunity. Its enormous popularity gave its accusers access to wide national publicity. Its product was not constitutionally protected under the First Amendment guarantees of free speech and free press (the *Mutual Film* decision of 1915 still defined the movies' constitutional status). And nearly everyone believed, in those pre-television days, that movies had a greater influence on public values than any other medium. Only a few observers and the victims themselves recognized that the attack on Communism in Hollywood, if successful, would achieve what special-interest groups had been seeking for half a century—effective outside control over movie content and personnel.

In 1947, when the House Un-American Activities Committee returned to Hollywood, the movie community had gone through great changes since Martin Dies' visit, seven years before. Ideological lines had been drawn between political extremes. Major strikes had further exacerbated old conflicts. The man who in 1940 accused movie workers of Communist leanings had not been connected with the industry; the producers had resisted his charges, and the persons named had been given a chance to clear themselves in private. In the drastically altered postwar atmosphere, the accusers were important figures in the movie community; the attitude of the producers was uncertain, and the accused were called to defend themselves in the glare of floodlights and before a bank of movie cameras.

The crack in Hollywood's united front began in 1944 with the formation of the Motion Picture Alliance for the Preservation of American Values (MPA), an organization of politically conservative movie workers who proposed to defend the industry against Communist infiltration. Congressman Rankin praised its members as "oldtime American producers, actors and writers," which may have been more revealing of Rankin's prejudices than the Alliance's, since the group included Jews and immigrants of conservative persuasion.[7]

The MPA provided HUAC with something no outside critics ever had, a body of supporters within the industry willing to testify publicly against their colleagues. For more than a decade there had been left-wing

---

[7] Quoted in John Cogley, *Report on Blacklisting: I. Movies* (1956), p. 11.

political activity in the movie community, but Communist party members and their sympathizers had basically formed alliances and sought influence within already established organizations, like labor guilds and unions. Their opposition, therefore, had come largely in the context of intraorganizational debates—for example, within the Screen Writers Guild. The sole purpose of the Alliance, however, was to combat Communism in general, and it gave the anti-Communist forces more concentrated purpose than the Communists themselves possessed.

This strength immediately became apparent in the bitter labor struggles that erupted near the end of the war. As usual, the conflict was over union jurisdiction, whether certain workers should be organized by the studio-wide union, the IATSE, or by one of the AFL craft unions. The pendulum of labor power had swung back to the craft unions, and in 1941 a Conference of Studio Unions was formed to give the craft unions some of the industry-wide unity IATSE already possessed.

During the war a struggle developed between CSU and IATSE over which would represent set decorators (a decade before, a similar conflict had erupted over sound technicians). In March 1945 the CSU affiliate in the dispute went out on strike, and nearly all the craft unions refused to cross its picket lines. At this point, in the intricate way of Hollywood labor battles, Communism became a major public issue in Hollywood, and the conservative MPA began to play a critical role.

What happened, quite simply, was that the newly arrived IATSE head, Roy Brewer, decided that his best tactic against CSU was to attack it as Communist-dominated. There was no question that CSU had consistently taken left-wing positions, but ironically, Communist-influenced studio unions opposed the CSU strike as a violation of their no-strike pledge during the wartime U.S.-USSR alliance. (Several months later, with the strike still on, the party line changed and the Communists began to support it.)

Brewer's strategy to make anti-Communism the bedrock of the IATSE public campaign against the strike led him to forge links with the MPA despite its antilabor views. Each partner in the alliance gained clear advantages: IATSE made some influential connections in the studios and the MPA significantly broadened its base, enlisting labor support for its assertion that Communists were trying to dominate the industry.

The strike lasted nearly eight months, and the studios maintained production by replacing CSU strikers with IATSE members. In October 1945, strikers attempted to block the entrance to Warner Bros., and police dispersed the pickets with tear gas and fire hoses. From a studio rooftop Jack L. Warner, the production head, looked down on the melee. His anger against the strikers spilled over into a determination to fight the Communists whom Brewer and the MPA claimed were behind the disorders, and he became the first major convert from the top of the industry's hierarchy to the anti-Communist front. A shorter but more violent CSU strike in the fall of 1946 hardened his antagonism, and Warner, along with two well-known political conservatives, Louis B.

THE MUSEUM OF MODERN ART/FILM STILLS ARCHIVE

Realism and a sense of social purpose were hallmarks of the wartime documentaries made by Hollywood directors in military service. One of the most striking films for its depiction of combat and its effect on civilians was John Huston's *The Battle of San Pietro* (1944), from which this frame enlargement is taken.

Mayer and Walt Disney, represented management among the "friendly" witnesses who testified before HUAC in October 1947.

HUAC may not have been willing to venture into Hollywood without the encouragement of influential supporters within the industry, but the goals of HUAC and of Hollywood's anti-Communist front were not always the same. The committee made its strategy apparent in March 1947—nearly two months before it took secret testimony from "friendly" witnesses—when it interrogated Eric Johnston.

The committee pressed Johnston along the path of logic the U.S. Chamber of Commerce pamphlet had only partially laid out. The first premise was that every Communist party member was an agent of a foreign ideology seeking to overthrow the American form of government and substitute its own, and that any such person employed in the entertainment and information media would undoubtedly use his or her position to attack American principles and put forward Communist ideals. Therefore, the congressmen maintained, the motion-picture industry should get rid of every Communist it employed. Johnston balked at this final step in the argument. "There is nothing," he protested, "which will enable us to discharge a person in Hollywood because he is a Communist."[8] He reiterated the Chamber of Commerce position that exposure of Communists would be sufficient. Yet he could not bring himself, any more than the Chamber report could, to spell out the consequences of exposure. If audiences knew an actor was a Communist, Johnston faintly suggested, they could show their displeasure by staying away from his films.

Johnston was caught in an unpleasant trap. He did not want to fire Communists, but the alternative he seemed to advocate, a selective boycott, invited economic disaster for the industry he represented. Moreover, his solution was open to the criticism that the allegedly most dangerous subversives were writers whose work was not as obvious to the moviegoing public as that of actors. Johnston's dilemma was to become all too familiar to liberals in many fields during the years of anti-Communist oppression. Once one accepts the basic anti-Communist premise—that Communists are disloyal—then any conclusion short of dismissal is merely a squeamish refusal to face the consequences of one's judgment.

As usual, Rankin put the committee's aim most bluntly: "Everyone whose loyalty was questioned I would certainly get them out of the moving-picture industry."[9] Various other committee members tried to mount their favorite hobby-horses during the hearings: Chairman J. Parnell Thomas, persisting in his efforts to show that the New Deal was Communistic, tried unsuccessfully to prove that the Roosevelt Administration had twisted arms in Hollywood to get pro-Russian movies pro-

---

[8] U.S. Congress, House. Committee on Un-American Activities, *Investigation of Un-American Propaganda Activities in the United States* (1947), p. 293.

[9] *Ibid.*, p. 302.

duced during the war, in particular *Song of Russia* (MGM) and *Mission to Moscow* (Warner Bros.). "Large numbers of moving pictures that come out of Hollywood carry the Communist line," Rankin had said on the floor of the House, and the investigators occasionally talked grandly of documenting that assertion, though it's clear they never tried.[10]

But all the issues the hearings raised—the lack of anti-Communist films made by Hollywood (this was Congressman Richard M. Nixon's singular interest) and the possibility that Communists sidetracked such projects; the role of high-salaried Hollywood Communists in contributing funds to the party; efforts by Communists to deprive anti-Communists of work—were subordinated to the committee's central purpose, the barring of all Communists from Hollywood employment. This, in a single stroke, would solve all problems.

The witnesses, "friendly" and "unfriendly," knew from the beginning they would have to take a stand on the committee's demand for an employment blacklist. On the eve of the October public hearings in Washington, Johnston told attorneys for the nineteen "unfriendly" witnesses who had been subpoenaed, "As long as I live I will never be a party to anything as un-American as a blacklist."[11] The industry's stance appeared firm when Jack L. Warner opened the hearings as the first "friendly" witness. In his secret May testimony he had boasted of having thrown more than a dozen Communist writers out of his studio. In October he said, "I have never seen a Communist, and I wouldn't know one if I saw one," and he explicitly opposed the suggestion of a blacklist.[12] Robert Stripling, the committee's chief investigator, inserted Warner's May testimony into the record to demonstrate the disparity between Warner's private views and his public adherence to the official industry line.

Louis B. Mayer would not compromise his conservative principles: he vowed that MGM would not employ any Communist party members. Among the remainder of the "friendly" witnesses there was no obvious unity on the question of a blacklist. Adolphe Menjou, the actor, said he saw no reason for a producer to fire a Communist writer: "He could be very carefully watched; this producer could watch every script and every scene of every script. We have many Communist writers who are splendid writers. They do not have to write Communistically at all, but they have to be watched."[13] Other "friendly" witnesses pleaded that it was the responsibility of Congress to make laws authorizing private employers to fire employees for political beliefs, since what the committee wanted the movie industry to do was in all likelihood illegal.

---

10 *Congressional Record*, 80th Congress, 1st Session, v. 93, pt. 3, p. 2900.

11 Johnston quoted in Gordon Kahn, *Hollywood on Trial* (1948), p. 6.

12 U.S. Congress, House. Committee on Un-American Activities, *Hearings Regarding the Communist Infiltration of the Motion Picture Industry* (1947), p. 11.

13 *Ibid.*, p. 105.

All told, twenty-three "friendly" witnesses appeared over a week's time, headed—at least in the eyes of the public crowding the hearing room—by stars like Gary Cooper, Robert Taylor, Robert Montgomery, Ronald Reagan and George Murphy. Their motives were varied. Some wanted to square old grievances, defend past decisions, get even with old enemies, advance their own careers or causes. More often than not their testimony was petty, mean, craven, even stupid. But some had also come to share a purpose they had not had in mind when they encouraged HUAC to enter their world: they wanted to limit the damage the committee was inflicting on their industry. If the wrath they had helped to unleash could be deflected toward the "unfriendlies," perhaps their industry could still survive the hearings with its powers and prerogatives intact.

Put yourself in the minds of the men called before the House Un-American Activities Committee in October 1947 as "unfriendly" witnesses. They were among the first witnesses deliberately subpoenaed because of their known hostility to views espoused by the committee. They were not full-time political activists or bureaucrats; they were men who made their living in an entertainment medium, as writers, actors, producers, directors. Years later, in the 1960s, a radical like Jerry Rubin could ridicule the committee by seeking to testify dressed as Santa Claus or as a guerrilla fighter, or like Dave Dellinger, could try to use the witness chair as a place to put forward a political perspective. But in 1947 the repression of left-wing political opinions had only just begun.

Nineteen "unfriendly" witnesses were subpoenaed from Hollywood by the committee. Eleven were called to testify during the second and final week of the motion-picture hearings. One, Bertolt Brecht, the German playwright, answered the committee's questions, denied he was a Communist and shortly thereafter returned to Europe, where he became one of the leading figures in East Germany. The others refused to answer whether they were then or had ever been members of the Communist party (the writers also refused to state whether they belonged to the Screen Writers Guild). They were cited for contempt of Congress, and after carrying their appeals unsuccessfully through the federal courts, two of them served prison terms of six months; the other eight served a full year. These are the "Hollywood Ten" of fact and legend.

The Hollywood Ten have been treated harshly in the historical accounts of the committee and its era. The extraordinary feelings of pain and powerlessness engendered, even a generation later, by the record of their confrontation with the committee has led to an all too understandable pose of blaming the victim: the feeling that they must have deserved what they got or they wouldn't have got it. They were rude, they were arrogant, they were cowardly—such are the charges leveled against them. It has hardly occurred to anyone that they may have been right in assessing their situation, and that their tactics were the only rational chance for a successful defense the moment allowed.

When the screen writer Alvah Bessie and his family arrived for a visit at his colleague Dalton Trumbo's ranch a short time after both men had been subpoenaed as "unfriendly" witnesses, they were shaken from having seen an automobile smash-up. Thinking they were worried about HUAC, Trumbo said, "Don't worry about the subpoena—we'll lick them to a frazzle." Later, after they had explained the cause of their upset, Bessie's wife asked Trumbo, "Do you really think we'll lick them to a frazzle?" "Of course not," Trumbo answered. "We'll all go to jail."[14]

More clearly than the others, Trumbo recognized the nature of the battle. The committee had firmly enunciated its demand that the motion-picture industry discharge every Communist party member in its employ, and in practice it rarely made fine distinctions between actual membership and the appearance of sympathy for Communist causes (no evidence was ever offered linking three of the original "unfriendly" nineteen with the Communist party). Once subpoenaed, the "unfriendly" witnesses were bound to suffer no matter what stance they took.

By refusing to state whether they were or had been members of the Communist party, they risked a contempt citation from Congress—this was the path they chose, and conviction and imprisonment were the result. Had they answered the questions negatively, they were likely to have been indicted for perjury (it is probable that all the Hollywood Ten had at one time been party members). There was a third alternative, and some later commentators have strongly condemned them for not telling the truth. If they had admitted party membership, it is argued, perhaps their candor and courage would have disarmed HUAC and rallied public support behind them. That prospect seems far-fetched. Had they confessed their party affiliations, it is far more likely they would have been grilled endlessly to name every other Communist in Hollywood and would not themselves have escaped reprisals unless they recanted their political beliefs.

Given the intransigence of HUAC and the evidence in newspapers and opinion polls indicating public disapproval of the committee's assault on civil liberties, their strategy to attack the committee's basic purpose as an unconstitutional infringement of First Amendment rights of free speech and free assembly was both expedient and high-principled. The committee responded that Communists had forfeited their right to constitutional protections. "At this ultimate point of conflict," Dalton Trumbo wrote in a pamphlet, "either the Committee or the individual is bound to be destroyed."[15]

The committee survived, and ten men went to jail. The crux of nearly all later criticism of the Ten centers on their demeanor before the committee. They behaved, it is said, in a manner Communists have tradi-

[14] Bessie, *Inquisition in Eden* (1965), pp. 185–86.

[15] Trumbo, "The Time of the Toad" (1949), p. 7.

tionally taken before such tribunals, turning the attack around against their accusers, filling the air with windy rhetoric, pugnacious belligerence and lofty incredulity that they should be suspected at all. There seems to be no question but that their performance on the witness stand cost the Ten critical support within the industry. But it must be remembered that during the first week of hearings, they had been forced to sit silently and observe Chairman Parnell Thomas' contempt for them, his raging temper, his own windy rhetoric and pugnacious bombast. It did not seem likely that even a saintly serenity could avail in the face of the committee's wrathful purpose. More than ever a tenacious offense appeared to be the most effective defense.

Thomas handled his side of the struggle cannily. As soon as the Hollywood hearings began, he and his committee were widely criticized in newspaper editorials for their violation of First Amendment rights. A Committee for the First Amendment was formed in Hollywood, and in an effort to sway public opinion it put a number of famous Hollywood stars on a special nationwide radio program after the first week of hearings and sent a delegation of movie players, including Humphrey Bogart and Lauren Bacall, to be present as the second week began, when Eric Johnston was scheduled to defend the industry. Thomas crossed them up: as soon as the stars appeared, he unexpectedly called John Howard Lawson, the first of the "unfriendly" witnesses, to the stand.

It is difficult, looking at newsreel clips of Lawson's testimony, to avoid the impression that he was deliberately abrasive, arrogant and unruly. He sought to begin by reading a statement, but Thomas demanded to look it over first and rejected Lawson's request after reading only the first sentence: "For a week, this Committee has conducted an illegal and indecent trial of American citizens, whom the Committee has selected to be publicly pilloried and smeared."[16] The two men shouted at each other across the hearing tables until Thomas ordered policemen to remove Lawson from the stand. After the committee's dossier on Lawson was read into the record, he was cited for contempt for refusing to answer questions on Communist party membership.

Lawson's tactics stunned the Hollywood stars who had come to protest the hearings, and they were further chagrined when they discovered that their presence made it appear to the press that they were linked to the strategy of the "unfriendly" witnesses. As further witnesses tried in the next three days to match Thomas' belligerence or to disarm it, their base of support from the movie community began to erode. Under pressure from their employers, several publicly identified leaders of the Committee for the First Amendment, including Humphrey Bogart, disavowed their roles. It was one thing to be a man or woman of courage, another to be unemployed.

The hearings ended abruptly on Thursday of the second week, with eight of the subpoenaed "unfriendly" witnesses still uncalled. Thomas

---

[16] Kahn, *op. cit.*, p. 72.

promised an early resumption, but it was not until nearly four years later, in the spring of 1951, after Thomas himself had served a prison term for padding his congressional payroll with relatives and accepting kickbacks from them, that Hollywood again came under HUAC's purview. The committee had never established that Communists had put propaganda into Hollywood movies, but it had accomplished its goal: it had successfully laid the groundwork for a purge of Communists and others suspected of disloyalty.

Less than a month after the hearings, Twentieth Century-Fox announced it would "dispense with the services" of Communists and all other persons who refused to answer questions about Communist party affiliation.[17] On November 24, 1947—the same day the House of Representatives voted overwhelmingly to approve HUAC's contempt citations for the ten "unfriendly" witnesses—the motion-picture producers association met at the Waldorf-Astoria Hotel in New York to discuss the fate of the Ten and formulate a policy on blacklisting. The following day they released a statement pledging, "We will not knowingly employ a Communist or a member of any party or group which advocates the overthrow of the Government of the United States by force, or by any illegal or unconstitutional method."[18]

The producers specifically deplored the behavior of the Ten: "Their actions have been a disservice to their employers and have impaired their usefulness to the industry."[19] They stated that they all would be discharged or suspended without pay pending the outcome of their cases.

It has frequently been said that the decision to institute a blacklist came not from Hollywood but from Wall Street bankers and the movie industry's New York business-office heads, but the distinction between East Coast moneymen and West Coast moviemen is in this case not worth drawing. The Hollywood producers' strategy under Will Hays's leadership had always been to avoid outside interference, keep power in their own hands and surreptitiously circumvent unpalatable declarations of principle as need required and circumstance permitted. Clearly, the blacklist policy was designed to further the same goals: if the Waldorf declaration could head off further congressional attacks on the industry, and particularly Thomas' announced probe into motion-picture content (as it seems to have done), then the sacrifice of a few heretofore valued employees might not seem such a high price to pay. Much the same thing had happened before, in the Arbuckle scandal and other such events.

But the movie industry's old bulwarks had never experienced such a storm as struck them in the postwar period on the issue of Communist infiltration. "In pursuing this policy," the producers said in their Wal-

---

[17] Bessie, *op. cit.*, p. 223.

[18] Kahn, *op. cit.*, pp. 184–85 for text of statement.

[19] *Ibid.*

dorf statement, "we are not going to be swayed by any hysteria or intimidation from any source." In all the history of hollow Hollywood words, few were emptier than these. The producers were more prophetic when they went on to say: "We are frank to recognize that such a policy involves dangers and risks. There is the danger of hurting innocent people, there is the risk of creating an atmosphere of fear. Creative work at its best cannot be carried on in an atmosphere of fear."[20] Those words read a little like an epitaph.

The problem was not so much the producers, whose limitations by then were well known, but the times and the nature of their antagonists. The period of anti-Communist madness in American life was a time when accusations without proof were immediately granted the status of truth; when guilt was assumed, and innocence had to be documented. Though anti-Communism was a tactic both major political parties used in pursuit of foreign policy and electoral goals, it was one that "respectable" people could not control. A perverse kind of democracy was practiced: all accusations, no matter from whom, were taken equally seriously. A housewife or a grocer, a "nobody," could by simply writing a letter jeopardize the career of a wealthy, glamorous movie star. When national organizations like the American Legion set themselves up as judges of the movie industry's ideological purity, the threat of a boycott, of picket lines before movie theaters, so frightened producers that they were willing to capitulate to any and all outside demands.

The anti-Communists were hard taskmasters. Myron C. Fagan, playwright and author of *Red Treason in Hollywood* (1949) and *Documentation of the Red Stars in Hollywood* (1950), made clear that he wanted to clean far more than Communist party members out of Hollywood. "As far as we are concerned," he said, "any man or woman who is a fellow traveler, or belongs to a Red front organization, or has supported Communism with financial or moral support . . . or has come out in open support of the ten branded men who defied the Parnell Thomas investigation, or associates with known Communists, openly or in secret is just as guilty of treason, and just as much an enemy of America as any outright Communist. In fact, more so! I have no fear of the known Communist! It is the rat that masquerades as a good American but who secretly nourishes the Communist's slimy cause, who is our greatest menace."[21]

As far as Fagan was concerned, to have joined the Committee for the First Amendment was an act of high treason. His list of "Stalin's stars" ran to almost two hundred—a figure close to the number of persons estimated to have been blacklisted over the years from the late 1940s to the mid-1960s. He was also, of all things, critical of the conservative Motion Picture Alliance, accusing it of being a tool of the producers. Of the producers themselves he was deeply suspicious, expressing the view

---

[20] *Ibid.*

[21] *Red Treason in Hollywood* (1949), pp. 47–48.

that they really wanted the Communists to remain in movie work (he was already aware that some studios were using blacklisted writers working under pseudonyms, although he did not mention that the writers were receiving a fraction of their former salaries). He himself was duped by producers, he wrote, who asked him to go easy with his charges, on the argument that if movie attendance dipped too far, studio managements would be replaced, and the new bosses wouldn't be as experienced at getting rid of Communists as the old. But he concluded that their plea was one more Red-tainted ruse.

It was a dark and difficult season for the industry. The anti-Communists naturally delighted in naming not little-known figures, like screenwriters, but big box-office stars. Actors and actresses, unlike writers, could not continue working under pseudonyms. Various groups in the movie community saw the necessity for a systematic procedure to deal with the many unsubstantiated charges pouring in from free-lance Red hunters. Gradually a system of "clearance" evolved. When faced with an accusation that might wreck a career, a person could, rather than flounder in ignorance, learn which conservative colleagues to approach, in order to begin the process of satisfying the accuser's demands. (Some accusers were never satisfied, but if the American Legion or HUAC approved, that was good enough.) For non-Communists, "clearance" required repudiating all liberal opinions and associations; former Communists were required to perform a humiliating public ritual of expiation by naming names of other Hollywood Communists.

The behavior of the studios during this period was contemptible, but given their unwillingness to take a stand on principle (along with nearly every American university, newspaper, radio and television station and the vast majority of intellectuals), what choice did they have? They might invest several million dollars in a movie, release it to the public and find that because its star—or writer or director or producer—had once signed a petition in the 1930s attacking Nazi Germany, the American Legion was ready to throw up picket lines throughout the country. To avoid adverse publicity and empty theaters, they quickly gave in.

Even so, the damage to Hollywood was very nearly fatal. For the first half-century of American movies the industry had had a fascinating and curious relationship with the American public. It had always stood slightly aslant the mainstream of American cultural values and expressions, seeking to hold its working-class audience while making movies attractive to middle-class tastes, and therefore never quite in step with other forms of cultural communication. Movies were always less courageous than some organs of information and entertainment, but they were more iconoclastic than most, offering a version of American behavior and values more risqué, violent, comic and fantastic than the standard interpretation of traditional cultural elites. It was this trait that gave movies their popularity and their mythmaking power.

And it was this trait that the anti-Communist crusade destroyed. Creative work at its best could indeed not be carried on in an atmosphere of fear, and Hollywood was suffused with fear. It dared not make any movie that might arouse the ire of anyone. One of the Payne Fund authors, Charles C. Peters, had argued in his *Motion Pictures and Standards of Morality* (1933) that movies ought not to challenge or deviate from prevailing moral norms. In the Cold War atmosphere of the late 1940s and 1950s, Hollywood went far beyond the standard Peters had asked of it: the studios tried to avoid making movies that would offend any vocal minority. As a result they lost touch both with their own past styles and with the changes and movements in the dominant culture at large. Let it not be said that television killed the movie industry: the movie industry must take that responsibility itself.

16

THE DISAPPEARING AUDIENCE AND THE TELEVISION CRISIS

In 1946, the first full peacetime year, American movies attained the highest level of popular appeal in their half-century of existence. Total weekly attendance climbed to nearly three fourths of their "potential audience"—that is, the movie industry's estimate of all the people in the country capable of making their way to a box office, leaving out the very young and very old, the ill, those confined to institutions, and others without access to movie theaters.

For the first time in the 1940s, the motion-picture industry began to study its audience systematically, and what it discovered was both surprising and pleasing. Contrary to received wisdom, researchers found that the more education a person had, the more often he or she went to the movies; people at higher income levels attended movies more frequently than people in lower brackets; as many men went to movies as did women; and (the least startling revelation) young people went to movies more than older people.

As the industry's analysts studied these data they could not help but be elated. Their audience was strongest among the prime consumers of entertainment in the country. Since all forecasts pointed to accelerated growth in disposable income, educational attainment and population, they had no difficulty at all in predicting continued expansion of the movies' popularity in the future.

There were, however, signs that might have led the motion-picture industry to temper its optimism. In 1945, radio marked a quarter century of commercial broadcasting: the medium had come of age as a mature and influential force in American communications, much the same way that movies had done in the early 1920s. And commercial television was just around the corner.

Comparisons between radio and movies in audience surveys ominously favored the former. One survey made in 1945 asked respondents which medium did the best job of serving the public during the war; 67 percent answered radio, 17 percent newspapers, and only 4 percent movies. This was not, of course, an entirely fair question: radio and newspapers served the public primarily with news, movies overwhelmingly with entertainment, and in wartime, news would naturally be considered of greater service. But another question asked: "If you had to give up either going to the movies or listening to the radio, which one would you give up?"[1] Eighty-four percent—more than four persons out of five—answered movies, only 11 percent radio, and 5 percent did not know.

With radio you didn't have to go out for entertainment—in particular, you didn't have to go into the dirty, crime-ridden, alien downtown districts where the opera houses, orchestra halls, legitimate theaters, museums and first-run movie houses were located. You could listen in your bathrobe or other informal attire at any time of day, in any kind of weather, at minimal additional cost (for electric current) beyond the original purchase price. While enjoying radio you could cook, clean, read, talk, exchange glances with family or friends, lie in bed; you could turn it on and off, adjust the volume, change stations at will.

Radio was to movies what automobiles were to streetcars. Of people interviewed in a national sampling in 1945, 87 percent owned radios in working order (an additional 4 percent had radios that were out of order), and the *average* of daily listening was reported to be 4.6 hours for men, 5.9 hours for women. In contrast, the average moviegoer in 1946, the peak year for movie attendance, went to the movies three times a month.

All these advantages were likely to be intensified in the case of television. By 1946, however, the movie industry had had two decades to worry about the possible effect of competition from commercial home television (the TV picture tube had been invented in the 1920s) and still the threat had not materialized. The state of television broadcasting remained primitive, like movies in the peep-show era: the screen was barely postcard-size with a fuzzy black-and-white image, and the receivers were enormously expensive, out of reach for the average American householder.

On balance, the movie-industry forecasters chose not to fear their media competition. The ratio of actual to potential audience for motion pictures had more than doubled in the decade 1935–1945 despite the growth of radio and wartime circumstances. In addition, research revealed the emergence of a social group with multiple media interests—that is, people who frequently used one medium were likely to be among the more frequent users of other media as well. The men and women who listened to radio many hours a week were also inclined to attend more movies and read more newspapers and magazines than the people who listened little or not at all. And these consumers belonged to the educated and affluent stratum that was expected to grow rapidly in postwar America.

The essential question was how the motion-picture industry would respond to its more accurate audience profile. For most of their careers the movie moguls had been indifferent to systematic investigation of their patrons' habits and desires, taking pride in their "seat of the pants" intuition about what pleased audiences, which was confirmed or con-

---

[1] Paul F. Lazarsfeld and Harry Field, *The People Look at Radio* (1946), p. 101.

founded by detailed study of box-office returns. Old show-business hands knew that audience tastes changed rapidly and unpredictably; audiences crave novelty, but they usually don't know what they'll like until some entrepreneur gives it to them.

Nevertheless, over the years the movie trade had constructed an image of its fundamental audience, one with obvious sentimental ties to the working-class and immigrant patrons who were its first supporters. As Terry Ramsaye, one of the medium's pioneer publicists, wrote in 1947, the movies continued to appeal primarily to "the great illiterate and semiliterate strata where words falter, fail, and miss."[2] The audience-survey data exploded this image.

It seems likely, in retrospect, that the nature of the motion-picture audience may have changed significantly in the decade from 1935 to 1945, when attendance rose from 31 percent of "potential audience" to 73.6 percent. More and more of the movies Hollywood made in that period appealed to an educated audience in the higher-income groups—sophisticated comedies, historical and biographical melodrama. The enormous increase in attendance appears to have come from people in the middle and upper-middle strata of American society.

Yet there were some myths that the Hollywood studio management cherished too much to let go. One was the belief in their fundamental role as servants to the masses. Every movie was made with the idea of reaching the maximum possible audience. The concept of "potential audience" was no mere statistical device; it was a moral imperative that every able-bodied American should be considered a member of a movie's potential audience.

Now here was evidence that movies were appealing most of all to the more educated and economically comfortable groups. Logically, if Hollywood wanted to attract those people not currently attending movies, it would seek to make pictures more appealing to men and women with less education and income—those whom Terry Ramsaye condescendingly described as illiterate and semiliterate. If such a policy were put into practice, however, it would risk alienating the most frequent moviegoers—the young, educated and affluent.

This was a dilemma the moguls seem never to have grasped. They were trapped in a traditional conception of their public as rigid as any plot convention in their movies, in which "the intellectuals" were their antagonists and "the people" their friends. The studio managers were not exactly complacent in 1946. They knew they had potentially serious problems confronting them—the government's longstanding antitrust case against the major studios, which had gone to trial in October 1945; the reconstruction of a foreign market in a confusing postwar situation; competition from television. But they persisted in deluding themselves as to the nature of their following.

---

[2] "The Rise and Place of the Motion Picture," *The Annals of the American Academy of Political and Social Science*, Vol. 254 (November 1947), p. 1.

That fundamental error left them unprepared to cope effectively with postwar changes in American social and political behavior. When HUAC directed its anti-Communist attack on the movie industry and when the great population shift to the suburbs began, the producers shaped their responses with the idea of retaining a foundation of support that in reality did not exist. Unwittingly they helped to turn away their principal audience. As the country prospered, Hollywood did not.

After 1946, attendance and box-office receipts began to fall, even before television made its significant impact around 1949 or 1950. By 1953, when 46.2 percent of American families were estimated to own television sets, motion-picture attendance had dropped to almost exactly half the 1946 high-water mark. But it is important to bear in mind that Hollywood had problems that would seriously have challenged its popularity and earning power even if television had never existed.

The essential structure of the movie industry had once again become a problem when the Justice Department renewed its antitrust suit against the eight principal producer-distributor organizations in 1944. By bringing the industry back into court, the government made clear its dissatisfaction with the compromises it had accepted on a trial basis in the consent decrees of 1940. Once again the government claimed that the only way to prevent the monopolistic abuse of power in the motion-picture business was to break up the vertical integration of the industry—to divorce the major studios from ownership of theaters.

In the consent decrees of 1940 the studios had agreed to eliminate blind-booking, limit block-booking and curtail further acquisition of theaters. This halted the cast against them and severed them as co-defendants from the separate actions against exhibitor chains, but these latter cases continued in the courts, and their progress was not good news for the industry's status quo. The first such case reached the Supreme Court in 1944, and it is possible that the Court's decision that year in *United States v. Crescent Amusement Co.* influenced the Justice Department to reactivate its struggle with the producers.

The Court held that Crescent and eight other affiliated firms had illegally conspired with the studios to gain a monopoly over first-run exhibition in seventy-eight towns in five Southern states. Because the exhibitor combines owned all the theaters in most of these towns, they were able to force distributors to give them monopoly power in competitive situations, demanding exclusive rights to first-run bookings and inordinately long clearance periods. In seeking to enjoin the defendants from exercising monopoly, the Court ordered each exhibitor company to divest itself of any financial interest in the others, forcing them to compete on the same footing as other independents. In 1945, when the case against the studios returned to litigation, the Justice Department asked for divesture of theaters from producer-distributors as the answer to studio monopoly as well.

United States v. Paramount Pictures, Inc., et al went to trial in October before a three-judge panel of the Federal District Court in the Southern District of New York. In their decision the following June the judges held that the movie industry's distribution system did violate the Sherman Act, but they refused to order the studios to divest themselves of theater holdings. They took the position that a number of other remedies—prohibiting forced block-booking, the fixing of admission prices, "unreasonable" clearances, and various franchise, formula and master agreements between distributors and their own or other large exhibitor chains—would eliminate the monopoly. Henceforth, they declared, every film should be offered for exhibition to all comers through competitive bidding.

The Justice Department appealed, and the Supreme Court heard the *Paramount* case along with two earlier actions against exhibitors. Building on the *Crescent* decision, Associate Justice William O. Douglas, who wrote the Court's opinion in all three cases, took a stronger stand against motion-picture monopoly than any lower court had yet done. In the first opinion he reversed a lower-court decision in favor of the defendant exhibitors, arguing that it was not necessary to show specific intent to violate the antitrust laws before it could be held that a violation had occurred. In the second, in which a lower court had ordered a large theater chain to divest itself of monopoly holdings, Douglas affirmed divesture but remanded the case so that the district court could ascertain which holdings had been acquired as a result of antitrust violations and order them divested first. These two opinions set the stage for the Court's consideration of the *Paramount* case.

Douglas affirmed nearly all the lower court's specific findings, but he disagreed with its solution. Competitive bidding by exhibitors would not work, he argued, because the lower court's plan did not provide rules for comparing bids and would therefore burden the courts with an impossible task of administering the distribution system. It would also leave untouched the real heart of monopoly power. It was true, he said, that the five major studios—Paramount, Warner Bros., MGM-Loew's, RKO and Twentieth Century-Fox—owned only 17 percent of all theaters in the United States, but what the *Paramount* case was really about was monopoly over *first-run* exhibition in the large cities, and that was overwhelmingly dominated by studio-affiliated theaters. He remanded the case to the lower court to reconsider whether breakup of vertical integration in the motion-picture industry was not the proper course.*

On reflection, the district court agreed. Circuit Judge Augustus N.

---

* Justice Douglas did, however, grant the movie industry one small victory. He stated, almost parenthetically: "We have no doubt that moving pictures, likes newspapers and radio, are included in the press whose freedom is guaranteed by the First Amendment." *United States v. Paramount Pictures, Inc., et al*, 334 U.S. 131 (1948), at 166. Thus he declared the Court's readiness to overturn the *Mutual Film* decision of 1915, which had excluded movies from First Amendment protection. The actual step of granting First Amendment rights to movies was taken by the Court in *Burstyn v. Wilson*, 343 U.S. 495 (1952).

Hand declared on July 25, 1949—nearly eleven years after the *Paramount* case had begun—that separation of the studios from exhibition was a necessary remedy. The Justice Department thereupon set about dismantling the house that Adolph Zukor built. By 1954 the five major producing firms had divested themselves of ownership or control of all their theaters.

But the advent of free enterprise in the booking of first-run features dawned too late for independent theater owners. By the time the federal court's rulings went into effect, theater attendance was in its second year of decline, and the small neighborhood theaters were hit most seriously. There has been more speculation than data on why movie patronage had begun to slip even before the impact of television, but it seems likely that the postwar spurt in the birth rate (the late 1940s "baby boom," during which young adults committed their time and money to home- and family building) led this prime consuming group to curtail its moviegoing habits. It has sometimes been assumed that people gave up movies for more active leisure pursuits, such as bowling or golf, yet a study of postwar recreation and entertainment expenditures indicates that spending on spectator and participation sports was less, on a percentage basis, in 1953 than in 1946.

Moreover, the small independent theaters had to raise their prices to compete for first-run films. As prices went up at every theater, the lower economic groups, the people producers considered their most faithful supporters, could not afford to go to the movies as frequently as in the past. More than four thousand "four-wall" theaters closed in the decade from 1946 to 1956, and though their loss was almost completely balanced by the construction of new drive-ins, these could not replace the inexpensive neighborhood theaters for inner-city lower-income residents. By 1953, according to a survey, only 32.4 percent of all theaters were making a profit on admission income. Another 38.4 percent were losing money at the box office but breaking into the black through sales of food, popcorn, candy and beverages, and the remainder, 29.2 percent, were just plain losing money.

Out in Hollywood the studio heads were beginning to feel like Caesar in the Forum or Richard III at Bosworth Field: the wounding stabs began to come from everywhere at once. In the middle of their struggle with the Justice Department came the HUAC investigators; and just as they were preparing for the congressional confrontation came an all-out attack from their most lucrative foreign market, Great Britain. Small wonder they were unable to give serious thought to television's implications.

For Hollywood, victory in war had meant, among other things, the reopening of European theaters to American movies. Before the war, American studios had gained as much as 40 percent of their total box-office revenues outside the United States and Canada; during the war, they had been able to maintain high profits through access to the Latin

American market and increased domestic attendance. With the end of hostilities in Europe, the studios expected overseas returns to leap back to the prewar high. It was an apparently ideal situation: an insatiable demand, created by years of deprivation, and a nearly unlimited backlog of pictures.

In 1946 Italy imported an astounding 600 feature films from the United States; two years later the figure was 668, more than half again as many as the total American production for those years, which suggests that hundreds of wartime and even prewar movies were belatedly earning lire for Hollywood. From British bookings, American producers began almost immediately to earn $60 million annually. The State Department extracted an agreement from France canceling the prewar import quotas and substituting a provision reserving screen time in French theaters for French films. In the case of Occupied Germany, the American military government opposed the studios' plans to take profits out of the country and gain control of German filmmaking; Hollywood was resentful, and at the end of 1946 only 43 American films had been released for showing in the American-occupied zone.

Unfortunately, these triumphs of business enterprise conflicted with the other countries' desire to nurture their own national film production, and in the precarious economic conditions of the immediate postwar years, the extraction of huge profits by Hollywood was among the factors threatening several nations with financial calamity.

Great Britain, whose balance-of-payments deficit was so severe that it had to find ways to stop the outflow of dollars, was the first to act. In August 1947 the British government declared that henceforth imported films would be required to pay a customs duty equal to 75 percent of their "value"—meaning their expected box-office earnings in Great Britain. Immediately the Motion Picture Export Association, a newly founded arm of the producers organization, proclaimed an embargo on further film exports to Britain. For seven months the British public was deprived of American movies. To fill the gap the British film industry rapidly increased its production. The boycott ended in 1948 after negotiations produced an agreement stipulating that Americans could import films freely but could remove only $17 million in earnings annually. At the same time, Britain, France and Italy took steps to reimpose quotas on the importation of foreign films to encourage their own domestic production.

By 1950, when television first began to make serious inroads on domestic attendance, overseas revenues had ceased to be the traditionally easy profits for Hollywood studios and became instead the margin between profit and loss for a majority of Hollywood films. Although a number of countries had placed restrictions on the removal of box-office earnings, most of them encouraged American producers to spend blocked profits by making films in their studios. Such ventures not only gave American filmmakers access to their earnings but could bring down production costs in comparison with Hollywood's high wage scales, and at the same time feature locations and players who would appeal to overseas audiences. In earlier years American-controlled foreign production companies had made "quota quickies." By the 1950s overseas locations and American investment in foreign production had become essential elements in Hollywood's financial survival.

Studio executives responded to Great Britain's import duty with a greater sense of panic, according to Hollywood observers, than to any other problem besetting them. It was clearly a case of taking out anxieties on a relative trifle, to which they would magisterially reply by withholding films, when the far more serious legal, political and technological challenges were too intractable and threatening to allow a free expression of feeling. The most obvious and imminent danger of all, that free home entertainment on television would render theater movies obsolescent, was too frightening even to think about.

With the advent of television, the history of motion-picture production and exhibition appeared in an entirely new light, not so much a fulfillment of the nation's entertainment needs as a diversion, an accidental detour caused by a temporary technological inadequacy. It was ironic that a home-entertainment medium dreamed of as a solution to middle-class dilemmas had turned into a theatrical medium controlled by immigrant entrepreneurs for the benefit of working-class audiences. Now it was even more ironic that the theatrical medium had achieved respectability and an audience of the educated and affluent, while the home-entertainment medium was on its way to becoming an almost universal possession of Americans of all races, nationalities and economic classes.

Could motion-picture production and exhibition maintain themselves in the face of television? McLuhan was later to say that the content of television is movies (as the content of movies is printed prose), but such a dictum does not necessarily imply the survival of Hollywood or of motion-picture theaters—the content of television could be old movies or movies made especially for TV. (Several studios did in fact sell or lease older films to TV stations in the early days of the new medium, and then found themselves in the nightmarish position they rarely permitted in theatrical booking: allowing an old product to draw the audience away from a current product. Later, when television had emerged triumphant in the competition between the two, selling or leasing television rights became a principal source of revenue for movie producers.)

The prevailing opinion seems to have been that natural gregariousness would keep the American people going out to movie theaters in preference to staying home. Only in 1949, when television could no longer be ignored, did producer Samuel Goldwyn dare to say the unsayable: "It is a certainty that people will be unwilling to pay to see poor pictures when they can stay home and see something which is, at least, no worse."[3]

---

[3] Samuel Goldwyn, "Hollywood in the Television Age," *Hollywood Quarterly*, Vol. 4 (Winter 1949), p. 146. Reprinted from the *New York Times* (February 13, 1949).

Goldwyn and others who turned at last to confront the challenge of television envisioned three possible courses of action: ownership of television stations by studios; large-screen television in theaters; and pay television. The first and third alternatives seemed advantageous to studios, the second to exhibitors, but no suggestion was made that would have been favorable to both.

One of the curious sidelights of mass-communication history is that the most powerful motion-picture company of its time almost became a leader in radio and television as well, two decades before television eclipsed movies. The company was Paramount, and the man who saw the future implications of electronic media was once again Adolph Zukor. This suggests that what has seemed one of Zukor's major errors, the lateness in shifting from silent to sound production, occurred because Zukor was preoccupied with even more far-reaching technological innovations.

In 1927, the year Warner Bros. pioneered the transition to sound, Zukor was negotiating to invest Paramount money in a radio network. For an $80,000 commitment (a drop in the bucket, in motion-picture terms) he wanted the network to be named the Paramount Broadcasting System and to locate its studios in the Paramount Theater Building in Times Square—then he would try to get New York City to change the square's name to Paramount Plaza. Nothing came of the deal, but when the network, with other funds, organized as the Columbia Broadcasting System, Zukor acquired a 49 percent share in exchange for movie-company stock. Unfortunately, when the Great Depression struck, Paramount, with its vast theater holdings, fell into even more difficult economic straits than the fledgling radio network, and in 1932, when the movie giant was about to go into bankruptcy, CBS bought back Paramount's holdings.

Except for that aborted effort, the Hollywood studios took no great interest in the electronic media. For a time they refused to allow their contract players to appear on radio, but in the late 1930s that broke down as radio began to reach an even larger audience than the movies, and radio performances by movie stars obviously became prime sources of publicity for current movies. In the late 1930s the major networks began to have producing studios in Hollywood, and writers and performers moved more freely between the two media. By then it was much more difficult for studio management to take a financial interest in the newer media; even if opportunities had presented themselves, the Justice Department's antitrust action would have made the producing companies cautious about acquiring control of a different kind of exhibition outlet. Some studios later did buy stock in individual television stations but were careful not to take an active part in management.

Of the other two options, pay-TV was obviously the more attractive to Hollywood, especially after the studios were forced to divest themselves of their theaters. In the late 1940s the system was called "phonovision" because it entailed cooperation between the producers and AT&T,

and the use of telephone wires for the delivery of programs into individual homes. Under the plan, a television signal would be carried on a leased telephone wire, and the TV sets of participating viewers would be wired into the telephone system. A home viewer who wanted to see a program had simply to dial a telephone number that would make the connection to the TV set. Program charges would appear on each month's telephone bill.

The attraction of pay-TV would be the opportunity to see current first-run movies at home without network television's commercial interruptions. Once enough customers had subscribed, it would be possible, even charging a per-set fee lower than the equivalent theater price (assuming more than one viewer at most sets), for a full length movie at one pay-TV screening to gross far more than its negative costs. A quarter century after the idea was first put forward, however, it had hardly been tried beyond the experimental stage and remained caught in competitive conflict with not only sponsored network television but also the new cable systems, a different version of pay-TV where customers pay a monthly fee to receive an expanded choice of conventional programs over wired sets.

As far as the studios were concerned, large-screen theater television came even less close to getting off the ground, although it has been used increasingly for showing sports events and for specialized nontheatrical screenings (closed-circuit televising of a speech, for example, to overflow crowds who cannot see the speaker in person). The potential advantage to studios would have been largely in distribution, since one print, carried by television over leased wires, could be screened simultaneously in thousands of theaters around the country. In the late 1940s, however, such saturation booking still seemed anathema to distributors accustomed to carefully orchestrating consecutive runs, and Hollywood's entrepreneurial energies remained committed to struggling against conventional television rather than innovatively adapting television to the movie industry's use.

Everywhere one looked, television raised questions or posed challenges to Hollywood's traditional methods of operation. Television, like radio, was financed by selling air time for commercial messages. The entire cost of a program's production might be borne not by the producing company itself, but by the program's sponsors. It was a no-loss, guaranteed-profit proposition, whereas moviemaking was more like book publishing: one could not always be sure whether the individual product would lose or make money. The movie producers, however, seem to have given little or no thought to commercial sponsorship of theatrical motion pictures.

Over the years, moviegoers have sometimes had reason to wonder whether a particular manufacturer may have paid a producer to display his product on the screen—a brand of whiskey, say. But no conclusive evidence has yet appeared. More common in the early days of movies was the showing of separate advertising slides or short films in theaters;

it was considered a highly promising way for exhibitors to increase their profits. In a number of countries, commercial advertising films—for department stores, restaurants or vacation spots, for example—remain a fixture, but in the United States, at some point and for no obvious reason, such films were regarded as beneath the dignity of a self-respecting exhibitor and almost entirely disappeared from American screens.

When studios began cutting down feature-movie production in the late 1940s, a number of movie workers found employment in television. They were surprised to discover that the new medium did not greet them as masters arriving to bestow wisdom on neophytes. Television required a much more rapid work pace than Hollywood people were accustomed to, and allowed much less tolerance for error—since most dramatic productions were screened live in the days before videotape, you couldn't retake flubbed dialogue or edit out scenes where the microphone boom appeared in the picture.

In 1949 one television commentator claimed that movie workers breaking into television would have to learn to produce thirty minutes' screen time a day instead of their usual two minutes. As norms, both figures are clearly exaggerated, but the point was well taken: the art of television was different from what had become the art of motion pictures. No more the long hours of make-up and fittings, the slow deliberations over camera setups, the steady procession of takes and retakes. Now it would once again be like Keystone and Biograph in the early days, more frantic, more spontaneous, more improvised, but with an immediacy of life that made the postwar Hollywood product look, to paraphrase André Bazin, cramped and isolated within the bright artificial world of an aquarium.

Once the box-office returns for 1947 were in, with the incontrovertible news that movies were losing patronage for the first time since the Depression, Hollywood at once came up with an explanation which had nothing to do with television or British customs duties or antitrust suits or HUAC hearings: the reason people stayed home was that there weren't enough good pictures.

It's difficult to know whether this was merely a cliché aimed at self-deception—there's nothing wrong with us a few good pictures won't cure—or a perceptive statement of an apparent and troubling fact: American movies were not as good as they used to be. Perhaps there was something of both perspectives in the movie community's answer: good pictures would have had a favorable effect on motion-picture attendance, but movie workers were beginning to question whether they knew how to make good pictures any more.

In the early postwar years, Hollywood made a number of films rightly regarded as classics, among them Hitchcock's *Notorious*, Ford's *My Darling Clementine*, Capra's *It's a Wonderful Life*, Hawks's *The Big Sleep*, all in 1946; Chaplin's *Monsieur Verdoux* in 1947, otherwise a below-par year; and in 1948 Max Ophul's *Letter from an Unknown*

Woman, Hawks's *Red River*, Welles's *Lady from Shanghai*, and Abraham Polonsky's neglected *Force of Evil*. Yet even the best Hollywood films displayed some of the curious visual and thematic flaws that appeared as more glaring defects in run-of-the-mill productions.

Hollywood movies of the postwar period seem in retrospect, to this viewer at least, to possess a visual tone and feel unlike anything before or since. "Everything, even the actors," as André Bazin wrote about one of Jean Renoir's American films, "seem[s] like Japanese flowers under glass."[4] It was as if the technological skills of studio filmmaking had developed to a point of diminishing returns. Even exterior scenes were routinely shot inside sound stages: with the end of wartime restrictions, sets were once again extensively lighted, but the wartime feeling of claustrophobia persisted in the midst of dazzling brightness. Hollywood's capacity to make its images look more and more real had the paradoxical effect of giving American movies an unintended surreal look. One reason for the stunning impact of Italian neorealist films in this period was the simplicity and directness of their location shots in comparison to Hollywood's highly elaborated but increasingly unconvincing artifice.

The same problem applied to Hollywood's treatment of human behavior, and again the Italian postwar films provided a sharp contrast. After their wartime experience making documentary and propaganda films, a number of Hollywood workers were determined to tackle fundamental human issues in their postwar movies, and films on anti-Semitism, like *Gentleman's Agreement* and *Crossfire* (both 1947), and on race, like *Intruder in the Dust* (1948) and *Pinky* (1949), were the laudable result. Yet when Hollywood tried to combine its formula characterizations with complex social and psychological themes, the situations and resolutions, like the settings, appeared contrived. Italian films like De Sica's *The Bicycle Thief* (1948) possessed by comparison an unmistakable sense of human and social reality.

What Hollywood had learned to do supremely well—comedy, musicals, genre Westerns and crime pictures, melodramas, popularizations of classics—did not provide many lessons for a new era of seriousness and responsibility. Hollywood's triumph had been overwhelmingly a triumph of formula, and the novelty and freshness of American commercial movies had come from the inventive new ways in which formulas were reshaped to meet the times. Formulas worked beautifully in their place—and continue to do so—but formulas and significant social themes did not mix effectively (even though films like *Gentleman's Agreement* and *Pinky*, perhaps because of the novelty and sensationalism of their subjects, were box-office hits).

One of the most startling aspects of Hollywood's postwar slump was the trouble filmmakers were having in a basic aspect of their craft—story continuity. There was an increasing trend in the 1940s to use voice-over narratives to tell a story that shots and dialogue themselves appar-

---

[4] *Jean Renoir* (1971; English translation, 1973), p. 94.

Billy Wilder's *Sunset Boulevard* (1950) combined nostalgia for Hollywood's glorious past with a curious demonstration of the troubles it was having with story continuity in the post–World War II period: in macabre fashion the film is narrated by a voice from beyond the grave. Gloria Swanson played the aging former star and William Holden the young scriptwriter she ensnares.

ently could not be made to do. At best the voice-over is a distancing device; it destroys the illusion of the screen image's presentness and forces the narrator's interpretation of visual experience on the viewer instead of allowing him or her to feel directly. In *Sunset Boulevard* (1950), Billy Wilder added an additional macabre element by having his narrator tell the story from beyond the grave. *Sunset Boulevard* is a remarkable example of Hollywood's crisis of confidence, not only in its nostalgia for Hollywood's golden past, but in its inability to let the moving image—which is, of course, what movies are all about—speak for itself.

At the end of the 1940s there were, as usual, additional complicating factors for Hollywood. The first to make itself felt, immediately after the war, was the desire of many directors and performers to set up independent producing companies. Their motives were both practical and idealistic. Since Hollywood's top-ranking movie workers were among the highest-salaried employees in the country, they were in the highest income-tax brackets. By incorporating as part of independent filmmaking companies they could earn income as a percentage of profits rather than as a salary, reducing their tax liability. In addition, having worked outside studio supervision on their wartime documentary assignments, many directors wanted to become their own bosses.

Independent production began to become important in Hollywood again just as the antitrust cases were drawing to a close, and the divesture of theaters from studios had a significant impact on the independents' independence. With block-booking outlawed, distributors—that is, the major studios—had to market every film individually, something they had not done in more than forty years. Without the guaranteed income that block- and blind-booking provided, producers also had to finance each film individually. This put the independent filmmakers in a bind. Banks would not provide funds without assurance that a major distributor would handle a film. Distributors would not agree to handle a film unless they thought they could market it, and that often meant demands for changes in script and casting. The result was that the independents were tied to formulas to an even greater extent than before.

After 1948 the old assembly-line method of making movies gradually came to an end. As more and more small neighborhood theaters closed their doors, there was no longer need to produce scores of "B" Westerns and melodramas to fill screen time in inexpensive houses. When the transcontinental cable was completed in the early 1950s, the television networks took advantage of Hollywood's pool of talent, and "B" movie workers and styles shifted over to weekly genre comedies, mysteries and Westerns on the small screen.

Meanwhile studio managers sought some way to halt the decline of motion-picture-theater attendance. MGM took the lead in using survey-research techniques to discover what moviegoers wanted to see. A wartime survey showed that musical comedies were favored over all other story types, so MGM revived the genre. With Gene Kelly and Fred

Astaire as its leading male dancers, MGM defied television's competition for half a decade with handsome, sophisticated musical productions in color, of which two and sometimes three a year ranked among the industry's top box-office hits from 1948 to 1952. The series culminated in two of the classic American musicals, *Singin' in the Rain* (1952) and *The Bandwagon* (1953)—both, ironically, steeped in nostalgia for Hollywood's great days gone by.

Other genres were less highly rated in the poll of audience preferences, yet genre films had an obvious allure for Hollywood in its crisis of confidence. Crime stories, cowboy stories and love stories were what movie entertainment, at its core, had always been about, and the country's repressive postwar political climate conspired with economic need to push Hollywood back to its familiar forms—neither overseas audiences nor the American Legion would appreciate movies on current American social problems, so why continue to make them?

Westerns, though among the least popular story types in the audience survey, nevertheless made a resurgence in the postwar period, and several of John Ford's U.S. Cavalry epics with John Wayne, as well as Fred Zinnemann's *High Noon* (1952) and George Stevens' *Shane* (1953), were popular hits. War pictures, comedies and costume melodramas also proved to be box-office favorites. For the first time in their history, American commercial movies became principally what they had once been only partially—an escape from reality into the familiar structures of genre formula. Their role in propagating alternative modes of social behavior seemed to have been completely abandoned, a casualty of the Cold War and a vanishing audience.

The idea that better pictures would reverse the box-office trend gave way gradually to a more basic show-business conviction: the only way to keep audiences coming back was by feeding their craving for novelty. Television was the new toy that entranced them at the moment, but the way to beat a gimmick was with a better gimmick. Entrepreneurs began searching inventors' workshops for the technological breakthrough that would bring people flocking to theaters. As with sound and color, further advances in motion-picture technology had been held up in laboratories, waiting for a time when commercial necessity would overcome the industry's reluctance to break with familiar patterns of success. In the wake of television that time had come.

The first novelty to reach the screen conquered the last outpost of the nineteenth-century vision of motion-picture realism—stereoscopic three-dimensionality. The technique of achieving three-dimensionality was relatively simple and had been grasped in the earliest days of filmmaking—like the old-fashioned wooden steroscopic viewers, the 3-D process consisted in essence of two images, and special lenses to superimpose one on the other. Public experiments with 3-D movies had been conducted at various times over the years, but the industry's businessmen had probably been correct in judging that moviegoers would not like wearing the spectacles necessary to attain 3-D vision.

THE MUSEUM OF MODERN ART/FILM STILLS ARCHIVE

Genre movies made a comeback in the 1950s as Hollywood struggled to recover its essential audience appeal in years of continually declining attendance. Westerns and musicals were among the strongest box-office attractions of the period. Fred Zinnemann's *High Noon* (1952) was a notable Western (top); Gary Cooper (right), the aging sheriff, wins the climactic gunfight with Ian MacDonald, while Grace Kelly has fallen on the ground between them. Fred Astaire and Cyd Charisse (bottom) are paired in the memorable "Girl Hunt" number from Vincente Minnelli's *The Band Wagon* (1953), one of the best musicals MGM made after the war.

FROM THE MGM RELEASE *The Band Wagon* © 1953 LOEW'S INCORPORATED

Even in the 1950s the major studios did not consider 3-D a gamble worth taking, but an independent producer went ahead and made an African adventure melodrama, *Bwana Devil* (1952), complete with naked savages throwing spears at the audience, and audiences thronged into theaters to see it. But like Hale's Tours, the simulated railway-car theater of half a century before, 3-D was one of those gimmicks that, once experienced, did not attract many patrons again. Its allure lasted only a few months, suggesting that nineteenth-century notions of realism no longer interested a motion-picture audience accustomed to fantasy and idealization.

Another multiple-projector, multiple-lens process, Cinerama, found more influential backing, perhaps because it created an illusion of three-dimensionality without the necessity of special eyeglasses. For more than two decades since its 1952 debut, it has played a successful, though limited, role in motion-picture exhibition, largely as a tourist attraction in a few metropolitan centers.

What the industry as a whole desired, clearly, was a simpler gimmick—something that could be installed without prohibitive expense, and adapted to the standard of single-camera filming and single-projector exhibition. The answer was found in a wide-angle lens that created a much larger screen image. The first wide-angle process was introduced by Twentieth Century-Fox in 1953 under the trade name CinemaScope; similar devices went by such names as VistaVision and Panavision.

It was a good gimmick—one that accentuated the difference between a vast motion-picture screen with a color image augmented by stereophonic sound and the smaller black-and-white television picture, without varying too far from traditional movie techniques and styles. Wide-screen processes were widely used for large-budget spectacles, but smaller screen sizes were still preferred by directors seeking an image that could effectively portray human interaction.

With so much novelty appearing at once in motion-picture theaters, box-office receipts climbed in 1953 for the first time since 1946. It was, however, a temporary remission. Though attendance and box-office figures occasionally rose over the years to follow, basically their direction was down—and the rises in admission prices and in total population only masked the even more precipitous decline on a comparative scale. By the early 1960s a survey of audience attitudes toward television asked respondents to name the product or service they were "personally most satisfied with" from among automobiles, TV programs, popular music, movies and women's fashions. Only 2 percent named movies, the lowest expression of preference among the five choices. When the researchers sought to compare television with other "major media . . . for the mass dissemination of information and entertainment," they listed radio, magazines and newspapers, and did not bother to mention motion pictures at all.[5]

---

[5] Gary A. Steiner, *The People Look at Television* (1963), pp. 29–30.

17

HOLLYWOOD'S COLLAPSE

Hollywood kept so bright a public face during its long decline that many moviegoers never realized the industry's travail. Changes in technology and public taste affected other great institutions of culture and commerce much more ignobly. The nation's railroads allowed their passenger service to deteriorate so scandalously that the federal government finally took over. Major magazines like *Life* and the *Saturday Evening Post* foundered not because they were losing their audience, but because their advertisers deserted them for television. There came a time, as the last third of the twentieth century began in the United States, when it was hard to find a decent railway car or a familiar magazine, but the movies were always there when one wanted them, bigger, noisier, more expensively produced and, so the industry proclaimed, better than ever. The trouble was that people did not want them nearly so much as before.

One had to read the trade papers or the financial pages to grasp the enormity of Hollywood's troubles. Suburbanites may even have imagined movies were prospering. Handsome new theaters were going up in the shopping centers, and when people went out on Saturday night they found long lines for the movie they wanted to see. They weren't likely to pass by the scores of shuttered theaters in old downtown neighborhoods (urban renewal was probably razing them, anyway) or notice how few customers their favorite theaters had on weekday nights. The stars were still getting their marriages and divorces on page one; people were constantly talking about movies on the television talk shows; the drugstore racks were filled with movie-star fan magazines. Hollywood was Hollywood; it was part of the national life.

Even in the movie community itself, where the facts of economic life were clear to everyone, signs of the true depth of Hollywood's troubles were not all that easy to find. Anxiety was endemic, of course, but then, everyone had always been anxious in Hollywood, even in the best of times. What was more significant, as hard times set in, was the necessity to keep up appearances—and appearances were not entirely deceiving: some people still made money in Hollywood, and the gold-rush mentality remained as strong as ever.

A principle of self-protection, always strong in Hollywood, became even more prominent. The new straitened circumstances impelled successful movie workers to raise their salary demands higher than ever. For it was not that every picture was earning less money than pictures had in the past: the public was going to fewer movies, and the total attendance for movies was dropping, but a smaller number of popular movies drew bigger crowds than ever. With higher admission prices, the favored movies turned bigger profits. The gold was there to be mined, only fewer people could share in it.

Under the impact of the *Paramount* decision, business methods changed rapidly and one had to keep one's eye on the target. The studio system of production was coming to an end, and it was still unclear what would replace it. In the production sphere, the absolute suzerainty of the studio managers had been invaded over the years by three countervailing forces: the banks, organized labor, the agents.

During the years of vertical integration, the studios had a cozy relationship with banks, particularly California's powerful Bank of America, which had grown to prominence in part through successful investments in movie production. The situation after the *Paramount* decision was drastically different: since each picture had to be marketed individually, there was no guarantee of first-run play dates until after the picture had been completed and previewed, and no idea of total bookings until after the first-run returns. These uncertainties made Hollywood's bankers retreat. To win their approval a picture had to have proven box-office stars and traditionally effective stories or formulas, and there is no question that the emphasis on these helped make Hollywood's product more timid, trite and conventional.

The increasing importance of box-office favorites gave more power to actors, and through them, to their agents. As the studios began to pare the lists of contract players, directors and writers, the balance of power in the generation-long struggle between agents and studios at last swung to the agents. They had the clients, they held the cards. As long as one of their clients was deemed necessary to a production before a bank would finance it, the agent could call the shots: he could determine the amount and method of payment to the star, and insist on approval of other players, the director and the script.

As the power of agents grew almost boundless, the larger agencies began to short-cut the negotiating process and put together a production package from among their own clients—players, writer, director, perhaps even producer—and offer it simultaneously to a bank and a studio. Eventually agencies like MCA and William Morris were doing every production task the studios had once done, and MCA ended up taking over Universal Studios. When the Justice Department threatened antitrust action, MCA kept Universal and let its agency operations go.

The agencies became one of the few sources of innovation or daring in beleaguered Hollywood of the 1950s and 1960s. If a box-office star wanted to do a certain script, the agency put together a package and convinced a studio to distribute a film which, had the production decision been in the studio's hands, would probably never have been approved. On the other hand, the power of stars to ruin promising productions by insisting on script changes or unsuitable co-performers was just as great, and undoubtedly exercised more often.

Like the banks, the last of the three countervailing forces, the unions, tended to be wholly conservative in the postwar years. The Communist issue helped to destroy labor militancy in Hollywood, and the cutbacks in studio personnel beginning in 1947 put the unions on the defensive. They needed to preserve what they had in a period of diminishing demand. This took the form of bargaining for job security with an industry that was itself less and less secure, and rigidly limiting the entry of newcomers into their fields. Costs of labor became an increasingly vexing problem for producers; they were one reason among many why more and more productions were filmed overseas, where wages were lower and work rules more flexible. For Hollywood's skilled workers, and for the vast majority of performers, writers and directors as well, the problem became not wages and working conditions, but underemployment and unemployment.

These challenges to the studio system coincided with another critical change in Hollywood's power structure: a generation of leaders was growing old. It was remarkable how much authority had habitually been wielded over moviemaking by young men. Almost all the principal studio executives and producers had made it to the top before they were forty, and many at a much younger age than that.

Once before, during the crisis in the movie industry engendered by the Great Depression, a group of men grown old in their jobs had been pushed out—Carl Laemmle, William Fox and Adolph Zukor among them—and a second generation of young men led Hollywood into its golden ages. Now at mid-century these men, too, had ruled two decades or more, and the movie community was sliding into a depression all its own. There are few targets so satisfying to aim at as men who are down, after they have exercised enormous arbitrary power.

The case against the aging moguls was built up of innumerable individual hurts and resentments—the anthropologist Hortense Powdermaker heard so many awful tales against the studio heads during her postwar stay in Hollywood that she concluded they were totalitarian tyrants. In the eyes of their employees, the bosses bore the blame for everything that was wrong with the movies; Hollywood would never abandon its adherence to banal old formulas, never give its creative workers a chance to make quality pictures, until the rulers were dethroned.

The stockholders' chief resentment was over salaries: now that earnings were falling, the principle of taking care of insiders first was clearly detrimental to the outsiders who considered themselves, as the folklore of American capitalism taught them, owners of the company. Studio managers paid themselves the highest salaries in the country, and when a man earning half a million dollars a year no longer produced profits for his company, he was vulnerable to the argument that a younger, less expensive executive could do no worse, and might do better.

Louis B. Mayer, once the mightiest of the moguls, was the first to go; his resignation from MGM was forced in 1951. He was sixty-six years old. Harry Cohn fought off his stockholders at Columbia—since the studio had never owned theaters, it coped better with post-1948 marketing patterns than other studios—until his death in 1958, age sixty-seven. Samuel Goldwyn gave up filmmaking in his mid-seventies. David O. Selznick made his last picture in the mid-1950s, having produced only four films after 1945; Darryl F. Zanuck resigned as production head of Twentieth Century-Fox in 1956 after several bad years for the company, though he was later to re-emerge as a powerful figure at the studio. Barney Balaban at Paramount and Jack Warner at Warner Bros. held on to their reins until the 1960s.

The new generation who succeeded them did not find solutions to the studios' problems any easier. They inherited a situation where fewer and fewer pictures were being made, and fewer still made money, but those that captured the box office earned enormous sums. It was as if the rules of baseball had been changed so that the only hit that mattered was a home run. The studios became interested only in the motion-picture equivalent of a home run.

This meant essentially enormous box-office power in a single production: big-name stars, proven formula, pre-sold title from a best-selling novel or Broadway hit musical or play. The right combination of these elements continues to have enormous popular appeal—*The Godfather* and *The Exorcist* are examples from the early 1970s. But what if a fickle public did not find the combination just right? Production heads were as likely to try to copy success in the 1960s and 1970s as their predecessors had been in the 1930s, making musicals in the wake of *The Sound of Music* or gangster pictures after *Bonnie and Clyde*. The difference was in the cost of production. Millions, sometimes tens of millions, were riding on each picture, and though the studio heads seemed more cautious in their approach to picture material than ever, what they were doing was carrying Hollywood's traditional gambling spirit to a suicidal extreme: a multimillion-dollar flop could endanger the stability of a company.

The third generation of studio heads lasted little more than a decade. By the 1960s the continuing decline in motion-picture revenues left the studios weak and vulnerable to outside financial manipulation, as had happened in the 1930s. In the age of conglomerates they became attractive targets for acquisition, and a number of movie companies were absorbed by mammoth corporations: Paramount by Gulf & Western, Warner Bros. by Kinney, United Artists by TransAmerica. MGM was purchased by a hotel magnate. Yet a fourth generation of young men came forward as studio executives.

The motion-picture studios the conglomerates bought were often little more than expensive shells—underutilized sound stages requiring enormous overhead expenses to maintain; idle back lots worth more for real estate than for picture making. (Twentieth Century-Fox in the late 1950s had turned over much of its studio property in West Los Angeles for the development of a commercial complex, Century City; in the early 1970s both Fox and MGM auctioned off their props and wardrobes.) But although they had lost their theaters and largely abandoned production, the studios retained one essential role: they remained the most important distributors. In the 1970s all the traditional majors except RKO continued as the big names in the field, and as distributors they kept the familiar names alive by putting their symbols prominently on every independent production they handled.

Their influence on the Hollywood product therefore continued to be enormous. As distributors they exercised ultimate financial control—except for that of the audience—over productions they handled. They planned the advertising and marketing strategies; they received the returns from exhibitors and made payments to producers after deducting their costs. An independent production that a studio had contracted to distribute but did not like (or understand) might receive indifferent handling, or never get off the shelf at all, on the ground that no exhibitor was interested. A picture might be pulled from circulation after its distributing studio had reaped what it considered adequate returns, to make way for new products, even though additional bookings might have been possible.

By the 1970s the structure of the movie industry had reverted to what it had been back in the days before World War I, to the system that W. D. Hodkinson had begun to construct before Adolph Zukor seized power at Paramount: exhibition, distribution and production were all separate from each other, with the distributor at the center of the business. Producers found themselves in exactly the position Zukor had fought his way out of in 1916: at the mercy of distributors. There were solutions to their dilemma, but through television rather than theatrical release. If a producer wanted a large-screen outlet for his picture, the only alternative to studio distribution was independent distribution, and it was a distinction without a difference.

In their guidebook for novices in the trade, *The Movie Industry Book: How Others Made and Lost Money in the Movie Industry* (1970), Johnny Minus and William Storm Hale outline some of the pitfalls producers faced. They call attention to a fact familiar to movie showmen for more than half a century: cheating can begin the minute the patron slides his money through the box-office window. Cashiers, theater managers, exhibitor chains, all may try to sweeten their share of the take at the expense of others. The studios had minimized that risk when they had integrated vertically. By the 1970s the risk was maximum for the people at the end of the money chain, the independent producers. They did not begin to see their profits until the distributor had met his own costs. Sometimes a picture seemed to be raking in box-office grosses, but the distributor's expenses rose uncannily to wipe out any chance of profit for the producer. The new breed of independent commercial filmmakers found, contrary to their expectations, that they were often more successful at making motion-picture art than motion-picture money.

THE MUSEUM OF MODERN ART/FILM STILLS ARCHIVE

Anarchic violence returned to the screen during the years of cultural and political upheaval in the late 1960s. Two films that unexpectedly gained enormous popularity with youthful audiences were Arthur Penn's *Bonnie and Clyde* (1967) and Dennis Hopper's *Easy Rider* (1969). Faye Dunaway and Warren Beatty played romanticized versions of 1930s bandits Bonnie Parker and Clyde Barrow in Penn's film, shown (top) with Michael J. Pollard, at left, during a getaway. Hopper, co-star as well as director, lies slain by Deep South rednecks (bottom) at the end of *Easy Rider*.

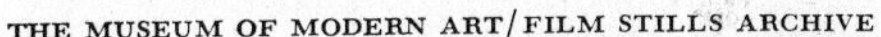

THE MUSEUM OF MODERN ART/FILM STILLS ARCHIVE

* * *

Art—or rather the name "art"—had re-entered the American movie world in the postwar period by way of Europe. Few people, in or out of Hollywood, were comfortable with the idea that commercial moviemaking was one of the arts, although the movie community appropriated the term to itself in various ways, as in the Academy of Motion Picture Arts and Sciences, or the language of studio contracts, which referred to players, writers and directors as "artists." But the word "art" was fraught with meanings that could not be accommodated with Hollywood's reality: the factory system of production, mass audiences, enormous profits, producer domination of movie workers, collaborative creation—or with a lingering skepticism about the ability of Americans to produce art. Since it was widely believed in universities and intellectual circles that art came to America from Europe, there was a predisposition to imagine that cinema as art would stem from across the Atlantic, too.

The international history of motion pictures gave some support to this view. The French and Italians had taken the lead in filmmaking, only to be waylaid by World War I. After the war, German and then Soviet silent cinema had set new standards for artistry, but Hollywood disposed of this competition by hiring away the leading German players and directors, and by introducing sound. Though the British with their superior dramatic tradition might have been expected to challenge American supremacy in the sound period, Hollywood cut off the threat by controlling British studios and concentrating their efforts on "quota quickies."

For some years American audiences did not have much opportunity to see European films. After the wave of excitement over post–World War I German features like *The Cabinet of Dr. Caligari*, foreign films rarely played first-run theaters but were limited to specialty houses in New York City and foreign-language theaters in immigrant neighborhoods. The situation began to change for British films in the mid-1930s when J. Arthur Rank, a prominent British financier, extended his British film-company holdings to become a substantial partner in Universal Studios. At the same time United Artists began to distribute British films more extensively in the United States, particularly productions of Alexander Korda.

In the immediate aftermath of World War II, British films first recalled the attention of American audiences to the qualities of foreign films—more precisely, perhaps, Hollywood called attention to British films by awarding several of them Oscars in 1946. Three different British pictures won awards, and Laurence Olivier was given a special award for his accomplishment as a producer, director and leading actor in *Henry V* (1945). Though one or two British films had won minor Oscars in the late 1930s, one wonders at the movie community's generosity to its English-speaking rival. One possibility is that Hollywood was recognizing the most important new power and influence in its affairs (outside of HUAC and the Justice Department), J. Arthur Rank.

Rank's British productions, released predominately through Universal, displayed the versatility, quality and entertainment value that producers like Selznick had brought to Hollywood's prewar period. In the first three postwar years, Rank dominated Hollywood's prestige productions with two Noël Coward adaptations, *Blithe Spirit* and *Brief Encounter* (1945; released in 1946 in the United States), both directed by David Lean; Lean's *Great Expectations* (1947); Carol Reed's brilliant thriller *Odd Man Out* (1947); and in 1948 two great American box-office hits, Olivier's *Hamlet* and *The Red Shoes*, directed by Michael Powell and Emeric Pressburger. *Hamlet* won the Oscar for best picture, the first time a foreign film had won in competition with Hollywood products.

The previous year Hollywood had also made a special gesture to the foreign cinema by awarding Vittorio de Sica's neorealist film, *Shoeshine* (1946), a prize for exceptional quality. Thereafter, in every year but 1953, an award was voted for the best foreign-language production released the year before in the United States. In 1951 the Oscar went to *Rashomon*, the Japanese film directed by Akira Kurosawa. Twice more in the 1950s—in 1954 for Teinosuke Kinugasa's *Gate of Hell* and in 1955 for Hiroshi Inagaki's *Samurai*—the awards were given to Japanese movies. Japan had become an unexpected new factor in the development of cinema as an art; it was also a major importer of American movies.

By the early 1950s, interest in British and foreign-language films was strong enough to support the first significant innovation in audience segmentation since the arrival of talking pictures—the rise of "art houses" devoted exclusively to non-Hollywood movies. These were generally small neighborhood theaters in university towns or large cities which could not have survived in their old role as inexpensive late-run outlets for Hollywood films but discovered that they could draw a steady audience for first-run foreign films at higher prices than they used to charge for double features. There may have been no more than four or five dozen such theaters in the country, but that was enough to encourage small independent distributors to bring in foreign films.

The art houses marked an important break with Hollywood's way of doing business. Over the years, Hollywood's critics had asserted that American companies would never produce intellectually respectable films as long as every one of their products was tailored to the tastes of a mass audience. What was needed was a recognition of separate audiences and films catering to various levels of taste and intelligence. Films made for discriminating audiences, it was argued, would not make big money, but there was a potential audience large enough at least to recover the costs of production.

To the art houses came the cream of European moviemaking: Italian neorealism; British comedies starring Alec Guinness and Alastair Sim; Jean Renoir's great films of the 1930s, *The Grand Illusion* (1937) and

Rules of the Game (1939), widely shown in the United States for the first time in the 1950s; Jacques Tati's comedy *Mr. Hulot's Holiday* (1953); the early films of Federico Fellini, such as *La Strada* (1954); Ingmar Bergman's *The Seventh Seal* (1957). An audience of university students and educated city dwellers coalesced around these offerings.

This audience probably did not realize it was seeing only the tip of the European iceberg, that banal genre romances and melodramas played as large a part in the production schedules of London, Paris or Rome as of Hollywood, and were considerably less skillfully made than their Hollywood counterparts. Moreover, in the welter of Hollywood releases with which American moviegoers were surrounded one had to do on one's own the task that distributors did for foreign films: separate the wheat from the chaff. The job was doubly difficult because the great American movies of the period were often triumphs within genre frameworks, and an audience newly attuned to art in cinema had trouble recognizing the artistry in a John Ford Western or an Alfred Hitchcock thriller, particularly when Hollywood's promotional ballyhoo was aimed at attracting mass audiences for those films.

The result was that the art-house audience which developed in the 1950s was convinced that only Europeans understood the cinema as an art. There was very little in daily or weekly film reviewing that could help them think otherwise, and critical writing on American movies was almost nonexistent. Outside of afternoon TV and the Late Show, it was almost impossible, except at a tiny handful of college cinema societies and big-city revival houses, to discover that Americans had once made sparkling sophisticated comedies, skillful renderings of classical literature, films with social and political content. Hollywood had always given short shrift to its own past, and as its present seemed more and more in jeopardy, it was incapable of demonstrating to a new generation of moviegoers, smaller but more discerning than earlier audiences, that it had anything to contribute.

Not all European imports to the United States were superior works of art. The tendency in motion-picture production and exhibition had always been to get away with as much risqué and socially disreputable behavior as the vigilance of censors would allow and economic necessity dictated. For nearly two decades after 1934, the Production Code Administration had maintained stringent control over Hollywood productions, and rising box-office figures through 1946 seemed to confirm that clean family entertainment was the road to prosperity. But as families found their clean entertainment on the TV screen, there was a natural impulse in the movie trade to revert to shock and titillation. The code remained in force, but not necessarily for European productions, if distributors and exhibitors wanted to take the risk of showing a foreign picture without the code seal.

Movies by directors like Fellini and Bergman were already much more straightforward about sexual behavior than anything the code permitted

Hollywood to make, but they remained limited to coterie audiences. What some enterprising distributors and exhibitors wanted were films that could break through the art-house barrier and appeal to general audiences. Their quality wouldn't necessarily matter if they offered something else audiences wanted to see—for example, nudity or scenes of copulation.

They found what they wanted in a sentimental and, indeed, highly moralistic Swedish film by Arne Mattsson, *One Summer of Happiness* (1951). The young couple in the film overcome the repressive prudery of their rural Swedish setting to achieve their sexual union, but the woman is killed in a motorcycle accident and the man is left with the responsibility and grief. Audiences endured the melodrama to get a glimpse of the couple bathing nude in a lake and lying together afterward, shown from the waist up during lovemaking. That scene created a sensation wherever it was shown, in Europe as well as the United States. Another box-office gold mine was struck by Roger Vadim's *And God Created Woman* (1956), which showed Brigitte Bardot in the nude. Unclothed human bodies were a spectacle audiences could not see just as well, and more cheaply, on television.

At the same time producers in Hollywood were struggling with the shackles of the code. The first important challenge to the Breen Office came in 1953 with Otto Preminger's production *The Moon Is Blue* (1953), an adaptation of a hit Broadway play. What seemed startling about the film was its off-color language—the use of words like "seduce" and "virgin"—but as Jack Vizzard pointed out in his revealing memoir of his years at the Production Code Administration, *See No Evil: Life Inside a Hollywood Censor* (1970), the Breen Office was more concerned with the film's implication that unmarried sexual relations were not an issue of morality. Joseph Breen, at the end of his long career as Hollywood's conscience, refused code approval for the picture. United Artists, the distributor, resigned from the producers association and released the picture without a code seal.

This marked the beginning of the end of Hollywood's self-censorship. Shortly thereafter Breen retired, to be replaced by Geoffrey Shurlock, a Briton who took the iconoclastic view that the code should not stand in the way of scenes depicting real human behavior on the screen, if they were not gross or offensive to audiences. Shurlock's approach placed the Production Code Administration in conflict for the first time with the Catholic Legion of Decency, which had instigated the Breen Office, and with Martin Quigley, the Catholic layman who had written most of the code. The dispute revealed, as Vizzard noted, how much the code's purpose had been to impose a theological standard on the movies, to permit the depiction only of human behavior that conformed to an otherworldly morality (at issue was a scene of a woman attempting suicide with sleeping pills).

After the Production Code Administration gave its seal of approval to Elia Kazan's 1956 film *Baby Doll*, the Legion came out with a direct attack on the administrators for disregarding the provisions of the code. As Vizzard wrote: "The Legion had thrown sham aside and had assumed a proprietary stance over the machinery of an American industrial entity."[1] The question became whether a church organization ought to consider itself empowered to meddle in the affairs of an independent private enterprise. Within Catholic circles the question was debated and finally answered in the negative. Martin Quigley himself, in a late-career turnabout, agreed to assist the producer of Stanley Kubrick's *Lolita* (1962) in obtaining a seal of approval from the code administrators.

By 1962 it may have been more important to a movie-industry veteran like Quigley that a picture with box-office potential be released than that it be moral. For Hollywood, the possibility that Catholic clergy might order their parishoners to boycott a film—a specter raised again in the 1950s—was no longer a threat; it was likely to provide notoriety and increase audience desire to see the picture. Hollywood was falling back more and more on elements moviemakers had known from the first would draw a crowd when every other attraction failed: sex and violence. The code administration tried for a time to preserve its relevance by approving sexually explicit or especially violent films with the added proviso, "Suggested for mature audiences." But that carried little weight at the ticket window.

People who worried about the potential of movies for corrupting youth were a vanishing breed. The battleground for the minds and hearts of children had shifted to Saturday morning TV, and a series of landmark Supreme Court decisions in obscenity cases had severely limited the reach of censorship bodies. The general popular definition of obscenity was likely to be much more restrictive than the Supreme Court doctrines allowed, but with the liberalization of the Legion of Decency's attitude there was no coherent organizational basis for censorship efforts. The issue arose only when local district attorneys sought to make a name for themselves by prosecuting a film or theater over alleged obscenity on the screen.

For several years after Eric Johnston's death in 1964, the Motion Picture Producers Association was without leadership, while attendance figures, after a brief upswing in 1964, dropped more steeply than ever, and producers mingled sex and violence in various proportions (usually more of the latter than the former) hoping to find a formula for renewed success. In 1966 the producers picked Jack Valenti, a presidential assistant to Lyndon B. Johnson, as their new head: American society had changed enough since the selection of Will H. Hays that the movies' frontman did not need to be an Anglo-Saxon Protestant, but the realities of power still required a man with influence in Washington.

One of Valenti's first tasks was to see what could be done about the code. After two years of further erosion of the code's prohibitions,

---

[1] *See No Evil* (1970), p. 209.

Valenti decided to junk it. He put in its place a rating system modeled after Great Britain's, but with more, and less precise, categories: G for general audiences; M for mature audiences (later changed to PG, parental guidance suggested, as a concession to producers who thought M ratings kept too many people away); R for restricted, persons under seventeen not admitted without a parent or guardian; and X for no one under eighteen admitted.

The rating system had the effect of calling special attention to X-rated films and deterred scrupulous exhibitors, or those who counted on youthful patrons, or those in areas where local censorship bodies persisted, from booking them. Thus the ratings became an arena for industry self-censorship with more flexibility than the old code. The rating board could bargain with a producer: so many cuts of nudity or foul language would reduce a rating from X to R, or R to PG, thus increasing the possibility of bookings and potential audience. The values of the new board, however, reflected the old code's standards—sex fell into the X or R category, depending on type and extent; swearing rated R; but violence, often of the most sadistic and gruesome kind, rarely scored other than PG.

The pace of change in motion-picture content was dizzying. By the mid-1960s many of the European directors who had first appeared on art-house screens were making films for distribution by major Hollywood studios to first-run theaters. Art houses faced the prospect of going back to late-run double features or closing their doors. Many tried the former or succumbed to the latter, but in California a few managers and small distributors imagined a more fortunate fate: they would fill their screens with X-rated titillation films made in Europe or by independent commercial producers in Hollywood. Why not candidly make a virtue of the sexual sensationalism that the rating system was designed to curb? An X-rating, far from being a warning to moviegoers, would be like the old pink permits in Chicago during the World War I era, a badge to display as a guarantee of customer satisfaction.

Russ Meyer, as William Rotsler points out in his *Contemporary Erotic Cinema* (1973), is regarded as the pioneer maker of X-rated films. It was he who brought sex for the sake of sex out of the illicit stag-movie category and onto the big screen. His films featured a great deal of lustful action, female nudity and simulated copulation, and the formula was so strikingly successful—and Hollywood so desperate—that in 1970 Twentieth Century-Fox lifted Meyer into the mainstream movie world by distributing his *Beyond the Valley of the Dolls*.

But by 1970 it was difficult to know where the mainstream movie world began and ended any more. By then R- and even X-rated sex films had become fixtures in many of the nation's drive-in theaters. As one former drive-in owner said, "We'd play a really fine picture from a major company and do nothing and we'd play a piece of junk and everybody would come out to see it. That proved to me that drive-in

As motion-picture attendance continued to dwindle, movie studios resorted more and more to sexual titillation to draw a crowd. But they didn't go as far as the independent makers of small-budget sex films, who began in the 1970s to show close-ups of male and female genitals in copulation. Hard-core filmmakers hit the jackpot in 1973, when *Deep Throat* and *The Devil in Miss Jones* were among the leading money-making films of the year, according to *Variety*. Los Angeles, a center of hard-core filmmaking and exhibition, offered a wide variety of sex films, and the Los Angeles *Times* advertised them in a special section; ads for "adult" films covered two thirds of a page in this edition of June 11, 1974.

theater audiences were looking for a specific type of entertainment—action, violence, a certain amount of sex."[2]

The problem—and the opportunity—lay in the propensity of the public to grow jaded. Hale's Tours, 3-D, naked breasts, each had its brief fling of popularity, only to give way to a search for other novelties or more basic qualities of entertainment and emotional catharsis. The sexploitation filmmakers, as they came to be called, had neither the talent nor the resources to create effective motion pictures, so they opted for novelty. San Francisco, the frontier of American sexual display, led the way, leaving behind the drive-ins but turning the art houses into adult film houses—first with shots of female genitals, then of limp male penises, and then, in the early 1970s, of actual copulation, oral and anal intercourse, with close-ups of genitals filling the screen.

At first the hard-core sex pictures attracted a special kind of audience. "Frankly, when we first started out," one adult-theater operator said, "you had the coat-and-tie stereotyped engineer coming in for the afternoon. A very good day business and a very poor night business."[3] The same people would show up week in and week out, a limited but loyal clientele, willing to pay $5 a ticket when the first-run theaters were charging only half that much, and willing also to risk occasional police raids, but not a large enough audience to sustain more than an occasional theater: in Los Angeles some adult houses switched back to late-run double features, and others began to specialize in male homosexual films.

Then, in 1973, two hard-core films scored major breakthroughs to the general movie audience and mass-media attention—*Deep Throat* and *The Devil in Miss Jones*. Neither film offered much more as cinema than the average sex picture. What made the difference seems to have been the willingness of the films' producers actively to promote their leading women players, Linda Lovelace in *Deep Throat* and Georgina Spelvin in *Miss Jones*, as movie stars, something theretofore shunned by the hard-core trade for the same reason producers avoided naming players in the early twentieth century: because low-paid players who became stars demanded more money. This piqued the interest of television, mass magazines and newspapers like the *New York Times*, themselves constantly seeking novelty as a means of maintaining audience interest. Thousands of men and women—particularly in the educated, affluent classes—went to hard-core sex films for the first time to see one or both of these pictures. *The Devil in Miss Jones* ranked sixth in box-office grosses in 1973 among all films released in the United States, according to *Variety*'s compilations, and *Deep Throat* was eleventh.

In the span of no more than a couple of years, hard-core sex had become one of the most popular audience attractions in the motion-picture field—an incredible change in the mores of public entertainment

---

[2] David F. Friedman, quoted in William Rotsler, *Contemporary Erotic Cinema* (1973), p. 173.

[3] Ed Karsh, quoted, *ibid.*, p. 121.

and therefore in the values of American culture at large. Yet some aspects of the culture remained more constant. One was the prosecutory zeal of local law-enforcement officials against allegedly obscene movies, and the desire of state legislative bodies to tighten their laws against obscenity. (*Deep Throat* was brought into the courts in a number of states, and would likely have ranked much higher than eleventh in box-office popularity had not many exhibitors been afraid to show it lest they be raided and prosecuted.)

The other constant was the desire of hard-core-movie producers, like their Hollywood predecessors, to maximize their profits, and their infinite flexibility where money was concerned. If *Deep Throat* could gross over $4 million in a year, even when many theaters refused to play it, what might a movie gross that could play in many more theaters? An R-rated film might have access to ten times as many bookings as an X-rated film. *Deep Throat II*, starring Linda Lovelace, came out in 1974 with an R-rating, showing little sex or nudity and nothing for which the original *Deep Throat* was notorious. With a sexual content no different from scores, if not hundreds, of Hollywood mainstream films, and lacking the wit, skill or style that Hollywood could still attain on occasion, the film sank without a trace.

It was understandable but faulty logic. Linda Lovelace in 1974 was not Mary Pickford in 1914: it was illusory to imagine her a star without the sexual performance that made her famous. There was no easy retreat for hard-core filmmakers into the soft-core class, and no evidence that soft-core sex would ever come close to the success of *Deep Throat* and *Miss Jones*. There seemed to be no new subject for the hard-core filmmakers to tackle. Having shown just about every form of sexual act on the screen, the next step would be to present the same material live on stage, which would surely be entertainment, but not, alas, motion pictures.

While attendance at motion-picture theaters was falling lower and lower, a seeming paradox occurred in the worlds of publishing and academics: a sharp rise of interest in motion pictures as a subject for books, newspaper and magazine criticism, and university courses. Of course, books about the movies and university film courses could thrive on an essentially coterie audience; but the only way movies could survive (except for low-budget hard-core sex films) was to reach a mass audience, and fewer and fewer new films seemed to contain the entertainment values that would lure people to theaters.

Yet there were glimpses of hope for moviemakers. In the 1960s the children of the postwar baby boom—the infants who kept their parents home from movies in the late 1940s—began to come of age. They themselves had grown up in the television era and had logged tens of thousands of hours before the small screen. Oriented to visual media as no previous generation had ever been, they had experienced a steady diet of entertainment equivalent to the "B" movies of the 1930s. When members of this new generation began to encounter classic European and

Hollywood movies through college courses or cinema societies, many were astounded by the wonders of past movies—another tip of the iceberg—in comparison with television shows. They were recruited to the ranks of movie fans.

Could this interest in the Marx Brothers or Humphrey Bogart be translated into a desire to support current films at the box office? There were clues to an answer from overseas: films by acknowledged masters, like Antonioni's *Blow-Up* (1966) did well among youthful audiences, but so did a curious film with a director and players virtually unknown in the United States, *Morgan! or a Suitable Case for Treatment* (1966), directed by Karel Reisz, with David Warner and Vanessa Redgrave. *Morgan!* was not well liked by reviewers, but its wacky behavior, its radical yet ambiguous approach to psychological and political issues, caught the fancy of a college audience awakening to a sense of generational difference in sexual and political values. The challenge to Hollywood was to come up with offerings of its own to please this potential new audience.

Hollywood's answer was to reach back to its genre traditions, and in 1967 it created several films that brought movies once again to the center of national attention. One was *Bonnie and Clyde*, directed by Arthur Penn; another was *The Graduate*, directed by Mike Nichols; a third was *Planet of the Apes*, directed by Franklin J. Schaffner. The first was a gangster picture; the second a boy-meets-girl, boy-loses-girl, boy-gets-girl; the third, science fiction. All three, significantly, were made with an eye to drawing the largest possible mass audience, from all classes and age groups. Yet they were also particularly attuned to the political and social values emerging in the college generation of the 1960s.

Bonnie and Clyde was a cultural phenomenon. It seems clear that Warner Bros., the distributor, did not particularly like the film and booked it to play to Midwestern audiences and draw some revenue from the popcorn-chewing middle-American audience before the expected negative reviews when it opened in New York. The expectations were fulfilled: *Newsweek* and the liberal weeklies, among others, panned it for its violence. (The one reviewer who grasped the meaning of the film most fully was the one with the most extensive knowledge of the American genre tradition, Pauline Kael of *The New Yorker*.)

Yet a bad press did not kill the film: it was as if audiences understood better than either the distributor or the critics the emotional power of the film's anarchic individualism, its depiction of the awesome force of violent authority, its stereotyped but skillful evocation of past movies and past time. *Bonnie and Clyde*'s triumph was, among other things, a small victory for the independent judgment of audiences against the guiding advice of mass journalism, and it led to the unusual experience of mass periodicals, not wishing to lose their aura of omniscience, shaming themselves and coming out in favor of the film.

In 1967–1968, the season of *Bonnie and Clyde* and *The Graduate*, motion-picture attendance rose significantly for the first time since

1945–1946. Writers began speaking of the emergence of a "film generation." University film courses surged from the scores to the thousands. Movie reviewers became subjects of public interest and debate. An American Film Institute, funded by the National Endowment for the Arts, began operations in Washington and Beverly Hills, dedicated to the preservation and enhancement of the American film heritage. Movies appeared to be entering their renaissance.

Appearances, unfortunately, were deceiving. The following year, movie attendance fell to a new low. The new pattern of motion-picture patronage proved unshakable: of the scores of movies released every year, only a handful captured the attention of the public. In 1972, the year of *The Godfather*, the top twenty-five films did almost half the business in the nation's movie theaters.

Nevertheless, the audience *was* there for a few pictures, and no one had yet figured out a foolproof way to guess which films, or what kind of films, would be the lucky ones. Every year big-budget pictures with top stars and "sure-fire" box-office potential flopped miserably. Every year a low-budget film with no clear expectations of success brought crowds. It was like playing the lottery—somebody always won, and though your chances were small, you still bought a ticket in the hope lightning would strike you.

The landmark movie of 1969 was *Easy Rider*, a film about two heroin dealers who take the profits from their last sale and motorcycle across America, looking for meaning to their lives, to a background sound track of contemporary rock-music hits. They end up murdered by Deep South rednecks, and the film, though open to other interpretations, captured the imagination of young audiences who identified the cyclers' rootlessness and alienation from American society with their own. Costing $400,000 to produce, the film earned more than twenty-five times that amount and propelled its principals—Dennis Hopper, the director and co-star, with Peter Fonda; Jack Nicholson, whose supporting role as an alcoholic Southern lawyer turned him into a major box-office attraction; and Bert Schneider, whose BBS Productions financed the film—into a vanguard who appeared to be taking over Hollywood for the young generation.

All these men were in their thirties. Union restrictions and a declining pool of labor had worked to keep young people out of mainstream Hollywood during most of the postwar period, but suddenly youth was at a premium. *Easy Rider*'s example, in the age-old Hollywood way, impelled others to copy its formula—gather up a youthful cast and crew, give them a story about youthful alienation and struggles with a repressive know-nothing society, and you'll bank a 2,500 percent profit, or thereabouts. A movie gold rush began anew in Hollywood for a few noncommercial filmmakers, television directors, free-lance screen writers and off-Broadway performers. It lasted until the imitations of *Easy Rider* nearly all turned out to be box-office disasters.

Still, the passing years could not help but bring forward new faces in

THE MUSEUM OF MODERN ART/FILM STILLS ARCHIVE

Hollywood in the 1970s still provided opportunities for aspiring young male filmmakers (though not for women). Two of the most successful were Peter Bogdanovich and Francis Ford Coppola, who often functioned as writers and producers as well as directors. Bogdanovich coaches Cybill Shepherd (top) on the set of *The Last Picture Show* (1971), a film he directed and wrote with Larry McMurtry. Coppola directed the big box-office hit of 1972, *The Godfather*, with Marlon Brando in the leading role. Brando dances with Talia Shire (bottom) in a shot from the film's opening wedding sequence.

© PARAMOUNT PICTURES CORPORATION

commercial moviemaking. There were still producers and directors who continued to make films in the traditional Hollywood way and be successful at it (the top-grossing picture of 1973 was *The Poseidon Adventure*, a melodrama about a sinking ocean liner), but there were also efforts to appeal to other specialized audiences besides the college generation—notably the urban black population, for whom a number of sex-and-violence films (sometimes called blaxploitation pictures) were made in the 1970s in a mingling of the gangster genre with the newly popular genre of Oriental martial arts originating in Hong Kong.

In the mid-1970s two men still in their early thirties came to the fore as the leaders of a new Hollywood generation—Peter Bogdanovich, director of, among other films, *The Last Picture Show* (1971), and Francis Ford Coppola, director of, among other films, *The Godfather*. Their ascendance marked in some ways a return to the early atmosphere of Hollywood: they were filmmakers in a sense the highly segmented movie industry had rarely known for decades, not only directors but also writers and producers of their pictures, men who created films in a way few Hollywood figures had done since the days of D. W. Griffith. They were followed by other, still-younger men, like Martin Scorcese, whose *Mean Streets* was one of the memorable films of 1973. (But in the years of the women's movement it was disturbing that Hollywood closed its doors to women filmmakers more tightly than ever.) The commercial spirit would never cease to dominate Hollywood as long as there were profits to be earned; but as the big rewards for moviemaking continually narrowed, the machinery of production unexpectedly offered room for some young men of ambition and talent to try to create, as European filmmakers had done, a personal cinema within the framework of movie commerce.

18

THE FUTURE OF MOVIES

"Personal cinema" is an ambiguous term with no precise counterpart in other forms of aesthetic expression. It came into use to describe what were once rarities in the motion-picture world, movies made for goals other than profit, as expressions of individual creativity. But the creative act in motion pictures has never been clearly defined. At one extreme, "personal cinema" can mean a Hollywood film directed by a person with some share of artistic control over the finished product; at the other, it signifies an abstract film conceived, recorded, developed, assembled and printed by a single creator working entirely alone.

The status of movies among the creative arts has always been anomalous. The motion picture sprang from two disparate forms, theater and photography, neither of which, at the end of the nineteenth century when movies were invented, served as a model for aesthetic endeavor. Theater was a public art that directly sought an audience, photography had hardly begun to be considered as a possible medium for artistic expression; where it was not simply commercial, it belonged to a private realm that was defined as recreational rather than creative: the taking of photographs for amusement or self-enhancement as a hobby or pastime.

In theoretical terms, movie cameras were as easily adaptable to amateur use as still cameras, but circumstances delayed the emergence of moviemaking as a private activity for more than a quarter of a century. One was the expense of the equipment, which inhibited persons of average means from acquiring movie cameras and projectors until 16mm and 8mm sizes became available in the 1920s. Another was the effort of Edison and his partners to limit distribution of motion-picture equipment through patent monopolies. And even people who could afford movie cameras in the early days of the medium were led into the arena of public communication by the ideological aura surrounding motion pictures.

The rhetoric of the inventors and promoters claimed that movies made visible the unseen world and recorded subjects that would otherwise be lost to posterity. This repeated emphasis on their social utility and historical significance established a climate that militated against exclusively private uses of the new equipment. Such private subjects as were recorded became, because of the novelty of the medium and the larger-than-life-size images it projected, of intrinsic interest to the public. Even when the goals of early filmmakers were not to turn a profit, they were still drawn into producing films for public dissemination.

Personal cinema was thus in the beginning inseparable from public cinema: the earliest explorations of motion-picture aesthetics came in the work of commercial moviemakers like D. W. Griffith and the Germans who collaborated on *The Cabinet of Dr. Caligari* (1919).

Even when Surrealist and Dadaist painters and poets began making independent experimental films in the 1920s, their purpose was as much to present public messages about the nature of art and visual experience as it was to express personal visions. When the climate of art and culture shifted in the early 1930s, the avant-garde movements went in new directions, and the filmmakers proceeded to other things—some to make documentary and propaganda films in the service of political causes; others, like René Clair and later Luis Buñuel, to direct feature films; still others to lend their talents in abstract film design to Hollywood. The avant-garde filmmakers of the 1920s inaugurated the history of experimental films but laid no foundation for a tradition of personal cinema.

In the decade after 1931, only a very small number of experimental films were made in North America, Great Britain and Europe, and those largely in 35mm, the standard gauge of commercial filmmaking, which the avant-garde of the 1920s also used. Then, as the newer, smaller and less expensive gauges became increasingly available, manufacturers of movie cameras began to encourage consumers with no training or particular interest in the medium to extend the snapshot habit to the moving image, to make "home movies." Thus the first extensive practice of personal cinema was in a realm oblivious to either profit or art.

The promotion of movie equipment for mass consumption stressed the private rather than the social value of the camera. Yet the visionary tradition of writing about motion pictures made it difficult in practice to separate the private from the social. Béla Belázs, the European film theorist, had spoken of the motion picture's subject as *der sichtbare Mensch* —the human being made visible in a way no other medium could. Élie Faure, the French critic, wrote of the promise of the medium if "instead of permitting itself to be dragged by theatrical processes through a desolating sentimental fiction, it is able to concentrate itself on plastic processes, around a sensuous and passionate action in which we can all recognize our own personal virtues."[1]

A small minority of men and women began to use movie equipment in these ways. In the years during and after World War II, what came to be known as the New American Cinema movement—sometimes also called "underground film"—was born in the United States. (Its postwar expansion was aided, curiously, by the availability of surplus 16mm cameras and projectors the armed forces had used for making documentary records and showing propaganda films and features to troops during the war.)

The New American Cinema was unequivocally and intimately personal. "Our movies come from our hearts," said Jonas Mekas, who, as

---

[1] *The Art of Cineplastics* (1923), p. 44.

filmmaker, exhibitor, distributor, publisher and critic, did more than any one else to foster the movement. "Our movies are like extensions of our own pulse, of our heartbeat, of our eyes, our fingertips."[2] And yet Mekas, like Walt Whitman, insisted that

> All I mark as my own you shall offset it
> with your own,
> Else it were time lost listening to me.

Expression of the self did not achieve its goals unless it led others to self-discovery and self-expression too.

"We want to remind [man] that there is such a thing as home," Mekas said, "where he can be, once in a while, alone and with himself and with a few that he loves close to him, and be with himself and his soul—that's the meaning of the home movie, the private visions of our movies. We want to surround this earth with our home movies."[3]

Edison wanted to bring the movie image into the home; Mekas wanted to put the home into the moving image. In one sense avant-garde home movies were meant to be like everyone else's home movies: expressions of personal vision, of family events, of communal experience. From this perspective, no distinctions were to be drawn between one film and another, between professional and amateur, artist and hobbyist. Film indeed became the democratic medium, where all men and women with cameras in hand were not merely created equal, they remained equal. To make judgments among films was to make invidious comparisons among souls. You would not claim that your dreams are better, more imaginative, more artful than mine, or mine than yours: they are unique to our personal histories and inner compulsions, hence incomparable. The same with personal cinema: at one point in the 1960s, Andy Warhol put forward the view that every frame of film was just as good as any other frame.

For viewers, of course, the democratic theory of filmmaking often failed to work. They found some films fascinating, others boring; some skillfully assembled, others technically inept. Up to a point, anyone was permitted to show his or her films at the screening rooms and festivals of the New American Cinema movement or list them in catalogues published by filmmakers' cooperatives. But distinctions were continually being made. One primary distinction that could not be suppressed was between amateur and artist. It was not merely a matter of some filmmakers preferring one designation and some insisting on the other; it was rooted in different ways of making films.

For amateurs, filmmaking could take several forms. It could be a means of recording life experience, fulfilling what Parker Tyler called,

---

[2] Mekas, "Where Are We–The Underground?" in Gregory Battcock, ed., *The New American Cinema* (1967), p. 20.

[3] *Ibid.*

in his study on underground films, one of the "most neglected functions" of the film camera, "that of invading and recording realms which have to some degree remained taboo—too private, too shocking, too immoral for photographic reproduction."[4] (Commercial sexploitation films in the early 1970s largely usurped this aspect of the underground filmmaker's role.) It could also be a means of organizing and experiencing life: filmmaking not only for the purpose of making images on celluloid, but as an opportunity to put one's dreams and desires into practice before the camera.

The artists of the New American Cinema may have shared in both these modes of filmmaking, but they brought to them, and to other forms of motion-picture work, different aims and aspirations. They wanted to do what modern artists in other media have attempted, not merely to make visible the unseen, but to create new ways of seeing. They claimed an equal status for cinema with poetry, painting and fiction within the tradition of the modern. "There is a pursuit of knowledge foreign to language and founded upon visual communication," the filmmaker Stan Brakhage wrote, "demanding a development of the optical mind, and dependent upon perception in the original and deepest sense of the word. . . . In the present time a very few have continued the process of visual perception in its deepest sense and transformed their inspirations into cinematic experiences. They create a new language made possible by the moving picture image."[5]

"A very few" are a far cry from Warhol's egalitarianism or Mekas' image of home movies girdling the globe. And the contradiction is more than implicit. Mekas' rhetoric is overtly antimodern, directly opposed to the claims Brakhage makes for the cinema artist. "There is pain in the arts of the last few decades," Mekas said, ". . . we want an art of light."[6] In a way, Mekas seemed to be demanding a cinema of satisfying and self-enhancing images—this from a filmmaker who, only two years before those words were spoken, made one of the most painful and harrowing works of art in the history of cinema, a film of Kenneth Brown's play *The Brig* (1964).

The distinction between artist and amateur did not account for the difference between painful and joyful films, though Mekas' language may appear to make that claim. All new visioning is in a sense painful, forcing the viewer through the arduous task of dismantling and reconnecting the intricate lines from eye to brain and brain to eye. Given that fact, it is remarkable how much the art of the New American Cinema has fulfilled Mekas' mandate, if not always to be joyful, then to give satisfaction to the learning and discerning spectator. Of all the distinctions in the realm of personal cinema, from abstract one-person films to

---

[4] *Underground Film* (1969), p. 1.

[5] Brakhage, "The Camera Eye—My Eye," in Battcock, *op. cit.*, pp. 212–13. An excerpt from Brakhage's *Metaphors on Vision* (1963).

[6] Mekas, *op. cit.*, p. 21.

commercial feature productions, the most significant is that between works of art and all others, for art has the capacity, no matter what its subject matter or mode of expression, to provide its audience with the emotional fulfillment of catharsis.

For all the emphasis on universal and equal creativity in the pronouncements of some of its leaders, the history of American underground cinema since World War II is the story of a small group of innovators and pathbreakers, an avant-garde. To a degree unusual in the arts, however, their aesthetic heritage and practical situation reinforced each other and led their filmmaking in a similar direction: as adherents of the modern movement in the arts and as impecunious artists working alone in a complex and expensive medium, it was almost inevitable that their work styles and films would be suffused with the themes and images of romantic individualism.

In his indispensable study of the underground-cinema movement from the 1940s to the 1970s, *Visionary Film: The American Avant-Garde* (1974), P. Adams Sitney tells tale after tale of economic vicissitudes: of important films being made with discarded scraps of raw film and borrowed cameras; of masterworks truncated for want of funds. The poet-and-novelist bohemians of San Francisco's North Beach or New York's Greenwich Village or the Left Bank of Paris seem plutocrats compared to underground filmmakers: all they needed to be artists were a few coins for pen and paper.

Financial stringency led some underground filmmakers to technological expedients which became new directions in film aesthetics. Gregory Markopoulos developed the assembling of a film—often when the image changed from frame to frame—within the camera; other filmmakers created films without using cameras, by applying their images, by drawing, scratching or overlaying collage materials directly on the film. For an understanding of avant-garde films it is often as important to know the manner of their making as to study the image on the screen.

Sitney's analysis is a necessary starting point for a brief account of the American avant-garde film—though it should be noted that he explicitly excludes major underground filmmakers whose work is either more social or more technologically impersonal than that of the "visionary company" with whom he is primarily concerned. In Sitney's view, the New American Cinema moves from dream to ritual films, or as he puts it, from trance to mythopoeia, a movement that can be defined chronologically as dividing the 1940s from the 1960s but can also be noted in the development of individual filmmakers. In the 1960s, following the full emergence of the mythopoeic film, came a radical departure from it, into the structural film. ". . . by affirming the priority of the mechanics of the tools over the eye of the film-maker," he wrote, "the structural film terminates the dialectics of the lyrical and mythopoeic forms."[7]

---

[7] *Visionary Film* (1974), p. 207.

A curious aspect of the American underground cinema is the thematic similarity of its early films to a pervasive tone in Hollywood films of the same period—the 1940s trance films are more intense, private, and candid explorations of the unconscious than the claustrophobic psychodramas Hollywood made in the same period. Moreover, several of the most important trance films, including Maya Deren's *Meshes of the Afternoon* (made in 1943 with her husband Alexander Hamid, a professional movie worker), Kenneth Anger's *Fireworks* (1947) and Gregory Markopoulos' *Swain* (1950), were created by filmmakers who had been at least peripherally connected with Hollywood: Deren through her husband, Anger as a child actor, Markopoulos as a student in film courses taught by Josef von Sternberg at the University of Southern California.

"The trance film," Sitney wrote, "is by nature an erotic quest, and its quest figure is either a dreamer or in a mad or visionary state."[8] It was through dreams that the trance films began to invade and record, as Parker Tyler suggested, the taboo realms of the unconscious: in Anger's *Fireworks*, homosexuality; in Stan Brakhage's *Flesh of Morning* (1956), masturbation; in Deren's *Meshes of the Afternoon*, the premonition of and wish for death. The difficulty of the trance films lies in their solipsism: they are expressions of psychic interiors, which, like dreams, require interpretation and may evoke analysis from viewers rather than feeling.

The trance films carried viewers into the inward beings of their on-screen protagonists and then left them there: they denied rather than affirmed the traditional rhetoric about the visionary nature of movies, which emphasized their effect on the viewer. Around the end of the 1950s, avant-garde filmmakers shifted away from the trance film partially at least because they realized that trance films contradicted their visionary goals.

Nowhere was this change more apparent than in the films and writings of Stan Brakhage, the most persistent and articulate of all avant-garde filmmakers. From his early trance films Brakhage turned to a style that identified the visionary act as taking place not within the protagonist on the screen but in the filmmaker behind the camera. He created a field of vision upon which the spectator could exercise his imagination, not merely a record of his own imagination for the spectator to understand. Brakhage insisted that as a spectator, he was in no more privileged a position to grasp the meanings of his films than anyone else. ". . . even when I lecture at showings of past Brakhage films," he said, "I emphasize the fact that I am not artist except when involved in the creative process AND that I speak as viewer . . . of The Work."[9] This inventive stance effectively avoided the tendencies toward authoritarianism in the Romantic idea of the visionary artist, and reaffirmed the social as an integral

---

[8] *Ibid.*, p. 147.

[9] Brakhage, quoted, *ibid.*, p. 212.

THE MUSEUM OF MODERN ART/FILM STILLS ARCHIVE

Maya Deren directed (with Alexander Hamid) and performed in *Meshes of the Afternoon* (1943), a "trance film" depicting the interior psychic state of its protagonist, which was the beginning of the New American Cinema of avant-garde, noncommercial filmmakers.

part of the personal, and the democratic as an essential element of the cinema avant-garde.

The shift from trance to mythopoeic films was not uniform among underground filmmakers, and not all of those who followed that course shared Brakhage's commitment to the artist as originator and envisioner. For others, the movement into myth came out of their growing desire to express in their films their adherence to systems of occult theosophy and mysticism, systems that explicitly transmuted the role of filmmaker into something else. For Kenneth Anger, a follower of the mystic Aleister Crowley, the filmmaker became a magus, a figure who initiates others into the secrets of divinity; for Harry Smith, a student of the cabala, the filmmaker became a messenger for the Deity. "My movies are made by God," he said; "I was just the medium for them."[10]

Nearly all the major expressions of the mythopoeic form arose from mythical systems in Western literary traditions, even those of filmmakers like Brakhage and Gregory Markopoulos, who saw themselves as creators rather than intermediaries. As Anger's brilliant film *Inauguration of the Pleasure Dome* (Sacred Mushroom Edition, 1966) derived from Crowley, and Smith's *No. 12* (ca. early 1960s) from the cabala, Brakhage's *Dog Star Man* (completed 1965) and Markopoulos' *Twice a Man* (1963) drew on classical mythology. The richness of these sources contributed to the extraordinary detail and depth of the visual energy and treatment of subject in the mythopoeic film, in contrast to the spareness and stark images of the trance films.

Movies themselves are, of course, a new source of mythology in modern mass culture, and Hollywood also served as inspiration for the mythopoeic avant-garde films. Jack Smith's *Flaming Creatures* (1963) is a commentary on, an elaboration of and a homage to the visual images and structures of Josef von Sternberg's 1930s films with Marlene Dietrich, and to the "B"-movie actress Maria Montez. Kenneth Anger's *Scorpio Rising* (1963) is even more explicitly a film about Hollywood mythology. Its central core is the creation of the myth of the American motorcyclist, which derives not from the resources of classical or mystical traditions, but from the filmmaker's visual assertion of the superior power of his mythmaking in comparison to its sources in popular culture: the images of Hollywood's mythical creations, James Dean and Marlon Brando, as motorcyclists, are derided; and the values of Anger's motorcyclist are given humorous triumph over those of the Western Judeo-Christian tradition by intercutting shots of Christ from Cecil B. DeMille's silent *King of Kings* (1927) with the motorcyclist's violent and blasphemous versions of how he would act in the same events.

Earlier than either of these films Bruce Conner made *A Movie* (1958) and *Cosmic Ray* (1961), which use clips from old Hollywood pictures in a complex, ironic juxtaposition that evokes the spectator's expected

---

[10] Smith, quoted, *ibid.*, p. 294.

response to familiar footage to convey a meaning larger than, and opposed to, the overt content of the messages on the screen.

Parker Tyler has described one kind of underground filmmaking as "a way of living over again, with preposterous let's-pretend, the fixating hallucinations of popular movies when one was a teenager or still licking lollipops."[11] This curious symbiosis between underground and Hollywood took a new turn in the early 1970s when Andy Warhol, one of the most significant avant-garde filmmakers of the 1960s, entered commercial production with "preposterous let's pretend" movies like *Andy Warhol's Frankenstein* (1974).

One way to avoid the temptation of going Hollywood, metaphorically or actually, was vigorously to cut from one's films the essential element of commercial features, the narrative line—in Hollywood's terms, the story; another was to give up the representation of human life and landscape entirely. The first alternative, which Andy Warhol pioneered in his films of the mid-1960s, was later developed by other filmmakers into the form known as structural film. The second has a longer heritage, going back to graphic films made in the early 1920s and continuing through the decades in the effort of certain filmmakers to depict design in motion. In recent years, nonrepresentational graphic cinema has taken a new turn through new technologies—television, computers and holography among them—under the name "expanded cinema."

Warhol's early films, the precursors of structural cinema, were to some degree responses to the issues of creative imagination and audience reaction raised by the postwar movement of avant-garde films from trance to mythopoeia. How much the films were intended as expressions of the filmmaker's imagination—as protagonist, artist or mythmaker—and how much as stimulants to the exercise of a viewer's imagination remained in question. At a critical transition point, Stan Brakhage effectively tried to unite these polarities by separating his role as an artist when he was alone from his role as viewer when he was one among many. Warhol's answer was to eschew the role of artist entirely.

In his early films, like *Sleep* (1963) and *Empire* (1964), Warhol stationed the camera in a fixed position—directed in the first film at a sleeping person, in the second at the Empire State Building—set it going and let it roll until the reel ran out. Then he put in a new reel and continued. *Sleep* ran for over six hours of fixed-frame viewing of an essentially stable subject, *Empire* for eight hours of a definitely stable object. It was in duration itself, as Sitney has suggested, that Warhol established the framework for audience response: the very length of the single image would impel the viewer to a new awareness of perceptual experience.

Warhol later shifted his attention to the narrative of human interac-

[11] Tyler, *op. cit.*, p. 52.

tion and character, notably in *The Chelsea Girls* (1966), which retains the fixed image but projects two images side by side. Other filmmakers carried forward the structural principles Warhol had suggested in his early films, in particular Michael Snow, whose *Wave Length* (1967), a forty-five-minute film of a slow zoom from a fixed camera position, established him as the leading practitioner of a cinema whose subject matter was the moving lens of the camera as a metaphor for consciousness itself. In *The Central Region* (1971), a film comprised of 360-degree sweeps of a barren landscape by a stationary camera, Snow carried the structural film even deeper into the interior of the self than the trance film, into a consciousness completely disconnected from contact with the world it can omnisciently perceive.

The graphic film, in contrast, is one in which the camera is at best a recording device and at other times quite unnecessary to the communication of motion pictures. Early graphic experimenters in Europe like Hans Richter in *Rhythmus 21* (1921) and Viking Eggeling in *Symphonie Diagonale* (1921–1924) created their designs in motion like animators, by making a movie, frame by frame, of still images. Len Lye, in a series of films made in Great Britain, beginning with *Colour Box* (1937), was the first abstract filmmaker to create images by drawing directly on the film surface. (In the early days of commercial movies, directors like D. W. Griffith also attained added effects by having portions of their films hand-tinted, frame by frame.) Thereafter animation and design-on-film techniques became part of the lexicon of avant-garde filmmakers, as in the films of Harry Smith. On the other hand, motion graphics as a principle in itself did not play a significant role until the development of expanded cinema.

The expanded-cinema filmmakers were men and women for whom the creative act took place not primarily with camera or celluloid, but with computers, video equipment or laser beams. Expanded-cinema exhibition went beyond the horizontal projection of a single image onto an opaque screen to new kinds of settings and situations for looking at films: multiple projections, vastly enlarged screens, vertical screens, 360-degree screens, and the combining of movies with live theater in the same field of vision (as part of Happenings, or, more formally, intermedia). At expositions and at the Disney amusement parks, there was even introduced the holographic projection of three-dimensional images into space, the ultimate illusion attained so far in the efforts to make motion pictures reproduce reality.

Through the mid-1970s expanded cinema was limited to a handful of filmmakers because of high costs and the difficulty of access to the required technology. Much of the equipment and specialized knowledge was held by private corporations, and the significant pioneers in computer and video graphics—John Whitney, Stan VanDerBeek and Scott Bartlett, among others—made many of their films under corporate aegis: Whitney with the collaboration of IBM, VanDerBeek with Bell Telephone Laboratory (and later with WGBH-TV in Boston), Bartlett by using the control room of a California television station. Holography remained entirely in the hands of corporate employees or university researchers.

Though Bartlett's extraordinary videographic films, among others, may be considered significant works of American avant-garde filmmaking, it is an obvious sign of the ambiguous status of expanded cinema that Sitney completely omitted computergraphic and videographic filmmakers from his company of visionary artists. Indeed, traditional notions of creativity may not encompass the filmmaker who works with a light pen on a computer display console, by inserting programmed punch cards into a computer, or by mixing images on a video control panel. "To get emotionally involved creatively at the computer," John Whitney said on the sound track of one of his computer films, "is not easy."[12]

In the most comprehensive work so far on the new modes, Gene Youngblood's prophetic and polemical *Expanded Cinema* (1970), the author stresses that technology can liberate the artist to concentrate on imagination: "In the new conceptual art, it is the artist's *idea* and not his technical ability in manipulating media that is important." On the other hand, he suggests that computers are already capable of making "autonomous decisions on alternative possibilities that ultimately govern the outcome of the artwork."[13]

The unsettled status of expanded cinema as art should not distract attention from its importance. We stand in the last quarter of the twentieth century in a position similar to the men and women in the last quarter of the nineteenth century who sought the intellectual, emotional and technological means to alter their ways of seeing the world, and in the process created a new medium. The computer, videographic and holographic films of the early 1970s may no more resemble the cinema of the future than Muybridge's row of separate still cameras to catch all four horse's hooves off the ground related, except in principle, to the motion-picture technologies that followed. "99.9 per cent of all that is now transpiring in human activity and interaction with nature," Buckminster Fuller has written, "is taking place within the realms of reality which are utterly invisible, inaudible, unsmellable, untouchable by human senses."[14] There is still more than meets the present-day eye to occupy the technologists and visionary artists of cinema.

From its beginnings the motion picture stimulated the prophetic fancy of its advocates. What is curious is how many forecasts about the future role and influence of expanded cinema were first sounded three quarters of a century before, at the very dawning of the medium: its power to replace spoken and written language as a central method of communica-

---

12 *Experiments in Motion Graphics* (1968), sound track.

13 Pp. 193, 191.

14 From Fuller's "Introduction," Youngblood, *op. cit.*, pp. 25–26.

tion, to expand consciousness, to express the full potential resources of the human mind. This similarity may suggest—Youngblood's *Expanded Cinema* makes the point explicitly—that the history of motion pictures in the United States up to now has been a diversion from the promise and capacity of cinema to improve the quality, indeed to transform the nature, of human life.

This book has a somewhat different point: that the movies have fulfilled much of what has been dreamed about them, though sometimes in quite unexpected ways. But it is unclear whether what the movies have done in their fourscore years remains a relevant or adequate model for what is required from them in the future.

Throughout their history the movies have served as a primary source of information about society and human behavior for large masses of people. So significant a medium of communication should naturally reflect dominant ideologies and interests, and the American movies have often done so. But what is remarkable is the way that American movies, through much of their span, have altered or challenged many of the values and doctrines of powerful social and cultural forces in American society, providing alternative ways of understanding the world.

There have been people at all points on the political and cultural spectrum who have been contemptuous of the messages American movies have delivered, who have found fault with their formulas, evasions and untruths. The value of such criticism depends, in the perspective of cultural history, on a number of related issues, among them the comparative formulas, myths, evasions and untruths of textbooks, sermons, newspapers, political statements and other modes of disseminating information in the society, and on one's judgment about the need for entertainment, stories, and fictional heroes and heroines in a culture.

My own view is that there is nothing disreputable about creating stories for the entertainment, edification and uplifting of mass audiences. That so many American movies have been mediocre or venal or false has to do with the profit motive that dominates them, and it is short-sighted to speak of transforming commercial entertainment without first transforming social ideologies. The small number of American movies that deserve preservation and study for their quality (as opposed to their putative value as cultural documents) rank with the best work that has been produced in American art and thought.

Despite the challenge of radio and TV, the commercial motion picture is likely to survive for some time on the annual success of several dozen highly popular entertainment films in traditional narrative forms. As to the larger role movies might play in the culture, one partial answer has already been given by the proliferation of personal cinema. Much of what has been exhibited as personal cinema is of course open to the same objections that have been made to the majority of commercial films: they are trite, poorly made, false. In the production of art, as in the production of commercial entertainment, the ability to create works of quality is vouchsafed to only a few.

Nevertheless, the rise of personal cinema is significant. It has clearly demonstrated the capacity of cinema artists to fulfill the promise of the medium, to develop a new visual language and expand the consciousness of their viewers. There is also a positive value in the dissemination of cinema equipment, the placing of a tool of communication in the hands of more and more people. Gene Youngblood foresees cinema as the language of the future, image-exchange as the mode of communication: "Through the art and technology of expanded cinema we shall create heaven right here on earth."[15]

Beguiling as such teleological visions are, they often unwittingly obscure the social, cultural and economic processes by which change is accomplished in the media field. New technologies, such as video cassettes, are controlled by private corporations, and their potential role in the transformation of human life is often postponed or reshaped by such mundane issues as competition, profitability and the state of the national economy.

There is no question, however, that the tools of a technological revolution are already in the hands of the people. Millions now own still and movie cameras, tape recorders, and of course, video monitors (otherwise known as TV sets). It is not so much that the existence of technology changes our consciousness, as the technological determinists believe, but that our consciousness of technology needs to change before there can be any transformation in the way it is used.

No one knows what the nature of communications and information distribution would be like if visual media were used with the frequency and dexterity of pen or typewriter. No doubt there would be a great deal of waste and confusion, and inessential messages would besiege our eyes. Still, it would be a remarkable event in human history if American men and women could give up their roles as passive spectators before the motion-picture or television screen, as they once gave up their status as colonial subjects of a foreign king. It would be another great experiment to see if, without bondage to the power of commerce, a democratic cinema could come into being.

---

[15] Youngblood, *op. cit.*, p. 419.

NOTES ON SOURCES

These notes comprise a selective list of sources directly useful in writing this book, and more generally, of writings on American movies. Not all the books, articles and other materials consulted in research are listed, even less do they provide a comprehensive bibliography on American motion pictures, either of which would require another volume in itself. No such volume has appeared in more than a generation, since the bibliography compiled by workers in the WPA New York City Writers' Project, *The Film Index: A Bibliography*, Vol. 1, *The Film as Art* (1941). In the decade since 1965, meanwhile, probably more books have been published on motion pictures than in the previous seventy years. A few volumes have begun to chronicle or provide introductions to this material, among them Frank Manchel, *Film Study: A Resource Guide* (1973); Peter J. Bukalski, *Film Research: A Critical Bibliography with Annotations and Essay* (1972); Ronald Gottesman and Harry M. Geduld, *Guidebook to Film: An Eleven-in-One Reference* (1972); George Rehrauer, *Cinema Booklist* (1972) and a 1974 supplement volume; and two volumes by Mel Schuster, *Motion Picture Performers: A Bibliography of Magazine and Periodical Articles, 1900–1969* (1972) and *Motion Picture Directors: A Bibliography of Magazine and Periodical Articles, 1900–1972* (1973). In the notes below, a number of works already cited in the text are not repeated.

1. THE BIRTH OF A MASS MEDIUM

On the invention of motion pictures perhaps the most important secondary work is Gordon Hendricks, *The Edison Motion Picture Myth* (1961), the chief service of which was to demolish the standard notion that Thomas A. Edison invented movies, and thus cleared the way for a reconsideration of E. J. Marey and Eadweard Muybridge. An important article on Muybridge is Harlan Hamilton, "'Les Allures du Cheval': Eadweard James Muybridge's Contribution to the Motion Picture," *Film Comment*, v. 5 (Fall 1969), pp. 16–35; it takes its title from the first published article on Muybridge's Palo Alto photographs, Gaston Tissandier, "Les Allures du Cheval: Représentées par la Photographie Instantanée," *La Nature* (December 14, 1878), pp. 23–26. The best approach to Marey is through his own writings: in English translation, *Animal Mechanism* (1874) for his early work, and for his later studies "The History of Chronophotography," Smithsonian Institution, *Annual Report for 1901* (1902), pp. 317–40; see also his 1878 paper, "Moteurs Animés: Expériences de Physiologie Graphique," in *La Nature* (September 28, 1878, pp. 273–78, and October 5, pp. 289–95). Marey's letter about Muybridge's photographs is in *La Nature* (December 28, 1878, p. 54), and Muybridge's reply in the same journal (March 22, 1879, p. 246). The intellectual and cultural dimensions of movement studies are discussed in Siegfried Giedion, *Mechanization Takes Command* (1948), pp. 14–30; the analogy between Duchamp and Marey was made in "Frozen Movies," *Independent*, v. 77 (March 2, 1914), p. 311.

Edison acknowledged his debt to Marey and Muybridge in a note appended to Antonia and W. K. L. Dickson, "Edison's Invention of the Kineto-Phonograph," *The*

Century, v. 48 (June 1894), p. 206. Gordon Hendricks continued his exploration of Edison's movie work in *The Kinetoscope* (1966). Considerable material on the marketing of Edison's motion-picture equipment and press response to exhibitions of early movies may be found in the Raff and Gammon Papers, Harvard Business School Library. For Edward Bellamy's media visions, see *Looking Backward: 2000–1887* (1888) and his short story "With the Eyes Shut," *Harper's Monthly*, v. 79 (October 1889).

Contemporary discussions of technical and commercial aspects of early movies include C. Francis Jenkins, *Animated Pictures* (1898); Henry Hopwood, *Living Pictures* (1899); Cecil M. Hepworth, *Animated Photography* (2d ed., 1900); and J. Miller Barr, "Animated Pictures," *Popular Science Monthly*, v. 52 (December 1897), pp. 177–88. Gordon Hendricks' third volume of pioneering research is *The Beginning of the Biograph* (1964).

On early vaudeville and motion-picture exhibition, the works of Robert Grau are valuable starting points; see his *The Businessman in the Amusement World* (1910), *The Stage in the Twentieth Century* (1912) and *The Theater of Science* (1914). Albert F. McLean, Jr., *American Vaudeville as Ritual* (1965), is a useful secondary work on vaudeville and its patrons. Albert E. Smith is the source of information on swiftly increasing profits for the Vitagraph company; see his *Two Reels and a Crank*, in collaboration with Phil A. Koury (1952), pp. 250–51. Early New York City exhibition statistics are listed in John Collier, "Cheap Amusements," *Charities and the Commons*, v. 20 (April 11, 1908), pp. 73–76. Two volumes in the Pittsburgh survey give interesting reactions to moviegoing in working-class districts—Vol. 1, Elizabeth Beardsley Butler, *Women and the Trades: Pittsburgh, 1907–1908* (1909), pp. 332–33, and Vol. 4, Margaret F. Byington, *Homestead: The Households of a Milltown* (1910), pp. 110–12.

2. NICKEL MADNESS

In the 1950s more than three thousand theretofore "lost" American films of the pre-1912 period, stored as paper rolls at the Library of Congress, were successfully transferred to 16-mm. film, making possible—and necessary—significant revisions of the standard history of early film production. I screened hundreds of these films at the Library, and at the Academy of Motion Picture Arts and Sciences in Los Angeles, and my treatment of styles and themes in the early films is based on this direct observation. A catalog of the Library's resources is Kemp R. Niver, *Motion Pictures from the Library of Congress Paper Print Collection 1894–1912* (1967). Niver also presents interesting highlights from the films in *The First Twenty Years* (1968).

American filmmaking before World War I is also discussed in Anthony Slide, *Early American Cinema* (1970); George C. Pratt, *Spellbound in Darkness* (rev. ed., 1973); Fred J. Balshofer and Arthur C. Miller, *One Reel a Week* (1967), a very useful joint memoir; A. Nicholas Vardac, *Stage to Screen* (1949); Edwin Wagenknecht, *The Movies in the Age of Innocence* (1962); and in the principal general histories of American movies: Lewis Jacobs, *The Rise of the American Film* (1939); Terry Ramsaye, *A Million and One Nights* (1926); Benjamin B. Hampton, *A History of the Movies* (1931); A. R. Fulton, *Motion Pictures* (1960); and Kenneth Macgowan, *Behind the Screen* (1965).

On Méliès, the most extensive studies are in French: Maurice Bessy and Lo Duca, *Georges Méliès, Mage* (1961), and Georges Sadoul, *Georges Méliès* (1961). We still lack a full-scale study of Edwin S. Porter; for a brief overview, see Robert Sklar, "Edwin S. Porter," in *Dictionary of American Biography*, Supplement 3, 1941–1945 (1972), pp. 606–8.

The popularity of chase films was noted in an illuminating article about the making of one, which was also among the first such articles to appear in a national magazine: Theodore Waters, "Out with a Moving Picture Machine," *Cosmopolitan*, v. 40 (January 1906), pp. 251–59. Early British filmmaking is covered in Rachel Low and Roger Manvell, *The History of the British Film 1896–1906* (1948), and Low, *The History of the British Film 1906–1914* (1949); Low lists film releases in Great Britain in 1909 by country (pp. 54–55). Georges Sadoul, *French Film* (1953), claims Pathé Frères dominated the American market before World War I.

The new industrial city in which movies found their working-class audience has been the subject of considerable recent study, well summarized in Peter G. Goheen, *Victorian Toronto, 1850–1900* (1970), pp. 3–20; I am indebted to Sam Bass Warner, Jr., for this reference. The response of reformers to the lure of movies, especially for children, may be found in such works as Jane Addams, *The Spirit of Youth and the City Streets* (1909); Louise de Koven Bowen, *Five and Ten Cent Theatres* (1911); and, with the most outrage, Chicago Vice Commission, *The Social Evil in Chicago* (1911). Articles on early censorship efforts include John Collier, "Cheap Amusements," and an interesting account of the New York Review Board in action, Charles V. Tevis, "Censoring the Five-Cent Drama," *The World To-Day*, v. 19 (October 1910), pp. 1132–39.

A number of articles in national magazines between 1908 and 1912 discussed movies as a source of cultural uplift and unity; see, for example, "The Drama of the People," *The Independent*, v. 69 (September 29, 1910), pp. 713–15; George Ethelbert Walsh, "Moving Picture Drama for the Multitude," *The Independent*, v. 64 (February 6, 1908), pp. 306–10; and Lucy France Pierce, "The Nickelodeon," *The World To-Day*, v. 15 (October 1908), pp. 1052–57.

3. EDISON'S TRUST AND HOW IT GOT BUSTED

The full story of the motion-picture business before World War I remains to be told. One central aspect of it, the Motion Picture Patents Company and the antitrust struggles, is discussed in detail in Ralph Cassady, Jr., "Monopoly in Motion Picture Production and Distribution: 1908–1915," *Southern California Law Review*, v. 32 (Summer 1959), pp. 325–90. Hampton's *A History of the Movies* is also an essential source, though it, like Ramsaye's *A Million and One Nights*, plays down Edison's role, which deserves much more thorough investigation. The principal clues to Edison's pecuniary interests are in the legal decisions rendered in his suits against the American Mutoscope and Biography Company between 1901 and 1907.

Most accounts of the rise of the motion-picture industry concentrate on the Jewish immigrant entrepreneurs who became the movie moguls. Philip French, *The Movie Moguls* (1969), is a perceptive brief introduction to their careers and behavior; Norman Zierold, *The Moguls* (1969), tells all the good anecdotes. There are a number of biographies, generally written during the subjects' lifetime, of varying candor and informativeness: John Drinkwater, *The Life and Adventures of Carl Laemmle* (1931); Will Irwin, *The House that Shadows Built* (1928), on Zukor, and see also Zukor's autobiography, with Dale Kramer, *The Public Is Never Wrong* (1953); Upton Sinclair, *Upton Sinclair Presents William Fox* (1933), which deals primarily with Fox's financial struggles after 1928; Alva Johnston, *The Great Goldwyn* (1937), and see the ghostwritten book signed by Goldwyn, *Behind the Screen* (1923); Bosley Crowther, *Hollywood Rajah* (1960), on Louis B. Mayer. Robert Grau's three volumes also provide much useful information on the early careers of several of these figures. Lectures by some of these men at Harvard Business School, along with others, are collected in Joseph P. Kennedy, ed., *The Story of the Films* (1927). Thomas H. Ince, an all-but-forgotten movie pioneer, tells his own story in an unpublished document, "History and Development of the Motion Picture Industry" (1921), in the UCLA Theater Arts Collection.

The standard scholarly studies and government reports on the movie industry generally skimp the early years and concentrate on the rise of the Hollywood studios; see Howard T. Lewis, *The Motion Picture Industry* (1933); Mae D. Huettig, *Economic Control of the Motion Picture Industry* (1944); and Daniel Bertrand, W. Duane Evans and E. L. Blanchard, *The Motion Picture—A Pattern of Control* (1941), a report by the Temporary National Economic Committee.

On motion-picture theaters, there are two informative and beautifully illustrated recent studies, Ben M. Hall, *The Best Remaining Seats* (1961), exclusively on the United States, and Dennis Sharp, *The Picture Palace* (1969), primarily on Great Britain but with considerable material on the United States as well. The rapid growth of interest in ornate movie theaters is reflected in two early books, Arthur S. Meloy, *Theatres and Motion Picture Houses* (1916), and Edward Bernard Kinsila, *Modern Theatre Construction* (1917). Berlin movie theaters are described and illustrated in Hans Schliepmann, *Lichtspieltheater* (1914).

4. D. W. GRIFFITH AND THE FORGING OF MOTION-PICTURE ART

After years of neglect the D. W. Griffith bibliography is rapidly expanding. Since 1969 there have appeared the first full-scale biography, Robert M. Henderson, *D. W. Griffith, His Life and Work* (1972), and a more detailed monograph by the same author, *D. W. Griffith, The Years at Biograph* (1970); Griffith's uncompleted autobiography, edited and annotated by James Hart, *The Man Who Invented Hollywood* (1972); memoirs by Lillian Gish, *The Movies, Mr. Griffith, and Me* (1969), with Ann Pinchot; by Billy Bitzer, *Billy Bitzer, His Story* (1973); and by Karl Brown, *Adventures with D. W. Griffith* (1973); and brief collections and studies such as Paul O'Dell, *Griffith and the Rise of Hollywood* (1970), and Harry Geduld, ed., *Focus on D. W. Griffith* (1971). More is to come, and undoubtedly more is needed on the first great artist of the motion pictures.

My account of Griffith's development as a motion-picture director derives from screening more than a hundred one- and two-reel and feature films in the Library of Congress Paper Print Collection and at the Museum of Modern Art. I have also utilized the museum's archive of Griffith's personal and business papers.

Earlier writings on Griffith which I have found essential include Iris Barry, *D. W. Griffith, American Film Master* (1940, 1965); Mrs. D. W. Griffith (Linda Arvidson), *When the Movies Were Young* (1925); Seymour Stern, "Griffith: I—*The Birth of a Nation*," *Film Culture*, no. 36 (Spring-Summer 1965); Theodore Huff, "*Intolerance*": *The Film by D. W. Griffith: Shot-by-Shot Analysis* (1966); the section in Anita Loos's entertaining autobiography, *A Girl Like I* (1966), on her work as a screen writer with Griffith; and the most penetrating essay on Griffith's film aesthetics I know of, Sergei Eisenstein, "Dickens, Griffith, and the Film Today," in his *Film Form* (1949), pp. 195–255. For other works on Griffith, and a list of his writings, see the valuable bibliography in Geduld, *Focus on D. W. Griffith* (pp. 171–79).

5. HOLLYWOOD AND THE DAWNING OF THE AQUARIAN AGE

The development of Hollywood, like so many other aspects of American movies before the sound era, awaits its historian. Perhaps the best brief account of the movie community in its surrounding geographical, cultural and economic setting is in Carey McWilliams, *Southern California Country* (1946); an earlier guide, Basil Woon, *Incredible Land* (1933), adds useful information. Michael Regan, *Stars, Moguls, Magnates* (1966), illustrates the development of lavish mansions in Beverly Hills. Edwin O. Palmer, *History of Hollywood* (1937), in two volumes, devotes little more than a dozen pages to movies (Vol. 1, pp. 190–204).

Early discussions of acting styles may be found in Frances Agnew, *Motion Picture Acting* (1913), in which the comedian John Bunny gives his views; Mae Marsh, *Screen Acting* (1921), describes Griffith's training on pp. 116–19; Sessue Hayakawa compares kabuki to movie acting in "Hayakawa, Japanese Screen Star," *Literary Digest*, v. 55 (November 3, 1917), pp. 70–72.

On movie aspirants, the first sign of popular concern was William A. Page, "The Movie-Struck Girl," *Woman's Home Companion*, v. 45 (June 1918), pp. 18, 75. Valentia Steer, *The Secrets of the Cinema* (1920), describes a similar desire among young British women to break into movies. How-to books, with ample warnings about pitfalls, include Marilynn Conners, *What Chance Have I in Hollywood?* (1924);

Charles Reed Jones, ed., *Breaking into the Movies* (1927); and Inez and Helen Klumph, *Screen Acting* (1922).

The basic compendium of Hollywood's sex, drug and other scandals is Kenneth Anger, *Hollywood Babylon* (1965); it names names, as do occasional memoirs like Colleen Moore, *Silent Star* (1968). Most other scandal-mongering works, like the anonymous *Sins of Hollywood* (1922), leave the reader to speculate. Works devoted less sensationally to Hollywood's culture include Perley Poore Sheehan, *Hollywood as a World Center* (1924), in which Hollywood is described as the vanguard of a new Aquarian Age; Dr. E. Debries, *Hollywood as It Really Is* (1932), is the European who calls the movie community unspiritual. See also Jack Richmond, *Hollywood* (1928); Alice M. Williamson, *Alice in Movieland* (1928); Herbert Reimherr, *Hollywood and the Moving Pictures* (1932); and [Sylvia Ullback], *Hollywood Undressed* (1931), an inside story by a masseuse.

Fiction about moviemaking can provide interesting insights into cultural beliefs and attitudes. The first stories about movies, curiously enough, were written for children by the prolific Victor Appleton and Laura Lee Hope. Their series on the Motion Picture Chums, the Motion Picture Girls and the Motion Picture Boys were launched into several dozen volumes by 1915, when what appear to be the first adult fiction books about movies were published: the anonymous *My Strange Life*, about an actress working in films in New York, and Charles E. Van Loan, *Buck Parvin and the Movies*, urbane and knowledgeable stories about Hollywood which had originally appeared in the *Saturday Evening Post*. Perhaps the best novel on the silent period of moviemaking is Harry Leon Wilson's charming *Merton of the Movies* (1922).

Working conditions in the studio are another little-studied subject. Murray Ross, *Stars and Strikes* (1941), is the principal secondary work on the early period. See also "The Groans of the Movie Actors," *Literary Digest*, v. 75 (November 4, 1922), p. 33, and Edmund DePatie, "Out of the Silents," in the Oral History Project, UCLA Special Collections Library.

6. THE SILENT FILMS AND THE PASSIONATE LIFE

More than seven thousand American films are briefly described in Kenneth W. Munden, ed., *The American Film Institute Catalog: Feature Films 1921–1930* (1970), the first two volumes of what promises to be a complete filmography of the American commercial cinema. But the list of studies on the silent film of the 1920s is surprisingly skimpy. Kevin Brownlow's immense *The Parade's Gone By* (1969) is made up largely of interviews with survivors, and has the merit of broad and varied interest in the unheralded but essential workers, like film cutters and stunt men, as well as the famous stars and directors. David Robinson, *Hollywood in the Twenties* (1968), is a brief introduction to films and directors of the period. George Pratt's documentary history of the silent film, *Spellbound in Darkness*, goes through 1929. General accounts of Hollywood films of the 1920s may also be found in the works by Jacobs, Hampton, Ramsaye, Fulton and Macgowan noted earlier, as well as in Paul Rotha, *The Film Till Now* (1930 and later editions). Marjorie Rosen, *Popcorn Venus* (1973) and Molly Haskell, *From Reverence to Rape* (1974), discuss the treatment of women in the decade's movies.

Walter Benjamin, "The Work of Art in the Age of Mechanical Reproduction," (1936), in his *Illuminations* (1955; English translation, 1969), provides a theoretical framework for considering the role of movies in broader cultural perspective. For a brief account of mass cultural as part of 1920s culture, see Robert Sklar, *The Plastic Age: 1917–1930* (1970), Introduction, pp. 1–24.

The rapidly expanding body of writings by and about directors and performers still does not provide great depth on the 1920s. On Cecil B. DeMille, see *The Autobiography of Cecil B. DeMille* (1959); William C. DeMille, *Hollywood Saga* (1939); Gabe Essoe and Raymond Lee, *DeMille* (1970); and Charles Higham, *DeMille* (1973). Works on other important personalities of the decade include Thomas Quinn Curtiss, *Von Stroheim* (1971); Irving Shulman, *Valentino* (1967); and S. George Ullman,

Valentino as I Knew Him (1926); John Bainbridge, *Garbo* (1955); Alistair Cooke, *Douglas Fairbanks* (1940), and Richard Schickel, *His Picture in the Papers* (1973), also on Douglas Fairbanks, Sr. King Vidor, *A Tree Is a Tree* (1953), is one of the most interesting of directors' autobiographies. On Robert Flaherty, see Richard Griffith, *The World of Robert Flaherty* (1953), and Arthur Calder-Marshall, *The Innocent Eye* (1963). Ernst Lubitsch and his films are extensively discussed in Herman G. Weinberg, *The Lubitsch Touch* (1968).

7. CHAOS, MAGIC, PHYSICAL GENIUS AND THE ART OF SILENT COMEDY

There has been very little effort to explore the connections between movie comedy and the traditions of American humor; on this theme, see Robert Sklar, "Humor in America," in Werner M. Mendel, ed., *A Celebration of Laughter* (1970), pp. 9–30. On the history of American humor, see Constance Rourke's classic study, *American Humor* (1931), and Kenneth S. Lynn, *Mark Twain and Southwestern Humor* (1959), on the elite humorists. Anthologies of American humor include Walter Blair, ed., *Native American Humor (1800–1900)* (1937), and Lynn, ed., *The Comic Tradition in America* (1958).

A useful brief study of American silent comedy is Donald W. McCaffrey, *4 Great Comedians: Chaplin, Lloyd, Keaton, Langdon* (1968). More general works on movie comedy are Gerald Mast, *The Comic Mind* (1973), and Raymond Durgnat, *The Crazy Mirror* (1969).

Mack Sennett and the Keystone comedies have been the subjects of two books by Kalton C. Lahue, *Mack Sennett's Keystone* (1971), and with Terry Brewer, *Kops and Custards* (1968). Much of Mack Sennett's autobiography, *King of Comedy* (1954), as told to Cameron Shipp, appears to have been drawn from Gene Fowler, *Father Goose* (1934). Sennett's career and his films await serious study.

Charles Chaplin has been more fortunate. There is a thorough treatment of his career through *Monsieur Verdoux* by Theodore Huff, *Charlie Chaplin* (1951), and a fascinating psychoanalytic interpretation by Parker Tyler, *Chaplin* (1948). Chaplin's own *My Autobiography* (1964) makes good reading. Among scores of other books and articles on Chaplin, see Robert Payne, *The Great God Pan* (1952), and the essay by Jim Tully in his *A Dozen and One* (1943).

A fine biography of Buster Keaton is Rudi Blesh, *Keaton* (1966); other studies include David Robinson, *Buster Keaton* (1969); and J.-P. Lebel, *Buster Keaton* (1967). With Charles Samuels, Keaton wrote *My Wonderful World of Slapstick* (1960). Harold Lloyd wrote, with Wesley W. Stout, *An American Comedy* (1928). Lloyd is the subject of a recent work by Richard Schickel, *Harold Lloyd* (1974). For Harry Langdon, see Robert Sklar, "Harry Langdon," in *Dictionary of American Biography*, Supplement 3, 1941–1945 (1972), pp. 443–44.

A British attack on American slapstick comedy appeared as early as 1914 in Harry Furniss, *Our Lady Cinema*, pp. 152–59; see also M. Jackson Wrigley, *The Film* (1922), pp. 82–83. An example of the more complacent American attitude toward ethnic, racial and class comedy in the silent movies is J. J. White, *Moviegrins* (1915), a joke-book containing, among others, jokes about Jews, Irish and blacks.

8. MOVIE-MADE CHILDREN

A large body of books, pamphlets, articles and official reports on the social and psychological aspects of movies in the United States through the 1930s, largely polemical and almost entirely anti-movie, comprises the primary source material for this chapter; many of these works are cited in the text and will not be repeated here. A thorough bibliography of writings on the social and psychological aspects of movies, in several languages, is in I. C. Jarvie, *Movies and Society* (1970).

Among recent studies of film censorship are Ira H. Carmen, *Movies, Censorship and the Law* (1966); Richard S. Randall, *Censorship at the Movies* (1968); and Murray Schumach, *The Face on the Cutting Room Floor* (1961). A useful bibliography of early writings on the subject is J. R. Rutland, *State Censorship of Motion Pictures* (1923). In addition to works cited in the text, see also Donald Ramsay Young, *Motion Pictures: A Study in Social Legislation* (1922); William Sheafe Chase, *Catechism on Motion Pictures in Inter-State Commerce* (1922); Robert O. Bartholomew, *Report of Censorship of Motion Pictures and of Investigation of Motion Picture Theatres of Cleveland* (1913); and Morris L. Ernst and Pare Lorentz, *Censored* (1930). Ivor Montagu, *The Political Censorship of Films* (1929), is a study of British suppression of Soviet silents. Montagu also wrote "The Censorship of Sex in Films," *Proceedings of the 3rd International Congress of the World League for Sexual Reform* (1929).

Before the 1930s there were few social-science studies on movies. The pioneer behaviorist psychologists Karl S. Lashley and John B. Watson wrote a government report on audience responses to an anti–venereal-disease movie, *A Psychological Study of Motion Pictures in Relation to Venereal Disease Campaigns* (1922), and concluded that the film had little effect; Charles Arthur Perry, *The Attitude of High School Students toward Motion Pictures* (1923), was sponsored by the National Board of Review and therefore biased in favor of the movie industry. Robert and Helen Merrill Lynd briefly discussed movies in their classic *Middletown* (1929), considering them significant but less influential than the automobile in bringing about social change. See also Solomon P. Rosenthal, *Changes of Socio-Economic Attitudes under Radical Motion Picture Propaganda* (1934), which indicates that students in an experiment were swayed by a pro-Russian, anti-American newsreel.

The Payne Fund studies comprise eleven separate projects combined in eight volumes. They are popularly summarized in Henry James Forman, *Our Movie Made Children* (1933), and in more scholarly fashion by W. W. Charters, *Motion Pictures and Youth* (1933). Other works are Perry W. Holaday and George W. Stoddard, *Getting Ideas from the Movies*; Edgar Dale, *How to Appreciate Motion Pictures*; Wendell S. Dysinger and Christian A. Ruckmick, *The Emotional Responses of Children to the Motion Picture Situation*; Charles C. Peters, *Motion Pictures and Standards of Morality*; Ruth C. Peterson and L. L. Thurstone, *Motion Pictures and the Social Attitudes of Children*; Frank K. Shuttlesworth and Mark A. May, *The Social Conduct and Attitudes of Movie Fans*; Samuel Renshaw, Vernon L. Miller and Dorothy P. Marquis, *Children's Sleep*; Herbert Blumer, *Movies and Conduct*; Blumer and Philip M. Hauser, *Movies, Delinquency, and Crime* (all 1933); and two works by Edgar Dale, *Children's Attendance at Motion Pictures* and *The Content of Motion Pictures* (both 1935). A twelfth study, Paul G. Cressey and Frederick M. Thrasher, *Boys, Movies, and City Streets*, appears never to have been published.

9. THE HOUSE THAT ADOLPH ZUKOR BUILT

Most of the works mentioned as sources for the pre–World War I history of the motion-picture industry (Chapter 3, above) are also the primary works for the 1920s. See in particular Hampton, *A History of the Movies*; Kennedy, *The Story of the Films*; Lewis, *The Motion Picture Industry*; Huettig, *Economics of the Motion Picture Industry*; Bertrand *et al.*, *The Motion Picture Industry—A Pattern of Control*; French, *The Movie Moguls*; and the biographies of individual moguls. On the Federal Trade Commission's ruling against Paramount, see Howard Thompson Lewis, *Cases on the Motion Picture Industry*, Vol. 8, Harvard Business Reports (1930), pp. 226–62.

The economics of theaters and motion-picture exhibition has received almost no attention. I have found especially useful several guides to theater management, including Harold B. Franklin, *Motion Picture Theater Management* (1927), and Frank H. (Rick) Ricketson, Jr., *The Management of Motion Picture Theatres* (1938). See also E. M. Glucksman, *General Instructions Manual for Theatre Managers* (1930).

The advent of sound is discussed from a technical perspective, and occasionally from an economic or cultural viewpoint as well, in several contemporary books, in particular Harold B. Franklin, *Sound Motion Pictures* (1929). See also Garry Allighan, *The Romance of the Talkies* (1929); Bernard Brown, *Talking Pictures* (1931); and John Scotland (pseud.), *The Talkies* (1930). George Groves, "George Groves: Sound

Director," Oral History Project, UCLA Special Collections Library, is an interesting first-hand account of the changeover to sound in the studios. "Color and Sound on Film," *Fortune*, v. 2 (October 1930), pp. 33–35 ff., is a detailed account of the financial impact of sound on the studios. James L. Limbacher, *Four Aspects of the Film* (1968), briefly summarizes the history of the development of sound films (pp. 197–229).

Ivor Montagu, *With Eisenstein in Hollywood* (1967), is a fascinating memoir of the Soviet director's experience in Hollywood, and contains the scenarios of Eisenstein's two American projects, *Sutter's Gold* and *An American Tragedy*.

10. THE MOGULS AT BAY AND THE CENSORS' TRIUMPH

A basic source of statistical information on the motion-picture industry in the early years of the Great Depression is Daniel Bertrand, *Work Materials No. 34–The Motion Picture Industry* (1936), a publication of the National Recovery Administration. A brief but succinct analysis of the movie studios on the eve of the Depression is Eleanor Kerr, *The First Quarter Century of the Motion Picture Theatre* (1930). F. D. Klingender and Stuart Legg, *Money Behind the Screen* (1937), make the case for banking control of the movie industry, and Sinclair, *Upton Sinclair Presents William Fox*, is one of their essential sources.

The Film Daily, Cavalcade (1939) provides authorized short histories of each studio with varying degrees of candor. *Fortune* published a series of in-depth studies of major studios during the decade: "Metro-Goldwyn-Mayer," v. 6 (December 1932), pp. 50–64 ff.; "Paramount," v. 15 (March 1937), pp. 86–96 ff.; "Warner Brothers," v. 16 (December 1937), pp. 110–15 ff.; and "Loew's Inc.," v. 20 (August 1939), pp. 24–31 ff.

Aspects of the relation between the government and the movie industry in the 1930s are covered in Louis Nizer, *New Courts of Industry* (1935), on the NRA motion-picture codes; and Ross, *Stars and Strikes*, particularly on the code's labor provisions. On the antitrust suit, see Ralph Cassady, Jr., "Impact of the Paramount Decision on Motion Picture Distribution and Price Making," *Southern California Law Review*, v. 31 (1958), pp. 150–80, for the legal background and ramifications, and Bertrand *et al.*, *The Motion Picture Industry—A Pattern of Control*, for its justification.

Labor conditions and union activity in the movie industry during the 1930s require extensive further study.

Olga J. Martin, *Hollywood's Movie Commandments* (1937), is a semi-official explication and justification of the Motion Picture Production Code. On the adoption of the code and the founding of the Production Code Administration, see Will H. Hays, *The Memoirs of Will H. Hays* (1955), and Raymond Moley, *The Hays Office* (1945).

11. THE GOLDEN AGE OF TURBULENCE AND THE GOLDEN AGE OF ORDER

There have been a number of brief efforts to link American movies of the 1930s with the economic, political and cultural changes of the Depression period; one of the best remains Richard Griffith's chapter "The American Film: 1929–1948" in the 1949 and subsequent editions of Paul Rotha, *The Film Till Now*. Andrew Bergman has written a stimulating book, *We're in the Money* (1971), on Depression America and its films, though I often find myself in disagreement with it—for example, on the social themes of gangster films; see also the relevant chapters in Jacobs, *The Rise of the American Film*. John Baxter, *Hollywood in the Thirties* (1968), has the merit of organizing production by studios, thus re-emphasizing how much moviemaking continued to be governed by traditional styles and formulas. A great deal of additional information may be gleaned from works on genres–Western, gangster, musical–and individual directors and players. Andrew Sarris' incisive brief comments on directors in *The American Cinema: Directors and Directions, 1929–1968* (1968) are often of great value on 1930s filmmaking; see also the brief film reviews in Pauline Kael, *Kiss Kiss Bang Bang* (1968), and remarks on the 1930s in her other works.

No study of either the Marx Brothers or Mae West has yet done justice to their remarkable films. On the Marx Brothers, see Allen Eyles, *The Marx Brothers* (1966), among many others; for Mae West, see her autobiography, *Goodness Had Nothing to Do With It* (1959), and a useful chapter in Alexander Walker, *The Celluloid Sacrifice* (1966; paperback title, *Sex in the Cinema*). The screwball comedies of the late 1930s also deserve considerably more attention; Ted Sennett has begun the task in his *Lunatics and Lovers* (1973).

Bob Thomas has written biographies of three producers and studio heads who rose to prominence in the 1930s: *King Cohn* (1967), on Harry Cohn; *Thalberg* (1969); and *Selznick* (1970); yet a good deal more work could usefully be done on these figures and others, like Samuel Goldwyn. On Selznick, see also Rudy Behlmer, ed., *Memo From: David O. Selznick* (1972). Mel Gussow has written a biography of Darryl F. Zanuck, *Don't Say Yes Until I Finish Talking* (1971).

12. THE MAKING OF CULTURAL MYTHS: WALT DISNEY AND FRANK CAPRA

That motion pictures communicate cultural information is a fact universally assumed and widely discussed, but not so far sufficiently studied in a thorough way. This chapter is intended as an introductory effort. One of the major new methodological approaches to the study of motion-picture communication is the application of semiotics (a mode of studying language) to movies. On semiotics, see Roland Barthes, *Elements of Semiology* (1964; English translation, 1967) and *Mythologies* (1957; English translation, 1972), and for its application to movies, Christian Metz, *Film Language* (1974), and Peter Wollen, *Signs and Meaning in the Cinema* (1969). The psychological or sociological approach to film studies is exemplified in Siegfried Kracauer, *From Caligari to Hitler* (1947), and André Bazin, *What Is Cinema?* (English translation, 1967, of essays written in the 1940s and 1950s).

On Walt Disney, see Richard Schickel, *The Disney Version* (1968), which is invaluable as almost the only extensive work not sponsored or authorized in part by the Disney studio. A lavishly illustrated example of the latter kind is Christopher Finch, *The Art of Walt Disney* (1973). See also Leonard Maltin, *The Disney Films* (1973).

I have written on Capra from a somewhat different perspective in Robert Sklar, "The Imagination of Stability: The Depression Films of Frank Capra," in Richard Glatzer and John Raeburn, eds., *Frank Capra* (1975), pp. 121–38; the Glatzer and Raeburn volume is a collection of essays and reviews on the director and several interviews with him. Capra's highly readable autobiography is *The Name Above the Title* (1971). See also Bruce Henstell, ed., *Frank Capra*, The American Film Institute, Discussion #3 (1971).

13. SELLING MOVIES OVERSEAS

The economic and cultural aspects of American movie exports before World War II have received almost no attention since John Eugene Harley, *World-Wide Influences of the Cinema* (1940), a work primarily devoted to a country-by-country account of government censorship practices. The most extensive sources on the subject are the reports published by the Motion Picture Section of the Bureau of Foreign and Domestic Commerce, a division of the Commerce Department; some twenty-two reports appeared between 1927 and 1933 on various areas of the globe, and annual volumes covered the entire world thereafter. Kracauer, *From Caligari to Hitler*, discusses the financial interest of Hollywood studios in German production during the 1920s; see also George A. Huaco, *The Sociology of Film Art* (1965), on the German film industry in the 1920s. R. G. Burnett and E. D. Martell, *The Devil's Camera* (1932), a British work which deplores the influence of American (and British) movies on colonial subjects, may be the most extended attack on movie content of any book published on motion pictures in English. See also L. A. Notcutt and G. C. Latham, *The African and the Cinema* (1937). A number of magazine articles proclaimed the triumph of American movies in the world market, particularly right after World War I when Hollywood's success overseas was fresh news; see especially two articles cited in the text. The suggestion that the motion-picture industry was one of the few with a universal world-wide standard was made in C. H. Claudy, "The Romance of Invention II: Sixteen Per Second," *Scientific American*, v. 121 N.S. (September 13, 1919), pp. 252 ff.

The efforts of a filmmaker to make and exhibit feature films in a small country whose cinemas were dominated by Hollywood are recounted in Robert Sklar, "Rudall Hayward, New Zealand Film-maker," *Landfall: A New Zealand Quarterly*, no. 98 (June 1971), pp. 147–54.

14. THE HOLLYWOOD GOLD RUSH

Hollywood in the 1930s was the subject of a highly useful sociological study, Leo C. Rosten, *Hollywood: The Movie Colony, The Movie Makers* (1941). Bob Thomas, *Selznick*, has some good information on Myron Selznick and the rise of the talent agency, and on David O. Selznick's tactics as a producer. Otherwise information on life in the movie community comes largely from personal memoirs. In addition to the works by Hecht and Priestley cited in the text, see, among others, Salka Viertel, *The Kindness of Strangers* (1969), which is particularly valuable for its perspective on the European émigrés in Hollywood and their reactions to the rise of Hitler and the coming of war; Anita Loos, *Kiss Hollywood Good-by* (1974), which demonstrates the importance of women screen writers at MGM; S. N. Behrman, *People in a Diary* (1972), on his relations to Hollywood; and Garson Kanin, *Hollywood* (1974).

George Eells, *Hedda and Louella* (1972), is a good dual biography of the gossip columnists. Parsons wrote about herself in *The Gay Illiterate* (1944) and *Tell It to Louella* (1961), Hopper in *From Under My Hat* (1952) and *The Whole Truth and Nothing But* (1963). On the movie fan magazines, see the collection edited by Martin Levin, *Hollywood and the Great Fan Magazines* (1970).

Hollywood screen writers have been the special subject of study by Richard Corliss. He wrote *Talking Pictures* (1974) and edited *The Hollywood Screenwriters* (1972), an expanded version of a special issue of *Film Comment*, v. 6 (Winter 1970–1971), although some material from the magazine does not appear in the book.

On Hollywood fiction, see Virgil L. Lokke, *The Literary Image of Hollywood* (unpublished Ph.D. dissertation, University of Iowa, 1955), and Jonas Spatz, *Hollywood in Fiction* (1969). For Fitzgerald's *The Last Tycoon*, see Robert Sklar, *F. Scott Fitzgerald* (1967), and on West's *The Day of the Locust*, see Jay Martin, *Nathanael West* (1970).

Upton Sinclair gives his version of the movie industry's propaganda campaign against him in William J. Perlman, ed., *The Movies on Trial* (1936), pp. 189–95. Rosten, *Hollywood*, gives a sympathetic account of the rise of political activism in Hollywood during the late 1930s; quite a different perspective may be found in Eugene Lyons, *The Red Decade* (1941), pp. 284–97. See also the Senate hearings, *Propaganda in Motion Pictures* (1942), fully cited in the text.

15. HOLLYWOOD AT WAR FOR AMERICA AND AT WAR WITH ITSELF

Hollywood's relation to the military effort in World War II is treated in a number of contemporary works: The Truman Committee hearings on the national defense program, cited in the text; The Editors of *Look*, *Movie Lot to Beachhead* (1945); Francis S. Harmon, *The Command Is Forward* (1944); Gussow, *Don't Say Yes Until I Finish Talking*, on Darryl F. Zanuck's wartime activities; an article by Bosley Crowther in Jack Goodman, ed., *While You Were Gone* (1946), pp. 511–32; and Dorothy B. Jones, "The Hollywood War Film: 1942–1944," *Hollywood Quarterly*, v. 1 (October 1945), pp. 1–19. Barbara Deming, *Running Away from Myself* (1969), is a fascinating psychological interpretation of wartime film content. Parker Tyler also brings a psychoanalytic perspective to films of the wartime years in his provocative early books on Hollywood, *The Hollywood Hallucination* (1944) and *Magic and Myth of the Movies* (1947). Charles Higham and Joel Greenberg, *Hollywood in the Forties* (1968), another in the series of surveys of American films by decades, organizes the period's production by genre; see their treatment of "black cinema," (*film noir*), pp. 23–31.

A lucid summary of the immediate background to the postwar congressional investigations of Hollywood, particularly the wartime union conflicts in the movie industry, is in John Cogley, *Report on Blacklisting I. Movies* (1956). The Chamber of Commerce of the United States launched an attack on alleged Hollywood subversives in *Communist Infiltration in the United States* (1946). The 1947 House Un-American Activities Committee hearings, which led to the indictment, conviction and imprisonment of the Hollywood Ten, are fully cited in the text; excerpts may be found in Eric Bentley, ed., *Thirty Years of Treason* (1971), and Gordon Kahn, *Hollywood on Trial* (1948). Bentley is unsympathetic to the "unfriendly" witnesses, as is Walter Goodman in his *The Committee* (1968) and Murray Kempton, *Part of Our Time* (1955). Personal statements and recollections by members of the Ten include Dalton Trumbo's important pamphlet, "The Time of the Toad" (1949), and his letters, Helen Manfull, ed., *Additional Dialogue* (1970), and Alvah Bessie, *Inquisition in Eden* (1965). Personal papers of the Hollywood Ten and other materials relating to their struggle are collected at the State Historical Society of Wisconsin, Madison.

On the blacklist, the essential works include Cogley, *Report on Blacklisting I. Movies* and a special issue of *Film Culture* on "Hollywood Blacklisting," no. 50-51 (Fall and Winter 1970). See also Stefan Kanfer, *A Journal of the Plague Years* (1973). Myron C. Fagan lobbied for a Hollywood purge in *Red Treason in Hollywood* (1949) and *Documentation of the Red Stars in Hollywood* (1950).

16. THE DISAPPEARING AUDIENCE AND THE TELEVISION CRISIS

Motion-picture audience habits and preferences were first extensively studied in Leo A. Handel, *Hollywood Looks at Its Audience* (1950); another valuable statistical compilation is Sindlinger & Co., Inc., *An Analysis of the Motion Picture Industry, 1946–1953*, Vol. 1 (1953). A varied group of articles on these and many other aspects of the postwar movie scene are collected in "The Motion Picture Industry," *The Annals of the American Academy of Political and Social Science*, v. 254 (November 1947). Comparisons between radio and movie audiences were made in Paul F. Lazarsfeld and Harry Field, *The People Look at Radio* (1946), and Lazarsfeld and Patricia L. Kendall, *Radio Listening in America* (1948). See also two volumes edited by Lazarsfeld and Frank N. Stanton, *Radio Research 1941* (1941) and *Radio Research 1942–1943* (1944). Evidence on how far motion pictures were to slip in the hierarchy of mass entertainment may be found in Gary A. Steiner, *The People Look at Television* (1963).

The final chapters in the government's antitrust action against the motion-picture industry are detailed in Michael Conant, *Anti-Trust in the Motion Picture Industry* (1961), and Ralph Cassady, Jr., "Impact of the Paramount Decision . . ." See also the various Supreme Court and federal lower court opinions. On Hollywood's activities in foreign film markets after World War II there is a detailed study, Thomas H. Guback, *The International Film Industry* (1969).

For Hollywood's relation to radio and television broadcasting before World War II, see the first two volumes of Erik Barnouw's History of Broadcasting in the United States, *A Tower in Babel* (1966) and *The Golden Web* (1968). After the war the problems of television and of the perceived slump in motion-picture quality were discussed in a number of articles: Anthony H. Dawson, "Motion Picture Economics," *Hollywood Quarterly*, v. 3 (Spring 1948), pp. 217–40; Frederic Marlowe, "The Rise of the Independents in Hollywood," *Penguin Film Review*, v. 3 (1947), pp. 72–75; Max Knepper, "Hollywood's 1948 Line-Up," *Penguin Film Review*, v. 7 (1948), pp. 113–16; Samuel Goldwyn, "Hollywood in the Television Age," *Hollywood Quarterly*, v. 4 (Winter 1949), pp. 145–51; Richard J. Goggin, "Television and Motion Picture Production—and Kinescope Recordings," *Hollywood Quarterly*, v. 4 (Winter 1949), pp. 142–59; Rodney Luther, "Television and the Future of Motion Picture Exhibition," *Hollywood Quarterly*, v. 5 (Winter 1950), pp. 164–77. A two-part article by

John E. McCoy and Harry P. Warner, "Theater Television Today," *Hollywood Quarterly*, v. 4 (Winter 1949, pp. 160–77, and Spring 1950, pp 262–78), details various strategies movie studios might employ to use television for motion picture exhibition. On technological novelties in motion-picture production, see Limbacher, *Four Aspects of the Film*, and Charles Higham, *Hollywood at Sunset* (1972).

17. HOLLYWOOD'S COLLAPSE

An admirable brief account of the motion-picture industry and its various components in the 1960s and 1970s is William Fadiman, *Hollywood Now* (1972). The long Hollywood boom was beginning to burst when Hortense Powdermaker studied the community in 1946–1947, and the resentments welling up in her informants led her to exaggerate the "totalitarian" character of studio leadership in her otherwise useful *Hollywood: The Dream Factory* (1950). Powdermaker reconsidered her Hollywood experience in her autobiography, *Stranger and Friend* (1969). A collection of articles on Hollywood's changing scene is Richard Dyer MacCann, *Hollywood in Transition* (1962). Two close-up looks at filmmaking, nearly two decades apart, are Lillian Ross's classic *Picture* (1952), on John Huston's *The Red Badge of Courage*, and John Gregory Dunne, *The Studio* (1969), on a year in the life at Twentieth Century-Fox. Edward Thorpe, *The Other Hollywood* (1970), is an account of everyday life along Hollywood Boulevard and its run-down side streets. See also Higham, *Hollywood at Sunset*; Ezra Goodman, *The Fifty-Year Decline and Fall of Hollywood* (1961); and Pauline Kael, "On the Future of Movies," *The New Yorker*, v. 50 (August 5, 1974), pp. 43–59.

The revived interest in film as art in the 1950s set the stage for daily and weekly movie reviewers to collect their once ephemeral judgments between hard covers. The posthumous publication of James Agee's reviews, *Agee on Film: Reviews and Comments* (1958), seems to have been the first of what has now become several shelves of volumes by Kael, Sarris, John Simon, Dwight Macdonald, Stanley Kauffmann, Richard Schickel, Renata Adler and other critics, as well as collections of older works by such writers as Otis Ferguson, William Pechter and Manny Farber. The National Society of Film Critics annually gathers outstanding examples of its members' work in a single volume. A historical compilation is Stanley Kauffmann with Bruce Henstell, *American Film Criticism: From the Beginnings to "Citizen Kane"* (1972).

Jack Vizzard chronicles the decline and fall of the Production Code Administration in his interesting memoir, *See No Evil* (1970). On the rise of hard-core commercial moviemaking, see William Rostler, *Contemporary Erotic Cinema* (1973).

Bonnie and Clyde and the controversy over it are detailed in John Cawelti, ed., *Focus on Bonnie and Clyde* (1972). On the popularity of young directors in Hollywood after the success of *Easy Rider*, see Robert Sklar, "Hollywood's New Wave," *Ramparts*, v. 10 (November 1971), pp. 60–66.

18. THE FUTURE OF MOVIES

Over the years I have developed many of my perspectives on the avant-garde cinema by viewing historical and contemporary films screened by the University of Michigan Cinema Guild and at the incomparable annual Ann Arbor Film Festival.

In the first half-century of motion pictures there were a number of works suggesting the aesthetic possibilities in noncommercial cinema. See, for example, Elie Faure, *The Art of Cineplastics* (1923); Leonard Hacker, *Cinematic Design* (1931); and of course the writings of Eisenstein, Pudovkin, Vladimir Nilsen and other Soviet film workers. The first effort to treat the experimental film in its historical aspect is Frank Stauffacher, *Art in Cinema* (1947), the catalog of a film series at the San Francisco Museum of Art, still an indispensable reference work; Lewis Jacobs followed with an essay, "Experimental Cinema in America, 1921–1947," *Hollywood Quarterly*, v. 3 (Winter 1947–1948, pp. 111–24, and September 1948, pp. 278–92), more readily available in the 1968 paperbound edition of his *The Rise of the American Film*.

P. Adams Sitney, *Visionary Film* (1974), is an impressive study of the romantic, individualist strand of American avant-garde filmmaking, and Gene Youngblood, *Expanded Cinema* (1970), covers computer- and video-graphics and experiments in holography. Richard Meran Barsam has studied *Non-Fiction Film* (1973); see also G. Roy Levin, *Documentary Explorations* (1971). A brief history of avant-garde filmmaking in Europe and the United States since the beginning of movies is David Curtis, *Experimental Cinema* (1971); on more recent American films, see Parker Tyler, *Underground Film* (1969); Sheldon Renan, *An Introduction to the American Underground Film* (1967); and Gregory Battcock, ed., *The New American Cinema* (1967).

INDEX

ABOUT THE AUTHOR

Robert Sklar was born in 1936 and was educated in the public schools of Long Beach, California, and at Princeton University. After working as a reporter for the Los Angeles *Times*, he received his Ph.D. in the History of American Civilization from Harvard University in 1965. Mr. Sklar is a historian and writer on twentieth-century American culture and society, and is the author of *F. Scott Fitzgerald: The Last Laocoön*, and editor of *The Plastic Age*, an anthology on 1920s culture. He has held a Guggenheim Fellowship and has taught overseas in New Zealand and Japan. Currently the holder of a Rockefeller Foundation Humanities Fellowship, he lives in New York, and is the father of two children.